THE NATURE OF COMPUTATION:

AN INTRODUCTION TO COMPUTER SCIENCE

THE NATURE OF COMPUTATION:

AN INTRODUCTION TO COMPUTER SCIENCE

Ira Pohl
University of California at Santa Cruz

Alan Shaw
University of Washington

COMPUTER SCIENCE PRESS

Computer Science Press, Inc.
11 Taft Court
Rockville, Maryland 20850

    3 4 5 6   86 85 84 83 82

Library of Congress Cataloging in Publication Data

Pohl, Ira.
  The nature of computation.

  (Computer software engineering series)
  Bibliography: p.
  1. Electronic data processing. I. Shaw, Alan C.,
1937–   joint author. II. Title. III. Series.
QA76.P58   001.64   80-18433
ISBN 0-914894-12-9

Cover design by Ruth Ramminger

To my parents
Mae and Morris
Ira Pohl
To my mother Sybil
Alan Shaw

PREFACE

This book is a rigorous introduction to computer science, suitable for the beginning major. As a general introduction, it has three objectives: to provide a survey of the field; to provide an initial literacy in the language and methods of computer science; and to present an historical, philosophical, and social perspective. The principal subjects treated are algorithms and their description, data and its representation, Boolean algebra, computer circuits and organization, programming languages and systems, computability theory, analysis of algorithms, and applications and implications of computing.

Our primary theme is that computer science is the study of algorithms. The technical foundations and applications are covered chiefly by constructing and studying a number of basic algorithms for each topic. Examples are Euclid's algorithm, number conversion, computer arithmetic, text manipulation, various machine simulations, elementary Turing machines, polynomial evaluation, sorting, and binary search. The purpose is not only to understand and apply the algorithms but also ultimately to analyze their complexity and prove their correctness. In order to describe algorithms, we define a small Algol-like programming notation, dubbed "Algolic," that most closely resembles a subset of Pascal.

Because computer science and technology are intimately tied to a societal context, we discuss the history, applications, and social implications of various technical developments. Significant contemporary work as well as the contributions of pioneers such as Babbage, Turing, and von Neumann are described. Also introduced are some of the philosophical, moral, and social controversies surrounding advances in computing, including those related to non-computability, artificial intelligence, computer modelling, and data banks and privacy.

Programming is introduced in the book through many examples and exercises. The progression of Algolic and examples is constructed to allow a parallel course in programming; alternatively, a programming course may follow our first course. Both approaches have been used successfully.

The present text evolved from a set of notes originally developed by I. Pohl in 1971. Early drafts of this book have been used by the authors as the text for the basic introductory course in computer science at the University of California at Santa Cruz since 1971 and at the University of Washington since 1975. After some experimentation, we have found that a one-term course in calculus provides the minimum mathematical sophistication for the material. The entire book can be covered in a year-long course, or selected parts can be used for a single term offering.

Contents

Chapter 1

COMPUTER SCIENCE

1.1 ORIGINS OF COMPUTER SCIENCE

Revolutionary advances in both science and engineering have changed the content and methodology of almost all technical fields during the current century, including physics, biology, medicine, electrical engineering, chemistry, transportation, communication, textiles, energy, agriculture, and computing. Most of the advances and changes have been incorporated quite naturally within traditional subject areas, and rarely has a major new discipline been created. Computer science is one of these rarities.

While computer science is undoubtedly the youngest of the sciences, its origins can be traced back many years. The most significant events of recent historical interest were the constructions of the first digital computers during and immediately after World War II. In the sense that the *science of X is the study of X*, computer science is devoted to the study of those devices called computers; the field could not exist until the first machines were built in the 1940's. However, hardware ideas about computers were expounded much earlier. The most prominent example is the work of C. Babbage who derived the basic principles of computer organization and designed a machine in the early 19th century.

Much of the theoretical foundations of computer science started with the research of A. Turing in the 1930's. He developed a mathematical model of a universal computing device and proved some remarkable properties of this abstract device. Turing's "machine" is still the accepted theoretical model of a computer. In summary, the modern origins of the field are the construction of the first computers and the independent formulation of an adequate mathematical model of machines.

The subject was recognized as a separate academic discipline in the mid 1960's when computer science departments were created at a number of universities in the U.S.A., and graduate programs, usually leading to the Master of Science and Doctor of Philosophy degrees, were introduced. In 1968, the Association for Computing Machinery, the largest professional and scientific organization of computer scientists, published a model undergraduate curriculum; this became the basis for many college and university programs throughout the world. It did not take long for computer science to become established, with all the trappings of a traditional discipline such as many technical journals and conferences, academic departments at most institutions of higher education, scientific and professional associations, and thriving research laboratories in academia, industry, and government.

Why is computer science a separate major field? After all, a computer is *just* a grand calculating device. Previous calculators, such as slide rules, were only considered as computing tools and never seriously treated as a new basic area of knowledge. Other significant technical innovations such as automobiles, television, and lasers have not led to separate disciplines; instead they just became part of the existing fields of mechanical engineering, electrical engineering, and physics, respectively. At one level, it is difficult to answer our question without assuming some familiarity with this book. However, we can make two main points that should be comprehensible now and can be profitably reread later.

Our first point is a technical one, dealing with the content of the field. Surprisingly, *computers are universal problem solving machines.* Any procedure that is precisely formulated can be implemented on a computer; such computational procedures are called *algorithms*. As a consequence of this universality, the computer has permitted scientists to focus on all aspects of technical problem solving. These include languages and notations for describing problems and their solutions, the efficiency and optimality of various problem solving schemes, the classes of computing devices required for different types of problems, the inherent complexity of specific problems, the existence or non-existence of solutions to well-posed problems, and a host of other related questions. Like mathematics, computer science provides the necessary tools for many technical endeavors. Unlike mathematics and similar to engineering and the natural or social sciences, computer science also has the very practical goals of understanding and applying real world phenomena—those surrounding computers and algorithmic problem solving.

The second point that accounts for the creation of a computer science is social. The impact of computers on society has been enormous but not well understood. It is evident that the computer "revolution" is still in progress. The ultimate effects on our political, cultural, economic, and moral lives are unpredictable, other than acknowledging that they will be substantial and potentially range from very beneficial to very hazardous. Since much of our economy relies on automatic information processing, there is a need for people who are technically trained in computers. At a different level, it is recognized that a new computer ingredient has been introduced in our societies, and that every well-educated person should have a basic understanding of these machines and some of their implications.

1.2 ON DEFINING COMPUTER SCIENCE

The science of any subject is concerned with the accumulation and organization of information about the subject and with the derivation and discovery of principles and methods. Most sciences have a pure aspect that is devoted entirely to the expansion of knowledge for its own sake, and an applied component that is oriented towards using this knowledge. The range covered by computer science is very broad. At one end of the spectrum, we have theoretical, and sometimes philosophical, investigations on the ultimate capabilities of machines and on the properties of various general problems and algorithms; the more applied end deals with techniques for the design and construction of computer systems, i.e. computer engineering, and with advanced applications.

The computer scientist, in his applied role, has been characterized as a *toolmaker*. As such, he develops methods and machines that others use in solving their problems. The theoretical computer scientist, while also involved in toolmaking, studies the nature of the tool. In a natural science, some part of the given natural or physical world is investigated. Computer science, by contrast, is an *artificial science* since we are studying one of man's own creations. As a result, the interest is not so much in observed facts and the discovery of laws, as it is in methods for the analysis and design of these creations and the derivation of their properties.

Computer science has been defined in many different ways. Following are three definitions that have been proposed.

1. Device-centered
   This is the straightforward definition that was mentioned in the last section.
   "Computer science is the study of computers."
   Thus the science focuses on the device and on questions surrounding it, such as how to design, analyze, construct, and use computers.
2. Information-centered
   Information or data is considered the central notion here.
   "Computer science is the study of information."
   This leads to questions about the representation, storage, organization, transmission, and processing of data.

3. Program-centered

A *program* is a set of computer instructions for solving a specific problem. Computer programs are also referred to as *software*.

"Computer science is the study of programming."

In this view, the emphasis is on programming issues such as appropriate languages for expressing programs, the correctness and efficiency of programs, machines for executing programs, and programming techniques.

All these definitions are "correct" in that most computer science topics are encompassed by any of them. The first definition emphasizes real and abstract machines, the second the data that machines work with, and the third the programs used to communicate with machines. Because their emphases are different, they are subject to misinterpretation and can easily be construed as too narrow or too broad.

What is desired is a definition that gracefully includes all of the above views without unduly emphasizing any. The unifying notion of an algorithm, informally defined in the last section, satisfies this requirement.

4. Algorithm-centered

"Computer science is the study of algorithms."

Computers are machines for implementing algorithms, information is the "stuff" that algorithms manipulate and produce, and programming is the means for describing algorithms. The algorithm concept also easily includes the theoretical parts of computer science.

Algorithms are the theme of this book and we shall see that all computer science questions can be naturally formulated as questions about algorithms.

1.3 CORE TOPICS: TECHNICAL, APPLICATIONS, AND SOCIAL

The theory and practice of computer science covers technical, applications, and social issues. The relations among these three aspects of the field are illustrated in Figure 1.1. Thus technical advances lead to applications and social questions, and, in turn, the technical side of computing is strongly influenced by applications and social pressures. Similarly, social problems feed back to applications development and technical questions. While concerned primarily with scientific or technical problems, the computer scientist must be aware of all three contexts of his work.

In this section, we introduce some of the main computer science topics in the above three areas. A summary of the core topics is presented in

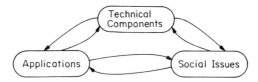

Figure 1.1   Relations Among computer Science Topics

Table 1.1. Our list should not be considered static but one that is constantly expanding as the field progresses and new insights are made.

The technical component can be summarized as the design, implementation, analysis, and theory of algorithms. A computer scientist attempts to answer some of the following questions:

1. What is an appropriate machine design for efficiently executing algorithms?
2. What is a good programming language for writing algorithms?
3. How can one design and implement good algorithms?
4. Is a particular algorithm correct for all possible cases?
5. How efficient is a particular algorithm?
6. What is the best possible algorithm for a given problem?
7. Does there exist an algorithm to solve a particular problem?
8. How does one define the syntax (form) and semantics (meaning) of a programming language?

Computer science research takes place within the framework of certain applications that are a source of computing problems of general interest. Scientific computing, which deals with algorithms for the numerical solution of mathematical equations, was the original application of computers, with a history stretching far back to antiquity and the earliest calculating devices. Another source of, usually numeric, algorithms is in problem solving by simulation; real world predictions are attempted by creating and executing a computer model of the phenomenon being studied. Investigations of nonnumeric algorithms, algorithms that manipulate symbols rather than numbers, arise naturally in the fields of artificial intelligence and database systems. The goal of artificial intelligence research is to produce computer systems that exhibit "intelligent" behavior; this ambitious, and often controversial, goal has generated a rich set of problems in game-playing, symbolic mathematics, theorem proving, and natural language understanding. The last application in our list, database systems,

Table 1.1   Some Core Topics of Computer Science

A. Technical Components
   1. Design: machines, programming languages and systems, programs
   2. Analysis: correctness, efficiency
   3. Theory and Foundations: automata theory and computability, complexity, formal languages
B. General Applications
   1. Scientific Computing
   2. Modelling and Simulation
   3. Artificial Intelligence
   4. Database Systems
C. Social Issues
   1. Machine Intelligence
   2. Automation
   3. Privacy
   4. Planning with Computer Models

---

refers to large information storage and retrieval systems; examples are systems for libraries, airline reservations, automobile design, income tax, credit, and banking.

At least four related social issues are direct and serious consequences of computer science developments. The possibilities and implications of machine intelligence are the subject of countless popular and scholarly discussions; these may stress, for example, the assault on man's ego caused by intelligent machines, the benefits of a benevolent intellectual collaboration between men and machines, or the horrors of being ruled by computers. As more and more tasks become automated and delegated to computers, society must deal with the undesirable effects such as possible widespread unemployment and the desirable aspects such as increased leisure time. The existence of large database systems containing detailed personal data has already caused great concern about the loss of privacy and potential for misuse; the prospects of "big brother" keeping track of one's every movement and transaction appeal to few, yet these systems also produce considerable economic and social benefits. The last issue stems from the increased reliance on computer modelling for economic and social planning. Large computer models give planning agencies much better information for intelligent decision-making. On the other hand, some simulations and models are so complex that few understand the underlying assumptions in the model and can interpret the results sensibly; the danger is that the computer output of such models is accepted and used on faith alone.

The nuclear and biological sciences have painfully learned that science is not value free and that the social implications of research directions and advances must be considered. Computer science is also fundamentally tied to its societal context and the relationships between the science and society cannot be ignored.

1.4 OUTLINE OF THIS TEXT

The chapters and topics in our book are sketched in Figure 1.2. The arrows in the figure indicate prerequisites.

The introductory part in the next three chapters presents some basic material on algorithms, data, and Boolean algebra. Following this are the central technical subjects: machines, software, theory of computation, and analysis of algorithms. The last two chapters deal with applications and the societal implications of computer technology and science. In order to give a deeper feeling for the dynamics of computer science—its creation and evolution—and also to acknowledge the major contributing pioneers, we also discuss the history of each development.

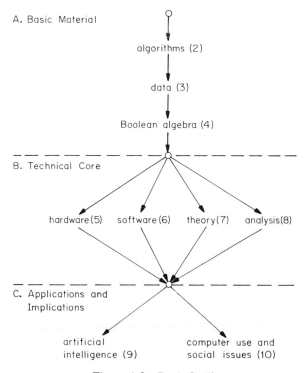

Figure 1.2   Book Outline

The technical foundations are covered chiefly by constructing and studying a number of basic algorithms relevant to each topic. To describe algorithms, we use a precise language called *Algolic*. Algolic is defined informally in the next few chapters; a more formal specification and summary is given in the Appendix.

The end of each chapter has an Exercise section and a list of references for additional reading.

EXERCISES

1. Make a list of all the interactions you have with computers, e.g., utility bills, automatic mailing lists, class scheduling, . . .

2. Discuss the following two statements:
    (a) "The computer, like a hammer, is only a tool that may be applied to study other disciplines. Therefore, there is no computer science."
    (b) The study of computers is just a fad similar to the earlier fad involving the study of automobiles."
    (Note: It is possible to agree with either of these two statements.)

3. Give a detailed step-by-step procedure, i.e., an "algorithm," for each of the following tasks or problems:
    (a) travelling from your place of residence to school or work
    (b) manually dividing one number by another (long division)
    (c) taking an unordered set of numbers and putting them in ascending sequence, i.e., "sorting" the numbers in ascending sequence
    (d) playing, and never losing, the game of tic-tac-toe.

ADDITIONAL READINGS

Newell, A.; Perlis, A. J.; and Simon, H. A. "Computer Science." *Science,* vol. 157, 1 September 1967, 1373–1374.

Pohl, I., and Shaw, A. "Introducing Computer Science: An Alternative." *Proc. IFIP 77,* North-Holland, Amsterdam, 1977, pp. 53–56.

Chapter 2

ALGORITHMS

Our principal theme is that computer science is the study of algorithms. The field is centrally concerned with such topics as the theory and properties of algorithms, methods for the design and analysis of algorithms, programming and other languages for describing algorithms, systems and techniques for representing algorithms as programs, machines for executing algorithms, and the societal implications of computer science and technology. In this chapter, we discuss the concept and characteristics of an algorithm, introduce several notations for expressing algorithms including the language *Algolic* used throughout the book, and define a simple computer than can execute algorithms. The material is presented mainly by constructing and studying a variety of example algorithms.

2.1 ALGORITHMS, PROGRAMS, AND COMPUTATIONS

Informally, an *algorithm* is a list of instructions for performing a specific task or for solving a particular type of problem. Algorithm-like specifications for problem solving and task performance are commonly found in our everyday experiences. Examples include the detailed instructions for knitting a sweater, making a dress, cooking a favorite meal, registering for classes at a university, travelling from one destination to another, and using a vending machine. It is instructive to examine one of these examples.

Consider the following recipe for preparing a meat roast:

Sprinkle the roast with salt and pepper. Insert a meat thermometer and place in oven preheated to 150°C. Cook until the thermometer registers 80°C-85°C. Serve roast with gravy prepared from either meat stock or from pan drippings if there is a sufficient amount.

The recipe is typically imprecise—what does "sprinkle" mean, where is the thermometer to be inserted, what is a "sufficient amount" of pan drippings?

However, it can be more precisely formulated as a list of instructions or steps, by taking some liberties and reading "between the lines":

1. Sprinkle roast with $1/8$ teaspoon salt and pepper.
2. Turn oven on to 150°C.
3. Insert meat thermometer into center of roast.
4. Wait a few minutes.
5. If oven does not yet register 150°C, go to step 4.
6. Place roast in oven.
7. Wait a few minutes.
8. Check meat thermometer. If temperature is less than 80°C, go to step 7.
9. Remove roast from oven.
10. If there is at least $1/2$ cup of pan drippings, go to step 12.
11. Prepare gravy from meat stock and go to step 13.
12. Prepare gravy from pan drippings.
13. Serve roast with gravy.

There are three categories of instructions and activities in the above steps—those that involve manipulating or changing the ingredients or equipment, those that just examine or test the "state" of the system, and those that transfer to the next step. Steps 1 and 6 are examples of the first category; the temperature test in step 8 and the pan dripping test in step 10 are instances of state testing; and the transfers in steps 5 and 8 ("go to step x") are examples of the last class.

By using suitable graphical symbols for each of these categories, a simple two-dimensional representation of our cooking "algorithm" can be obtained as shown in Figure 2.1. Such a figure is called a *flow chart*. In order to perform the algorithm (prepare the roast), one just follows the arrows doing the instructions noted in each box. The manipulation activities are contained in rectangular boxes, the tests are placed in diamonds, and the transfer or *flow of control* is determined by the arrows. Because of their visual appeal and clarity, flow charts are often used instead of lists of instructions for informally describing algorithms. There have even been cookbooks that employ flow charts extensively.

Our recipe for preparing a roast can still not be called an algorithm in a strictly formal sense, primarily because the individual instructions are too loosely specified. Let us study another example—one that manipulates numbers instead of food. A different number is initially placed in each of three boxes, labelled a, b, and c, respectively. The purpose of the algorithm is to rearrange or *sort* the numbers so that the final number in box a is less

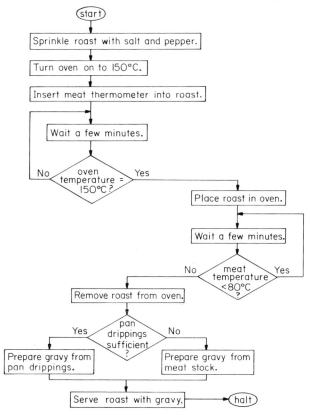

Figure 2.1 Flow Chart for Preparing a Roast

than that in box b, and the number in box b is less than that in box c. Initial and final states for a particular set of numbers are illustrated in Figure 2.2.

An algorithm for performing this sorting task is given by the following steps:

1. Place first number in box a.
2. Place second number in box b.
3. Place third number in box c.
4. If the number in a is not larger than the number in b, go to step 6.
5. Interchange the number in a with that in b.
6. If the number in b is larger than the number in c, then go to step 7; otherwise halt.
7. Interchange the numbers in b and c.

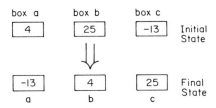

Figure 2.2   Sorting Three Numbers

8. If the number in a is larger than that in b, then go to step 9; otherwise halt.
9. Interchange the numbers in a and b.
10. Halt.

Let us execute this algorithm with some specific numbers. Suppose the three numbers are, in order, 17, 6, and 11. We always start with the first instruction. To execute step 1, we place the first number, 17, in box a; similarly, at the end of instruction 3, the 6 has been inserted into b, and c contains 11. Since 17 is larger than 6, the condition tested in step 4 is false and we proceed to instruction 5; the step switches the values of a and b so that a now contains 6 and b has 17. Figure 2.3 shows the contents of the three boxes at various stages of execution. Step 6 has now been reached and we compare the number in b (17) with that in c (11); 17 is greater than 11 and a transfer is made to instruction 7. The numbers in b and c are then interchanged so that b has 11 and c has 17. The test in step 8 fails (6 is not larger than 11) and the computation then halts. The three numbers are sorted in ascending sequence, i.e., $6 < 11 < 17$. The reader should convince himself that this algorithm will work correctly for *any* three numbers.

A flow chart of this sorting algorithm is presented in Figure 2.4. Several new notational conventions are introduced in the figure. The instruction "$x \leftarrow e$" means to take the *value* of e and place it in box x. If e is the name of box, its value is its contents; if e is an algebraic expression, for example $(z + 15)/a$, we mean to evaluate the expression and use the resulting value. The test "$a > b$" is interpreted as a comparison between the *contents* of boxes a and b. Finally, we have decomposed the operation of interchanging two numbers into three more primitive instructions. The box t is used as temporary or scratch storage to hold intermediate results. In order to interchange or switch two numbers a and b, we first temporarily store one of the numbers, say a, in t ($t \leftarrow a$); next the other number is stored in a ($a \leftarrow b$)

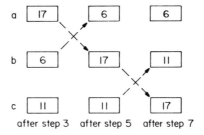

after step 3   after step 5   after step 7

Figure 2.3   Execution of the Sorting Algorithm

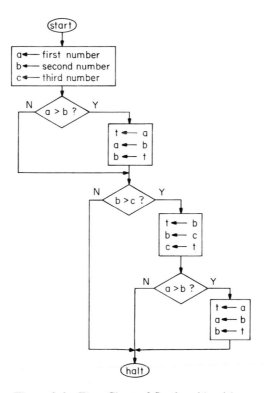

Figure 2.4   Flow Chart of Sorting Algorithm

and, last, the first number is placed in b ($b \leftarrow t$). Note that the instruction sequence "$a \leftarrow b$; $b \leftarrow a$" will not interchange a and b since the first instruction effectively destroys the old value in a. In computer terms, the labelled boxes are analogous to *memory* or *storage* areas that can contain values.

We have executed the sorting algorithm by acting as an agent mechanically following a list of instructions. This is called *hand simulation,* an important technique for developing and checking algorithms. The execution of a set of instructions by an agent is called a *computation*. Usually the agent is a computer; in that case, the set of instructions is a *program*. A specification of a computation that *terminates* is an *algorithm*.

The sorting algorithm has a number of other features that are characteristic of all algorithms:

1. Instructions are precise. Each instruction is unambiguous and subject to only one interpretation.
2. Instructions are possible to perform. Each instruction is within the capabilities of the executing agent and can be carried out exactly in a finite amount of time; such instructions are called *effective*.
3. Inputs and outputs. An algorithm has one or more outputs ("answers") that depend on the particular input data. The input to the sorting algorithm is three integers, while the output is the same numbers rearranged in ascending order.

It is easy to encounter lists of instructions that violate some of the above. Non-termination is especially common. Consider the following instructions:

1. Place the number 1 in the box labelled a.
2. Add 2 to the contents of a.
3. If a contains 10, then halt.
4. Go to step 2.

Each step is precise and effective, but the computation never terminates since a successively contains 1, 3, 5, 7, 9, 11, 13, ... Thus this specification cannot be considered an algorithm. It is the looping or repetitive nature of the computation that causes termination problems, but almost all interesting algorithms contain instruction sequences that are to be repeated until some condition is satisfied.

An imprecise instruction might be "Divide the contents of a by the contents of b", where there is either no guarantee that $b \neq 0$ or no further instructions on how to proceed if $b = 0$. An example of an instruction beyond our capabilities is "If there exists a fast general algorithm for playing an optimal game of checkers, then go to step 5". This instruction is not effective since no one knows whether or not such an efficient checker-playing algo- rithm exists. (It is strongly suspected that a fast, optimal algorithm does not exist; the instruction is also imprecise since we did not specify what "fast" means here. These issues are discussed further in Chapter 8.)

The description of a computation in a form that may be also executed by a computer was earlier called a program. There is a variety of languages— *pro- gramming languages*—for expressing programs, but the most generally useful ones are those that are suitable for both machine and human con- sumption. We need such a language in this book so that our algorithms may be easily understood, designed, implemented as computer programs, and analyzed. The language or notation we have devised is called *Algolic* and will be introduced more systematically at the end of this chapter. Below, we il- lustrate the language by presenting the sorting algorithm in Algolic.

```
algorithm Sort3; {Sort 3 numbers in ascending sequence.}
a, b, c, t : integer; {Each variable may take on integer values.}
begin
    read(a, b, c); {Read 3 numbers into a, b, and c.}
    write(a, b, c); {Display or print the 3 numbers.}
    if a > b then
        begin {a > b here}
                {Interchange a and b.}
                t := a; {Replace the value of t by the value of a.}
                a := b; b := t {a ≤ b after these statements}
        end;
    if b > c then
        begin {b > c here}
                {Interchange b and c.}
                t := b; b := c; c := t; {b ≤ c now}
                if a > b then
                begin {Interchange a and b.}
                        t := a; a := b; b := t
                end
        end;
    {Values are sorted so that a ≤ b ≤ c.}
    write(a, b, c) {Display the numbers in sorted order.}
end.
```

The Algolic form is somewhat longer than necessary here because we have inserted many explanatory remarks; these appear within the braces "{" and "}". The second line *declares* the variables of the program and states that each variable may only take on integer values; the variables have the same characteristics as the labelled boxes used previously. The *read* statement provides for the algorithm inputs and indicates that some external source inserts 3 values into the variables. The *write* statements are used for output and have the effect of displaying or printing the values of the variables on some external medium. Finally, the ":=" symbol represents *assignment,* having the same meaning as the arrow " ← " used in the flow chart of Figure 2.4. If the algorithm is executed with input data 17, 6, and 11, the output displayed by the two write statements during the computation will be:

$$17 \quad 6 \quad 11$$

$$6 \quad 11 \quad 17$$

The term "algorithm" has a long, involved history, originally stemming from the name of a well-known Persian mathematician of the 9th century. It later became associated with arithmetic processes and, then more particularly, with Euclid's algorithm (discussed in the next section). Since the development of automatic digital computers, the word has taken on a more precise meaning that defines a real or abstract computer as the ultimate executing agent—any terminating computation by a computer is an algorithm and any algorithm can be programmed for a computer. Chapter 7 examines some of the theoretical ideas and implications surrounding this correspondence, and also gives a completely formal definition of algorithm. In this section, we have developed an equivalent but informal definition as a set of instructions with four properties: termination, precision, effectiveness, and inputs and outputs.

2.2 DESCRIPTION AND ANALYSIS OF ALGORITHMS

The last section presented several different ways to describe algorithms—instructions in a natural language (i.e., English), flow charts, and programs. We now study these description schemes in more detail and also introduce several important analysis issues.

2.2.1 Euclid's Algorithm

The greatest common divisor (*gcd*) of two positive integers m and n, denoted $gcd(m,n)$, is defined as the largest integer that divides both m and n. For example:

$$gcd(20,28) = 4 \quad gcd(5,10) = 5 \quad gcd(14,33) = 1$$

The *gcd* appears frequently in pure mathematical studies and also is used in some computing techniques. Euclid's algorithm is a procedure for finding the *gcd* that was developed in antiquity (approximately 300-400 B.C.) and described in Euclid's *Elements*. The algorithm is noteworthy not only because of its history and application but also because it exhibits so clearly the required characteristics of algorithms. D. Knuth describes it as "the oldest nontrivial algorithm which has survived to the present day" and as "the world's most famous algorithm". We will use it as a pedagogic example for examining various description and analysis topics.

The algorithm is based on the following two theorems;

Theorem 1: Given positive integers m and n, there exist unique integers q and r such that $q \geq 0$, $0 \leq r < n$, and $m = qn + r$.

Discussion: q is conventionally called the quotient and r the remainder, resulting from the division of m by n. For example, if $m = 20$ and $n = 8$, we have $20 = 2 \times 8 + 4$. This is a fundamental theorem of arithmetic and is used implicitly when performing elementary divisions.

Theorem 2: Given positive integers m and n and the unique integers q and r such that $q \geq 0$, $0 \leq r < n$, and $m = qn + r$, then
(1) if $r = 0$, then $gcd(m, n) = n$ and
(2) if $r \neq 0$, then $gcd(m, n) = gcd(n, r)$

Proof:
(1) $r = 0$. Since $gcd(m, n) \leq n$ and $m = qn$ $(r = 0)$, $gcd(m, n) = n$.
(2) $r \neq 0$. We prove that $gcd(m, n) = gcd(n, r)$ by arguing in two directions:
  a. Show that if some integer k divides m and n, then k also divides n and r. This assures us that the divisors of m and n are retained in n and r.
  b. Show that if some k divides n and r, then k also divides m and n. This guarantees that n and r do not contain any "extra" divisors not in m and n.

Proof of a: Let k divide m and n so that $m = c_1 k$ and $n = c_2 k$ for some positive integers c_1 and c_2. Since $m = qn + r$ for some integers $q \geq 0$ and $0 < r < n$, we have $c_1 k = qc_2 k + r$. Therefore $r = k(c_1 - qc_2)$ and is clearly divisible by k.

Proof of b: Let k divide n and r so that $n = c_1 k$ and $r = c_2 k$ for some positive integers c_1 and c_2. Therefore, we have $m = qc_1 k + c_2 k = k(qc_1 + c_2)$. Therefore k divides m. $\qquad\square$

Example: Let $m = 20$ and $n = 8$; then $m = 2 \times 8 + 4$. Therefore $gcd(20,8)$
$= gcd(8,4)$

The algorithm iteratively uses the calculations implied by Theorem 2 until r becomes zero. That is, it computes a sequence $r_0, r_1, r_2, \ldots$ of remainders:

$$r_0 = m - q_0 n \qquad (q_0 \geq 0, 0 < r_0 < n)$$
$$r_1 = n - q_1 r_0 \qquad (q_1 \geq 0, 0 < r_1 < r_0)$$
$$r_2 = r_0 - q_2 r_1 \qquad (q_2 \geq 0, 0 < r_2 < r_1)$$
$$\vdots$$
$$r_i = r_{i-2} - q_i r_{i-1} \qquad (q_i \geq 0, 0 < r_i < r_{i-1})$$
$$\vdots$$

continuing until a zero remainder, say r_k, is obtained. Then $gcd(m, n) = r_{k-1}$ (assume $n = r_{-1}$), because $gcd(m, n) = gcd(n, r_0) = gcd(r_0, r_1) = gcd(r_1, r_2) = \ldots = gcd(r_{k-2}, r_{k-1}) = r_{k-1}$ if $r_k = 0$.

Example:

$$m = 121 \qquad n = 330$$

i	$r_i = r_{i-2} - q_i r_{i-1}$
0	$121 = 121 - 0 \times 330$
1	$88 = 330 - 2 \times 121$
2	$33 = 121 - 1 \times 88$
3	$22 = 88 - 2 \times 33$
4	$11 = 33 - 1 \times 22$
5	$0 = 22 - 2 \times 11$

$$\therefore gcd(121, 330) = 11$$

Euclid's algorithm is simple but certainly not obvious. Does it always terminate? Termination can be proven by showing that the value of the remainder r_i decreases by at least one at each step; since $r_i \geq 0$ always, this will establish that the remainder eventually decreases to zero. Consider the formula given by Theorem 1:

$$r_{i-2} = q_i r_{i-1} + r_i \qquad \text{where} \quad 0 \leq r_i < r_{i-1}$$

Letting $m = r_{-2}$ and $n = r_{-1}$, this formula holds for all $i = 0, 1, 2, \ldots$ throughout the computation. Since $r_i < r_{i-1}$, the new remainder r_i at each step is at least one smaller than the old remainder r_{i-1}.

We have described Euclid's algorithm in a mixture of mathematics and English, and shown how it produces the *gcd* and terminates. Before the advent of computers, the above description and analysis were adequate. However, these are not sufficient today and we need more precise descriptions and further analysis of the execution properties of the algorithm.

Euclid's Algorithm as a List of Instructions and Flow Chart

A step by step formulation that may be mechanically executed by some agent is:

1. Divide m by n and obtain the remainder r.
2. If $r = 0$, then halt. The answer is n.
3. Replace m by n ($m \leftarrow n$) and n by r ($n \leftarrow r$).
4. Go to step 1.

This description is perhaps not an entirely evident translation of the mathematics/English presented before, mainly because it has eliminated much unnecessary notation and verbiage. It is obtained by noting that $gcd(m, n) = gcd(n, r)$ when $r \neq 0$; therefore, one can substitute n and r for the roles of m and n, respectively, and repeat the main computation and test.

It is often very difficult to be confident of the validity of an algorithm without first trying it out manually on some actual data. This "hand-simulation" is also an effective way to understand the algorithm. Below is a transcript or *trace* of the instructions for the data $m = 121$, $n = 330$.

Steps	m	n	r
1	121	330	121
2, 3	330	121	
4, 1	330	121	88
2, 3	121	88	
4, 1	121	88	33
2, 3	88	33	
4, 1	88	33	22
2, 3	33	22	
4, 1	33	22	11
2, 3	22	11	
4, 1	22	11	0
2		(11)	

Figure 2.5 expresses the instructions in flow chart form. Instead of saying "take the remainder on dividing m by n", we use a new operator **mod** which is assumed to perform this function. If x and y are positive integers, then x **mod** y can also be defined:

$$x \bmod y = x - (x \div y) \times y,$$

where $\div$ indicates integer division (i.e., fractions are disregarded; equivalently, the result of the division is *truncated*).

2.2.2   Correctness

While hand-simulation is useful for understanding an algorithm and for discovering some errors, it is rarely sufficient. Similarly, running a program on a computer with actual data is one way to uncover some, but usually not all, errors that may exist in the program or algorithm. This standard *debugging* method can only confirm the "presence of errors, not their absence". In order to guarantee correctness, the algorithm must be formally proven on a step by step basis. We will introduce the standard methodology using Euclid's algorithm as our example.

Consider the annotated flow chart given in Figure 2.6. An additional box has been inserted at the beginning to distinguish the original input values, denoted by M and N, from the placeholders m and n that change as the computation proceeds. The A_i, $i = 0, \ldots 6$, are *assertions* or statements about the *state* of a machine executing the flow chart; one such assertion is attached to each edge of the chart. The assertion on a particular edge is a statement that is supposed to be true whenever execution passes through that edge. The initial assertion, A_0, expresses the constraints on the algorithm inputs, while the final assertion A_4 describes the desirable relations that must hold when the computation reaches the halt box.

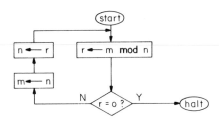

Figure 2.5   Euclid's *GCD* Algorithm

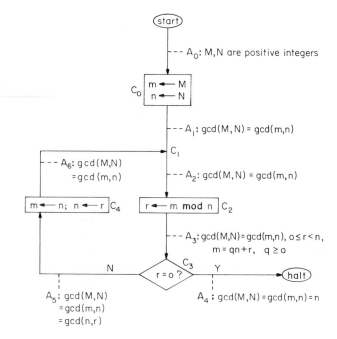

Figure 2.6   Correctness of Euclid's Algorithm

It must be proven that if a box is entered through an edge whose assertion is true and the box is executed, then it will exit through an edge whose assertion is true at that time. Then, by mathematical induction on the number k of boxes or commands executed (C_i in the flow chart), the assertion on the exiting edge of the kth command will be true for all $k \geq 0$, provided that the assertion on the entering edge of the flow chart is true; in particular, if the last edge of a command execution sequence leads to a halt box, the assertion on that edge will be true.

Let us apply these ideas to Figure 2.6. Consider each box in turn:

1. If A_0 is true and C_1 is executed, then A_1 is true since $M = m$ and $N = n$ at that point.
2. $A_1 = A_6 = A_2$.
3. If A_2 is true and C_2 is executed, then A_3 is true by Theorem 1 (Section 2.2.1).
4. If A_3 is true and the test in C_3 returns "Yes," then A_4 is true by the first part of Theorem 2 (Section 2.2.1).

If A_3 is true and the test in C_3 returns "No," then A_5 is true by the second part of Theorem 2.

5. If A_5 is true and C_4 is executed, then A_6 is true since $gcd(m, n) = gcd(n, r)$ before the replacements of C_4.

This establishes the required local relations A_1 through A_6.

Consider now a particular case. Executing the flow chart on the initial data, $M = 20$ and $N = 8$, yields the command execution sequence:

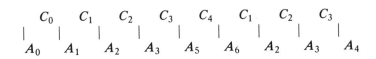

where the assertions have been inserted for clarity. Then, since A_0 is assumed true, our local proofs for each individual box have established that each A_1, A_2, ... A_4 is successively true as execution proceeds. Therefore, on termination, A_4 is true.

For any command sequence of any length, the assertion on the exiting edge of the last command will be true by mathematical induction. Thus, command sequences ending at C_3 and output edge leading to the halt box will always have A_4 true. If A_4 accurately describes the intent of the algorithm, i.e., describes the required relations between the input M and N and the output n, the algorithm is considered correct.

This general procedure can be applied to any algorithm expressed as a flow chart. The most difficult and creative part is to determine the appropriate assertions. Note that we have not proved that the algorithm always terminates; we have only shown that if it reaches the halt box, it will produce a correct answer. Generally, termination is handled separately. For gcd, the proof relies on the termination arguments discussed in the last section.

2.2.3   Program Descriptions

One Algolic program that directly follows the preceding descriptions for Euclid's algorithm is:

algorithm *GCD*0; {Call the algorithm "GCD0".}
m, n, r : *integer*; {Variables take on integer values.}
begin
    read(*m, n*); {Read two integers into *m* and *n*. Assume that they are
                positive.}
    write('*m* = ', *m*, '*n* = ', *n*); {Display *m* and *n*, properly identified.}
1: *r* := *m* **mod** *n*;
    if *r* ≠ 0 **then** {*r* ≠ 0 here}
    begin {Replace *m* by *n* and *n* by *r*.}
            m := *n*; *n* := *r*;
            go to 1 {Transfer back to statement 1 above.}
    end;
    {*r* = 0 here and *n* contains the *gcd*.}
    write('*The gcd is* ', *n*) {Print answer.}
end.

The *read* statement obtains two numbers and inserts them into *m* and *n*. The quoted elements in the *write* statement are printed literally with the values of the variables named in the 2nd and 4th fields; for example, if *m* = 20 and *n* = 8, this output might appear as follows:

$$m = 20 \quad n = 8$$

The last *write* displays the string "The gcd is ", followed by the value of *n*. The statement "*r* := *m* **mod** *n*" is *labelled* or explicitly identified by the integer 1 so that it may be referenced elsewhere in a **go to** statement; the "**go to**" interrupts the normal sequential execution of statements and causes execution to continue at the particular labelled statement.

In general, there are many different ways to solve the same problem and each algorithm will have different characteristics. For example, if Euclid's algorithm had not been known, we might have devised the following straightforward procedure:

1. Set *g* equal to *n* (*g* ← *n*).
2. If *g* divides *m* and *n*, then halt. *g* is the *gcd*.
3. Decrement *g* by 1 (*g* ← *g* − 1).
4. Go to step 2.

The instruction "*g* ← *g* − 1" can be best explained in terms of our earlier labelled box analogy (Section 2.1): Take the contents of *g*, subtract 1 from it, and insert the result back into box g. In Algolic form (and omitting the declarations and input-output statements), this algorithm is:

algorithm *SimpleGCD*;
    ⋮
  $g := n$;
1: **if not** $((m \bmod g = 0)$ **and** $(n \bmod g = 0))$ **then**
    begin { g is not a divisor of both m and n. }
        $g := g - 1$;
        go to 1
    end;
{ g is the *gcd*. }
    ⋮
end.

Which algorithm is better, Simple*GCD* or Euclid's algorithm? In order to answer this question, we must agree on some quantitative definition of "better." Intuitively we may want to use either the amount of work expended in performing the algorithm (a *time* measure) or the amount of storage required for any temporary data and the instructions (a *space* measure), or some combination of time and space. Time measures are commonly employed; these are usually formulated in terms of the number of operations performed (e.g., arithmetic, testing, ...) as a function of the input data. With this criterion, Simple*GCD* is less efficient (in time) since it tests every integer between n and the $gcd(m, n)$, while Euclid's algorithm eliminates many of the intervening integers by taking the remainder as the next candidate; the Simple*GCD* tests are also more complicated than in Euclid's algorithm, requiring two divisions (m **mod** g and n **mod** g) for each candidate. For example, $gcd(20, 8)$ is obtained in two passes through the loop with Euclid's algorithm and five passes using *SimpleGCD*. The time (or space) "complexity" can be divided further under such categories as worst case, best case, and average behavior.

Another important set of questions is concerned with optimality. Is a given algorithm the best possible, according to some measure of "best"? Euclid's algorithm is better than Simple*GCD*, using most reasonable definitions of "better," but is it the very best? Apparently not so, since at least one *gcd* algorithm exists which appears superior.[1] The search for optimality is extremely difficult and has only occasionally been successful; one important area where optimality results have been obtained is in general sorting algorithms.

---

[1] A detailed discussion of the greatest common divisor appears in Volume 2 of D. Knuth's series, *The Art of Computer Programming* (Addison-Wesley, 1969).

In the same way that there may be several different algorithms for the same problem, there are many different ways to express the same algorithm as a program in a given language. Below is another, and in some ways better, Algolic program for Euclid's algorithm:

```
algorithm GCD1;
m, n, r : integer;
begin read(m, n); write('m=', m, ' n=', n);
      while n ≠ 0 do {Perform loop as long as n ≠ 0.}
      begin  r := m mod n;
             m := n; n := r
      end;   {gcd is in m.}
      write('The gcd is ', m)
end.
```

The new construct "**while** *condition* **do** *S*" has the meaning:

1. If *condition* is true, then execute *S*; otherwise go to step 3.
2. Go to step 1.
3. Execute statement following "**while** *condition* **do** *S*".

The **while** construct was devised to provide a high-level means of expressing this extremely common desired behavior. While the same behavior can be obtained using **go to**'s and labelled statements (e.g., *GCD*0 program), the **while** form is normally easier to understand and use, especially for larger programs.

As a final example, we present the *gcd* algorithm in a programming language that differs radically from the Algolic shown so far, but can be viewed as an extension to this notation. The functional form of program below together with the facility to define a function in terms of itself, permits a description that closely resembles the original mathematical basis of the algorithm:

```
function gcd(m, n : integer) : integer;
gcd := if n = 0 then m
       else gcd(n, m mod n);
```

This definition can be interpreted: "The function *gcd* has two integer parameters *m* and *n* and returns an integer value. If $n = 0$, the function's value is *m*; otherwise, the value is obtained by substituting *n* for the first argument, the value of *m* **mod** *n* for the remaining argument, and invoking the function again."

Such functions that invoke themselves are called *recursive*. Note how this type of definition, which uses features available in many programming languages, can almost be directly translated from Theorem 2 of Section 2.2.1.

2.3 PERFORMING ALGORITHMS ON COMPUTERS

Human beings can act as universal computing agents in the sense that they can perform any well-specified set of instructions involving logical and arithmetic operations and tests. The best known non-biological device with this capability is the *digital computer*. Digital computers operate in discrete counting steps; hence the term "digital." There is another class of machines, called *analog* computers, that compute by measuring; a slide rule is a well-known, but obsolete, example of an analog device. We are concerned exclusively with digital computers. In this section we will outline the general structure and operation of a computer. The analogy with human calculating methods is sufficiently close that it is illuminating to first present a pencil, paper, and desk calculator process.

Suppose that our computing tools were pencil, paper, and a desk calculator. In order to manually compute, say *gcd*(121, 330) with these tools, we might organize the paper as shown in Figure 2.7. At the top of the page is the *gcd* algorithm, expressed as four instructions; the successive results for *m, n,* and *r* are written on the bottom of the page as we execute the instructions. An arithmetic operation, such as computing the remainder, is performed on the desk calculator; this machine has an illuminated *register* that indicates either

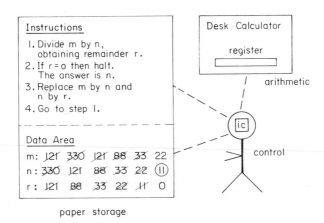

Figure 2.7   Computing *GCD* with Pencil, Paper, and Calculator

the current value being inserted into the calculator or the results of an operation. The execution of the algorithm is controlled by the human who transfers data to and from the desk calculator, writes the correct values of m, n, and r onto the paper, and decides what to do next. As the computation proceeds, we might mentally update an *instruction counter* (*ic*) that points to the next instruction to be executed. (Note that we are not stating that a human will go through this procedure, only that a human could.) The execution history for *gcd*(121, 330) can be characterized by the sequence of instructions executed; this gives the sequence:

$$1\ 2\ 3\ 4\ 1\ 2\ 3\ 4\ 1\ 2\ 3\ 4\ 1\ 2\ 3\ 4\ 1\ 2\ 3\ 4\ 1\ 2\ 3\ 4\ 1\ 2.$$

A digital computer has a similar organization as shown in Figure 2.8. Internally, it consists minimally of three main components:

1. arithmetic unit
   This part is capable of performing various arithmetic and other operations, as well as testing and comparing the values of data. It contains one or more registers for storing operands and results.
2. storage
   This is the "memory" part of the machine where both the instructions or *program*, and the data are stored. Information can be written into storage and also read from memory. Storage consists of a large number of boxes or *cells*, each of which can be individually accessed.
3. control
   The control unit is responsible for initiating arithmetic operations and storage accesses, for reading and interpreting instructions from storage, and, in general, for managing the operation of the entire computer system. It has several internal registers of which the most important is the instruction counter (*ic*).

The computer is connected to the external world through a console containing a variety of switches and displays, and also typically through some input-output devices, such as typewriter terminals. These facilities permit information to be entered into the system, results to be printed from the system, and external control of the computer's operation.

A simple hypothetical machine is now defined. Storage consists of 10,000 cells or words, each capable of holding five decimal digits plus a sign. Examples are given in Figure 2.9. Every word is uniquely labelled or *addressed* with a number from 0000 to 9999; thus one can reference, for example, the word with address (location, label) 1,473. Depending on the interpretation

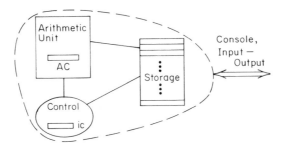

Figure 2.8   Computer Organization

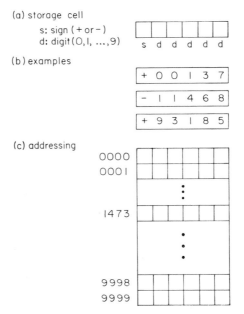

Figure 2.9   Storage

by the control unit, a given word can be treated as an item of data or as an instruction.

Our machine has what is called a "single-address" instruction format. Every instruction consists of an *operation* and, at most, a single *operand*; the operation may be arithmetic, testing, or transfer of control, and the operand is specified by a storage address. An instruction word is broken into these two fields according to the format of Figure 2.10(a). Most instructions implicitly refer to an *accumulator* register, denoted AC, that is part of the arithmetic unit. The AC is used to store the results and one of the operands of an arithmetic operation, and to hold a number that is to be compared against zero. The instruction repertoire and meaning of each instruction is given in Figure 2.10(b). In the figure, the notation $[\alpha]$ means "the contents of the location given by the 4-digit address α."

Examples of Instructions:

1. Let [0572] be +00025 (i.e., address 0572 contains the number +25) and let the AC contain 12.

    + 3 0 5 7 2   The operation code is +3 and the operand field is 0572 for this instruction. It results in the addition 12 + 25 = 37. The AC contains 37 after execution. Location 0572 still contains 25.

2. Let [1619] = −11111 and AC = +03123.

    + 1 1 6 1 9   Load the AC with [1619]. AC = −11111 (and [1619] is unchanged) after the load is performed.

3. Let [1619] = −11111 and AC = +03123.

    + 2 1 6 1 9   Store the AC into [1619]. [1619] = +03123 (and AC remains unchanged) after the store operation.

4. + 5 0 3 7 6   Transfer ("unconditionally") to location 0376 to get the next instruction to be executed, and continue the execution sequence at that point.

5. Let AC = −00325.

    + 7 0 3 7 6   Continue execution at the instruction following this one (the instruction at the next sequential address after this one), since AC is not greater than zero.

6. + 0 7 0 3 2   The computer halts on executing this instruction. Note that the address is irrelevant for a halt.

In the interests of simplicity, we have not bothered to include any input-output instructions or more elaborate arithmetic ones. However, the overall instruction set of this machine is sufficient for any computational task[2] and for illustrating the most significant elements of a machine's operation.

How does the computer work? The *control* or executive part of the system continuously executes the following loop, termed the *instruction cycle*:

---

[2] For *any* computational task, we also need an unbounded amount of "auxiliary" storage with input and output operations. (Chapter 7 presents the appropriate model and theory.)

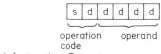

operation   operand
code

(a) Instruction Format

Operation Code	Meaning of Instruction (α denotes operand field)
+ 0	Halt the machine.
+ 1	AC ← [α] (load)
+ 2	[α] ← AC (store)
+ 3	AC ← AC+[α] (add)
+ 4	AC ← AC −[α] (subtract)
+ 5	go to α (transfer)
+ 6	if AC=0 then go to α (transfer on AC=0)
+ 7	if AC>0 then go to α (transfer on AC>0)
+ 8	if AC<0 then go to α (transfer on AC<0)

(b) Instruction Set

Figure 2.10   Machine Instructions

1. Get instruction, say I, from the storage location addressed by the in-struction counter ic.
2. Update instruction counter to point to next instruction. ($ic \leftarrow ic + 1$)
3. Execute the instruction previously retrieved. (Execute instruction I.)
4. Go to step 1.

Step 3 involves the interpretation of I according to Figure 2.11(b). The four branch or transfer instructions (operations +5, +6, +7, and +8) will reset the ic to the transfer address if the branch is taken.

Assuming that a program and any required data have somehow been placed ("loaded") into storage, the execution is initiated by setting the ic to the address of the first instruction of the program and then pressing the computer's "start" button; the ic can be set from switches on the computer console. Let us now program this machine to solve a familiar problem.

Euclid's Algorithm in Machine Language

Since we have deliberately omitted any division and **mod** operations in the computer, Euclid's algorithm must first be rephrased in terms of addition and subtraction only. The most straightforward technique is to express **mod** as a sequence of subtractions and tests:

Let m and n be positive integers. Then m **mod** n is computed in Algolic by:

$r := m$;
while $r \geq n$ **do** $r := r - n$ {Divide by successive subtractions.} ;
$\{r = m \bmod n\}$

To translate the Algolic into our machine language, we must select addresses for m, n, and r. If m is stored in address 1000, n in 1001, and r in 1002, then the following machine language code will realize this computation:

Address	Instruction	Remarks
0201	+ 1 1 0 0 0	Load m into AC.
0202	+ 4 1 0 0 1	AC ← AC − n.
0203	+ 8 0 2 0 5	If $(r - n) < 0$, then go to 205.
0204	+ 5 0 2 0 2	$r \geq n$. Repeat at 0202.
0205	+ 3 1 0 0 1	$(r - n) < 0$. Add n back in.
0206	+ 2 1 0 0 2	Store result in r.

We have arbitrarily chosen the storage locations for m, n, and r, and also arbitrarily selected address 0201 for the first instruction of the program. The general idea is to load the value of m into the AC, do all the arithmetic and tests with the contents of the AC and n, and finally store the result in r.

As before, a hand simulation leads to greater understanding. Let $m = 20$ and $n = 8$. Starting with the ic at 201, we have:

Instruction Address	Values after Execution of Instruction				
	AC	m	n	r	ic
0201	20	20	8	—	0202
0202	12	20	8	—	0203
0203	12	20	8	—	0204
0204	12	20	8	—	0202
0202	4	20	8	—	0203
0203	4	20	8	—	0204
0204	4	20	8	—	0202
0202	−4	20	8	—	0203
0203	−4	20	8	—	0205
0205	4	20	8	—	0206
0206	4	20	8	4	0207

gcd also requires that we replace *m* by *n* and *n* by *r*. Assuming *m, n,* and *r* are stored above, this replacement is accomplished by the following four instructions:

Instruction	Remarks
+ 1 1 0 0 1	Load *n* into AC.
+ 2 1 0 0 0	Store in *m*.
+ 1 1 0 0 2	Load *r* into AC.
+ 2 1 0 0 1	Store in *n*.

The complete *gcd* program can now be constructed by combining these code segments with some minor changes:

Address	Instruction	Remarks
		gcd Program
		1. Compute remainder.
0201	+ 1 1 0 0 0	AC ← *m*
0202	+ 4 1 0 0 1	AC ← AC − *n* (*r* − *n*)
0203	+ 8 0 2 0 5	Transfer if (*r* − *n*) < 0
0204	+ 5 0 2 0 2	Transfer back to 202.
0205	+ 3 1 0 0 1	Add *n* back in.
		2. Test for termination.
0206	+ 6 0 2 1 3	Go to end if *r* = 0.
0207	+ 2 1 0 0 2	Store AC into *r*.
		3. Replace *m* by *n* and *n* by *r*.
0208	+ 1 1 0 0 1	AC ← *n*
0209	+ 2 1 0 0 0	*m* ← AC
0210	+ 1 1 0 0 2	AC ← *r*
0211	+ 2 1 0 0 1	*n* ← AC
0212	+ 5 0 2 0 1	4. Return to main loop.
0213	+ 0 0 0 0 0	5. Halt. Answer is in *n*.

In order to execute this program, we must:

1. Load the instructions into storage, starting at location 0201.
2. Load the values of *m* and *n* into addresses 1000 and 1001, respectively. (*r* does not have to be initialized externally since its value is computed from *m* and *n*.)
3. Set the *ic* to 0201.
4. Press the "start" button.

When the machine halts, the *gcd* will be stored in word 1001.

This simple computer can be programmed to perform any algorithm. While it is not an exact replica of any existing machine, it has many of the essential features of computers and could be easily constructed with electronic components.

Symbolic Programming Languages and Higher-Level Machines

The machine language version of *gcd* is clearly a detailed and tedious description of the algorithm. The programmer is concerned with many seemingly arbitrary problems, such as where to place the instructions and data in storage and the translation of familiar operations into numeric operation codes. One of the first programming advances was the development of symbolic languages at the machine level. Instead of writing, say, $+ \; 1 \; 1 \; 0 \; 0 \; 1$ for the instruction to load *n* into the AC, one might write: *LD N*, where *LD* stands for the "load" operation and *N* is a programmer-defined name for some data address. This type of symbolic language is called *assembly language.* An assembly language program for computing the remainder (*m* **mod** *n*) might be:

Address	Instruction		Remarks
	LD	M	AC ← M
LOOP	SUB	N	AC ← AC − N
	TLZ	OUT	Transfer out of loop if AC < 0.
	TR	LOOP	Transfer back to *LOOP*.
OUT	ADD	N	Add *N* back in.
	ST	R	Store result in *R*.

Another program, an *assembler*, is used to translate assembly language into machine language. The assembler takes care of allocating machine locations to symbols and translating symbolic operations and operands into their numeric codes.

Higher-level symbolic languages, such as Algolic, are realized on computers by providing more complex translators that produce equivalent machine language programs. These languages relieve the programmer of responsibility for many machine details and permit him to concentrate on his problem and algorithm. Chapter 6 discusses a number of issues and techniques in programming languages, translators, and other programming aids.

Translator programs and other programming utilities are called *software*, to distinguish them from the *hardware* components of a computer system.

One trend in computer design is to implement some of this software as hardware, so that the computer itself appears as a higher-level language machine to the user.

2.4 INTRODUCTION TO THE ALGOLIC LANGUAGE

Algolic is the name of our notation for *describing* algorithms. Since the algorithms of this book are to be read, understood, analyzed, and developed by *humans*, Algolic is a convenient high-level problem solving language that is independent of the idiosyncrasies and details of any particular machine. However, it is still an easy task to implement an Algolic "program" on any computer.

Algolic derives from a language called *Algol-60* that was designed by an international group of computer experts in the late 1950's. (The acronym "Algol" stands for *algo*rithmic *l*anguage.) Translators for Algol-60 have been constructed for many machines, but, more importantly, the language and some of its modern variations, has served as an international standard for communicating algorithms through the published literature. The best-known successor to Algol-60 is the *Pascal* language developed by N. Wirth in 1970. Algolic strongly resembles a subset of Pascal.

All Algolic programs have the form:

algorithm *identifier;*
   declarations
   statements.

identifier is an arbitrary name that serves to identify the algorithm. The *declarations* part lists the variables of the program and specifies the set of possible values each variable may take. The actions of the algorithm are listed in the *statements* component. Comments or explanatory remarks that are not part of the formal algorithm description are enclosed in braces "{" and "}", and may appear anywhere in a program.

Example:
algorithm *ComputeInterest*; {identifier is "ComputeInterest"}
{Given the number of *days* and the *principal*, *ComputeInterest* will compute the amount of *interest* earned at a rate of 5%.}
days : *integer*; *principal, interest* : *real*; {declarations}
begin {statements}
   read(*principal, days*);
   interest := (*days*/365) × 0.05 × *principal*;
   write('*The interest earned for', days, 'days at* 5% *on the principal amount', principal, 'is', interest, 'dollars'*)
end.

In the above example, the program is written in a particular *style*. Notice how the layout allows the reader to readily understand the program. For example, variable names, such as "days" and "interest" were chosen to indicate their use. Names such as "x1" and "x2" could have been used without affecting the meaning but would have made the program less understandable. We also indented the statements appearing between the **begin** and **end**. This is again stylistic and promotes clarity and readability.

The programs in this book are meant to illustrate good programming style. As an extreme example of bad form, let us rewrite the above program:

algorithm *QX*;*QY*: *integer*;*Q1*,
Q2:*real*;**begin** *read*(*Q1*,*QY*); *Q2* := (
QY/365) × 0.05 × *Q1*; *write*('*The interest earned for*',
 QY,'*days at* 5% *on the principal amount*', *Q1*, '*is*',
Q2,'*dollars*') **end.**

2.4.1 Variables and Expressions

A *variable* identifies a storage cell that can hold *values*. The name of a variable is given by a variable *identifier*, which may be any sequence of characters starting with a letter. A variable can only have one value at a time.

Examples of variable identifiers: *A, Harry, main,* $x15$, *InterestRate.*

Associated with each variable v is a *type* that defines the permissible values that v may hold. We will initially allow two types:

1. integer: the set of integers.
2. real: a subset of the real numbers.

Thus if a variable x is of type integer, x may take on or hold any integer value; if x is of type real, it can hold any "real" value (defined below).

The permissible integers and reals are defined more precisely:

1. An *integer* is any positive or negative whole number, including zero. Examples: 0, -3276, $+575$, 13.
2. A *real* number is given by a finite sequence of digits, possibly preceded by a sign and containing a decimal point, and optionally followed by an exponent part consisting of the letter E followed by an integer. The exponent part denotes a power of 10. A representation aEb, where a is the (signed) digit sequence and b is the exponent power, denotes the number $a \times 10^b$.
   Examples: 15.7, 35, -0.0037, $10.0058E-17$, $0.00025E1278$, $-0168E-13$. The last three numbers represent 10.0058×10^{-17}, 0.00025×10^{1278}, and -168×10^{-13}, respectively.

Note that any integer value is also a real value; the integers are a subset of the reals.

The name and type of each variable used in an Algolic program must be listed or declared in the declarations part at the beginning of the code. Each declaration in this part consists of one or more variable identifiers followed by a colon (:) and then a type; semi-colons are used to separate each declaration.

Examples:

1. *a* : *integer*; *x3* : *real*;
   This declares the variable *a* to be of type integer and *x3* to be of type real.
2. *r1, r2, r3* : *real*; *int, m* : *integer*;
   r1, r2, and *r3* are of real type, while *int* and *m* are declared to be of type integer.

An *expression* is a collection of variables, constants, and operators that may be *evaluated* to produce a value. *Arithmetic expressions* are expressions involving only variables and constants of type real or integer and the operators $+$, $-$, $\times$, $/$, $\div$, and **mod**. Parentheses may be used for grouping.

Examples of arithmetic expressions:

$(x3+15.2)/root$, $a \times (b \div c)$ **mod** 6, y, $-13.32E15$,
$(days/365) \times 0.05 \times principal$.

Arithmetic expressions are normally evaluated from left to right, except that the operators $\times$, $/$, $\div$, and **mod** take precedence over $+$ and $-$. Thus $a + b \times c$ is evaluated as $a + (b \times c)$, and $a/b \times c$ is computed as $(a/b) \times c$. The operators $+$, $-$, $\times$ and $/$ may have either integer or real operands, while $\div$ performs division with truncation producing an integer quotient. Given two integers a and b with $b \neq 0$, the operators $\div$ and **mod** satisfy:

$$a = (a \div b) \times b + (a \bmod b)$$

where $0 \leq a \bmod b < b$. ($a \div b$ is the quotient and $a \bmod b$ is the remainder on dividing a by b).

The second type of expression that we have used appears in **if** statements, **while** statements, and other statement types where it is necessary to test the truth or falsity of some logical conditions. The expressions describing these conditions are called *Boolean expressions*, after the logician George Boole;

they evaluate to either *true* or *false*. Boolean expressions may take any of the four forms:

$$(ae_1 \ominus ae_2), \quad b_1 \text{ and } b_2, \quad b_1 \text{ or } b_2, \quad \text{not } b$$

where ae_1 and ae_2 are arithmetic expressions, $\ominus$ is a *relation* from the set $\{ =, \neq, >, <, \geq, \leq \}$, and b, b_1, and b_2 are Boolean expressions. $(ae_1 \ominus ae_2)$ is *true* only if the relation $\ominus$ holds between ae_1 and ae_2; otherwise the value of the expression is *false*.
b_1 **and** b_2 is *true* only if *both* b_1 and b_2 are *true*.
b_1 **or** b_2 is *true* if either b_1 or b_2 is *true*.
not b is *true only* if b is *false*.

Examples of Boolean expressions:

$(n \neq 0)$ **or** $(a + b \geq c)$, **not** $(k < y + z)$,
not $((m \bmod g = 0) \text{ and } (n \bmod g = 0))$, $n < m$

Boolean expressions are developed in more detail in Chapter 4.

2.4.2   Statements

The *declarations* section of an Algolic program describes the data of the algorithm while the *statements* part contains the instructions to be performed. Statements are executed in the order that they appear unless directed otherwise. A program terminates after its last statement has been executed.

If S_1 and S_2 are statements, then S_1; S_2 indicates that S_2 is to be executed immediately after S_1; the semi-colon is used as a statement separator. A sequence of statements may be grouped together and treated as a unit by bracketing them with **begin** and **end**. The group is then called a *compound statement* to distinguish it from the simple or basic statements of the language. The statements section of an Algolic algorithm consists of either a simple or a compound statement; in the latter case, it has the form:

$$\textbf{begin } S_1; S_2; \ldots ; S_n \textbf{ end}$$

where the S_i are statements.

In this section, we will define assignment, **go to**, **if/then/else**, and input-output statements. These are the most basic statement types and are sufficient for any algorithm. Some additional statements, such as the **while** statement introduced earlier, are covered in succeeding chapters.

Assignment Statement

Assignments are specified by statements of the form:

$$variable := expression$$

When an assignment statement is executed, the *expression* part is evaluated and the resulting value is assigned to the *variable* given on the left side of the ":=" symbol. The old value of the *variable* is destroyed by the assignment. Let the following declarations be valid:

a, b, c : integer; x, y, z : real

1. Suppose *a* has the value 15. Execution of

$$a := a + 1$$

   proceeds by

   (1) first evaluating the expression $a + 1$, yielding a result of 16, and
   (2) then assigning 16 to *a*.

   The result of performing this statement is that *a* now has a value of 16.
2. Let *a* and *b* have values of 145 and 17, respectively. Execution of

$$b := (a \div 10) \times 10$$

   assigns a new value of $(145 \div 10) \times 10 = 14 \times 10 = 140$ to *b*. *b*'s old value (17) is destroyed.
3. Let *x, y,* and *z* have the values 3.14159, 20, and 3.51*E*-978, respectively. The assignment

$$z := (x \times y \times y)/4$$

   assigns the new value 314.159 to *z*.

The symbol ":=" is used rather than "=", or "←", or some other symbol, for several reasons. Some programming languages employ "=" for the assignment operation but this can cause confusion with the ordinary mathematical meaning of "=" which denotes equality and the resulting natural use of "=" to express relations in Boolean expressions. The character set handled by the early machines was relatively small and did not include new appealing characters such as "←". The combination of two available characters ":" and "=" was selected and it has remained the assignment symbol in many programming languages for historical reasons.

go to and Labelled Statements

The **go to** statement is the analogue of the arrow line in a flow chart. Normally, an Algolic program is executed in sequence from top to bottom. A **go to** statement changes this normal "flow of control" and causes execution to continue at the *target* identified in the **go to**. The form is:

go to label

where *label* specifies the target statement. The *label* may be any string of characters starting with a letter or it may be an unsigned integer.

A statement S is identified with a label L by preceding S by L and a colon (:), i.e.,

$$L : S$$

The same label can only be used for one statement.

Example:

$$x := y + z;$$

> **go to** 15; {Transfer to 15.}
>
> *mainloop*: $y := y + 1$; {statement labelled by *mainloop*.}
> $\vdots$
>
> 15: **go to** *mainloop*; {Transfer to *mainloop*.}
> $\vdots$

The **go to** statement is quite primitive and low level, compared to the other statements of Algolic. We will see in the next chapter that many of its uses are subsumed by some other higher-level statements. Nevertheless, we will keep it in Algolic because:

1. It can be used to clearly describe some machine level activities.
2. It is useful for defining higher level constructs.
3. There are some algorithms that can only be described awkwardly without **go to**'s.

if Statements

Much of the power of computers and algorithmic notations derives from their ability to conditionally execute instructions. This facility is provided in Algolic through the **if/then** and **if/then/else** statements.

The **if/then** statement has the form:

if Boolean expression **then** statement

where *statement* may be either a simple or a compound statement.

Examples:

if $a > 15$ **then begin** $x := y + z; a := a + 1$ **end**
if $(b1 = b2)$ **or** $(b3 \leq y)$ **then go to** 76

The **if/then** specifies that the *statement* portion is to be executed only if the *Boolean expression* is *true*; otherwise execution continues after the statement. An equivalent flow chart is given in Figure 2.11(a).

The **if/then/else** is a generalization of the **if/then** statement which permits a sequence of (Boolean expression, statements) pairs. It has the form:

if B **then** S_1 **else** S_2

where B is a Boolean expression and S_1 and S_2 are statements. The statement is equivalent to:

> **if** B **then**
> **begin** S_1; **go to** *elsepart* **end**;
> S_2;
elsepart: ...

Figure 2.11(b) gives the corresponding flow chart.

Note that S_2 itself can be an **if/then** or an **if/then/else** statement. Programs will frequently contain long sequences of **if/then/else**'s such as **if** B_1 **then** S_1 **else if** B_2 **then** S_2 **else** ... **else if** B_n **then** S_n **else** S_{n+1}.

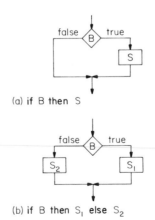

(a) if B then S

(b) if B then S₁ else S₂

Figure 2.11 Flow Charts for **if** Statements

Input/Output Statements

There are two ways to change the value of a variable. The first is to assign it a new value using the assignment statement. The second method is to "read" a value from some source external to the algorithm (or computer); the source could be a human or it could be some other machine. In Algolic, we describe this "reading" by the statement:

$read(v_1, \ldots, v_n)$

where $v_1, \ldots, v_n$ are variable names. The effect is to read values sequentially from some external source, assigning the first value to variable v_1, the second to v_2, and so forth. For example:

Examples: $read(A1)$, $read(a, x, z)$.

The inverse of reading a value from an external source is to display or write a value on some external medium. Here, the medium may be, for example, paper, a TV screen, or some magnetic storage device. Typically, we wish to display the values of variables and also some identifying information. This can be accomplished with the write statement:

$write(i_1, i_2, \ldots, i_n)$

where each item $i_1, \ldots, i_n$ is either a variable name or a quoted string of characters. If an item i_k is a variable, then its value is displayed; if i_k is a quoted string, then the string itself is displayed.

Examples:

1. *write(ab)*; {Display value of variable *ab*}
2. *write('ab')*; {Display the string *ab*}
3. Let *m* and *n* have the values 10 and 20 respectively.
   Then: *write ('Values of M and N are ', m, n)* causes the display:
   Values of *M* and *N* are 10 20

2.4.3   Examples of Algolic Programs

The examples of this section are meant to further illustrate the use of Algolic and to introduce some additional issues in the design of algorithms.

Example 1: Finding the Maximum, Minimum, and Average

Let *S* be a set of real numbers. We desire an algorithm that computes the smallest number, largest number, and mean or average of all the numbers in

S. Suppose *S* contained only a few elements, say three. Then, a suitable Algolic algorithm is not difficult to design. One could, for example, sort the three numbers using the program *Sort 3* given in Section 2.1, and then the minimum and maximum are directly available. Another approach, that avoids the interchanges of *Sort 3* and can be generalized into a more efficient algorithm for larger sets, involves computing a "current" maximum and minimum as each number is read. Thus, if *x* is the next number examined, and *min* and *max* contain the current smallest and largest numbers examined so far, the following statement will update these variables:

if $x > max$ **then** $max := x$ **else if** $x < min$ **then** $min := x$

This idea leads to the algorithm:

algorithm *Find3*;
a, b, c, max, min, average : *real*;
{*a, b*, and *c* will contain the 3 elements of *S*. *max, min*, and *average* will hold the largest, smallest, and mean of the numbers.}
begin
    read(a); {Read 1st number into *a*.}
    $max := a$; $min := a$; {Initialize *max* and *min* to 1st number.}
    read(b); {Read 2nd number into *b*.}
    if $b > max$ **then** $max := b$ **else if** $b < min$ **then** $min := b$;
    read(c); {Get 3rd number and store in *c*.}
    if $c > max$ **then** $max := c$ **else if** $c < min$ **then** $min := c$;
    $average := (a + b + c)/3$;
    write('largest =', max, 'smallest =', min, 'mean =', average)
end.

Find 3 works correctly for *any* three numbers. However, we usually want our algorithms to apply more generally. (After all, the output of *Find 3* can be obtained almost instantaneously by inspection and a small amount of manual arithmetic.) Assume now that *S* contains *n* real numbers, where *n* is *any* positive integer, and that the data is arranged in the order:

$$n \; x_1 \; x_2 \; \cdots \; x_n$$

where the x_i are the elements of *S*. The central part of our new algorithm is a loop that is executed *n* times, once for each element of *S*. Inside the loop, the current maximum (*max*), current minimum (*min*), and the sum of all the numbers read to that point (*sum*) are computed. At the end of the k th time through the loop, these variables will have the values:

min = minimum of $(x_1, \ldots, x_k)$
max = maximum of $(x_1, \ldots, x_k)$

$$sum = \sum_{i=1}^{k} x_i$$

The Algolic is:

algorithm *MaxMinMean*;
index, n : integer; x, min, max, sum : real;
begin {First initialize variables.}
   read(n); {*n* is the size of the set *S.*}
   index := *n*; {*index* will control the looping.}
   max := $-10E500$; *min* := $10E500$;
   {Assume that $-10E500 < x < 10E500$ for all x in *S.*}
   sum := 0;
   next: read(x); {Get next number in *S.*}
     if $x > max$ **then** *max* := *x*; **if** $x < min$ **then** *min* := *x*;
     sum := *sum* + *x*; {Accumulate the sum.}
     index := *index* $-$ 1; {Decrement loop count.}
     if *index* $\neq$ 0 **then go to** *next*;
   {*index* = 0 and loop has been performed *n* times.}
   sum := *sum/n*; {Compute the average.}
   write('min = *', min, 'max* = *',max, 'mean* = *',sum)*
end.

Two aspects of this program warrant some further comments. The first is the initialization code at the beginning which sets *index, max, min*, and *sum* to their values. A frequent and frustrating programming error is either to initialize variables incorrectly or to forget the initialization. The assignments to *max* and *min* are a little tricky; the intent is to ensure that *max* and *min* will be reset to the value of x the first time through the loop. This trick can be avoided by also performing one "*read(x)*" and then setting *min, max*, and *sum* to x, all during the initialization.

The second interesting aspect is the loop control. It is often the case that a set of statements is to be repeated a fixed number of times. This can be implemented using an index or count variable (*index* in *MaxMinMean*) that is incremented or decremented by 1 at each time through the loop and tested against some upper or lower limit. Because of the frequent need for this type of repetitive execution, a special statement is available in most programming languages to automatically perform "looping with an index;" special looping statements are introduced in the next chapter.

Example 2: Fibonacci Numbers

Consider the following problem in population growth. Assume:

1. A colony starts with one pair of fertile rabbits.
2. Each pair of fertile rabbits produces a pair of offspring every month.
3. A new pair becomes fertile in one month.
4. Rabbits never die.

What is the minimum number of months n that it will take for the colony to attain a population of m rabbit pairs, where $m \geq 2$?

This problem appeared in a book by the Italian mathematician L. Fibonacci in the 13th century and leads to a sequence of numbers, now called Fibonacci numbers. After the first month, there will be two rabbit pairs, the original pair and their offspring. After the second month, there will be three pairs, the original and their first offspring plus a new second offspring of the original pair—recall that it will take one month for the first offspring pair to become fertile. After the third month, there will be five pairs—the three pairs remaining from the second month, a new offspring from the original, and a new offspring from the now fertile first offspring of the original pair. In general, the population at the end of any month, say the $(n + 2)$nd month, will consist of the colony existing at the end of the $(n + 1)$st month plus the new offsprings of all the fertile rabbits; the latter is equal to the population at the end of the nth month.

The size of the colony at the end of any month is a *Fibonacci number.* The Fibonacci numbers F_n, $n \geq 0$, are defined:

$$F_{n+2} = F_{n+1} + F_n, \text{ where } F_0 = 0 \text{ and } F_1 = 1.$$

Examples:

$$n: \quad 0\ 1\ 2\ 3\ 4\ 5\ 6\ \ 7\ \ 8\ \cdots$$
$$F_n: \quad 0\ 1\ 1\ 2\ 3\ 5\ 8\ 13\ 21\ \cdots$$

The population problem is then equivalent to finding a number n such that $F_{n+2} \geq m$ and $F_{n+1} < m$. A straightforward algorithm is to try each month in succession until the above conditions are satisfied; this leads to the program:

```
algorithm RabbitColony;
n, m, Fn1, Fn2, t : integer;
begin read(m); {Assume m ≥ 2.}
       Fn1 := 1; Fn2 := 1; n := 0; {Initialization.}
       newmonth: if Fn2 < m then
                      begin  n := n + 1; t := Fn2;
                             Fn2 := Fn2 + Fn1; Fn1 := t;
                             {Fn2 = F_{n+2}.}
                             go to newmonth
                      end;
       write('The colony will contain', m, 'pairs in a minimum of ', n,
       'months')
end.
```

In order to prove the correctness of this algorithm, it must be shown that $F_{n+2} \geq m$ and $F_{n+1} < m$ at the termination of the main loop. The central idea behind the proof is that $Fn2 = F_{n+2}$ at the beginning of each execution of the main loop.

Fibonacci numbers appear surprisingly often in combinatorial mathematics and in computer science. There is an extensive literature on their theory and they are used in practical computing areas such as sorting, searching, and storage management. Interestingly enough, some analysis of the performance of Euclid's *gcd* algorithm leads to formulae involving Fibonacci numbers.

Example 3: Roots of a Quadratic Equation

Let a, b, and c be any real numbers.[3] The problem is to produce an algorithm that computes the roots of the quadratic equation $ax^2 + bx + c = 0$. When first confronted with this problem, most people regenerate the solutions $(-b \pm \sqrt{b^2 - 4ac})/(2a)$. After a little reflection, we separate out the case where the discriminant $b^2 - 4ac$ is negative 0 and, therefore, the roots are imaginary. But, what happens if $a = 0$? or $b = 0$? or $c = 0$? or some combination of a, b, and c are each zero? A general algorithm for **any** a, b, and c must handle all of these possibilities, or at least eliminate explicitly those that are not of interest. This problem is not as trivial as it appears at first glance.

---

[3] More precisely, we mean that a, b, and c may be any of the permissible reals defined in Section 2.4.1.

The reader may verify that the solution can be divided into the following six cases depending on the values of a, b, and c:

1. $a \neq 0$ and $b^2 - 4ac > 0$
   The equation has two real distinct roots: $(-b + \sqrt{b^2 - 4ac})/(2a)$ and $(-b - \sqrt{b^2 - 4ac})/(2a)$.
2. $a \neq 0$ and $b^2 - 4ac = 0$
   The equation has one double root $b/(2a)$.
3. $a \neq 0$ and $b^2 - 4ac < 0$
   There are two imaginary roots: $-b/(2a) \pm (\sqrt{4ac - b^2}/(2a))i$, where $i^2 = -1$.
4. $a = 0$ and $b \neq 0$
   The quadratic equation has degenerated into a linear equation with one root $-c/b$.
5. $a = 0$, $b = 0$, and $c \neq 0$
   The equation has no roots; i.e., there is no value of x that satisfies $ax^2 + bx + c = 0$ in this case.
6. $a = 0$, $b = 0$, and $c = 0$
   Any number satisfies the equation. There are an infinite number of roots.

The algorithm includes the computation of a square root. We could develop a general algorithm that produces an approximation to the square root of any non-negative number, but this task would not be relevant to the main purpose of the example. Instead, we assume the availability of a function $sqrt(x)$ that computes the square root of its argument. Most programming languages and systems have "built-in" functions for the square root, trigonometric functions (e.g. sin, cos, tan), natural logarithm, and other commonly-used mathematical functions; these are designed by specialists in numerical analysis in order to produce accurate approximations and are often quite intricate.

The quadratic equation solver is presented as an Algolic program *segment* rather than the complete program. Declarations and input-output statements have been omitted.

{Algolic Segment to Find the Roots of a Quadratic Equation}

```
if a ≠ 0 then
begin
    discr := b × b − 4 × a × c; a2 := 2 × a;
    if discr > 0 then {case1 : two real distinct roots}
    begin  root1 := (−b + sqrt(discr))/a2;
           root2 := (−b − sqrt(discr))/a2;
           case := 1
    end
    else if discr = 0 then {case2 : double root}
    begin  root1 := −b/a2; case := 2 end
    else {case3, discr < 0 : imaginary roots}
    begin root1 := −b/a2; {Real parts are root1 and root1.}
           root2 := sqrt(−descr)/a2;
           {Imaginary parts are root2 and −root2.}
           case := 3
    end
end
else {a = 0}
begin
    if b ≠ 0 then {case4 : linear equation}
    begin  root1 := −c/b; case := 4 end
    else if c ≠ 0 then {case5 : no roots} case := 5
    else {case6, c = 0 : any x is a root.} case := 6
end
```

The Algolic code is written to avoid unnecessary computations. Thus instead of writing, say:

```
if b × b − 4 × a × c > 0 then {case1}
begin  root1 := (−b + sqrt(b × b − 4 × a × c))/(2 × a)
       :
```

we assign $b \times b - 4 \times a \times c$ and $2 \times a$ to *discr* and *a2*, respectively, at the beginning of the $a \neq 0$ section. Similarly, we have avoided some unnecessary variables; for example, we might have used $r1$, $i1$, $r2$, and $i2$ for the real and imaginary parts of each root, respectively. The variable *case* is convenient for interpreting *root1* and *root2* in any later computations.

EXERCISES

1. Write a flow chart of the following recipe for cooking baked beans (taken from *The Natural Foods Cookbook*, Nitty Gritty Productions, Concord, Calif., 1972).

   Bring apple juice and water to a boil and add beans so slowly that boiling doesn't stop. Reduce heat after beans are in water and simmer 2-2½ hours or until beans are almost tender. Drain beans, reserving liquid, and add other ingredients to beans. Place in oiled baking dish and bake covered 2-3 hours in 250° oven. Uncover for the last hour of cooking. If beans become dry, add a little of the reserved bean water. About 15 minutes before removing from the oven, add the fresh diced tomato.

2. Consider the step-by-step English description of the procedure for sorting three numbers presented in Section 2.1.

   (a) Trace the execution of the algorithm on the three numbers 25, 30, and 11 (in order). List every step that is performed, and show the contents of each box at the end of every step.

   (b) Give the maximum (worst case) and minimum (best case) number of steps that could ever be performed.

3. In the Algolic program *SimpleGCD* of Section 2.2.3, how many times is the loop executed in the worst case, as a function of m and n?

4. Let m and n be positive integers. Consider the following algorithm for computing the quotient q and remainder r on dividing m by n.

   1. Set q to zero ($q \leftarrow 0$).
   2. If $m < n$, then stop. q is the quotient and m is the remainder.
   3. Replace m by $m - n$ ($m \leftarrow m - n$).
   4. Increment q by 1 ($q \leftarrow q + 1$).
   5. Go to step 2.

   (a) Express the algorithm in flow chart form.

   (b) Prove the correctness of the algorithm using the techniques of Section 2.2.2. (Hint: Let $Q(m, n) = m \div n$ and $R(m, n) = m$ **mod** n, and find appropriate assertions involving Q and R).

   (c) Express the algorithm as an Algolic program.

   (d) Give the algorithm in the machine language presented in Section 2.3.

5. Trace the execution of the machine language program for the *gcd* on the numbers $m = 15$, $n = 10$.

6. Let B_1 and B_2 be arbitrary Boolean expressions and let S_1 and S_2 be arbitrary statements. Consider the following three code segments.

   (1) **if** B_1 **then** S_1; **if** B_2 **then** S_2;
   (2) **if** B_1 **then** S_1 **else if** B_2 **then** S_2;
   (3) **if** B_1 **then** S_1 **else** S_2;

   Explain the differences in executing each of the above. Show the execution of (1), (2), and (3) for the following four cases:

Case 1: B_1 and B_2 are both true.
Case 2: B_1 is true and B_2 is false.
Case 3: B_1 is false and B_2 is true.
Case 4: B_1 is false and B_2 is false.

7. Trace the execution of the program *MaxMinMean*, where the input data, in order, are the numbers 4, 20, -4, 70, 6. Show the values of the variables *index*, *x, min, max,* and *sum* after each execution of a *read* statement.

8. Change the initialization of the *MaxMinMean* program as suggested in Section 2.4.3.

9. Consider the Algolic *RabbitColony* program.
   (a) Express the program as a flow chart.
   (b) Prove the correctness of the algorithm.
   (c) Code the algorithm in the machine language of Section 2.3 (ignoring input and output).

10. Add the required heading and declarations, and appropriate input-output statements to the quadratic equation solver (Example 3, Section 2.4.3).

11. Let a rectangle that is aligned with the coordinate axes be represented by the coordinates of its lower left and upper right corners, $(xmin, ymin)$ and $(xmax, ymax)$, respectively, as shown in Figure 2.12. Given two such rectangles R_1 and R_2, devise an algorithm that finds the rectangle, if any, that is *common* to both R_1 and R_2. Express the algorithm as an Algolic program; the input data are the eight real numbers representing the coordinates of the rectangles' corners.

12. Suppose a line segment is represented by its two endpoints $P_1 = (x_1, y_1)$ and $P_2 = (x_2, y_2)$ $(P_1 \neq P_2)$. Given two line segments L_1 and L_2, devise an algorithm in Algolic that computes the coordinates of their point of intersection, if any. (Two line segments intersect if they have exactly one point in common.)

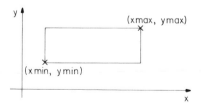

Figure 2.12   Exercise 11

ADDITIONAL READINGS

Forsythe, A.; Keenan, T.; Organick, E.; and Stenberg, W. *Computer Science: A First Course.* 2nd ed., New York: Wiley, 1975.

Knuth, D. *The Art of Computer Programming,* Vol. 1, *Fundamental Algorithms.* Reading, Mass.: Addison-Wesley, 1968.

Trakhtenbrot, B. *Algorithms and Automatic Computing Machines.* Boston: Heath, 1963.

Chapter 3

NUMBERS AND OTHER DATA

An algorithm defines a recipe for processing information. The *information* or *data* of an algorithm is represented by strings of symbols which are given appropriate interpretations.

Examples:

> '3'—the integer three
> 'hello'—common form of greeting
> 'π'—the real constant pi

In this chapter we describe commonly used computer representations of data. Number systems are particularly emphasized, but other simple forms of data are also introduced.

3.1 THE ORIGINS OF THE NUMBER SYSTEM

Pre-agrarian human civilization was a nomadic hunting-gathering society. Such a society had only a limited concept of number and counting. It was not until the rise of agrarian society (10,000 B.C.?) that a need for a more elaborate system of accounting and exchange led to number systems. The primieval farmer knew his herds as individuals, and his crops and lands were gauged by a rough sense of adequacy for feeding his family and tribe. The primitive agrarian society was communal and did not need to apportion finely tribal wealth. As this society enlarged to incorporate many families, private wealth and trading made bookkeeping necessary. Here began counting. By placing a pebble in a jar for each sheep they had, the shepherds kept their accounts.

Originally number sense was a part of the description of an object, not a separate symbolic system. Terms like "brace" included a number within their meaning (e.g., brace = 2). The detachment of number from object developed as civilization evolved. It was a consequence of accounting needs, calendar making, surveying, trading, and governing—all requirements of more organized stable human societies.

3.1.1   Ancient Civilizations and Their Number Systems

Early number systems were based on grouping simple tally marks. A group of such marks would then be replaced by a single symbol of higher value. For example, the Egyptian hieroglyphic system (c. 3500 B.C.) replaced 10 tally marks by the symbol ∩. The higher valued symbol could be grouped and, in turn, replaced by symbols of still higher value. The Egyptian system would replace 10 lower valued symbols by a new symbol. One of the largest valued of these symbols was an astonished man 𓁨 representing 10^6. To extend the Egyptian system, symbols must be invented for each higher power of ten. The system is convenient for addition but cumbersome for multiplication. The Egyptian decimal grouping system remains an archetype for grouping notations and is an earlier invention than the more familiar Greek and Roman mixed base grouping notations where 5 and 10 were both used for grouping. Table 3.1 contains the elements of both the Egyptian and late Roman systems.

Such grouping notations are convenient to read but are not easily extended. Frequently, this difficulty hampers scientific calculation. A case in point is Archimedes' calculation of the size of the heavens: for this problem, he was forced to invent a new scheme to express very large numbers.

Archimedes: The Sand-Reckoner ("Psammites")

Archimedes (289–212 B.C.) was antiquity's greatest mathematician. One of his finest arithmetic discoveries, for example, was the law of exponents, i.e., $a^n \cdot a^m = a^{n+m}$. But even such a great genius was hampered by the Greek grouping notation. In that notation, a new larger number always requires a new symbol—hence the difficulty in displaying large numbers. Archimedes decided to demonstrate that a number that completely eclipsed any known physical reality could be generated. In an essay titled "The Sand Reckoner," he calculated the number of grains of sand required to fill the known universe. For this purpose, he used the cosmology of his contemporary, Aristarchus of Samos, a Greek astronomer who hypothesized a heliocentric solar system; Aristarchus was able to estimate planetary distances, using a sun-centered system. Adopting Aristarchus' estimates, Archimedes calculated h, the diameter of the heavens, and h^3, the heavenly volume. His calculations were:

$$h = 10^4 \text{ diameters of earth}$$
$$\text{earth} = 10^6 \text{ stadia}$$
$$\text{stadia} = 10^4 \text{ fingerbreadths}$$
$$\text{fingerbreadths} = 40 \text{ poppyseeds}$$
$$\text{poppyseeds} = 10^4 \text{ sand grains}$$

$$h = 10^4 \times 10^6 \times 10^4 \times 40 \times 10^4 = 4 \times 10^{19} \text{ sand grains}$$

$$h^3 = 64 \times 10^{57} < 10^{59} \text{ volume of the universe (as estimated}$$
$$\text{by Aristarchus)}$$

He then shows a method of getting truly large numbers:
Define a cycle as the numbers

$$1, 2, 3, 4, \ldots, 10^8 = a,$$

a second cycle as the numbers

$$1 \cdot a, \ 2 \cdot a, \ 3 \cdot a, \ \ldots, \ 10^8 \cdot a = a^2,$$

and so on until

$$1 \cdot a^{a-1}, 2 \cdot a^{a-1}, \ldots, 10^8 \cdot a^{a-1} = a \cdot a^{a-1} = a^a = 10^{8 \times 10^8} = p.$$

The number p terminated the first Archimedian period. The second period is found by replacing a by p and performing the computation of the first period.

2nd period
$$1 \cdot p, 2 \cdot p, \ldots, 10^8 \cdot p = a \cdot p$$
$$1 \cdot a \cdot p, \ 2 \cdot a \cdot p, \ \ldots, \ 10^8 \cdot a \cdot p = a^2 \cdot p$$
$$1 \cdot a^{a-1} \cdot p, \ 2 \cdot a^{a-1} \cdot p, \ \ldots, \ 10^8 \cdot a^{a-1} \cdot p = p^2$$

This would continue until the ath period would produce the number $p^a = (10^{8 \times 10^8})^{10^8} = 10^{8 \times 10^{16}}$. So the number of grains of sand needed to fill Aristarchus' universe is found in the 8th cycle of the first period. Certainly this is a small number in the hierarchy Archimedes generated.

Babylonian and Mayan Place Value Notation

A most interesting number system was developed by the Sumerian-Babylonian civilization. The Sumerians (c. 3000 B.C.) had a grouping system

Table 3.1   Grouping Notations

	Egyptian Hieroglyphic	Late Roman
I	'	I
5	',','	V
10	n	X
50	n n n n n	L
100	e or 9	C
500	eeeee	D
1000	(symbol)	M
10^4	(symbol)	$\overline{X}$
10^5	(symbol)	$\overline{C}$
10^6	(symbol)	$\overline{M}$

1979 written in Roman and Egyptian:

    M   CM   L   XX   IX   ',',',','   nnnn
nnn   eee
eee
eee   (symbol)

   1000   900   50   20   9   9   7   900   1000

Note: Roman system uses a substractive abbreviation,
     e.g., IV = 4, IX = 9.

which progressed to a place value notation (c. 200 B.C.). The Babylonians were the ancient world's most gifted calculators. Many of the theorems attributed to Greek mathematicians were actually Babylonian discoveries. They were talented administrators, merchants, and astronomers. Each of these abilities relies on a mastery of numerical calculation.

The Sumerians used not only decimal grouping but also sexigesimal grouping (base 60). One conjectured reason for their use of such a grouping was its convenience for division. The base 60 is evenly divisible by 2, 3, 4, 5, 6, 10, 12, 15, 20, and 30. Their big unit was 60, and fractional transactions involving this unit came out evenly. The Sumerian-Babylonian civilization invented the earliest known place value notation—a uniform sexigesimal system (c. 2000 B.C.). The Babylonian and Sumerian systems are illustrated in Table 3.2. The value of a symbol was determined by its position. The same symbol, depending on context, could have different value. The major drawback of this system was its lack of a zero. For example, the number ∇ ∇

could be $60 + 1$ or $3600 + 1$ or $3600 + 60$. The reader of such a number would determine from the context surrounding the number what power each symbol represented. By the year 500 B.C., the Babylonians had partly rectified this situation by creating the symbol ":" to be used as a place holder, denoting the omission of the next power.

Examples:

1. $\triangledown : \triangledown$ could mean $60^2 + 1$ or $60^3 + 60$, but not $60 + 1$.
2. $\triangledown : \triangledown \ \triangledown$ could mean $60^3 + 60 + 1$, or $60^5 + 60^3 + 60^2$.

This place holder was only allowed in between symbols—one could not write $\triangledown$: to mean 60. It was not a symbol for zero—since it was not thought of as a number itself.

Mayan System

Despite the heights that mathematics achieved in the Old World civilizations, only the Babylonians approached a modern place value notation. This makes more remarkable the achievement of just such a notation in the New World by the Mayans. The Mayans were Central American Indians who developed an organized, agrarian-based, high civilization centered in the Yucatan, Guatemala, and Honduras. The Mayans, perhaps before 0 A.D. but certainly independent of any achievements in Europe or Asia, had a vigesimal (base 20) positional notation including a zero ⊖. They also had a highly accurate calendar, and their number symbols represented calendrical

Table 3.2 Sumerian-Babylonian Notation
(Cuneiform Writing: Stylus on Clay)

Sumerian (c. 3000 B.C.)

D	o	D	O	O
I	10	60	600	3600

Sumerian (c. 2000 B.C.)

$\triangledown$	◁	$\triangledown$	$\triangledown$◁
I	10	60	600

Babylonian positional notation with place holder (c. 500 B.C.) $\triangledown : \triangledown$

$60^2 + I = 3601$

cycles and deities. The system had mixed 20 and 18 radices. A common example of a mixed radix system is the use of inches, feet, yards, and miles to measure distances. In the Mayan system the digits were represented by a vertical grouping notation, the dot "·" being 1 and the bar "—" being 5. These represented the digits 1 through 20, e.g., $\underline{\underline{\cdots}}$ is 13.

Their calendar cycles were

1 kins	(day)
20 kins	1 uinal (month)
18 uinal	1 tun (year)
20 tuns	1 katun
20 katuns	1 cycle

The 18 uinal partition of the year made their positional notation nonuniform.

Examples:

$$20 \times 18 \times 20 + 20 \times 18 + 20 + 1 = 7581$$

$$360 + 0 + 2 = 362$$

$$20 \times 20 \times 18 \times 20 + 0 + 10 \cdot 18 \times 20 + 1 \cdot 20 + 0 = 147620$$

Exactly when and why this system was developed and, in parallel, how Mayan astronomy and geometry became so sophisticated are among the most intriguing of contemporary archaeological mysteries. Mayan achievements are a great cul-de-sac; for they had fully developed subtle notions which eluded the Old World civilizations without actually contributing these ideas to the mainstream of human intellectual tradition. The story of the conquest of zero must turn now to India in the East.

3.1.2   The Zero: Can Nothing Be Counted?

The necessity of zero in the modern place value system obscures the paradox of counting "nothing." Yet, the difficulty of seeing that "nothing" could be counted and thought of in the same way as other integers probably contributed to the prolonged hiatus between the invention of number systems (c. 3000 B.C.) and the development of the full place value notation (c. 600 A.D.). An even more important reason was that ancient cultures lacked the motivation to perform arithmetic calculation using written notation. Computation was performed on the abacus or counting board. Notational systems were used only for recording. The present day notation can be traced from its origins in India.

In certain ancient scripts, such as the Egyptian hieractic, a code symbol was used to abbreviate a hieroglyphic cluster, rather than repeating unit symbols, e.g., 111 in hieratic script was 𝟒. Often the letters of an ancient alphabet also stood for particular integers. This was (and is) the case in Hebrew where א , ב , ... stood for 1, 2, ... Our decimal digit notation is a lineal descendent of such an encipherment coding. India of the 5th through 8th century A.D. developed a decimal digit and positional system using 0 as a true number. The Indian zero may have been absorbed from Greek astronomical texts. In some of these texts (c. 200 A.D.) the Babylonian sexigesimal notation was used along with a symbol "o" as a place marker for the least significant positions. However, it is also hypothesized that the Indians invented the zero to designate an empty column on their counting boards. What is certain is that the decimal position notation was in common use in India before the 8th century A.D. One form of these digits is the Sanskrit-Devanagari digits.

𑁡	𑁢	𑁣	𑁤	𑁥	𑁦	𑁧	𑁨	𑁩	o
1	2	3	4	5	6	7	8	9	0

Distinct resemblance is seen between these digits and our own.

In the 8th century, the dynamic new Arab expansion touched on India. The nascent Arab-Moslem empire was promoting and importing the intellectual products of its newly conquered lands. The mathematical and astronomical writings of the Indians were brought to Baghdad and disseminated within the Arabic empire.

A Persian scholar, Abu Jafar Muhammed ibn Musa al-Khwarizmi, read an Indian astronomy text and comprehended the advantages of Indian place value notation. He wrote a text on arithmetic adopting the convenient Indian notation. This book was widely distributed in Arab cultural circles and entered western Europe via the Moslem foothold in Spain. There it was translated into Latin by monks in the 12th century. Al-Khwarizmi's directions for computing in place value notation entered medieval European culture where it competed with the continued use of the Roman numerals, a Latin inheritance that the church propagated. To understand such an unequal contest, the principles of computation by the abacus and counting board must next be explored.

Before we leave the story of the cultural transmission of zero from India to Baghdad to Europe, a final salute must be paid to "Mohammed the father of Jafar and the son of Musa, who comes from the province of Khoresm." In Latin, Al-Khwarizmi (the part of his name referencing his birthplace) became Algorismus. As his time's greatest mathematician, his name remains in the form of "algorithm" for his work on place value arithmetic.

3.1.3   The Abacus

The zero as a number was a difficult abstraction for people used to carving notches. However, later Babylonian science and Greek-Roman mathematics and technology were sophisticated enough to invent it, if it were needed. Two important advantages of the decimal place value system are, first, the ability to use only ten different symbols for any number, no matter how large; and second, the convenience of the routine arithmetic computations. As a notation for small numbers, a grouping system is often simpler and shorter, e.g., using M instead of 1000. More important is the second advantage—ease in computation. However, place value systems were not fully exploited due to the early invention of different forms of counting tables and abaci. Calculation was not handled by notational manipulations at all; instead, these elementary computing instruments were employed.

Some of the different forms of the abacus and counting board are illustrated in Figure 3.1. Devices of this form existed in ancient Greece, but physical evidence does not exist for the older Babylonian and Egyptian civilizations. Nevertheless, these devices probably predate 1000 B.C. in their use.

The Roman hand abacus in Figure 3.1(a) illustrates the basic principle of number representation. The upper bead represents five of whatever units its column stands for. The lower four beads count one apiece. The beads are counted if they are pushed toward the center. In essence the abacus is a place value system.

The medieval counting board in Figure 3.1(b) could represent two numbers side-by-side. From zero to four beads are placed near the bottom on a line on the table, and a second bead placed above this area represented five units. Each vertical sector was worth ten times the sector below. It is now easy to add these two numbers by pushing the representation of one number over the middle line, as shown in Figure 3.2. The beads would then be

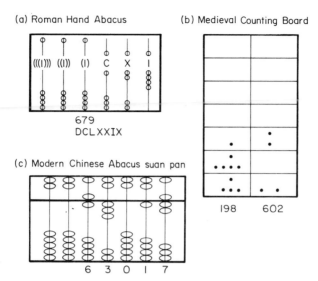

Figure 3.1   Counting board and abaci

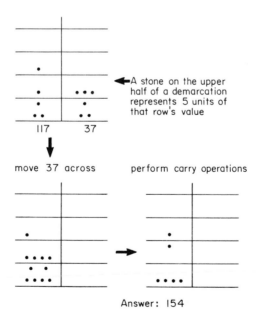

Figure 3.2   Using a medieval counting board to add 117 and 37

counted and the sum recorded in the Roman notation. Hence the abacus obviated the need for doing elementary calculation in the symbolism itself.

The convenience of counting boards and abaci is such that they prolonged the use of the Roman numeral system in Europe until Renaissance times. The 13th and 14th centuries saw the Algorismus, or place value system, spread slowly through learned European circles and counting houses.[1] The algorithmicist and abacist disputed the advantages of their respective systems. Final victory for the modern system was slow in coming, but the turning point was the invention of printing. Nevertheless, the abacus was too useful a device to die out and continues in use throughout Russia and Asia. It must be counted as the most successful computational engine up until the contemporary digital computer.

The Chinese suan pan (Figure 3.1(c)) is probably the most convenient form of the modern abacus. It has two "upper" beads, which allow the carry operation to be deferred. The abacus and the place value notations were used by trained professional calculators to perform the four basic arithmetic operations: add, subtract, multiply, and divide. The algorithms they used were not always the ones taught today. In the next section a miscellany of such methods is presented.

3.1.4   Ancient and Medieval Algorithms

In this section several unconventional arithmetic algorithms are described. Partly this description is for fun as these methods are exotic. More seriously, it demonstrates that contemporary methods are not the only way to perform these most basic operations. It is a significant observation that different algorithms exist for even the trivial operations and that they are related to the tools and representations available. This point is still relevant in modern times, for once again the digital computer causes us to rethink even basic algorithms and to discover new ones.

Multiplication by Doubling

The method was used by both abacists and algorithmicists and is related to binary notation. In the following examples, multiplication by doubling is illustrated for two products, 7×4 and 17×49. The arithmetician must only know how to add, double (multiply by 2) and halve (divide by 2).

---

[1] Leonardo of Pisa (known as Fibonacci, 1180–1250?) was instrumental in promoting the business use of the Hindu-Arab numbers. He wrote the *Liber Abaci* in 1202 describing arithmetic in the "new" notation.

Examples:

1. 7×4

double	halve
7	4
14	2
28	1 odd
result	28

2. 4×7

double	halve		
4	7 odd		4
8	3 odd		8
16	1 odd		16
		result	28

3. 17×49

double	halve		
17	49 odd		
34	24		17
68	12		272
136	6		544
272	3 odd		
544	1 odd	result	833

A "double" column is set up with one of the numbers and a "halve" column with the other number. On successive lines the previous number is doubled in the "double" column and halved in the "halve" column. If the halve column is odd, that line is marked odd and the number minus one is halved. Eventually the halve column reaches one. Then the double numbers, on lines marked odd, are added up and this is the product. The general algorithm is given in Algolic below:

```
algorithm HalveDoubleMPY;
    A, B, product : integer;
    {product = A × B, to be accomplished by the Egyptian doubling
    algorithm}
begin
    product := 0;
    read(A, B);
over: if B = 0 then write(product)
        else
        begin
            if (B mod 2) = 1 then product := product + A;
            A := 2 × A; {Double A.}
            B := B ÷ 2; {Halve B.}
            go to over
        end
end.
```

The doubling method is one of the first algorithms involving iteration. It was known to the Egyptians and as such is a candidate for the first algorithm involving a loop. Other computations of this period were mainly formulas, such as the area of a triangle.

The Diagonal Lattice and Chessboard Multiplication Schemes

While the method of doubling is conveniently done on an abacus, positional notation allows direct written calculation. The Hindus, Arabs, and the Renaissance Europeans all experimented with different tableaux for written multiplication. One of these methods is the chessboard method which is the one commonly used today.

Example: Chessboard method

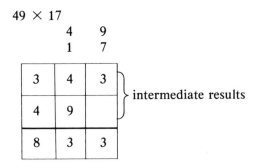

It was called the chessboard method because boxes were drawn to contain the intermediate results in their proper position.

A more elegant but less compact method is the diagonal lattice (or grating) method. The two numbers to be multiplied would be placed on two sides of a rectangle:

Example: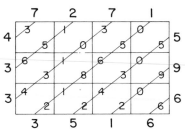

7271 x 596 = 4333516

One number is placed over the top of the rectangle, and the other number is placed on the right side of the rectangle. The rectangle is then lined with a grid of dimensions equal to the number of digits of the two numbers. A diagonal line is drawn through each box. Each box then contains the two digit product corresponding to its coordinates in the grid. The columns traced by diagonals are then added rightmost first. The result is then read off the left and lower sides of the rectangle.

Before we continue with a discussion of the abstract principles of modern number systems and their representation on computers, it is interesting to note that arithmetic was "higher" mathematics until very recent times. A person who could divide was an adept mathematician. A virtuoso of the abacus was the systems analyst of his day. It is easy to see that with the widespread use of computers a new set of skills will replace old knowledge.

3.2   RADIX POSITIONAL NOTATION

3.2.1   Decimal, Binary, and Other Systems

A positive integer written in the *decimal system* is a string of the form

$$a_n a_{n-1} a_{n-2} \cdots a_2 a_1 a_0,$$

where each a_i is one of the 10 decimal digits $\{0, 1, 2, 3, 4, 5, 6, 7, 8, 9\}$. The number is understood to have value

$$a_n \times 10^n + a_{n-1} \times 10^{n-1} + a_{n-2} \times 10^{n-2} + \cdots$$
$$+ a_2 \times 10^2 + a_1 \times 10^1 + a_0 \times 10^0$$

Examples:

   3 means 3×10^0
   300 means $3 \times 10^2 + 0 \times 10^1 + 0 \times 10^0$
   913 means $9 \times 10^2 + 1 \times 10^1 + 3 \times 10^0$

The decimal system is a *positional* notation because the digit's position in a string of digits determines its value. In the decimal system, the digit a_i is multiplied by 10^i. Since powers of 10 are used to multiply each digit, 10 is called the *base* or *radix* for this number representation.

Fractional numbers can also be expressed in the decimal system through the use of the decimal point. Thus a number between zero and one might be written as

$$0.a_{-1}a_{-2}a_{-3} \ldots a_{-m}$$

and would be understood to have value

$$a_{-1} \times 10^{-1} + a_{-2} \times 10^{-2} + a_{-3} \times 10^{-3} + \cdots + a_{-m} \times 10^{-m}.$$

Examples:

0.3 means 3×10^{-1} or $\dfrac{3}{10}$

0.913 means $9 \times 10^{-1} + 1 \times 10^{-2} + 3 \times 10^{-3}$ or $\dfrac{9}{10} + \dfrac{1}{10^2} + \dfrac{3}{10^3}$

A positive number in the decimal system would be written

$$a_n a_{n-1} a_{n-2} \ldots a_0 . a_{-1} a_{-2} \ldots a_{-m}$$

where the decimal point "." separates those digits multiplied by negative powers of 10 from those digits multiplied by positive powers of 10.

The Binary System

The binary system is a positional notation using radix 2 instead of radix 10. A binary number will be written

$$a_n a_{n-1} \ldots a_0 . a_{-1} a_{-2} \ldots a_{-m} \ 2$$

where each a_i is either 0 or 1. The value of the number is

$$a_n \times 2^n + a_{n-1} \times 2^{n-1} + \cdots$$
$$+ a_0 \times 2^0 + a_{-1} \times 2^{-1} + \cdots + a_{-m} \times 2^{-m}$$

The separator "·" is now called a binary point, instead of the decimal point, and the a_i are called *binary* digits or *bits*.

Examples:

$$101_2 \text{ means } 1 \times 2^2 + 1 \times 2^0 = 5$$
$$1100_2 \text{ means } 1 \times 2^3 + 1 \times 2^2 = 12$$
$$0.101_2 \text{ means } \frac{1}{2} + \frac{1}{2^3} = 0.625$$

$$0.1100_2 \text{ means } \frac{1}{2} + \frac{1}{2^2} = 0.75$$

Arithmetic in the Binary System

The arithmetic operations in the binary system are simpler than the corresponding decimal operations. In effect, the same algorithms are used, but the binary tables are simpler than the decimal tables. The addition and subtraction tables for a single bit are:

addition	*subtraction*
$0 + 0 = 0$	$0 - 0 = 1 - 1 = 0$
$0 + 1 = 1 + 0 = 1$	$1 - 0 = 1$
$1 + 1 = 0$ plus a carry	$0 - 1 = 1$ plus a borrow

Examples:

101_2	1010_2	1010_2	1111_2
11_2	101_2	-101_2	-111_2
1000_2	1111_2	101_2	1000_2

The multiplication table is also simple:

$$0 \times 0 = 0 \times 1 = 1 \times 0 = 0$$
$$1 \times 1 = 1$$

Therefore, a multiply of a binary number by the binary digit 1 requires only that the number be recopied. When multiplying two binary numbers, a *multiplicand* by a *multiplier*, the multiplicand is recopied and appropriately shifted for each occurrence of 1 in the multiplier. Finally, these results are added to give the binary product.

Examples:

$$101_2 \qquad 10111_2$$
$$\underline{10_2} \qquad \underline{10101_2}$$
$$1010_2 \qquad 10111$$
$$10111$$
$$\underline{10111}$$
$$111100011_2$$

Division is accomplished by writing out the most significant quotient digit, multiplying it by the divisor and subtracting from the dividend.

Examples: [2]

$$
\begin{array}{r}
1011 \\
101{\overline{)110111}} \\
\underline{101} \\
111 \\
\underline{101} \\
101 \\
\underline{101}
\end{array}
\qquad
\begin{array}{r}
1001 \\
100{\overline{)100100}} \\
\underline{100} \\
100 \\
\underline{100}
\end{array}
$$

There is nothing simpler than the binary system. A two-tendrilled intelligent alien will probably send us messages of greeting in this system. For example, the table of primes is a universal truth of mathematics, that all intelligent beings could be expected to discover in the course of their cultural development. Hence an appropriate first message might be 10, 11, 101, 111, 1011, 1101, 10001, 10011, ... These aliens would be amazed to find that Earthmen still use the awkward decimal system, an accident of local evolution.

The binary number system is also more convenient and simpler than the decimal one when used as a basis for automatic computing. The binary digits 0 and 1 are easily representable by electronic and electromagnetic devices; and elementary arithmetic and testing operations on binary numbers can be readily implemented electronically. Hence, almost all computers use this system or some variation of it at the lowest internal levels. Because other radices, such as those based on different powers of 2, are also very popular, it is useful to define positional systems for an arbitrary radix.

General Positional System

Let b be an arbitrary positive integer. A number in a positional system using radix b is written

---

[2] When the base is obvious, we will often omit it, thus writing 1011 instead of 1011_2.

$$a_n a_{n-1} \cdots a_0 \cdot a_{-1} \cdots a_{-m}{}_b$$

where each a_i is one of the b digits $\{0, 1, 2, \ldots, b - 1\}$. The number is understood to have value

$$a_n \times b^n + a_{n-1} \times b^{n-1} + \cdots + a_0 \times b^0$$
$$+ a_{-1} \times b^{-1} + \cdots + a_{-m} \times b^{-m}$$

Examples:

$$120_3 \text{ means } 1 \times 3^2 + 2 \times 3$$
$$120_7 \text{ means } 1 \times 7^2 + 2 \times 7$$
$$0.59_{16} \text{ means } \frac{5}{16} + \frac{9}{16^2}$$

The operation tables and algorithms for arithmetic in any base b can be produced in a manner similar to those for the decimal and binary systems.

Examples:

1. base 3

addition table

+	0	1	2
0	0	1	2
1	1	2	0 + carry
2	2	0 + carry	1 + carry

multiplication table

×	0	1	2
0	0	0	0
1	0	1	2
2	0	2	1 + carry

$$
\begin{array}{r}
101_3 \\
+\ 212_3 \\
\hline
1020_3
\end{array}
\qquad
\begin{array}{r}
212_3 \\
\times\ 12_3 \\
\hline
1201 \\
212 \\
\hline
11021_3
\end{array}
$$

2. base 8
$$346_8$$
$$+ \ 71_8$$
$$\overline{437_8}$$

3.2.2   Iteration and Arrays in Algolic

In order to express clearly many of our algorithms, we will need iterative constructions in Algolic. *Iteration* is the repeated execution of a set of instructions. A program segment which accomplishes iteration is a *loop*. The simplest form of a loop that appears frequently is given by the flow chart of Figure 3.3. In Algolic this is expressed:

> *entry*: **if** *Boolean expression* **then**
>   **begin**
>   *Computation*;
>   **go to** *entry*
>   **end;**
> *exit*:

This type of loop is so useful and commonly occurring that it has a simple equivalent statement in Algolic—the **while** statement. The general form of the **while** statement is:

while *Boolean expression* **do** *statement*

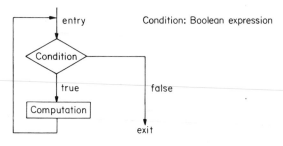

Figure 3.3 Simple loop

Examples:

1. {adding the integers 1 to 100}
   $sum := 0; n := 1;$
   while $n \leq 100$ **do**
      begin
         $sum := sum + n;$
         $n := n + 1$
      end
   The loop performs the computation: $sum = \sum\limits_{n=1}^{100} n.$

2. {Find the smallest integer of the form 2^k that is greater than or equal to 1000.}
   $twopow := 2;$
   while $twopow < 1000$ **do**
      $twopow := twopow \times 2$
   The Boolean expression '$twopow < 1000$' continues to be *true* until *twopow* is assigned the value 1024. At this point the **while** loop terminates.

3. The multiplication by doubling algorithm given in Section 3.1.4 can be presented more clearly using a **while** statement.
   $product := 0; read(A, B);$
   while $B \neq 0$ **do**
   begin
      if $(B \textbf{ mod } 2) = 1$ **then** $product := product + A;$
      $A := 2 \times A; B := B \div 2$
   end;
   $\{B = 0$ at termination of **while** loop.$\}$
   $write(product)$

Iteration is especially useful with a data structure called an *array*. An *array* is a collection of elements of the same type which may be selected or accessed by an integer expression called an *index*. A row of seats in a theatre is analogous to an array, with the seat number being the index of a particular seat. At any time the person occupying the seat would be the contents or value of that particular array element.

An array declaration has the form:

$$identifier: \textbf{array } [integer . . integer] \textbf{ of } type$$

An example is

$$X: \textbf{array } [1..5] \textbf{ of } \textit{real}$$

which declares the five separate variables

$$X[1], X[2], X[3], X[4], X[5]$$

all of real type. The first 'integer' in the declaration is the *lower bound* (*lb*) of the array and the second integer is the *upper bound* (*ub*). An array declaration creates as variables a set of elements identified by the index values *lb*, *lb* + 1, ..., *ub* − 1, *ub*. All other index values are in error. Thus an array declaration creates an array of size *ub* − *lb* + 1. The individual elements of an array can be used in the same way that a simple variable of the same type is used.

Examples:

1. $X[3] := 2.7$;
   {The element $X[3]$ is assigned the value 2.7}
2. $X[2] := X[3] + 6.1$;
   {The value stored in $X[3]$ + the value 6.1 is assigned to $X[2]$}
3. $read(X[1], X[2], X[3])$;
   {Three values are read in sequence into elements $X[1], X[2], X[3]$}
4. $write(X[i])$;
   {'i' is evaluated to an integer value—and providing $1 \le i \le 5$, the appropriate element in X is selected and its value written out}

Let us write a simple program for taking the average of 50 exam scores. We will make use of both arrays and iteration.

algorithm *testscore;*
   {program for finding average grade in class of 50}
   i, totscore:integer; average:real;
   exams:**array**[1..50] **of** *integer*; {to hold exam scores}
begin
   i := 1; {Initialize array index variable}
   while *i* ≤ 50 **do**
   begin *read(exams[i]);*
     i := *i* + 1 {*i* used as an index}
   end;
   i := 1; *totscore* := 0;
   while *i* ≤ 50 **do**
   begin {totscore is used to accumulate sum of exams}
     totscore := *totscore* + *exams[i];*
     i := *i* + 1
   end;
   average := *totscore*/50;
   write('average grade is', average)
end.

The program segment

   i := 1;
   while *i* ≤ 50 **do**
   begin *statement;*
     i := *i* + 1
   end

occurs twice in the above program. The integer variable 'i' is used to control the number of iterations. It is also used within the loop as an array index. This construction allows a program to process in a uniform fashion an arbitrary amount of data stored in arrays. As it is frequently occurring, Algolic has a special notation for this kind of iteration—the **for** statements:

     for *identifier* := *start value* **upto** *final value* **do** *statement*

and

     for *identifier* := *start value* **downto** *final value* **do** *statement*

The first form counts up and the second form counts down. The **upto** form is equivalent to the flow chart given in Figure 3.4.

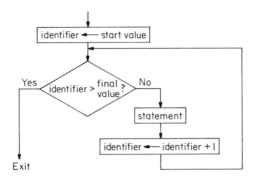

Figure 3.4   Meaning of **upto** Form of **for** Statement

Examples:

1. **for** $i := 1$ **upto** 50 **do** $read(exams[i])$
   {equivalent to **while** in testscore}
2. **for** $ind := 5$ **downto** 1 **do** $X[ind] := ind$
   {This loop performs the computations, in order:
   $X[5] := 5; X[4] := 4; X[3] := 3; X[2] := 2; X[1] := 1$}

The identifier controlling the loop is called the *control variable*. It is implicitly declared only within the context of that loop. It assumes all integer values between the *start value* and the *final value*. The control variable cannot be modified within the loop.

Example: {illegal}
                for $i := 3$ **downto** 1 **do**
                    $i := i + 2$

Unconstrained control variable modification can create situations which, as seen in the above example, easily lead to non-terminating loops and unclear algorithms.

Before returning to our treatment of number systems, let us display a non-trivial program that operates on arrays. Try to imagine the size and complexity of an equivalent program, if it were to be done without loops and arrays.

We wish to *experimentally* check the conjecture that:

$$\left(\sum_{i=1}^{n} a_i \right)^2 \geq \left(\sum_{i=1}^{n} a_i^2 \right)$$

The program will test the conjecture for values of n up to 100 and different values of the a_i.

algorithm *CheckConjecture;*
   n : integer;
   A, SUMA, SUMASQ : **array**[1 . . 100] **of** *real;*
begin
   read(n); {size of array $\leq$ 100 for test}
   for $i := 1$ **upto** *n* **do** *read(A[i]);*
   SUMA[1] := *A*[1]; *SUMASQ*[1] := *A*[1] $\times$ *A*[1];
   for $i := 2$ **upto** *n* **do**
      begin
      SUMA[i] := *A*[i] + *SUMA*[i − 1];
      SUMASQ[i] := *A*[i] $\times$ *A*[i] + *SUMASQ*[i − 1];
      if *SUMASQ*[i] > *SUMA*[i] $\times$ *SUMA*[i] **then go to** *fail*
      end;
   write('conjecture true');
   go to *finish;*
fail : write('conjecture false');
finish :
end.

The integer n is used to decide what portion of the 100 element array will be used. It is then used as a final value in the various **for** loops. The first **for** loop reads in n consecutive values into array A. The second **for** loop computes the two sums and compares them. An equivalent non-looping program would be n-times as long. Arrays, iteration, and indexing are a powerful addition to Algolic; in short program segments, one can specify the homogeneous processing of large amounts of data. Most programming languages have similar constructs.

Algorithm for Adding Two Binary Numbers

Arithmetic in the binary system was informally introduced in the last section. As another exercise in the use of arrays and loops, we present an Algolic program for adding two binary numbers on a bit-by-bit basis. Given the binary numbers

$$X = x_n x_{n-1} \cdots x_0{}_2 \quad \text{and} \quad Y = y_n y_{n-1} \cdots y_0{}_2,$$

the algorithm will produce the sum bits

$$S = X + Y = s_{n+1} s_n s_{n-1} \ldots s_0 \, {}_2$$

S will have one extra bit position because $(n + 1)$ bits may not be sufficient for $X + Y$.

Assume that the bits of X are stored in an array so that X is represented by the elements $X[n]$, $X[n - 1]$, ..., $X[0]$; Y and S are stored in a similar manner. Then the bits of S are produced by the Algolic segment:

```
Carry := 0; {Initialize the carry.}
for i := 0 upto n do
begin
    Temp := X[i] + Y[i] + Carry;
    S[i] := Temp mod 2; {sum bit in ith position}
    if Temp ≥ 2 then Carry := 1 else Carry := 0
    {Compute carry out of ith position.}
end;
    S[n + 1] := Carry
```

3.2.3   Converting Between Bases

We present some general methods for converting integers from one base b to another base B.

The Multiplication Method

A number N in base b, given by the place value notation

$$a_n a_{n-1} a_{n-2} \ldots a_1 a_0 \, {}_b$$

is evaluated as

$$N = a_n b^n + a_{n-1} b^{n-1} + \cdots + a_1 b + a_0$$

If the repeated additions and multiplications are carried out in base B, then the result is the representation of N in base B. The computation can be done efficiently by nesting

$$N = (\cdots (((a_n b + a_{n-1})b + a_{n-2})b + \cdots)b + a_0$$

Example: Convert 10110101_2 to decimal.

$$10110101_2 = ((((((1 \cdot 2 + 0) \cdot 2 + 1) \cdot 2 + 1) \cdot 2 + 0) \cdot 2 + 1) \cdot 2 + 0)$$
$$\cdot 2 + 1 = 181_{10}$$

Note that the multiplication starts with the *most significant digit,* i.e., the leftmost digit, and continues through the *least significant digit,* i.e., the rightmost digit. Furthermore, the arithmetic is done in decimal.

This conversion algorithm can be easily defined in a variation of Algolic, if we assume that the arithmetic can be done in base B:

algorithm *ConvertByMultiply*;
  i, v, b: *integer*;
  digits: **array** $[0..10]$ **of** *integer*;
  {*v* will be the value of *N* in base *B*; *digits*[10], *digits*[9], ..., *digits*[0] is
    a base *b* representation of *N*.}
begin
  read(b);
  for $i := 10$ **downto** 0 **do** *read(digits*[*i*]);
  {Initialize *v* to the most significant digit.}
  $v := digits[10]$;
  for $i := 9$ **downto** 0 **do** $v := v \times_B b +_B digits[i]$;
  {$\times_B$ and $+_B$ indicate arithmetic in base *B*.}
  write$_B$ (v) {*write$_B$* indicates writing in base *B*.}
end.

Let us work through the execution of this algorithm for converting the binary number 10101100101_2 to decimal. Initially, we have $b = 2$, *digits*[10] $= 1$, *digits*[9] $= 0$, *digits*[8] $= 1$, *digits*[7] $= 0$, *digits*[6] $= 1$, *digits*[5] $= 1$, *digits*[4] $= 0$, *digits*[3] $= 0$, *digits*[2] $= 1$, *digits*[1] $= 0$, and *digits*[0] $= 1$. $v = 1$ upon entering the **for** loop.

As the loop is executed, the values of v and i become successively:

v_{10}	i	digits[i]
2	9	0
5	8	1
10	7	0
21	6	1
43	5	1
86	4	0
172	3	0
345	2	1
690	1	0
1381	0	1

This method is fine for manually converting from radix b to B but is not suitable for computers because most computers represent numbers and perform arithmetic in a *fixed* base.

The Division Method

Consider what happens when a number N is divided by B. Let N be expressed as $a_n a_{n-1} \cdots a_{0\,b}$

$$\frac{N}{b} = \frac{a_n \times b^n + \cdots + a_0}{b} = a_n \times b^{n-1} + \cdots + a_1 + \frac{a_0}{b}$$

$$= N_1 + \frac{a_0}{b}$$

a_0 is the remainder upon division by b and N_1 is the integer quotient. If N_1 is now divided by b, the remainder is a_1. The repetition of this process thus generates the digits of N in base b, least significant first. The process terminates when the quotient is zero. This leads to an algorithm to convert a number N to its representation in any base b.

algorithm *ConvertByDivide*;
  i, N, b: *integer*;
  digits: **array** [0. .20] **of** *integer*;
  {Assume that the array is large enough to hold the base *b* digits}
  begin
    read(*b, N*);
    i := 0; {Assume $N \neq 0$ initially.}
    while $N \neq 0$ **do**
    begin
      digits[*i*] := *N* **mod** *b*;
      N := *N* ÷ *b*; *i* := *i* + 1
    end;
    i := *i* − 1;
    for *i* := *i* **downto** 0 **do** *write*(*digits*[*i*])
  end.

Let us convert 1381_{10} back to binary using the division algorithm. Initially $b = 2$ and $N = 1381$. The expressions in the **for** loop successively evaluate to the following:

i	$digits[i]$	N **mod** b	N ÷ b
0	1	1	690
1	0	0	345
2	1	1	172
3	0	0	86
4	0	0	43
5	1	1	21
6	1	1	10
7	0	0	5
8	1	1	2
9	0	0	1
10	1	1	0

Either of the two algorithms can be used for manual conversion between bases. While it is not necessary, it is generally more natural to use the division algorithm on whole numbers when going from a large base to a small base and to use the multiplication algorithm when going from a small base to a large base.

Example: Convert 121_3 to base 7

Using the multiplication algorithm in base 7, we get

$$(1 \times 3_7 + 2) \times 3_7 + 1_7 = (5 \times 3)_7 + 1_7 = 21_7 + 1_7 = 22_7$$

Combining the Multiplication and Division Methods

The ideas of the *ConvertByMultiply* and *ConvertByDivide* algorithms can be combined to produce a general Algolic program for base conversion. Let *bdigits*[*i*], $i = m, m - 1, \ldots, 1, 0$ be the base *b* representation of a number *N* and *Bdigits*[*i*], $i = n, n - 1, \ldots, 1, 0$ be the base *B* digits of *N*. In the last example we have

$$b = 3, \; bdigits[2] = 1, \; bdigits[1] = 2, \; bdigits[0] = 1$$
$$B = 7, \; Bdigits[1] = 2, \; Bdigits[0] = 2$$

The algorithm first converts *N*, by multiplication, to the (unknown) base of the Algolic "machine" and then converts this new representation to base *B*, using the division method. For example, if Algolic works in base 10, the conversion of the above numbers proceeds as:

$$121_3 \xrightarrow{\text{multiplication}} 16_{10} \xrightarrow{\text{division}} 22_7$$

The core of the algorithm is given by the following Algolic code fragment:

```
{Convert from base b to Algolic base.}
N := bdigits[m]; start := m − 1;
for i := start downto 0 do N := N × b + bdigits[i];
{Convert N to base B.}
i := 0; Bdigits[0] := 0; {just in case N = 0.}
while N ≠ 0 do
begin Bdigits[i] := N mod B;
      N := N ÷ B;   i := i + 1
end
```

Converting When Base B is a Power of Base b

Manual conversion becomes especially simple when $B = b^k$, for some positive integer *k*. We first illustrate this case informally using the common computer cases when $b = 2$.

Let $b = 2$ and $B = 8 = 2^3$. Base B here is called *octal*. We have, for example, $101\ 110_2 = 56_8$ and $3075_8 = 011\ 000\ 111\ 101_2$. Each octal digit is expressed as three binary digits and each group of three binary digits is directly mapped into octal, grouping from the right.

Octal and *hexadecimal* (base 16) are commonly used as computer representations. The standard way of writing the 16 hexadecimal digits, 0 through 15, is 0, 1, ..., 9, A, B, C, D, E, F. Each hexadecimal digit is equivalent to four binary digits. For example, $10\ 1110_2 = 2E_{16}$ and $1010\ 0011_2 = A3_{16}$.

Conversion between octal and hexadecimal can be accomplished by using binary as an intermediate notation.

Example:

octal

$$77_8 = \quad \overline{111}\overline{111}_2 = 3F_{16}$$

hexadecimal

In general, converting from base b to base $B = b^k$ is straightforward. Each base B digit is rewritten as k digits of base b.

Example: ternary (base 3) to base 9 ($3^2 = 9$)
$$12102_3 = (01)(21)(02) = 172_9$$

Why does this algorithm work? Let a number N be expressed $(a_n a_{n-1} \dots a_k a_{k-1} \dots a_0)_b$ in base b. Then $N \bmod b^k$, the least significant digit of N in base $B = b^k$, is $a_{k-1} \times b^{k-1} + \cdots + a_0$. Thus $(a_{k-1} \dots a_0)_b$ gives the first digit of base B digit of N. The quotient $N_1 = N \div b^k$ is $(a_n a_{n-1} \dots a_k)_b$. Repeating the ConvertByDivide algorithm on N_1 gives the next base B digit as $(a_{2k-1} \dots a_k)_b$ and so on.

3.3 CODING THE INTEGERS

The symbols 3, 'three', 11_2 and 'trois' all denote the integer three. Trois, the French for three, would not necessarily be understood by a Japanese. Writing 11_2 would almost certainly confuse most people who would mistake it for decimal eleven. All of these expressions for three are useful. Any confusion with a particular denotation is because of unfamiliarity and not because of conceptual difficulty. We will present a number of ways to code the integers and other numerical and non-numerical data; the methods discussed are most often used on computers. As with the above denotations, the computer encodings must be understood within a given stated context.

Computers are built from electronic and electro-magnetic components which have two readily distinguishable *states*. Thus it is natural to interpret the two states as the binary digits {0, 1}. A device capable of storing one binary digit is said to be one *bit* of storage. A computer is organized to handle contiguous strings of bits, called a *word*, where the number of bits is its *word length*. In some computers there are different length strings of bits which can be manipulated. One commonly used grouping is the eight bit unit called a *byte*. The byte is used both as a measure of wordlength (eight bits) and as a designation of a particular set of bits ("that particular byte"). For example, some computers have 32 bit words, each divided into four bytes; others have word lengths of 12, 16, 36, 48, or 60 bits.

An eight bit byte has 2^8 distinct strings. In order for the computer to operate meaningfully on the strings of binary digits stored in a word, it must assign a meaning to each distinct string. A scheme of assigning meaning to strings is called a *code*. Let us look at some binary codes for the integers.

Unsigned Binary

This code interprets a binary string as a positive binary positional number.

Examples:

$$0101 = 2^2 + 1 = 5$$
$$1001 = 2^3 + 1 = 9$$
$$1110 = 2^3 + 2^2 + 2 = 14$$

Sign-Magnitude

This code makes provision for both positive and negative numbers. It reserves the leftmost bit for the sign and uses the remaining bits as unsigned binary. A 0 bit is used for a plus sign and a 1 bit for minus.

Examples: Assume the strings are four bits in length. Then

$$0101 = (0)(101) = +5,$$
$$1001 = (1)(001) = -1, \text{ and}$$
$$1110 = (1)(110) = -6.$$

One's Complement

This code is useful on computers because it simplifies the computer hardware to do arithmetic. As in sign-magnitude, the leftmost bit is the sign with 0 representing "+" and 1 representing "−". The positive integers are coded as in sign magnitude. The negative integers are obtained by taking the code for the positive integer of equal magnitude and changing each 1 to a 0 and each 0 to a 1, i.e., "complementing" each bit.

Examples: $0100 = (0)(100) = +4$
$1011 = (1)(011) = -(100) = -4$
$1000 = (1)(000) = -(111) = -7$

In general, one speaks both of the *one's complement representation of a number* and the *one's complement of a bit string*. The one's complement of a bit string X is obtained by changing each 1 in X to 0 and each 0 to 1. If the string X is interpreted as a number, say N, then taking the one's complement of X produces the representation of $-N$, with the correct sign.

Examples:

1. If $X = 1011$, then $N = -4$.
   one's complement(1011) = 0100, representing the number $-(-4) = +4$
2. If $X = 0110$, then $N = +6$
   one's complement(0110) = 1001, representing the number -6

Two's Complement

This code is similar to one's complement. The two's complement representation of positive integers is the same as sign-magnitude. The two's complement representation of negative integers is obtained by taking the one's complement code and, treating the result as an unsigned binary number, adding 1 to it.

Examples:

1. $0100 = +4$
2. $1011 = 1010 + 1 = 1010 = -(101) = -5$

    two's   one's   sign

  complement   complement   magnitude

In the same way as in one's complement, we can also speak of taking the two's complement of a bit string. This can be done by taking the one's complement and adding 1. There is also another method that is particularly useful for manual work. Suppose that a bit string X is n bits in length. Then the two's complement of X is the bit string resulting from the operation $2^n - X$ (and ignoring the $(n + 1)$st bit after the subtraction).[3]

Example: $X = 11010$ $n = 5$

$$
\begin{array}{r}
2^n - X: \quad 100000 \\
-11010 \\
\hline
00110
\end{array}
$$

Comparison and Properties of the Various Integer Codings

Table 3.3 shows the integer interpretations of four bit strings in each of the codes that we have presented. On a machine with an n bit word length, the unsigned codes would represent the integers from 0 to $2^n - 1$. The sign magnitude and one's complement would represent the positive integers from 1 to $2^{n-1} - 1$, the negative integers from -1 to $-2^{n-1} + 1$, and 0 as both $+0$ and -0. The two's complement system does not have a code for -0 and instead uses the code $10\ldots0$ ($n - 1$ '0's) to represent -2^{n-1}. In the two's complement notation there is only one code for 0 and we are able to avoid any confusion arising from comparing $+0$ and -0. On the other hand, it is not totally symmetric since it has a code for -2^{n-1} but not for $+2^{n-1}$.

---

[3] To be precise, we should distinguish between the bit string X and the unsigned number, say N, denoted by X.

Table 3.3   Different Codes for the Integers

Code	The Represented Number			
4 bit word	unsigned	sign-magnitude	one's complement	two's complement
0000	0	0	0	0
0001	1	1	1	1
0010	2	2	2	2
0011	3	3	3	3
0100	4	4	4	4
0101	5	5	5	5
0110	6	6	6	6
0111	7	7	7	7
1000	8	−0	−7	−8
1001	9	−1	−6	−7
1010	10	−2	−5	−6
1011	11	−3	−4	−5
1100	12	−4	−3	−4
1101	13	−5	−2	−3
1110	14	−6	−1	−2
1111	15	−7	−0	−1

Both complement notations have the desirable property that

$$\text{complement}(\text{representation}(-N)) = \text{representation}(N)$$

for any integer N such that $|N| < 2^{n-1}$. They also permit addition to be performed in binary in a straightforward manner by just adding the representations:

$$\text{representation}(N) + \text{representation}(M) = \text{representation}(N + M)$$

for integers N and M.[4]

One major advantage of the complement notations is that subtraction can be performed by addition, thus allowing the same circuit to accomplish both operations. We have

$$\text{representation}(N - M) = \text{representation}(N) + \text{representation}(-M);[4]$$

therefore performing subtraction requires only complementation and addition.

---

[4] In one's complement, an extra addition is required if a carry occurs out of the leftmost bit of the result.

Example of 4 bit two's complementation subtraction:

$$7 - 3 = 7 + (-3) = 0111 + 1101 = 0100 = 4$$

There is a carry out of the leftmost bit but this can be ignored.

For one's complement, subtraction is performed by adding the one's complement of the subtrahend to the minuend and performing an "end around carry;" this is an addition of a carry out of the leftmost bit to the least significant bit position.

Example of one's complement 4 bit subtraction:

$$
\begin{array}{r}
3 - 2 = \quad 0011 \\
1101 \\
\hline
10000
\end{array}
$$

end around carry

0001 result

Addition and subtraction in sign-magnitude notation are much more complex. Let the sign-magnitude representation of an integer N be denoted $(sign(N), |N|)$, where the first element of the pair is $+$ or $-$ and the second element is the magnitude. Then addition requires an algorithm similar to the following, for integers N and M:

> $representation(N + M) =$
> **if** $sign(N) = sign(M)$ **then** $(sign(N), |N| + |M|)$
> **else**
> **if** $|N| > |M|$ **then** $(sign(N), |N| - |M|)$
> **else** $(sign(M), |M| - |N|)$

Binary Coded Decimal (BCD)

One less common form of coding the integers is BCD. In this code, the word is divided into four bit slices, each slice encoding a decimal digit.

Example: 16 bit BCD

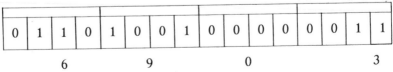

| 0 | 1 | 1 | 0 | 1 | 0 | 0 | 1 | 0 | 0 | 0 | 0 | 0 | 0 | 1 | 1 |

6   9   0   3

While this coding scheme enables computers to work directly in decimal, it is wasteful of storage. There are 16 distinct 4 bit strings and only 10 are used. So the 16 bit BCD encoded word can represent 10,000 integers rather than $2^{16} \approx 64,000$ integers.

3.4 FLOATING POINT NUMBERS

Scientific calculations range from very large numbers, such as the speed of light, $c = 2.998 \times 10^{10}$ cm/sec, to very small numbers, such as the gravitational constant, $k = 6.67 \times 10^{-8}$. Expressing c using decimal positional notation would require 11 digits, 29980000000 where seven digits are trailing zeros. We can capture the same information more conveniently in *floating point notation* which stores both a fraction and a power.

A floating point number is a real number of the form

$$\pm f \times b^e$$

where f is a *fraction*, $0 \leq f < 1$, b is an integer base, and e is a positive or negative integer *exponent*.

Examples: 0.2998×10^{11}, 0.667×10^{-7}, -0.873×10^6
0.003×10^{-2}, -0.300×10^{-4}

In floating point, we can represent the same number in different ways; the last two examples both denote 3×10^{-5}.

A *normalized* floating point representation is a representation where

$$f = 0 \cdot a_{-1}a_{-2} \ldots a_{-k} \quad \text{and} \quad a_{-1} \neq 0 \text{ unless } f = 0.$$

The k digits used to express f are the number's *significant* digits.

Examples: π in 3 significant digits $= 0.314 \times 10^1$ (normalized)
π in 5 significant digits $= 0.31416 \times 10^1$ (normalized)
π not normalized $= 0.0314 \times 10^2$

Fractional Conversion Algorithms

Our previous discussions of base conversion algorithms were concerned only with whole numbers. To treat the general case of real numbers, such as those expressed by floating point, it is necessary to handle fractional numbers. One approach would be to multiply the fraction by an integer, a *"scaling constant,"* that is sufficiently large to convert it to a whole number, use a whole number conversion method, and finally divide by the scaling constant. Yet another way, described below, is to adapt the multiplication and division methods to fractions.

Binary to Decimal by Division Method

A fractional number in binary

$$0 \cdot b_1 b_2 \ldots b_k \,_2$$

has value

$$\frac{b_1}{2} + \frac{b_2}{2^2} + \cdots + \frac{b_k}{2^k} = (\ldots ((b_k/2) + b_{k-1})/2 \ldots)/2 + b_1)/2$$

If the binary digits are stored in an array B, then an Algolic segment for computing its decimal expression would be:

$$f := B[k]/2; start := k - 1;$$
for $i := start$ **downto** 1 **do**
$$f := (f + B[i])/2$$

It is assumed that f is stored in decimal and that the arithmetic is in decimal.

Example: Convert 0.1011_2 to decimal.
Initially $k = 4, f = B[4]/2 = 0.5$.

i	$B[i]$	f
3	1	0.75
2	0	0.375
1	1	0.6875

Conversion to Binary by Multiplication Method

As before, a fraction in binary $0 \cdot b_1 b_2 \ldots b_k$ has value

$$f = \frac{b_1}{2} + \frac{b_2}{2^2} + \cdots + \frac{b_k}{2^k}$$

Suppose f is multiplied by 2. The result is:

$$2 \times f = b_1 + \frac{b_2}{2} + \frac{b_3}{2^2} + \cdots + \frac{b_k}{2^{k-1}} = b_1 + f_1$$

Thus the integer part of the result is b_1. The fraction part f_1 can again be multiplied by 2 to obtain b_2, and so on. This process can be repeated for as many digits as is required. We will give an Algolic program for this algorithm which will use the *transfer function* "trunc." A transfer function converts one data type to another data type. Trunc converts a real to an integer by retaining only its integer part.

Examples:
$$trunc(3.14) = 3$$
$$trunc(0.71) = 0$$
$$trunc(-2.6) = -2$$

The following algorithm produces the binary digits of a fraction f, starting with the first digit to the right of the decimal point.

```
algorithm ConvertFractionByMultiply;
  k, b : integer;
  f: real;
  begin
    read( f, k); {Assume f is a fraction.}
    for i := 1 upto k do
      begin
        b := trunc(2 × f);
        f := 2 × f − b;
        write('next digit', b)
      end
end.
```

Example: Convert 0.625 to binary.

Initially $f = 0.625$, $k = 4$.

i	$2 \times f$	b	$2f - b$
1	1.25	1	0.25
2	0.50	0	0.50
3	1.00	1	0.00
4	0.00	0	0.00

$0.625 = 0.1010_2$

Fractional Conversion Between Arbitrary Bases

The multiplication and division methods for fractional conversions can be easily modified to accommodate any pair of radices.

To convert a fraction f to a base B, we just successively multiply by B to obtain the base B digits. Let f be represented in base B by $0 \cdot b_1 b_2 \ldots b_k \ldots_B$. Then $f = b_1 \times B^{-1} + b_2 \times B^{-2} + \cdots + b_k \times B^{-k} \ldots$ and $f \times B = b_1 + f_1$, where b_1 is an integer and f_1 is a fraction. Thus, the general algorithm is just the *ConvertFractionByMultiply* program with B substituted for 2 in the main loop.

Let *bdigits*[1], ..., *bdigits*[m] be the representation in base b of a fraction f and *Bdigits*[1], ..., *Bdigits*[n] be the first n digits of f in base B. Then, in a similar manner as in the whole number algorithms, we can convert f from radix b to B by applying the multiplication and division algorithms in order.

Note that fractions which terminate in one base, i.e., fractions that have a finite number of non-zero digits in that base, do not necessarily terminate when expressed in another base. For example, 0.1_3 (1/3) in base 3 has a non-terminating representation $0.3333 \ldots_{10}$ in base 10, and $0.2_{10} = 0.001100110011 \ldots_2$.

Computer Word Representation of Floating Point

A floating point number is represented in a computer word in three parts: sign, exponent, fraction.

For example, in a 16 bit floating point representation, we may have:

(a) bit 15, the high order bit, is the sign of the number, where 0 denotes $+$ and 1 stands for $-$,

(b) bits 10 to 14 are the exponent in two's complement code, and

(c) bits 0 to 9 give the unsigned fraction in binary.

Assume that the number's exponent is base 2 and that the ten bit fraction is normalized. The five bit exponent can then represent the range (2^{15}, 2^{-16}). These are approximately the largest and smallest floating point numbers representable by this encoding.

Examples: 0 00001 10000 00000
$+\ 2^1$ 0.5 $= +0.5 \times 2^1 = 1$
1 00000 11010 00000
$-\ 2^0$ 0.8125 $= -0.8125 \times 2^0 = -0.8125$
1 11110 10100 00000
$-\ 2^{-2}$ 0.625 $= -0.625 \times 2^{-2} = -0.15625$

Instead of interpreting the previous example as a base 2 exponent, we might have used a base 8 exponent; then the exponent range would be $(8^{15}, 8^{-16})$. This is a substantially larger portion of the real line. Such a gain in magnitude is achieved by a loss in the density of representable numbers. Two fractions, f_1 and f_2, can differ by one in the least significant bit; for 10 bit binary fractions, and $f_1 \neq f_2$, we have

$$0.001 \approx 2^{-10} \leq |f_1 - f_2| < 0.5 = 2^{-1}.$$

This means that roughly 1000 distinct reals are representable per exponent. So using base 8, we would be able to represent numbers between 8^2 and 8^3 at intervals of approximately 0.45 $((8^3 - 8^2)/1000)$. The same range in base 2 is covered by 2^6, 2^7, 2^8, up to 2^9 and this would allow representation at intervals of approximately 0.15.

When computer designers decide on a floating point code, they must decide how a word is to be divided into its exponent and fractional parts, and further, they must select the base to use. Each decision affects the range and accuracy achievable in floating point computation. While we have not discussed these issues in any detail, floating point codes and arithmetic result in inexact representations of real numbers. Numerical analysts try to ensure that these approximations are accurate. In programming languages, such as Algolic, declaring a variable to be of type *real* implies that the variable is represented in floating point in the underlying computer.

3.5 CHARACTERS AND STRINGS

So far we have considered only numerical data. While numbers are obviously important, they are only one of the many kinds of data processed by computers. In fact, much of modern computing involves calculations and transformations on character information. This is understandable since most of our own information sources are expressed in natural language text. The actual processing of text is a major application of computing and is called "text editing" or "word processing."

In Algolic the data type *character* refers to any of the alphabet, digits, and special characters, including punctuation and special operators, that are explicitly listed in the language. These characters are also representable as a sequence of bits, typically stored one to a byte.

Three commonly used character codes are BCD (binary coded decimal), EBCDIC (extended binary coded decimal interchange code) and ASCII (American standards code for information exchange). BCD is a six bit code,[5] while EBCDIC and ASCII are eight bit codes. These codes are listed in Table 3.4. They are all used in a variety of computer and communication systems, and there is a frequent need to translate among them—much as there is a need to convert among number representations.

A typical machine might use EBCDIC and have four bytes per word. Consequently, a single word can store the EBCDIC encoding of four characters.

Example:

1100 0011	1100 1000	1100 0001	1101 1001
C	H	A	R

An Algolic variable of type character can have any of the allowable single characters as its value. As with other types, any variables that will be used in an Algolic program must first be declared.

Example: {declaration of two simple character variables}
               char, A : character ;

These variables can then be assigned either character constants or character variables, where constants are represented by quoted characters. Character variables and constants can also be used in comparisons in Boolean expressions, employing the relations = and ≠ .

---

[5] Note that this six bit BCD *character* code is different from the four bit BCD code for the *integers* discussed in the last section.

Table 3.4 BCD, EBCDIC and ASCII Codes

Character	BCD Code	EBCDIC Code	ASCII Code
blank	110 000	0100 0000	0010 0000
.	011 011	0100 1011	0010 1110
(	111 100	0100 1101	0010 1000
+	010 000	0100 1110	0010 1011
$	101 011	0101 1011	0010 0100
*	101 100	0101 1100	0010 1010
)	011 100	0101 1101	0010 1001
—	100 000	0110 0000	0010 1101
/	110 001	0110 0001	0010 1111
,	111 011	0110 1011	0010 1100
'	001 100	0111 1101	0010 0111
=	001 011	0111 1110	0011 1101
A	010 001	1100 0001	0100 0001
B	010 010	1100 0010	0100 0010
C	010 011	1100 0011	0100 0011
D	010 100	1100 0100	0100 0100
E	010 101	1100 0101	0100 0101
F	010 110	1100 0110	0100 0110
G	010 111	1100 0111	0100 0111
H	011 000	1100 1000	0100 1000
I	011 001	1100 1001	0100 1001
J	100 001	1101 0001	0100 1010
K	100 010	1101 0010	0100 1011
L	100 011	1101 0011	0100 1100
M	100 100	1101 0100	0100 1101
N	100 101	1101 0101	0100 1110
O	100 110	1101 0110	0100 1111
P	100 111	1101 0111	0101 0000
Q	101 000	1101 1000	0101 0001
R	101 001	1101 1001	0101 0010
S	110 010	1110 0010	0101 0011
T	110 011	1110 0011	0101 0100
U	110 100	1110 0100	0101 0101
V	110 101	1110 0101	0101 0110
W	110 110	1110 0110	0101 0111
X	110 111	1110 0111	0101 1000
Y	111 000	1110 1000	0101 1001
Z	111 001	1110 1001	0101 1010
0	000 000	1111 0000	0011 0000
1	000 001	1111 0001	0011 0001
2	000 010	1111 0010	0011 0010

Table 3.4   Continued.

Character	BCD Code	EBCDIC Code	ASCII Code
3	000 011	1111 0011	0011 0011
4	000 100	1111 0100	0011 0100
5	000 101	1111 0101	0011 0101
6	000 110	1111 0110	0011 0110
7	000 111	1111 0111	0011 0111
8	001 000	1111 1000	0011 1000
9	001 001	1111 1001	0011 1001

Examples of character assignment and comparison:

$char$:= 'A';
$char$:= ' '; {the blank character}
A := 'A'; {A is a character variable, 'A' is a character constant}
$char$:= A;
$char$:= '+'; {'+' is a character constant}
if X = '5' **then** i := i + 1 {Compare the character variable X with the
                                              character constant '5'.}

Character Strings

Single characters by themselves are of limited utility. More frequently, we encounter sequences of characters, such as the sentences of this text. These will be represented as arrays of characters, sometimes referred to as character strings.

Example: *SENTENCE*: **array**[1 . . 1000] **of** *character*

Let us work through a simple exercise using character arrays. Assume that the names of 100 students are stored in a character array whose identifier is *STUDENTS*. Each student's name is truncated to 10 characters and each name begins at index $k \times 10 + 1$, for $k = 0, \ldots, 99$, i.e., at 1, 11, 21, ..., 991. The purpose is to count the number of students whose name begins with 'T,' and print them out. An Algolic code fragment for this task is:

```
TCOUNT := 0; {integer variable used to count students whose name
  begins with T}
FIRSTLETTER := 1; {index into character array}
for i := 1 upto 100 do
  begin
    if STUDENTS[FIRSTLETTER] = 'T' then
    begin {found a name beginning with 'T'}
      TCOUNT := TCOUNT + 1; LASTLETTER := FIRSTLETTER
      + 9;
      for j := FIRSTLETTER upto LASTLETTER do
        write(STUDENTS[j])
    end;
    FIRSTLETTER := FIRSTLETTER + 10;
    {Advance index to first letter of next name.}
  end;
write('There are', TCOUNT, 'students whose names begin with T')
```

3.6 DATA AND STRUCTURE

We have now shown how numerical and character data may be represented in binary codes suitable for digital computer storage. In Algolic, the basic data types can be structured into single-dimensional or *linear* arrays; an array may be encoded by just concatenating together the representatives of each element.

The array structure is useful for processing large amounts of data in a uniform iterative manner. In languages more complex than Algolic, there are numerous other structuring methods which are both useful and readily encoded. We briefly introduce two of these more advanced data structures in this section.

Two and Higher Dimensional Arrays

While Algolic only provides one-dimensional arrays, most current computer languages allow higher dimensional arrays. In the theatre seat example of Section 3.2.2 where it is necessary to identify each seat, one could label both the row (one index) and the seat number within the row (a second index); for example, $SEAT[15, 37]$ might designate the 37th seat in the 15th row. A possible extension to Algolic would allow *two-dimensional* arrays of the form:

identifier: **array**$[lb_1 . . ub_1]$ **of array** $[lb_2 . . ub_2]$ **of** *type* or in abbreviated form

$$identifier: \textbf{array}[lb_1..ub_1, lb_2..ub_2] \textbf{ of } type$$

Examples:

1. *names*: **array** $[1..100, 1..10]$ **of** *character*
   {100 names each 10 characters long}
2. *scores*: **array** $[1..50, 1..3]$ **of** *integer*
   {3 exam scores for each of 50 students}

The second example declares *scores* to be an array of 150 (3×50) elements. A particular element is identified by providing two indices, one for the first dimension and the other for the second, e.g., *scores*[20, 2]. It is conventional to speak of the first dimension as the *row* of the array and the second dimension as the *column*; the array is then viewed as arranged in a rectangle (Figure 3.5). The array *scores* has 50 rows and 3 columns and the element *scores*[20, 2] is found at the intersection of the 20th row and the 2nd column.

For processing two or more dimensional arrays, one often uses a nested loop structure where each index takes on an appropriate sequence of values. Suppose that we are given the *scores* array containing exam scores and we wish to average the three scores for each student. An extended Algolic code fragment for this problem is:

```
{We assume scores is a two-dimensional array and average is a one-
   dimensional array. There are three scores to average and n students
   in the class.}
   {outer loop for processing n students}
   for i := 1 upto n do
     begin
       average[i] := 0;
       {inner loop for averaging three scores}
       for j := 1 upto 3 do
            average[i] := scores[i, j] + average[i];
       average[i] := average[i]/3
     end
```

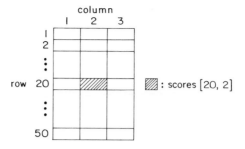

Figure 3.5   The Array *scores*[1..50, 1..3]

Linear Linked Lists

A list is a sequential structure whose basic element has two components, primitive data and *link* data. The primitive data could be any of the types we are familiar with, for example, integers. The link data is the means for accessing the next element of the list, and contains the address of this next element. An address used in this manner is called a *pointer*. Pictorially a list is:

header is a pointer (address) to the first element of the list; the last element has a special *null* link indicating the end of the list.

Lists have many applications, especially in the processing and storage of non-numerical data. We show the advantage of this structure compared with arrays, by illustrating the steps involved in inserting an element into the middle of a list. Suppose a new element e_{new} is to be inserted in a list between the elements e_i and e_j, as shown below:

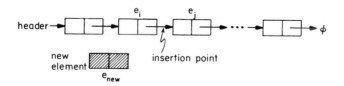

e_{new} is inserted by assigning e_{new}'s link component to point to e_j and re-assigning e_i's link to e_{new}:

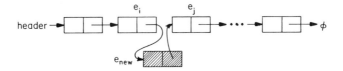

In contrast, inserting an element into the middle of a large array would require numerous data reassignments (everyone after the new element must move one 'seat' over in the array).

A linked linear list can be constructed from two arrays as follows. One array is used for the data fields, and the other array simulates the link field and is of type integer. An integer variable contains the value of the index of the first element of the list, and acts as the header; the special value 0 indicates the end of the list.

Example: *datalist*: **array** [1..100] **of** *character*;
linklist: **array** [1..100] **of** *integer*;
header: *integer*;

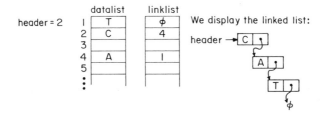

Chapter 6 contains a more detailed discussion of structuring concepts. The main point here is that there exists a variety of useful data structures that can be constructed from the basic data types.

EXERCISES

1. Write this year in Egyptian and Late Babylonian notation.

2. Give a list of words that contain a number in their meaning such as 'brace'.

3. Describe some ancient civilization's number system that was not included in this book.

4. Where in Archimedes' cycles would the following numbers appear?
   (a) diameter of the Earth?
   (b) diameter of the solar system?
   (c) diameter of the universe?

   Assume that the unit of measurement is a mile.

5. Using the doubling method, multiply 43 $\times$ 36 and 217 $\times$ 599. How many doublings are required for multiplying $m \times n$ for any positive integers m and n?

6. Hand simulate the algorithm *HalveDoubleMPY* given the values $A = 17$ and $B = 15$.

7. Express the following decimal numbers in binary: 29, 37, 6, 2, 102.

8. Express in decimal: 1_2, 1000_2, 1111_2, 1010_2.

9. Give two reasons for using binary on computers.

10. Perform the following binary additions, multiplications, subtractions and divisions:
    (a) $101 + 11$ (b) $10011 + 1111111$ (c) 101×11 (d) 10011×111
    (e) $1101 - 11$ (f) $1110111 - 110001$ (g) $111/10$ (h) $11001101/1010$

11. Convert from binary to octal:
    (a) 110101   (b) 1101   (c) 11   (d) 1110101110

12. Convert from hexadecimal to binary:
    (a) A1   (b) 98   (c) 9A   (d) E30F

13. Convert from hexadecimal to octal:
    (a) FF3   (b) 1073   (c) A123B   (d) ABC

14. Write an Algolic program that adds the negative integers -1, -2, ..., -100, producing the sum $\sum_{i=-1}^{-100} i$.

15. Let X be the array: X: **array**$[1..50]$ **of** *real*. Write a program to read values into X and to sum them into the real variable *total*. Give three versions using a) an **if/then** loop, b) a **while** loop, and c) a **for** loop, respectively.

16. Write a program to find the smallest value contained in the first n elements of an array X.

17. Rewrite **algorithm** *testscore* so that only *one* loop is required.

18. What is wrong with the following Algolic fragments?

    (a) **while** $i > 20$ **do**
            begin
                S_1; {some statement}
                $i := i + 1$
            end

    (b) **for** $i := 5$ **downto** 0 **do**
            begin
                $TOT := TOT + X[i]$;
                $i := i - 1$
            end

19. Display a set of values for array A in **algorithm** *CheckConjecture* that causes the program to write "conjecture false."

20. Hand simulate **algorithm** *ConvertByMultiply* for converting from ternary $(b = 3)$ to base $B = 7$. Use 212011_3 for the simulation.

21. Convert to decimal: (a) 1001.1101_2,   (b) 0.00101_2,
                          (c) 11.001_2,   (d) -1.000101_2.

22. Convert to binary: (a) 3.67, (b) 9.99, (c) −6.125, (d) 4.6038. Do not use more than 6 binary digits in the fraction of the binary representation.

23. Give a general algorithm in Algolic for converting a number $a_n a_{n-1} \ldots a_1 a_0 \cdot a_{-1} \ldots a_{-m}$ from base b to base B.

24. Display the following decimal numbers in one's complement, two's complement, and sign-magnitude, using an 8 bit representation:
    (a) 0   (b) −1   (c) 100   (d) −100.

25. Describe the floating point arithmetic of one of your local computers.

26. If you want to represent the integers −1000, −999, ..., −1, 0, 1, 2, ..., 1000, what is the minimum length binary word you would need?

27. The IBM System/360-370 computer series has a floating point representation of the form:

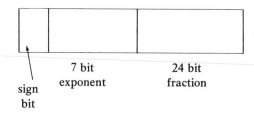

           7 bit   24 bit
           exponent   fraction
sign
bit

The fraction is a 6 digit normalized hexadecimal number, i.e., the leading hexadecimal digit must not be 0; e.g., .A10365 *but not* .0A1036. The exponent can range from 63 to −64 and the numbers are interpreted as being base 16. Therefore this representation results in values $\pm f \times 16^e$ where f is the fraction and e the exponent.

    (a) What is the largest magnitude number expressable?

    (b) What is the smallest positive non-zero number representable?

    (c) Represent the numbers 0.5, 1 and 16 in this code. (The 7 bit code for any exponent e is given by the binary representation of $64 + e$; this is called *excess 64* notation.)

28. To within what accuracy is $\frac{1}{3}$ representable on the IBM system/360-370 (see last exercise)?

29. Imagine using a second 32 bit word for eight hexadecimal digits of fraction added to the right of a first word as described in Exercise 27. This is called *double precision*. Now what is the answer to Exercise 28?

30. Let a bit string X be represented in Algolic as an array of integers. Give an Algolic program for taking the two's complement of X.

31. What would be the 16 bit BCD for the numbers:

    (a) 0   (b) 1   (c) 9999   (d) 4013

32. Reinterpret the codes in the last exercise as two EBCDIC characters.

33. Investigate for one of your local computers how data is represented in memory.

34. Write out the word CORE in EBCDIC, ASCII, and BCD codes.

35. Write an Algolic program which counts the number of occurrences of A, B, and C in a string of text stored in array $TEXT$ whose declaration is

$$TEXT: \textbf{array } [-50..49] \textbf{ of } character$$

36. Store in $ALPH$: **array** $[1..26]$ **of** *character* the letters of the alphabet. Using this array and the array $COUNT$: **array** $[1..26]$ **of** *integer*, write a program which counts all letters of the alphabet occurring in the array $TEXT$ defined in the last exercise.

37. Suppose a list is represented by arrays as shown in the Example of Section 3.6. Give an Algolic fragment that inserts a new element $(datalist[new]$, *link-list*$[new])$ immediately *after* the element with address i, i.e., immediately after the element $(datalist[i]$, $linklist[i])$.

ADDITIONAL READINGS

Knuth, D. E. *Seminumerical Algorithms*. Reading, Mass.: Addison-Wesley, 1969.

Menninger, K. *Number Words and Number Symbols*. Cambridge, Mass.: M.I.T. Press, 1969.

van der Waerden, B. L. *Science Awakening*. Clarendon: Oxford University Press, 1961.

Chapter 4

BOOLEAN ALGEBRA AND APPLICATIONS

A central question in philosophy is *what is truth*. Rationalists, such as Plato, Descartes, and Leibniz, believed that many truths could be discovered by logical reasoning. Given a set of *axioms* or true statements about the world, other true statements may be derived by the laws of reason. These derivable truths need not be checked by reference to the world provided that the axioms are true and that the derivation procedure is correct.

Example:

Given that
  1. the distance by direct flight between San Francisco and Boston is 2600 miles, and
  2. a road between two cities is at best the same distance as a flight path, then by logical reasoning it is true that
  3. a car trip from San Francisco to Boston would be at least 2600 miles.

The study of the principles of correct reasoning is called *logic*. Originally, it was a serious concern of philosophers and mathematicians. More recently, logic has also become an important theoretical and practical tool for computer scientists. Computers can be viewed abstractly as logical machines described by systems of axioms; a computation corresponds to that which is derivable in a finite amount of time by such a machine. This theory is elaborated in later discussions on abstract computability (Chapter 7) and on program proving (Chapter 8). In the present chapter, we are primarily concerned with the applications of logic in the Boolean expressions of programming languages and in the switching circuits that comprise some of the basic components of digital computers.

The next section introduces propositional logic, the logic of statements, and shows how it is used in proving mathematical theorems. Propositional logic forms the basis for defining and evaluating Boolean expressions in programming languages; this application is developed in Section 4.2. A Boolean algebra is then formally defined and shown to describe propositional logic, the algebra of sets, and switching algebra. The last section discusses switching algebra and combinational switching circuits.

4.1 PROPOSITIONAL LOGIC

The twin fountainheads of modern logic are the works of the Greek mathematicians as collected and elaborated by Euclid (300 B.C.), and the works of Aristotle (384-322 B.C.) on syllogism. The Greek mathematicians pioneered the idea of axiomatic-deductive proof; this is the same method used in a high school geometry class. In an entirely different direction, Aristotle explored the nature of logical argument in ordinary discussion. He categorized different forms of correct argument—that is, arguments that preserved truth. His fundamental scheme was the syllogism.

Example:

The following is a syllogistic argument.
Given that
1. all men are mortal, and
2. no angel is mortal,
then it can be concluded that
3. no man is an angel.

Aristotelian logic, with some elaboration by medieval logicians, remained the dominant theme in logic through the 17th century. Leibniz (1646-1716), the co-inventor with Newton of the integral and differential calculus, injected new vigor into logical studies by his proposal that all arguments could be settled by calculation. He suggested a universal language that could precisely encode any sentence; an encoded sentence could then be placed in a machine which would attempt a logical derivation, i.e., a proof, of the sentence. Leibniz was three centuries premature in his speculation.

George Boole (1815-1864), a British mathematician, realized part of Leibniz' vision in his 1854 publication, *The Laws of Thought*. This work contained a logical calculus, now called *propositional logic*. The logic can be viewed as a system of variables and operators which form expressions taking on the value 1 (true) or 0 (false). In this form, it is also known as an example of a *Boolean algebra.*

4.1.1 Elements of Propositional Logic

The statement "It is raining" is a *proposition*. It is either *true* or *false*; its truth is empirical. "It is sunny" is also a proposition. However, if "raining" implies that "it is not sunny," then the conjunction of the above statements, "It is raining" *and* "It is sunny," is logically false. This reasoning may be written symbolically:

symbolic representation	*statement*
1. P	It is sunny.
2. Q	It is raining.
3. $Q \supset \neg P$	It is raining *implies* that it is *not* sunny.
4. $Q \wedge P$	It is raining *and* it is sunny.

If 3. is considered as an axiom (always true), then $P \wedge Q$ is a *contradiction,* that is, $P \wedge Q$ is always false.

The reasoning of the syllogism example can also be formulated in propositional logic:

1. H	X is a man.
2. M	X is mortal.
3. A	X is an angel.
4. $H \supset M$	X is a man implies that X is mortal.
5. $M \supset \neg A$	X is mortal implies that X is not an angel.
6. $H \supset \neg A$	X is a man implies that X is not an angel.

Given 4. and 5. one can assert the truth of 6.

In the above examples, variables, such as P, Q, H, M, and A, are used to denote elementary propositions and symbols, such as $\wedge$, $\neg$, and $\supset$, denote logical connectives. A *propositional variable* is a variable having the *truth value T or F,* where T means "true" and F means "false." Propositional variables may be combined into more complex sentences with logical connectives. The most common connectives come from ordinary language use; these include "not," "and," "or," and "implies." Such connectives act as operations for a calculus of truth. Hence, in a manner similar to arithmetic operations, they can be defined by operation tables. These tables are called *truth tables.*

1. The operation *not,* also called *negation,* is written "$\neg$" and changes the truth value of its argument.

	Propositional Variable P	Statement ¬P
Truth	T	F
Values	F	T

2. The operation *and*, also called *conjunction*, is denoted "∧." It is a binary operation, i.e., an operation on two arguments. The conjunction of two propositions is true only when both are true.

P	Q	P ∧ Q
T	T	T
T	F	F
F	T	F
F	F	F

3. The binary operation *or*, also called *disjunction*, is denoted "∨." It is the analog of the natural language "inclusive or." A disjunction is true if either or both of its propositions are true.

P	Q	P ∨ Q
T	T	T
T	F	T
F	T	T
F	F	F

4. The binary operation *implication,* denoted "⊃," is the analog to the natural language "if P then Q" construct. P is called the *antecedent* and Q the *consequent*. P ⊃ Q is true whenever its consequent is true or whenever its antecedent is *false*.

P	Q	P ⊃ Q
T	T	T
T	F	F
F	T	T
F	F	T

The rationale for the definitions in the last two rows of the last table is often difficult to understand and is indeed controversial. Statements that are meaningless in everyday usage, such as, "If the earth is flat, then I am Napolean" (false antecedent and false consequent), or, "If the moon is made of cheese, then the earth is round" (false antecedent and true consequent), are logically true according to this accepted definition of implication. The truth of the statement has no relevance to the real world because the false antecedent allows the confirmation of any pronouncement. The key notion is that an implication $P \supset Q$ is false only when a true antecedent P implies a false consequent Q; the implication states that P is a sufficient condition for Q but not a necessary one.

5. The binary operation " $\equiv$ " is called *equivalence, if and only if,* or *equals.* Equivalence evaluates to true only when both arguments have the same truth value.

P	Q	$P \equiv Q$
T	T	T
T	F	F
F	T	F
F	F	T

Expressions may be formed using propositional variables, the constant truth values T and F, and the logical connectives. Truth tables are commonly used to evaluate such expressions, that is, to determine the truth value of the expression for different possible truth values of the variables.

Consider first the examples given at the beginning of this section. The sentence, "If it is raining, then it is not sunny, and it is raining and it is sunny," can be expressed in propositional logic as $(Q \supset \neg P) \wedge (P \wedge Q)$. The truth table for this expression can be derived:

P	Q	$(Q \supset \neg P)$	$(P \wedge Q)$	$(Q \supset \neg P) \wedge (P \wedge Q)$
T	T	F	T	F
T	F	T	F	F
F	T	T	F	F
F	F	T	F	F

The expression always evaluates to false, a *contradiction.*

The expression for the syllogism given earlier is $((H \supset M) \wedge (M \supset \neg A)) \supset (H \supset \neg A)$. Using a truth table to evaluate this expression, we have:

H M A	X	Y	X ∧ Y	Z	(X ∧ Y) ⊃ Z
T T T	*T*	*F*	*F*	*F*	*T*
T T F	*T*	*T*	*T*	*T*	*T*
T F T	*F*	*T*	*F*	*F*	*T*
T F F	*F*	*T*	*F*	*T*	*T*
F T T	*T*	*F*	*F*	*T*	*T*
F T F	*T*	*T*	*T*	*T*	*T*
F F T	*T*	*T*	*T*	*T*	*T*
F F F	*T*	*T*	*T*	*T*	*T*

where $X = (H \supset M)$, $Y = (M \supset \neg A)$, and $Z = (H \supset \neg A)$.

This expression always evaluates true. Such an expression is called a *tautology*. In ordinary mathematical usage, a tautology is a *theorem*. The general form of the syllogism rule expressed in propositional logic is $((P \supset Q) \wedge (Q \supset R)) \supset (P \supset R)$, for any P, Q, and R; this formula is a theorem or tautology.

The operators $\neg$, $\vee$, $\wedge$, $\supset$, and $\equiv$ are redundant in that it is possible to express some operators in terms of the others. For example, $P \supset Q$ has the same meaning as $\neg P \vee Q$. (More formally, $(P \supset Q) \equiv (\neg P \vee Q)$ is a tautology.)

P	Q	¬P ∨ Q
T	*T*	*T*
T	*F*	*F*
F	*T*	*T*
F	*F*	*T*

Similarly, $P \equiv Q$ is equivalent to $(P \wedge Q) \vee (\neg P \wedge \neg Q)$ and also to $(P \supset Q) \wedge (Q \supset P)$.

Expressions in propositional logic can be interpreted as functions that produce a truth value from truth-valued arguments; these functions are called *Boolean functions*. The truth table is an exhaustive tabulation of the function. For example, the last table above defined the function $f(P, Q) = \neg P \vee Q$. Within this framework, it can be shown that the connective set $\{\neg, \vee, \wedge\}$ is sufficient to describe any such propositional function; these connectives are then said to be functionally *complete*. Section 4.4.1 treats the issue of completeness in more detail.

4.1.2   Some Applications of Logic

Propositional logic provides much insight into the techniques of stating and proving mathematical results, both formally and informally. Theorems are often stated in the form "*if P then Q*"; for example, "*if m and n* are positive integers *then* gcd(m, n) = gcd(n, m **mod** n)." Proving a theorem of this form is equivalent to showing that $P \supset Q$ is true when P is true. (When P is false, we wish the theorem, but not necessarily the consequent Q, to be true; this provides another example of the rationale underlying the definition of implication.) Sometimes, it is easier to convert $P \supset Q$ to its equivalent *contrapositive* form ($\neg Q \supset \neg P$) and prove that the truth of $\neg Q$ implies the truth of $\neg P$. In proving implications, an extended syllogism rule is commonly employed; ($P \supset Q$) is proven by finding statements $P_1, \ldots, P_n$ such that $P_1 = P$, $P_n = Q$, and ($P_1 \supset P_2$) $\wedge$ ($P_2 \supset P_3$) $\wedge \cdots \wedge$ ($P_{n-1} \supset P_n$) is true.

Another common form of theorem statement is "*P if and only if Q;*" for example, "a number d divides the Fibonacci numbers F_m and F_n if and only if d divides F_{m+kn} and F_n, for any non-negative integer k." Proving this form of theorem is identical to showing that ($P \equiv Q$) is always true for the given P and Q. It is most often proven in two steps: (1) show *if P then Q*, (2) show *if Q then P*. That is, the formula ($P \supset Q$) $\wedge$ ($Q \supset P$) is proven for the given P and Q.

A third standard proof technique is proof by contradiction, also called a *reductio ad absurdum* argument. If the theorem is $P \supset Q$, one assumes the truth of P and the truth of $\neg Q$, and then derives a contradiction of the form $R \wedge \neg R$ where R is any statement. The only way out of this dilemma (the contradiction) is that the truths of P and $\neg Q$ are not valid; since P is assumed to be true when the theorem is used, we must conclude that $\neg Q$ must be false and Q is true. A simpler form of this method is to prove a statement Q by assuming $\neg Q$ and deriving a contradiction. We use this technique in Chapter 7.

Example:

We illustrate some of the above ideas with the simple raining/sunny example of the last section. Suppose we wish to prove the following theorem: "If it is sunny implies that it is not raining, then it cannot be sunny and raining at the same time." Symbolically, the theorem can be stated as: if $P \supset \neg Q$ is true, then $\neg(P \wedge Q)$ is true; i.e., ($P \supset \neg Q$) $\supset \neg(P \wedge Q)$. In contrapositive form, the theorem is:

if $(P \wedge Q)$ is true, *then* $\neg (P \supset \neg Q)$; *i.e.,* $(P \wedge Q) \supset \neg (P \supset \neg Q)$

(If it can be sunny and raining at the same time, then sunny weather does not imply the absence of rain.)

A *reductio ad absurdum* argument would assume the truth of both $(P \supset \neg Q)$ and $(P \wedge Q)$ and derive a contradiction. We can proceed as follows: Let $R_1 = P \supset \neg Q$ and $R_2 = P \wedge Q$. But $R_1 = \neg P \vee \neg Q = \neg (P \wedge Q) = \neg R_2$. (This can be verified using truth tables.) Since R_1 and R_2 are assumed true, we have the contradiction $R_2 \wedge \neg R_2$. One then concludes that $\neg (P \wedge Q)$ must be true.

Propositional logic and higher-order logics are also used for specifying and verifying computer programs. A logical calculus is employed to assert conditions existing at appropriate points during a program's execution and to prove program correctness. As a brief example, consider the following program segment for computing an integer approximation to $\sqrt{N}$, where N is a non-negative integer:

$\{P_0: (N \geq 0)\}$
$a := 0;$
$\{P_1: (a^2 \leq N)\}$
while $(a + 1) \times (a + 1) \leq N$ **do** $a := a + 1;$
$\{P_2: (a^2 \leq N) \wedge ((a + 1)^2 > N)\}$

P_0, P_1, and P_2 are assertions that specify relations among the program variables during execution. P_0 is the given initial condition while P_2 expresses the desired effect of the program. The correctness of the program is verified by proving that if an assertion preceding a statement is true and the statement is executed, then the assertion following the statement is true. We pursue these ideas further in Chapter 8. The next section shows how the notation and concepts of propositional logic have been applied to the definition and evaluation of Boolean expressions in programming languages.

4.2   BOOLEAN EXPRESSIONS IN PROGRAMMING LANGUAGES

In the program examples given in earlier chapters, we have informally introduced and used expressions that evaluate to *true* or *false*. These expressions are necessary parts of conditional statements and while statements, and they sometimes appear in assignment statements. For example, B is such an expression in the forms:

if B **then** S, **if** B **then** S_1 **else** S_2, and **while** B **do** S.

Because of the connection with propositional logic, the B's are called *Boolean expressions*, the constants *true* and *false* are called *Boolean constants,* and variables that can have Boolean values are termed *Boolean variables.* (Sometimes, the word "logical" is substituted for "Boolean"; e.g., logical expression, logical variable, logical constant.)

The elementary components of Boolean expressions are Boolean variables, Boolean constants, and relational expressions (defined below). These may be combined into more complex expressions using the *Boolean operators* $\lor$ (inclusive or), $\land$ (and), and $\neg$ (not); in some languages, other operators, such as $\supset$ (implies) and $\equiv$ (equivalence), are also included. The operators are defined in the same way as the analogous operators in propositional logic:

Let B_1 and B_2 be Boolean expressions:

1. $B_1 \lor B_2$ evaluates to true if either or both of B_1 and B_2 are true, and is false otherwise.
2. $B_1 \land B_2$ is true if both B_1 and B_2 are true, and false otherwise.
3. $\neg B_1$ is true if B_1 is false, and false if B_1 is true.

Relational expressions are used to compare the values of two expressions. They have the form $E_1 \ r \ E_2$ where E_1 and E_2 are the expressions being compared and r is a relation from the set $\{=, \neq, <, >, \leq, \geq\}$. A relational expression evaluates to *true* or *false*, according to whether or not the relation r is satisfied. When E_1 and E_2 evaluate to Boolean values (true or false) or to character strings, the relation r is often restricted to the set $\{=, \neq\}$; alternatively, orderings may be imposed on Boolean values and strings so that the other relations may be used; for example, by convention, the elements may be ordered such that *true* > *false*, 'T' > 'B', and 'CAT' > 'APPLE' all evaluate to *true*.

Examples of Boolean expressions:

test, true, $(a \leq 15) \land (b \neq c)$, $x = $ '*MAIN*'
$\neg (a + b = c) \lor e \land (f > g)$
test and *e* are Boolean variables; $(a \leq 15)$, $(b \neq c)$, $(a + b = c)$, $x = $ '*MAIN*', and $(f > g)$ are relational expressions.

In Algolic, a Boolean variable v is declared:
v:*Boolean*;

v can then take either of the Boolean constants, *true* or *false*, as its value.
Boolean expressions in Algolic are defined as follows:

Let v be a Boolean constant, Boolean variable, or relational expression, and let B, B_1, and B_2 be Boolean expressions.

1. v is a Boolean expression.
2. **not** B, B_1 **or** B_2, and B_1 **and** B_2 are Boolean expressions (**not, or,** and **and** correspond to $\neg$, $\vee$, and $\wedge$, respectively).
3. (B) is a Boolean expression.

In the absence of parentheses, **not** is given highest priority in evaluation, **and** has the next priority, and **or** has the lowest priority. Thus a **or not** b **and** c is interpreted as (a **or** ((**not** b) **and** c)).

Relational expressions in Algolic may have one of the forms:

1. $E_1 \; r \; E_2$, where E_1 and E_2 are *arithmetic* expressions and r is in the set $\{=, \neq, >, <, \geq, \leq\}$. E_1 and E_2 must be of the same type; that is, they must *both* be either integer expressions or real expressions.
2. $S_1 \; r \; S_2$, where S_1 and S_2 are *character* expressions and r is either $=$ or $\neq$. A character expression is either a character variable or a quoted character.
3. $B_1 \; r \; B_2$, where B_1 and B_2 are Boolean expressions and r is either $=$ or $\neq$. In evaluating expressions involving **or, and, not,** $=$, and $\neq$, the relational operators $=$ and $\neq$ are given highest priority. Thus a **and** $b = c$ **or** d is evaluated according to (a **and** ($b = c$)) **or** d, which is different from (a **and** b) $=$ (c **or** d).

Examples of Boolean expressions in Algolic:

$(i = 15)$ **and not** $(j + k \leq 3 \times (n - j))$
$(pi < 3.2)$ **and** $(x[i] = \text{'}C\text{'})$
$((b1 \; \textbf{and} \; (b2 \; \textbf{or} \; b3)) \neq \textbf{not} \; b4)$

In the Algolic statement forms **if** B **then** S, **if** B **then** S_1 **else** S_2, and **while** B **do** S, B is an arbitrary Boolean expression. The right part of an assignment statement may also be a Boolean expression; in that case, the left part must be a Boolean variable. For example, in the statement $x := B$, x must be a single or subscripted Boolean variable if B is a Boolean expression.

Examples:

$B1 := B2 \; \textbf{and} \; (i + 15 = j);$
$a[i] := \textbf{not}(b1 \; \textbf{or} \; c);$

There are at least two different methods for evaluating Boolean expressions of the forms $B_1 \vee B_2$ and $B_1 \wedge B_2$. The most straightforward technique first evaluates both operands and then applies the operator:

$$b_1 := Evaluate(B_1);$$
$$b_2 := Evaluate(B_2);$$
$$result := b_1 \vee b_2; \{B_1 \vee B_2\}$$

or

$$result := b_1 \wedge b_2; \{B_1 \wedge B_2\}$$

where $Evaluate(B)$ evaluates the Boolean expression B and returns a value of true or false.

This is not the most efficient method. For example, in evaluating $B_1 \vee B_2$, if B_1 is true, then the expression $B_1 \vee B_2$ is true and B_2 need not be computed. A more efficient method avoids these unnecessary evaluations:

1. {Evaluate $B_1 \vee B_2$}
   if $Evaluate(B_1)$ **then** *result* := *true*
   else *result* := $Evaluate(B_2)$
2. { Evaluate $B_1 \wedge B_2$}
   if $Evaluate(B_1)$ **then** *result* := $Evaluate(B_2)$
   else *result* := *false*

The Boolean values *true* and *false* are usually represented by either a single bit or a bit string inside computers. Typically, *true* is implemented as 1 and *false* as 0. Alternatively, *false* may, by convention, be coded as a string of all zero bits 00...0 and *true* by a string of bits containing at least one 1; the string may, for example, be one byte or one word in length. Boolean operations are then implemented by performing analogous operations or tests on bits.

We end this section with a program example that uses Boolean expressions. A string is a *palindrome* if it reads the same in both its forward (left-to-right) and backward (right-to-left) directions, examples are "OTTO" and "able was i ere i saw elba." The purpose of the following Algolic segment is to determine whether a string of characters is a palindrome.

```
string : array [1 . . 100] of character;
i, n : integer; {string[i], i = 1, . . ., n, contains the string, n ≤ 100}
palindrome : Boolean;
                ⋮
i := 1; palindrome := true;
while (i ≤ n − i) and palindrome do
begin
   palindrome := (string[i] = string[n − i + 1]);
   i := i + 1
end;
if palindrome then write('palindrome')
else write ('not palindrome')
```

4.3 BOOLEAN ALGEBRA

Several interesting and useful symbolic systems, including propositional logic, are instances of a particular type of algebra called Boolean algebra. By "algebra," we mean a set of symbols and operators that may be combined and manipulated according to some given rules, postulates, or axioms. Because Boolean algebras appear in so many different guises and contexts, it is useful to define them abstractly in an application-independent form.

A Boolean algebra is a set $B = \{a, b, \ldots\}$, two binary operators $+$ and $\cdot$, and a unary operator $'$, that satisfy the following rules:

Assume that a, b, and c are any members of B.
0. Closure. $a + b$, $a \cdot b$, and a' are members of B.
1. Commutative law. $a + b = b + a$ and $a \cdot b = b \cdot a$
2. Distributive law. $a \cdot (b + c) = (a \cdot b) + (a \cdot c)$ and $a + (b \cdot c) = (a + b) \cdot (a + c)$
3. Identity elements. B contains two distinct identity elements, denoted 1 and 0, with the properties: $1 \cdot a = a$ and $0 + a = a$
4. Complementary law. $a + a' = 1$ and $a \cdot a' = 0$

The closure postulate says that the result of *applying* any operator to member(s) of B is to produce another member of B; thus, when we state that $a + b$ is a member of B, we really mean that there exists some element c in B such that $c = a + b$. The remaining rules, which are all of the form $S_1 = S_2$, consequently are interpreted to mean: the member of B that results from applying the operators in S_1 to their operands is identical to that obtained by applying the operators in S_2 to their operands.

A number of other basic properties can be proven from the above rules. These include:

5. Associative property. $a + (b + c) = (a + b) + c$ and $a \cdot (b \cdot c) = (a \cdot b) \cdot c$
6. Idempotent property. $a + a = a$ and $a \cdot a = a$
7. The identity elements act as null elements. $a + 1 = 1$ and $a \cdot 0 = 0$
8. Involution property. $(a')' = a$
9. Absorption property. $a + (a \cdot b) = a$ and $a \cdot (a + b) = a$
10. De Morgan's laws. $(a + b)' = a' \cdot b'$ and $(a \cdot b)' = a' + b'$

Properties 5 through 10 are often given as part of the definition of a Boolean algebra, rather than as rules that can be proven from postulates 1 through 4. Let us prove several of the above properties using our definition above. In the proofs, the number in brackets after each line indicates the rule that has been applied to yield the result. By adopting the convention that $\cdot$ has priority over $+$, we can eliminate some parentheses in expressions; thus $a + b \cdot c$ will be interpreted as $a + (b \cdot c)$.

Proof of $a + a = a$
$$a = 0 + a \quad (3)$$
$$= a \cdot a' + a \quad (4)$$
$$= a + a \cdot a' \quad (1)$$
$$= (a + a) \cdot (a + a') \quad (2)$$
$$= (a + a') \cdot (a + a) \quad (1)$$
$$= 1 \cdot (a + a) \quad (4)$$
$$= a + a \quad (3)$$

Proof of $a + 1 = 1$
$$1 = a + a' \quad (4)$$
$$= a + 1 \cdot a' \quad (3)$$
$$= (a + 1) \cdot (a + a') \quad (2)$$
$$= (a + 1) \cdot 1 \quad (4)$$
$$= 1 \cdot (a + 1) \quad (1)$$
$$= a + 1 \quad (3)$$

Proof of $a \cdot 0 = 0$
$$a \cdot 0 = 0 + a \cdot 0 \quad (3)$$
$$= a \cdot a' + a \cdot 0 \quad (4)$$
$$= a \cdot (a' + 0) \quad (2)$$
$$= a \cdot (0 + a') \quad (1)$$
$$= a \cdot a' \quad (3)$$
$$= 0 \quad (4)$$

Proof of $a + a \cdot b = a$

$$
\begin{aligned}
a + a \cdot b &= 1 \cdot a + a \cdot b \quad (3)\\
&= a \cdot 1 + a \cdot b \quad (1)\\
&= a \cdot (1 + b) \quad (2)\\
&= a \cdot (b + 1) \quad (1)\\
&= a \cdot 1 \quad \text{(property 7, proven above)}\\
&= 1 \cdot a \quad (1)\\
&= a \quad (3)
\end{aligned}
$$

Proof of $(a + b)' = a' \cdot b'$

We proceed in two major steps:

(a) Show that $(a + b) + (a' \cdot b') = 1$ and $(a + b) \cdot (a' \cdot b') = 0$

(b) Show that if $x + z = 1$ and $x \cdot z = 0$, then $x' = z$

Proof of (a):

$$
\begin{aligned}
(a + b) + a' \cdot b' &= ((a + b) + a') \cdot ((a + b) + b') \quad (2)\\
&= (a' + (a + b)) \cdot (b' + (a + b)) \quad \text{(1 applied to each term)}\\
&= ((a' + a) + b) \cdot (b' + (a + b)) \quad \text{(5, see Exercise 7(e))}\\
&= ((a' + a) + b) \cdot ((b' + b) + a) \quad \text{(1 and 5)}\\
&= (1 + b) \cdot (1 + a) \quad \text{(1 and 4)}\\
&= 1 \cdot 1 \quad \text{(7, already proven)}\\
&= 1
\end{aligned}
$$

$(a + b) \cdot (a' \cdot b') = 0$ (Proof left as an exercise)

Proof of (b):

$$
\begin{aligned}
x' &= 1 \cdot x' \quad (3)\\
&= (x + z) \cdot x' \quad \text{(given that } x + z = 1\text{)}\\
&= x' \cdot x + x' \cdot z \quad \text{(1 and 2)}\\
&= x' \cdot z \quad \text{(4 and 3)}
\end{aligned}
$$

Similarly

$$
\begin{aligned}
x' &= 0 + x' \quad (3)\\
&= x \cdot z + x' \quad \text{(given)}\\
&= (x' + x) \cdot (x' + z) \quad \text{(1 and 2)}\\
&= x' + z \quad \text{(4 and 3) (*)}
\end{aligned}
$$

$\therefore$ substituting $x' \cdot z$ for x' in (*), we have

$x' = x' \cdot z + z = z$ (1 and 9, already proven)

The rules and properties can be used to deduce other properties. In particular, "expressions" formed by elements of B and the operators can often be reduced in complexity. For example,
$s = a \cdot b + a' \cdot c + b \cdot c \cdot d$ may be manipulated as follows:
$$s = a \cdot b + a' \cdot c + (a + a') \cdot b \cdot c \cdot d$$
$$= a \cdot b + a' \cdot c + a \cdot b \cdot c \cdot d + a' \cdot b \cdot c \cdot d$$
$$= a \cdot b \cdot (1 + c \cdot d) + a' \cdot c \cdot (1 + b \cdot d)$$
$$= a \cdot b + a' \cdot c$$

We now demonstrate that *propositional logic is a Boolean algebra*. To accomplish this, it is necessary to translate the symbols and operators of logic to those of the algebra and to show that rules 0 through 4 are satisfied. The set B contains the two truth values $B = \{T, F\}$. T corresponds to the element 1 and F to 0. The operators are given in the table below:

Operators

Boolean Algebra	Propositional Logic
$+$	$\vee$
$\cdot$	$\wedge$
$'$	$\neg$

The rules 0 to 4 are presented in the notation of logic. Assume that a, b, and c are any members of B; i.e., a, b, and c are in $\{T, F\}$.

0. $a \vee b$, $a \wedge b$, $\neg a$ are in B.
1. $a \vee b = b \vee a$ and $a \wedge b = b \wedge a$
2. $a \wedge (b \vee c) = (a \wedge b) \vee (a \wedge c)$ and $a \vee (b \wedge c) = (a \vee b) \wedge (a \vee c)$
3. $F \vee a = a$ and $T \wedge a = a$
4. $a \vee \neg a = T$ and $a \wedge \neg a = F$

Rule 0 follows from the defining truth tables given in Section 4.1.1. The remaining rules can be confirmed by truth tables.

Consider a completely different domain—that of *sets*. Let U be any set. The *power set* of U is defined as the set of all subsets of U (including the empty set $\emptyset = \{ \ \}$). The power set of a set U will be denoted $P(U)$; the power set of U is sometimes also denoted by 2^U. (For finite sets U, $P(U)$ contains $2^{|U|}$ elements, where $|U|$ is the number of elements in U).

Examples:

1. $U = \{x\}$, $P(U) = \{\emptyset, \{x\}\}$
2. $U = \{0, 1\}$, $P(U) = \{\emptyset, \{0\}, \{1\}, \{0, 1\}\}$
3. $U = \{a, b, c\}$, $P(U) = \{\emptyset, \{a\}, \{b\}, \{c\}, \{a, b\}, \{b, c\}, \{a, c\}, \{a, b, c\}\}$

Then, the *algebra of sets is a Boolean algebra* under the following interpretations:

Boolean Algebra	Set Theory (U is a given set)
B	$P(U)$
0	$\emptyset$
1	U
+	$\cup$ (union)
$\cdot$	$\cap$ (intersection)
$'$	$-$ (complement)

The standard set operations are defined:

$$X \cup Y = \{a : a \in X \quad \text{or} \quad a \in Y\}$$
$$X \cap Y = \{a : a \in X \quad \text{and} \quad a \in Y\}$$
$$\overline{X} = \{a : a \in U \quad \text{and} \quad a \notin X\}$$

The rules 0 to 4 can be confirmed from the operation definitions.

The algebra of sets has an appealing graphical representation that often
simplifies proofs and understanding. These are the *Venn diagrams*, invented
by the 19th century British logician John Venn. The set U is depicted by
a rectangle that is completely colored or shaded; the points in the rectangle
correspond to elements of U. A subset of U (i.e., a member of $P(U)$) is
represented by a colored disk inside the rectangle. The results of performing
the operations $^-$, $\cup$, and $\cap$ are presented by appropriately coloring the
disks and their surroundings; associated with each operator is a rule for
coloring the diagram. These ideas are illustrated in Figure 4.1.

Given an expression in the set algebra, a Venn diagram can be drawn by
representing each variable as a disk and following the coloring rules. Each
disk must be drawn in a general position in order to obtain valid results.
The disk of each variable should intersect that of every other variable and
also have a piece that overlaps no other variable. Figure 4.2 provides some
examples. The Venn diagram approach is practical when there are a

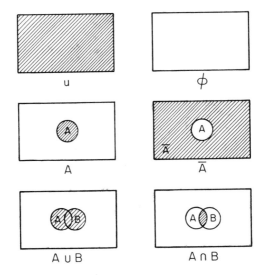

Figure 4.1   Venn Diagram Representation

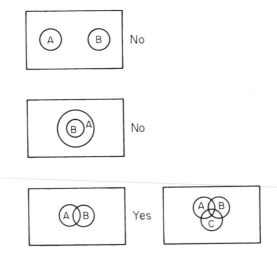

Figure 4.2   Correct Positioning of Disks

relatively small number of variables in the expression; otherwise, the diagram may become too complex.

Examples:

1. Prove $\overline{(A \cap (\overline{A} \cup B))} \cup B = U$
   An informal Venn diagram proof is given in Figure 4.3.
2. Show that $(A \cap B \cap C) \cup (A \cap B) \cup (B \cap C) \cup (\overline{B} \cap C)$
   $= (A \cap B) \cup C$
   Figure 4.4 contains the proof.

Venn diagrams may just as easily be used for *any* Boolean algebra. Thus Figure 4.3 could also be used to demonstrate that $\neg(A \wedge (\neg A \vee B)) \vee B$ is a tautology and Figure 4.4 shows that $A \cdot B \cdot C + A \cdot B + B \cdot C + B' \cdot C = A \cdot B + C$.

Another major application of Boolean algebra is the design of the combinational switching circuits which are some of the basic building blocks of digital computers. For this purpose, the particular instance of a Boolean algebra that is used is called *switching algebra*. The following symbols are employed in our switching algebra:

Boolean Algebra	Switching Algebra
B	$\{0, 1\}$
0	0
1	1
+	+ (or)
·	· (and)
'	' (not)

The operators are interpreted identically to those of propositional logic and can be defined by the following tables:

+	y=1	y=0
x=1	1	1
x=0	1	0

$x + y$

·	y=1	y=0
x=1	1	0
x=0	0	0

$x \cdot y$

x	x'
0	1
1	0

These tables could also be derived from the rules defining a Boolean algebra.

The next section discusses switching algebra and its applications.

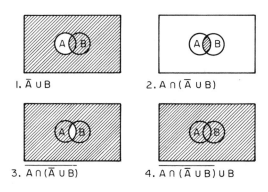

Figure 4.3   Proof of $\overline{A \cap (\overline{A} \cup B)} \cup B = U$

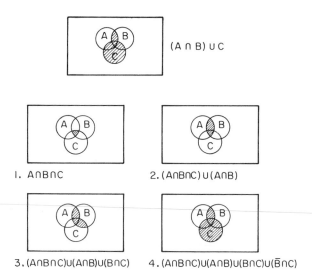

Figure 4.4   Proof of $(A \cap B \cap C) \cup (A \cap B) \cup (B \cap C) \cup (\overline{B} \cap C) = (A \cap B) \cup C$

4.4   SWITCHING ALGEBRA AND COMBINATIONAL CIRCUITS

The application of Boolean algebra to the design of switching networks was first developed by C. Shannon in his master's thesis at MIT in 1938. Shannon made many important contributions to the computer and communications fields, including some early work in artificial intelligence (Chapter 9); he is best known as the founder of information theory. The switching algebra defined at the end of the last section was used by Shannon for the design of electromechanical switching circuits found in telephone systems. We will be concerned with analogous electronic circuits in computers.

Suppose we wish to compute a binary-valued function of one or more binary-valued variables. These functions are called *switching functions.*

Examples:

1. Majority function:
$$M(a, b, c) = \begin{cases} 1 & \text{if at least two of } a, b, \text{ and } c \text{ are 1} \\ 0 & \text{otherwise} \end{cases}$$

2. Exclusive or:
$$XOR(a, b) = \begin{cases} 1 & \text{if either } a \text{ or } b \text{ is 1 not both} \\ 0 & \text{otherwise} \end{cases}$$

Such functions can be defined in terms of the switching algebra operators $+$, $\cdot$, and $'$. For the examples above, we have

$M(a, b, c) = a \cdot b + a \cdot c + b \cdot c$
$XOR(a, b) = a \cdot b' + a' \cdot b$

These may be verified by evaluating the function in a table form analogous to a truth table. For example:

a	b	$a \cdot b'$	$a' \cdot b$	$a \cdot b' + a' \cdot b = XOR(a, b)$
0	0	0	0	0
0	1	0	1	1
1	0	1	0	1
1	1	0	0	0

Circuits that realize switching functions are used throughout computers for manipulating and testing binary-valued data. Switching functions are

implemented electronically with basic circuits, called *gates*, for each operator. Figure 4.5 shows the usual pictorial symbols employed by engineers for
each type of gate. The input and output lines can be viewed as wires that
carry binary-valued signals. In the next chapter, we discuss the electronic
realization of storage elements (bits) and gates. Figure 4.6 gives a schematic
of circuits for the *M* and *XOR* functions. These circuits are termed *combinational* circuits (also called combinatorial circuits).

Given an expression in switching algebra, it is a straightforward task to
tabulate the function for all possible values of the input. However, it is
often necessary to work in the opposite direction—given the table, produce
an expression. Consider the table for the "odd parity" function on three
variables:

$$P(a, b, c) = \begin{cases} 1 & \text{if there are an odd number of 1's in } a, b, \text{ and } c \\ 0 & \text{otherwise} \end{cases}$$

a	b	c	$d = P(a, b, c)$
0	0	0	0
0	0	1	1
0	1	0	1
0	1	1	0
1	0	0	1
1	0	1	0
1	1	0	0
1	1	1	1

Consider the second line of the table, a line whose outcome (d) is 1. It
represents the expression $E_2 = a' \cdot b' \cdot c$ in that $E_2 = 1$ *if and only if*
$a = 0$, $b = 0$, and $c = 1$. Similarly, line 7 represents $E_7 = a \cdot b \cdot c'$;
$E_7 = 1$ if and only if $a = 1$, $b = 1$, and $c = 0$. Any line can be similarly
written as a *conjunct* ("product") of its variables or their negation; such a
conjunct evaluates to 1 *only* for the variable values of its corresponding
line. The switching function can then be expressed as the *disjunct* ("sum")
of those conjuncts corresponding to lines with outcome 1. Hence, $P(a, b, c) =$
$a' \cdot b' \cdot c + a' \cdot b \cdot c' + a \cdot b' \cdot c' + a \cdot b \cdot c$, with terms corresponding to
lines 2, 3, 5, and 8 of the table.

The above example leads to the following general algorithm for producing
an expression from a table:

1. For each outcome that is 1, write a conjunct where each variable occurs either negated if its value is 0 or not negated if its value is 1.
2. Connect all the conjuncts produced by step 1 as a disjunct.

This procedure yields a unique (or *canonical*) expression that is called *disjunctive normal form* (DNF). A similar algorithm exists for expressing a function as a conjunct of disjuncts; this form is called conjunctive normal form (see exercise). Note that DNF is unlikely to be a shortest length or minimal expression. One example is $M(a, b, c)$, the majority function, which has the DNF $M(a, b, c) = a \cdot b \cdot c + a \cdot b \cdot c' + a \cdot b' \cdot c + a' \cdot b \cdot c$; this can be reduced to $a \cdot b + a \cdot c + b \cdot c$. An extreme example is a function of n variables whose value is always 1; it can be expressed simply as 1, yet its DNF would contain 2^n conjuncts.

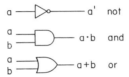

Figure 4.5 *and, or,* and *not* Gates

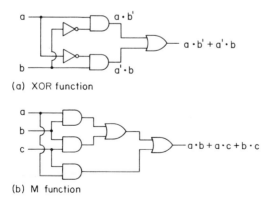

(a) XOR function

(b) M function

Figure 4.6 Combinational Circuits for *XOR* and *M*

Example: A Full Adder

Let us design the switching functions and corresponding combinational circuits for a *full one-bit adder* (*FA*). Recall the binary addition algorithm developed in Chapter 3. At each bit position, a sum bit S and a carry-out bit C_o are formed as a function of the "augend" and "addend" bits at that position, say X and Y, and the carry-in bit C_i; an *FA* performs these tasks. It has three inputs and two outputs as shown in Figure 4.7(a). The output functions, S and C_o, are defined by the following table:

X	Y	C_i	S	C_o
0	0	0	0	0
0	0	1	1	0
0	1	0	1	0
0	1	1	0	1
1	0	0	1	0
1	0	1	0	1
1	1	0	0	1
1	1	1	1	1

The DNF form of the switching functions for S and C_o are readily obtained from the table:

$$S = X' \cdot Y' \cdot C_i + X' \cdot Y \cdot C_i' + X \cdot Y' \cdot C_i' + X \cdot Y \cdot C_i$$
$$C_o = X' \cdot Y \cdot C_i + X \cdot Y' \cdot C_i + X \cdot Y \cdot C_i' + X \cdot Y \cdot C_i$$

(Note that S is identical to the odd parity function P and C_o is the same as the majority function M.)

The expression for C_o can be reduced as follows:

$$\begin{aligned} C_o &= X' \cdot Y \cdot C_i + X \cdot Y' \cdot C_i + X \cdot Y \cdot C_i' + X \cdot Y \cdot C_i \\ &= X' \cdot Y \cdot C_i + X \cdot Y \cdot C_i + X \cdot Y' \cdot C_i + X \cdot Y \cdot C_i + X \cdot Y \cdot C_i' \\ &\quad + X \cdot Y \cdot C_i \end{aligned}$$

(Using the idempotent property of a Boolean algebra.)

$$= (X' + X) \cdot (Y \cdot C_i) + (Y' + Y) \cdot (X \cdot C_i) + (X \cdot Y) \cdot (C_i' + C_i)$$
$$= Y \cdot C_i + X \cdot C_i + X \cdot Y \quad \text{(Complementary law)}$$
$$= (X + Y) \cdot C_i + X \cdot Y$$

Less obviously, the sum bit S can be conveniently expressed in terms of the exclusive-or function *XOR*:

$$S = XOR(XOR(X, Y), C_i)$$

The *XOR* function is often denoted by an operator $\oplus$:

$$XOR(a, b) = a \oplus b,$$

so that $S = (X \oplus Y) \oplus C_i$.

A combinational circuit implementing the final expressions for S and C_o is given in Figure 4.7(b). In the figure, the *XOR* box denotes the circuit of Figure 4.6(a).

4.4.1 Completeness

How many switching functions of n variables are there? Consider the case where $n = 2$. The table listing the function has $2^2 = 4$ rows, one row corresponding to each of the variable assignments 00, 01, 10, and 11. For each row, the switching function can have one of the two values 0 and 1. Consequently, there are $2^4 = 16$ different functions. The following table lists each function f_i, $i = 0, \ldots, 15$.

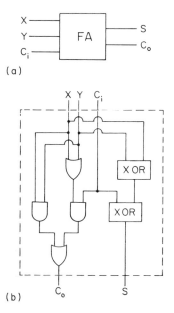

(a)

(b)

Figure 4.7 Combinational Circuit for a Full Adder

a	b	f_0	f_1	f_2	f_3	f_4	f_5	f_6	f_7	f_8	f_9	f_{10}	f_{11}	f_{12}	f_{13}	f_{14}	f_{15}
0	0	0	1	0	1	0	1	0	1	0	1	0	1	0	1	0	1
0	1	0	0	1	1	0	0	1	1	0	0	1	1	0	0	1	1
1	0	0	0	0	0	1	1	1	1	0	0	0	0	1	1	1	1
1	1	0	0	0	0	0	0	0	0	1	1	1	1	1	1	1	1

Another way of viewing the above is to consider each function output as a column of four bits. But four bits can represent 2^4 different "codes"; therefore, we have 2^4 different functions.

Suppose there are n variables, $n \geq 1$, in the switching function. The table will have 2^n rows, each row corresponding to a different binary number in the range 0 to $2^n - 1$. The outcomes for each function can be represented by 2^n bits, one bit for each row. Therefore, there are 2^{2^n} different switching functions of n variables. Some of these are tabulated below for the case $n = 3$.

a	b	c	f_0 $\cdots$	f_{11} $\cdots$	f_{113} $\cdots$	f_{148} $\cdots$	f_{255}
0	0	0	0	1	1	0	1
0	0	1	0	1	0	0	1
0	1	0	0	0	0	1	1
0	1	1	0	1	0	0	1
1	0	0	0	0	1	1	1
1	0	1	0	0	1	0	1
1	1	0	0	0	1	0	1
1	1	1	0	0	0	1	1

Some of the functions on *two* variables are quite familiar by now. For example, $f_5 = b'$, $f_6 = a \oplus b$, $f_{14} = a + b$, $f_8 = a \cdot b$. Others have been used in some of the Boolean algebras presented earlier; for example, $f_{11} = a' + b$ corresponds to logical implication ($\supset$) and $f_9 = a \cdot b + a' \cdot b'$ corresponds to logical equivalence ($\equiv$). Many of the functions have no specific "names," such as $f_2 = a' \cdot b$. An interesting question is whether all of the functions can be represented as an expression involving the operators $+$, $\cdot$, and $'$. The answer is clearly yes since the DNF form of the function can be readily produced from the table. Similarly, the operator set $\{+, \cdot, '\}$ is sufficient to describe any switching function of n variables, $n \geq 1$; again, this can be accomplished using the DNF algorithm described in the last section.

A set of operators is said to be *complete* if, and only if, all switching functions can be expressed with these operators. Thus $\{+, \cdot, '\}$ is complete. The notion of completeness is important because it assures us that *any* function can be expressed with the operators and, consequently, assures us that any function can be *implemented* if we have circuits that correspond to these operators.

The operator $\cdot$ can be removed from the set $\{+, \cdot, '\}$ and the resulting set is still complete. The easiest way to demonstrate the completeness of $\{+, '\}$ is to show how $\cdot$ can be expressed in terms of these:

$$a \cdot b = (a' + b')'$$

Similarly, the set $\{\cdot, '\}$ is complete since

$$a + b = (a' \cdot b')'$$

These results mean that combinational circuits for *or* and *not* gates (alternatively, *and* and *not* gates) are sufficient building blocks to realize any switching function.

An extremely interesting and practical result is that there exist *single* operators that are complete. One well-known complete operator is the *nand* operator $|$, defined as

$$a | b = (a \cdot b)'$$

To show completeness, we use the fact that $\{+, '\}$ is complete and express $+$ and $'$ in terms of $|$:

$$a' = a' + a' = (a \cdot a)' = a | a$$
$$a + b = (a' \cdot b')' = ((a|a) \cdot (b|b))' = (a|a)|(b|b)$$

Thus a single type of gate, such as a *nand* gate, is sufficient to implement any switching function.

EXERCISES

1. Translate the following sentences into symbolic expressions in propositional logic:

    (a) If all adults must work and children are not adults, then no child has to work.
    (b) The cat is either male or female (but not both).
    (c) x is a positive number if and only if $2x$ is positive.
    (d) Either John is not speaking and Mary is speaking or John is speaking and Mary is speaking.
    (e) If angels are not mortal and all men are mortal, then no angel is a man.

2. Give truth tables for the following expressions:

    (a) $(P \wedge \neg Q) \vee (\neg P \wedge Q)$
    (b) $P \wedge (P \supset Q)$
    (c) $(P \supset Q) \equiv Q$
    (d) $(\neg(P \supset Q) \wedge R) \vee (Q \equiv \neg R)$

3. Show by truth tables that

    (a) $A \supset (B \supset A)$ is a tautology
    (b) $\neg(A \wedge B) = \neg A \vee \neg B$
    (c) $A \supset B = \neg B \supset \neg A$
    (d) $(A \supset \neg B) \wedge (A \wedge B)$ is a contradiction
    (e) $\neg A \vee (B \wedge C) \vee ((A \vee B) \wedge (\neg A \vee C)) = \neg A \vee C$

4. Show that the extended syllogism rule is valid by proving that

    $((P_1 \supset P_2) \wedge (P_2 \supset P_3)) \supset (P_1 \supset P_3)$ is a tautology.

5. The relational expression $(a \neq b)$ has the same meaning as the Boolean expression $\neg(a = b)$; similarly, $(a \leq b)$ can be expressed as $(a < b) \vee (a = b)$. Express the relational operators $\geq$ and $>$ in terms of the Boolean operators, $\vee$, $\wedge$, and $\neg$ and the relational operators $=$ and $<$.

6. The Algolic **if** statement can be implemented with **while** and assignment statements as follows:

    [Simulate **if** B **then** S with a **while** statement.]
    $b := true$;
    while B **and** b **do begin** S; $b := false$ **end**;

    Show how the Algolic statement **if** B **then** S_1 **else** S_2 can be simulated with **while** and assignment statements.

7. Using the rules 1 to 4 defining a Boolean algebra, prove the following properties:

    (a) $a \cdot a = a$
    (b) $(a')' = a$
    (c) $a \cdot (a + b) = a$
    (d) $(a \cdot b)' = a' + b'$
    (e) $a + (b + c) = (a + b) + c$ (Hint: Let $x = a + (b + c)$ and $y = (a + b) + c$. Prove first that $a \cdot x = a \cdot y$ and $a' \cdot x = a' \cdot y$.)
    (f) $a \cdot (b \cdot c) = (a \cdot b) \cdot c$

8. Using the rules and properties 1 through 10, prove the following equalities:

    (a) $(a' + b) \cdot (b' + a) = a \cdot b + a' \cdot b'$
    (b) $a' + b \cdot c + (a + b) \cdot (a' + c) = a' + c$
    (c) $((a + b)' \cdot (a \cdot c)')' + b \cdot c = a + b$

9. (a) What is the power set of the power set of the set $U = \{0, 1\}$; i.e., list the elements of $P(P(U))$?
   (b) If U is a finite set, how many elements are there in $P(P(U))$?

10. Show that the algebra of sets satisfies rules 0 to 4 of a Boolean algebra.

11. Draw Venn diagrams representing the following set algebra expressions:
    (a) $(A \cap B) \cup (A \cap C) \cup (B \cap C)$
    (b) $(\bar{A} \cup \bar{B}) \cap (A \cap B)$
    (c) $(A \cap (\bar{B} \cup C)) \cup (\bar{A} \cap B)$
    (d) $\overline{(\bar{A} \cup B)} \cup C$

12. Use Venn diagrams to prove:
    (a) $A \cap (B \cup C) = (A \cap B) \cup (A \cap C)$
    (b) $(A \cap (\bar{A} \cup B)) \cap \bar{B} = \emptyset$
    (c) $(P_1 \cap \bar{P}_2) \cup (P_2 \cap \bar{P}_3) \cup (\bar{P}_1 \cup P_3) = U$

13. Draw combinational circuits that realize the following switching functions:
    (a) $f_1(a, b, c) = a \cdot b + b \cdot c + a \cdot c'$
    (b) $f_2(a, b) = (a \cdot b + a)' + a \cdot b$

14. Consider the "equality" switching function on two variables:

    $$E(a, b) = \begin{cases} 1 & \text{if } a = b \\ 0 & \text{otherwise} \end{cases}$$

    Tabulate the function for all values of its arguments, express the function in DNF, and draw a combinational circuit that implements $E(a, b)$.

15. For the combinational circuit in Figure 4.8:

    (a) Give the switching algebra expressions relating the outputs A and B to the inputs X and Y.
    (b) Draw an equivalent circuit containing less than four gates.

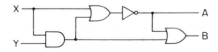

Figure 4.8 Exercise 15

16. Express the following switching functions in DNF:

(a) $f_1(a, b, c) = \begin{cases} 1 & \text{if there are an even number of 1's in } a, b, \text{ and } c \\ 0 & \text{otherwise} \end{cases}$

(even parity)

(b) $f_2(a, b, c, d) = \begin{cases} 1 & \text{if } ab \neq cd, \text{ where } ab \text{ and } cd \text{ are bit strings} \\ 0 & \text{otherwise} \end{cases}$

(unequal comparison)

(c) $f_3(a, b, c) = \begin{cases} 1 & \text{if the binary number represented by the bit string} \\ & abc \text{ is even} \\ 0 & \text{otherwise} \end{cases}$

17. Design a combinational circuit with five inputs $X_5, X_4, X_3, X_2,$ and X_1 and one output Y such that $Y = 1$ if the bit string $X_5X_4X_3X_2X_1$ is equal to the bit string $X_1X_2X_3X_4X_5$ and $Y = 0$ otherwise (i.e., $Y = 1$ if the input is a "*palindrome*").

18. When two binary digits b_1 and b_2 are subtracted ($b_1 - b_2$), difference and borrow digits are produced as follows:

b_1	b_2	difference	borrow
0	0	0	0
0	1	1	1
1	0	1	0
1	1	0	0

Now consider a *full one-bit subtractor*, analogous to the full one-bit adder.

(a) Fill in the following table expressing the *difference* and *borrow$_{out}$* digits as functions of b_1, b_2, and the *borrow$_{in}$* digit.

b_1	b_2	borrow$_{in}$	difference	borrow$_{out}$

(b) Express each of the *difference* and *borrow$_{out}$* functions as expressions in switching algebra.

(c) Draw the combinational circuits for the full one-bit subtractor.

19. List all possible switching functions of *one* variable. Write a switching algebra expression for each function.

20. Define a *minimal circuit* as one using fewest operators over the operator set $\{+, \cdot, '\}$ (e.g., $a + a$ is not minimal but a is). Construct minimal equivalent circuits for

  (a) $a \cdot b \cdot c + a \cdot b \cdot c'$
  (b) $a \cdot b + a \cdot b' + a' \cdot b + a' \cdot b'$
  (c) $a + a \cdot b' + b' \cdot c'$

21. (a) Tabulate the function given by the expression $(a \,|\, (b \,|\, c)) \,|\, 1$.
  (b) Give an expression for the majority function $M(a, b, c)$ that contains only the *nand* operator.

22. The *nor* operator $\|$ is defined: $a \| b = (a + b)'$.

  (a) Tabulate the function $(a \| b) \| c$.
  (b) Prove that the *nor* operator is complete.

23. Under the assumption that 0 and 1 are available as constants, prove the completeness of

  (a) the operator set $\{\oplus, \cdot\}$, where $\oplus$ is the exclusive-or operator
  (b) the operator $\Rightarrow$ (implication), defined: $a \Rightarrow b = a' + b$
  (c) the operator set $\{\equiv, +\}$, where $a \equiv b = a \cdot b + a' \cdot b'$

ADDITIONAL READINGS

Bertziss, A. T. *Data Structures: Theory and Practice.* 2nd ed. New York: Academic Press, 1975.

Hohn, F. E. *Applied Boolean Algebra.* New York: Macmillan, 1966.

Chapter 5

COMPUTER ORGANIZATION
AND DESIGN

Computing is among civilization's oldest activities and requirements. As quantitative explanations of the world became more successful and the organization of societies increased, more complex calculations were demanded by science, industry, commerce, government, and the military. It is only natural that many real and proposed devices were invented to simplify and mechanize computations. The culmination of these inventive efforts is the modern digital computer, an automatic universal computing machine capable of realizing any algorithm. The purpose of this chapter is to introduce the principal components and architectural features of these machines and some aspects of their design.

We start with a brief account of the origins and history of computers. Section 5.2 then presents a general structural decomposition of machine hardware, from the logical machine viewed by a programmer down to the electronic switching elements employed by a circuit designer. We then proceed from the "bottom" in Section 5.3 and describe some of the electronic components and circuits used in all computers. Digital logic is covered next, dealing with the design of combinational and sequential circuits that realize logical functions, and with storage systems. Section 5.5 outlines the design of an example machine and uses this design to discuss computer architecture. The final section is concerned with the various types of computer configurations that are commonly found and with some of the effects of technology on the organization, applications, and science of computing.

5.1 A SHORT HISTORY OF DIGITAL COMPUTERS

Automatic computing machines and other kinds of automata, such as robots, were visualized and designed in past centuries. However, their actual realization depended on the convergence of need, theory, and technology that occurred in the mid 1900's. The history of computers is similar in this respect to that of other technologies. For example, Leonardo da Vinci conceived of machines, such as the submarine, that his world could not construct; he was decidedly ahead of his time. A remarkable example in computing technology is Charles Babbage, an English mathematician and scientist who worked out all the principles of the general purpose digital computer and designed such a machine in the 19th century. Unfortunately, his machine was never completed because the available mechanical technology was just not adequate to implement his design. It remained for teams of scientists in the 1940's, working under the pressures and priorities of a world war and with an emerging electronic capability, to build the first operational general purpose computers. These machines had few conceptual innovations not already found in the designs of Babbage a century earlier.

The modern history of computers properly starts with the work of Babbage. However, some perspective is gained by briefly describing some pre-Babbage calculating devices first.

Pre-Babbage Devices

The most successful and ancient calculators were the various forms of manual abacus (see Section 3.1). These were found in practically all civilizations and are still in use today. It seems likely that shortly after a civilization invented a written number system, it also invented some form of counting board or abacus.

Antiquity was also not entirely lacking in mechanical calculators. For example, the Antikytheria orrery was a Greek device from about 100 B.C. for mechanically displaying the positions of the heavenly bodies; a method for constructing a geared odometer was illustrated by the mathematician Heron of Alexandria (approximately 60 A.D.). Both devices, the orrery and the odometer, used gear sprockets to store numbers and count.

Possibly the first mechanical adding machine was built by the eminent French philosopher, scientist, and mathematician, Blaise Pascal, in 1642. As a youth, he was employed by his father to compute numerous sums. Finding this a tedious activity, he devised a geared machine for the task. His machine did not differ significantly from Heron's odometer, but it did introduce mechanical calculation to the arithmeticists of Europe. Pascal's calculator was comprised of a series of wheels, each with 10 teeth; on the tenth tooth was a peg, which upon each full rotation of the gear, advanced the neighboring wheel one full notch. The peg was the mechanical implementation of a carry.

G. Leibniz augmented Pascal's design in 1671 to include a "multiply" operation—actually, by successive additions through the manual turning of a handle. Leibniz's and Pascal's calculators had little use until practical machine toolmen, like Gersten and Hahn, built a marketable product in the following century.

5.1.1 Charles Babbage

Charles Babbage (1792-1871) was a brilliant and unusually diverse scholar. His contributions ranged over such fields as astronomy, archeology, economics, geology, government, mathematics, physics, and theology. His work on computer design remains, however, his greatest legacy.

Babbage, like most mathematicians of earlier times, was intimately involved in calculations. In computing some astronomical values, he discovered numerous errors in the then standard tables. He recognized that such tables, which involved hundreds of thousands of manual calculations, would always contain errors. This led to Babbage's proposal in 1822 for a "Difference Engine" for mechanizing some table computations. The Difference Engine was to be a steam-driven machine for calculating sixth degree polynomials using finite difference techniques. It was designed to perform a chain of additions automatically rather than the single operations executed by a desk calculator; these additions would be arranged by the method of differences to produce a table of values for a specified polynomial.

He proposed that the English admiralty help finance the Difference Engine. The possession of a more accurate ephemeris—a table of the daily positions of the heavenly bodies—would allow more accurate navigation on the open seas. Babbage was given close to £ 20,000[1] by the Royal Navy to build his Difference Engine. In the process, a more elegant and general machine design occurred to him—the *Analytical Engine*. He never completed the Difference Engine but instead turned all his efforts to this new invention. (A Swedish machine tool maker did, however, construct a Difference Engine based on Babbage's design later in the 19th century.)

---

[1] 20,000 British pounds, which is roughly comparable to $1,000,000 today. This was among the earliest known government sponsored research contracts; such sponsorship has become routine only in this century.

An Aside on Finite Difference Methods

Polynomials are particularly useful because they can be used to approximate most other "normal" functions and they can be evaluated using only multiplication and addition operations.

A sixth degree polynomial, the function chosen by Babbage for his Difference Engine, has the form:

$$p(x) = a_6x^6 + a_5x^5 + a_4x^4 + a_3x^3 + a_2x^2 + a_1x + a_0$$

$$= \sum_{i=0}^{6} a_i x^i$$

Consider the following second order polynomial:

$$p(x) = 3x^2 + 2x + 5.$$

This function has the values:

x:	0	1	2	3	4	5	6
$p(x)$:	5	10	21	38	61	90	125

The *first differences* $\Delta p(x)$ of a polynomial are defined as

$$\Delta p(x) = p(x + 1) - p(x).$$

For our example, we have:

x:	0	1	2	3	4	5
$\Delta p(x) = p(x + 1) - p(x)$:	5	11	17	23	29	35

The *second differences* $\Delta^2 p(x)$ are the differences of the first differences:

$$\Delta^2 p(x) = \Delta p(x + 1) - \Delta p(x).$$

Taking second differences on our example polynomial, we obtain:

x:	0	1	2	3	4
$\Delta^2 p(x)$:	6	6	6	6	6

The second differences are constant. One can similarly define nth differences:

$$\Delta^n p(x) = \Delta^{n-1} p(x + 1) - \Delta^{n-1} p(x) \text{ for any } n > 1.$$

In fact, it is a theorem that the nth differences of an nth degree polynomial are constant.

How can these ideas be used to produce tables of function values, where the function is approximated by a polynomial? Consider our example polynomial again. Given the values of $p(x)$, $\Delta p(x - 1)$, and $\Delta^2 p(x - 1)$ for some integer x, it is a simple matter to produce $p(x + 1)$ by using the equations:

$$p(x + 1) = p(x) + \Delta p(x)$$

$$\Delta p(x) = \Delta p(x - 1) + \Delta^2 p(x - 1)$$

Confirming this numerically we have, for example, from the above tables:

$$p(6) = p(5) + \Delta p(5) = 90 + 35 = 125$$

$$\Delta p(5) = \Delta p(4) + \Delta^2 p(4) = 29 + 6 = 35.$$

Now, suppose we wish to find $p(7)$, which has not yet been calculated in the table.

$$p(7) = p(6) + \Delta p(6) = 125 + \Delta p(6) \text{ and}$$

$$\Delta p(6) = \Delta p(5) + \Delta^2 p(5) = 35 + 6 = 41$$

$$\therefore p(7) = 125 + 41 = 166$$

Thus instead of computing $p(7) = 3 \times 7^2 + 2 \times 7 + 5$, which requires four multiplications and two additions, we can obtain the result with only two additions using these *finite differences*—an enormous computational saving. Similarly, we can efficiently compute $p(8)$, $p(9)$, $p(10)$, ..., to produce a table of values for $p(x)$ at $x = 0, 1, \ldots$. Once we have $p(0)$, $\Delta p(0)$, and $\Delta^2 p(0)$, all the remaining entries are generated by repeated additions. For nth degree polynomials, $n > 0$, we require $p(0)$, $\Delta p(0)$, ..., $\Delta^n p(0)$ to get started.

Example:

Let $p(x) = x^3 + 4x + 3$. It is desired to tabulate $p(x)$ for $x = 0, 1, 2, \ldots$. To get started, we compute $p(0) = 3$, $p(1) = 8$, $p(2) = 19$, and $p(3) = 42$ and form the initial table below:

$$x: \quad 0 \quad 1 \quad 2 \quad 3 \quad 4 \quad 5 \quad \ldots$$

$$p(x): \quad 3 \quad 8 \quad 19 \quad 42 \quad -$$

$$\Delta p(x): \quad 5 \quad 11 \quad 23 \quad -$$

$$\Delta^2 p(x): \quad 6 \quad 12 \quad -$$

$$\Delta^3 p(x): \quad 6 \quad 6 \quad 6 \quad \ldots \text{ (constant)}$$

The next set of entries is easily computed:

$$p(4) = p(3) + \Delta p(3) = p(3) + \Delta p(2) + \Delta^2 p(2)$$
$$= p(3) + \Delta p(2) + \Delta^2 p(1) + \Delta^3 p(1)$$
$$= 42 + 23 + 12 + 6 = 83$$

This permits the further calculations:

$$\Delta p(3) = p(4) - p(3) = 83 - 42 = 41$$
$$\Delta^2 p(2) = \Delta p(3) - \Delta p(2) = 41 - 23 = 18$$

In a similar fashion, the table can be filled in for each successive value of x.

The Analytical Engine

Babbage's grander engine borrowed some key ideas that appeared in the automatic Jacquard loom. This loom, first constructed in France in 1801, was the end product of 200 years of development efforts in mechanized silk weaving. The Jacquard loom followed a pattern design "program" embodied in a set of holes that were punched on a pasteboard card. Each card specified a single weaving step and each hole represented a binary variable for a warp thread. Once a loom was programmed, the pattern could be repeated by reusing the corresponding set of pasteboard cards. One of the most famous such programs wove a portrait of Jacquard, himself, on a five foot square tapestry; 24,000 cards were used.

Babbage grasped that a similar system could guide or control an "arithmetic mill." In Babbage's own description:[2]

---

[2] Charles Babbage, *Passages from the Life of a Philosopher,* 1864, quoted in P. Morrison and E. Morrison, eds., *Charles Babbage and His Calculating Engines* (New York: Dover, 1961) p. 55–56.

"The Analytical Engine consists of two parts:

1st. The store in which all the variables to be operated upon, as well as all those quantities which have arisen from the result of other operations, are placed.

2nd. The mill into which the quantities about to be operated upon are always brought.

Every formula which the Analytical Engine can be required to compute consists of certain algebraical operations to be performed upon given letters, and of certain other modifications depending on the numerical value assigned to those letters.

There are therefore two sets of cards, the first to direct the nature of the operations to be performed—these are called operation cards: the other to direct the particular variables on which those cards are required to operate—these latter are called variable cards. Now the symbol of each variable or constant, is placed at the top of a column capable of containing any required number of digits.

Under this arrangement, when any formula is required to be computed, a set of operation cards must be strung together, which contain the series of operations in the order in which they occur. Another set of cards must then be strung together, to call the variables into the mill in the order in which they are required to be acted upon. Each operation card will require three other cards, two to represent the variables and constants and their numerical values upon which the previous operation card is to act, and one to indicate the variable on which the arithmetical result of this operation is to be placed.

But each variable has below it, on the same axis, a certain number of figure-wheels marked on their edges with the ten digits: upon these any number the machine is capable of holding can be placed. Whenever variables are ordered into the mill, these figures will be brought in, and the operation indicated by the preceding card will be performed upon them. The result of this operation will then be replaced in the store.

The Analytical Engine is therefore a machine of the most general nature. Whatever formula it is required to develop, the law of its development must be communicated to it by two sets of cards. When these have been placed, the engine is special for that particular formula. The numerical value of its constants must then be put on the columns of wheels below them, and on setting the Engine in motion it will calculate and print the numerical results of that formula.

Every set of cards made for any formula will at any future time recalculate that formula with whatever constants may be required.

Thus the Analytical Engine will possess a library of its own. Every set of cards once made will at any future time reproduce the calculations for which it was first arranged. The numerical value of its constants may then be inserted.''

The machine was to have a mechanical store or memory of 1000 words, with 40 decimal digits per word. The steam-driven mill was proposed to perform arithmetic operations at a rate of approximately one second per addition and one minute per multiplication. A Jacquard system of punched cards would direct the mill; punched cards were also used as "variable" cards and could be read into the store if more constants or variables were needed. A printing press was to print the computed values. Without delving further into the details of Babbage's machine, we can summarize his project and its achievements:

1. The scope and design of the Analytical Engine anticipated the contemporary digital computer.
2. The device was too sophisticated for a practical mechanical implementation at that time.

Babbage's work engaged the attention of other scientists, most notably the mathematician Ada Augusta, Countess of Lovelace and daughter of the great English poet, Lord Byron. She became an expert in "programming" the proposed Analytical Engine, showing how the machine could generate numerical functions. It is interesting that she also speculated on non-numeric computations, such as musical composition.

5.1.2   The Modern Computer: Contemporary Developments

Babbage's achievement was a cul-de-sac; his ideas had to await a more appropriate technology than the mechanical one prevailing in the mid 19th century. After Babbage, many advances in technology incrementally improved the state of computing machines. Herman Hollerith of the U.S. Census Bureau adapted the Jacquard punched card to data collection, and built a machine to tabulate the census of 1890. (This machine was also the subject of Hollerith's Ph.D. thesis at Columbia University.) In the early 20th century, Eccles and Jordan built the first electronic memory circuit, a "flip-flop" with two stable states that could be used to represent a binary digit. In the 1930's, various electronic and electro-mechanical computing devices were being proposed, including the Harvard Mark I designed by Howard Aiken and partially inspired by his reading of Babbage's papers. Similar projects were undertaken at Bell Laboratories and in Europe.

Developments accelerated during World War II. Substantial resources were applied to automating the calculations required by navigation and gunnery officers. A moving ship attempting to hit a plane with its anti-aircraft fire is a difficult estimation problem. Each weapon and target had different characteristics, and detailed ballistic tables for firing these weapons had to be produced.

ENIAC

The Ballistics Research Laboratory of the U.S. Army Ordnance Corps sponsored the construction of the first electronic computer,[3] named ENIAC for *E*lectronic *N*umerical *I*ntegrator *A*nd *C*alculator. ENIAC was a collaborative effort between John Mauchly and J. Presper Eckert at the Moore School at the University of Pennsylvania. Machine construction started in 1943 and was completed three years later.

ENIAC was impressive both in concept and in magnitude. It required approximately 18,000 vacuum tubes and consumed an enormous amount of power. (It was said that when ENIAC was turned on at night, the lights of West Philadelphia noticably dimmed.)

The computer worked but was cumbersome to program. In Babbage's Analytical Engine, operation cards were to feed into and control the mill; the card reading was to take fractions of a second, a speed matched to that of the machine's operations. ENIAC, on the other hand, was "programmed" on a wiring board which controlled the sequence of operations executed. It could execute arithmetic operations in a few hundred *microseconds* (millionths of a second), since data was retained in high speed electronic memory; however, it took one or two days to wire in the program. Why not place the program in high speed storage? This was a principal design innovation of some conferences held from about 1944 onwards devoted to the ENIAC and possible improvements. In addition to Eckert and Mauchly, these conferences were attended by John von Neumann.

von Neumann; EDVAC, IAS, EDSAC, . . .

The army liaison mathematician to the ENIAC project, Herman Goldstine, mentioned the project to von Neumann at a chance meeting in a train station. One of the great applied mathematicians of this century, von Neumann,

---

[3] While ENIAC is widely acknowledged as the first electronic computer, there is much controversy surrounding the history during World War II.

had become interested in computing devices and joined the Eckert-Mauchly group to help plan the ENIAC successor, called EDVAC. The group accomplished much but soon broke up. Eckert and Mauchly started their own computer company which eventually became the UNIVAC division within the Sperry Rand Corporation; von Neumann and Goldstine went to the Institute for Advanced Study at Princeton; and other members remained at the University of Pennsylvania where the EDVAC was completed.

In 1946, A. W. Burks, Goldstine, and von Neumann wrote a series of memos on their proposed machine, the IAS (*I*nstitute for *A*dvanced *S*tudy) computer. The IAS design was widely copied and became the template for the first generation of stored-program computers—often called a single address von Neumann machine. (It is difficult to know who really contributed each innovation described in the IAS memos. The established von Neumann has received most of the credit, with less frequent mention of the other scientists who contributed over a three year period to the ideas in ENIAC and its successors.)

The ENIAC could perform a multiplication in three *milliseconds* (thousandths of a second) and could internally store 20 numbers of 10 decimal digits each. It could punch out answers at a rate of 100 cards per minute, each card containing eight numbers; this is a factor of about 20 slower than the internal speed of the machine. The limited amount of internal storage meant that many problems would be constrained by this external rate. The effects of the imbalance between processing and output rates could be reduced if a larger internal memory were available. Then not only could more data be internally stored but also the program itself could be stored as if it were data. Developments in radar technology provided several possibilities for larger memories.

The first IAS memo, entitled "Preliminary discussion of the logical design of an electronic computing instrument," contained these ideas and others that greatly influenced computer design. We quote directly from the first section of this document:

1.1 Inasmuch as the completed device will be a general-purpose computing machine it should contain certain organs relating to arithmetic, memory-storage, control and connection with the human operator. It is intended that the machine be fully automatic in character, i.e., independent of the human operator ...

1.2 It is evident that the machine must be capable of storing in some manner not only the digital information needed ..., but also the instructions which govern the actual routine to be performed on the numerical data .... Hence there must be some organ capable of storing these program orders. There must, moreover, be a unit which can understand these instructions and order their execution.

1.3 Conceptually we have discussed above two different forms of memory: storage of numbers and storage of orders. If, however, the orders to the machine are reduced to a numerical code and if the machine can in some fashion distinguish a number from an order, the memory organ can be used to store both numbers and orders . . . .

1.4 If the memory for orders is merely a storage organ there must exist an organ which can automatically execute the orders stored in the memory. We shall call this organ the *Control.*

1.5 Inasmuch as the device is to be a computing machine there must be an arithmetic organ in it which can perform certain of the elementary arithmetic operations . . . .

The operations that the machine will view as elementary are clearly those which are wired into the machine . . . .

1.6 Lastly there must exist devices, the input and output organ, whereby the human operator and the machine can communicate with each other . . . .

The von Neumann machine was divided into four functional modules—control, storage, arithmetic, and input-output (Figure 5.1). Storage words were ordinarily treated as 40 bit two's complement integers but when transferred to the control, they were interpreted as two 20 bit instructions. The instruction stored in the FR controlled the computer's operation until its execution was completed. Upon completion of the current operation, the next instruction would be fetched from either the CR or from the word in memory addressed by the CC.

Example:

The effect of a "clear and add" instruction was expressed by the notation:

$$S(x) \rightarrow Ac^+$$

$S(x)$ denotes the contents of storage location number x; A is the accumulator; c means "to clear" or set to zero; and the superscript $+$ indicates that the number was to be added into A. The arrow, like the Algolic assignment, indicates a transfer of information between storage elements.

Execution of the instruction occurs as follows:

1. Place the number at $S(x)$ in the SR. (SR $\leftarrow S(x)$)
2. Clear the accumulator. ($A \leftarrow 0$)

3. Add the number in SR into A. $(A \leftarrow A + \text{SR})$

Thus, the instruction stores $S(x)$ into A.

Most instructions had a single address field that referred to a word in storage; typically, the contents of this word were operated upon by the arithmetic organ during instruction execution. This accounts for the designation "single address machine."

The first stored-program-computer that was actually operational was the EDSAC, completed at Cambridge University in 1949 under the direction of M. Wilkes; the EDSAC design was most directly influenced by EDVAC. The IAS machine, and a copy of it, the ORDVAC at the University of Illinois, were both completed in 1952. Throughout the 1950's, the EDVAC and IAS designs dominated the computer field.

Initially, computers were viewed primarily as mathematical instruments for automating scientific calculations; as such, the market appeared rather small in the early 1950's. The field began its explosive growth a few years

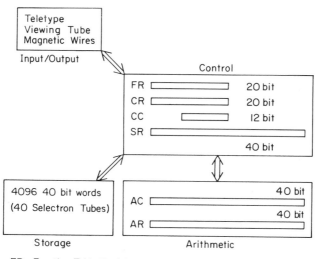

FR : Function Table Register – stored current instruction
CR : Control Register – stored next instruction
CC : Control Counter – stored address of next instruction
SR : Selection Register – stored word just fetched from storage
                          or word just sent to storage
AC : Accumulator – used for arithmetic operations
AR : Arithmetic Register – used in conjunction with AC

Figure 5.1 IAS Machine Organization

later when the computer was also recognized and marketed as a *data processing* system with unlimited accounting and record-keeping applications. Pushed by economic as well as military incentives, computer developments advanced rapidly, supported by private and public funds.

The "first generation" *vacuum tube* technology of the 1950's was replaced by *transistor* technology in the 1960's; this second-generation of computers was an order-of-magnitude[4] faster, consumed less power, and was more reliable than the first. Similar benefits were realized in the third generation starting in the mid 1960's, which was based on *integrated circuit* technology. The fourth generation of computers, first appearing in the early 1970's, used *large scale integration* (LSI) and vastly improved memory devices. Each successive generation has been characterized by dramatic increases in speed and capacity and by order-of-magnitude decreases in cost.

Many architectural innovations have also been implemented since the first machines. However, the basic concepts and logical structure of the von Neumann design can be found in virtually all modern computers.

5.2 HARDWARE STRUCTURE AND BUILDING BLOCKS

Computer hardware can be viewed at any of the four different levels illustrated in Figure 5.2. The structure is hierarchical in the sense that the functions performed at any level are realized by the levels immediately beneath it; level $(i + 1)$ is thus an *abstraction* of level i, for $i = 1, 2, 3$.

At the lowest *electronic* level, a computer is composed of many copies of a relatively small number of basic electronic devices and circuits. These elements provide for the definition, storage, transfer, and Boolean manipulation of binary signals, as well as clocks that produce timing signals. For example, logic gates, such as the *and, or* and *not* gates discussed in Section 4.4, are constructed at the electronic level.

The next level, *digital logic*, consists of combinational and sequential switching circuits, and storage systems. Level 2 is implemented with the electronic components of level 1. The combinational circuit for a full one-bit adder (Section 4.4) describes part of a computer at this second level of abstraction.

The *architectural* level treats the switching circuits and storage registers as indivisible units; it is concerned with the details of instruction retrieval and execution, including the flow of data among the various registers and subsystems. The top of the hierarchy, *programming*, describes the computer

---

[4] An "order-of-magnitude" is a factor of 10.

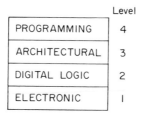

Figure 5.2   Levels of Computer Hardware

instructions and components at the functional level required by a programmer—this is the "black-box" user view of the machine. The computer presented in Chapter 2 (Section 2.3) was specified primarily at the programming level.

Example:

Recall the *add* instruction of the Chapter 2 machine. We can represent it symbolically by:

$$add \ \alpha$$

where α is a four decimal digit operand address.
It has the effect (*programmer*'s description):

$$AC \leftarrow AC + [\alpha]$$

At the *architectural* level, the execution of this instruction may involve the following steps:

1. Transfer α to the storage address register (SAR), in preparation for a storage "read". (SAR $\leftarrow \alpha$)
2. Perform a storage "read" operation. This reads the contents of the main storage word addressed by SAR, denoted M[SAR], into the storage data register (SDR). (SDR $\leftarrow M$[SAR]).
3. Initiate an add operation in the arithmetic unit. The contents of the SDR and AC are both "gated" to the adder, and the result is transferred back to the AC. (AC $\leftarrow$ AC + SDR)

The *digital logic* for implementing the above flow includes:

1. the main storage system and its logic for decoding addresses in the SAR, responding to the "read" signal, and transferring the result to the SDR,

2. switching circuits for moving the SDR and AC contents to the adder, and the sum to the AC,
3. the adder logic, and
4. timing and switching circuits for initiating each suboperation in the correct sequence.

The four level decomposition can also be used to distinguish the various classes of engineers and scientists involved in hardware design. The computer architect or designer is primarily working at levels 3 and 4, with a strong interest in 2. The logical designer or "chip" designer is concerned with level 2 and 3 issues, with a strong interest in level 1. The electronics engineer contributes at levels 1 and 2, while the applied physicist works at the electronics level. There has always been a large overlap between the technical domains of the computer architect and those of the logical designer, and it is not easy to establish a dividing line; for example, the building blocks provided by the logical designer may be microprocessors, which are complete central processing units of computers.

5.3 BASIC ELECTRONIC COMPONENTS AND CIRCUITS

Computers represent information in terms of binary electrical signals—that is, signals with two discrete states. One state is interpreted as the binary digit "0" while the other state denotes a "1". A particular system for example might adopt the convention that an electrical potential of -3 volts corresponds to a binary "1" and 0 volts to a binary "0", or that $+10$ and -25 volts correspond to "1" and "0", respectively. The reasons for selecting binary electrical signals, rather than say ternary, octal, or decimal signals, are not arbitrary. Inexpensive, reliable, and fast devices can be constructed that store, transfer, and perform logical operations on such signals. In this section, we briefly examine some of the components and circuits that produce, store, and manipulate binary electrical signals and that constitute the basic building blocks of computers.

Electronic circuits are composed of both passive and active elements. Passive components do not amplify signals. They include resistors, capacitors, and inductors, as well as devices such as diodes that can change their state when signals are applied to them. The active heart of most digital circuits is the *transistor*—an active semiconductor device that can amplify signals and switch states with great speed. Amplification is desirable so that signals may be transmitted through many circuits without serious degradation, while component switching speeds determine circuit speeds to a large extent. We will first outline the operation of transistors and then show how they can be used to implement logic gates and bit storage.

Transistor Operation

An *npn* transistor[5] has three electrodes, termed the base, collector, and emitter (Figure 5.3). The flow of current from the collector to the emitter, the *output*, is controlled by the *input* current that flows from the base to the emitter. A small amount of base current is sufficient to produce a much larger collector current, thus amplifying the input signal; if the base current is zero, the collector current also becomes zero and the transistor is "cut off".

These transistors are constructed by adjoining *n* and *p* type regions of "doped" silicon as sketched in Figure 5.3 (b). Silicon is said to be doped when certain impurities have been systematically introduced into the pure silicon crystals. In *n* type regions (*n* for negative), the impurities result in an excess of electrons in the crystal structure; a small voltage will energize these electrons to produce a current flow. Conversely, *p* type regions (*p* for positive) have a deficiency of electrons caused by their impurities. This deficiency, called "holes", has the effect of a positive charge which can also be mobilized into an electric current.

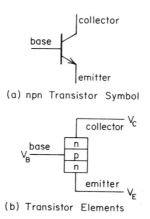

(a) npn Transistor Symbol

(b) Transistor Elements

Figure 5.3 *npn* Transistor

---

[5] The *npn* transistor is just one of several different varieties that have been constructed.

Suppose that the collector and base have positive voltages V_C and V_B respectively, relative to the emitter voltage V_E and that $V_C > V_B$. Since $V_B > V_E$, the "holes" in the p region will flow down to the emitter's n region and the electrons in this n region will flow into the p region; the net result is a base to emitter current. There will be no current between the base and collector because $V_C > V_B$. However, the electrons from the emitter will diffuse through the entire p region to the collector causing a large current flow from emitter to collector. If V_B is reduced to V_E or lower, then the base current will cease; this in turn cuts off the collector current.

Gates

Consider the circuit of Figure 5.4 (a). If the input X is at 0 volts, then the base and emitter have the same potential; consequently, base current is zero and the transistor is cut off. Therefore the output Y is at $+3$ V. When X is at $+3$ V, current flows through the transistor and the voltage at Y then becomes 0. Figure 5.4 (b) illustrates this behavior. Assume that $+3$ V represents a binary "1" and 0 V corresponds to the binary digit "0". The circuit then implements the switching function:

Input X	Output Y
0	1
1	0

$Y = X'$

It can thus be used as a *not* gate (Figure 5.4 (c)).[6]

By providing for multiple input lines, we can extend the *not* gate into a logical *nor* circuit as shown in Figure 5.5.[6] Base current flows if either or both of X_1 and X_2 are high ($+3$ V), yielding a low output (0 V); if both X_1 and X_2 are at 0 V, then the transistor is cut off and the output signal Y is $+3$ V. The circuit thus realizes the switching function:

Inputs X_1	X_2	Output Y
0	0	1
0	1	0
1	0	0
1	1	0

$Y = X_1' \cdot X_2' = (X_1 + X_2)'$

---

[6] The actual circuitry may be more complex for increased speed or reliability.

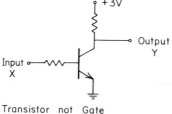

(a) Transistor not Gate

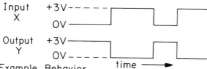

(b) Example Behavior

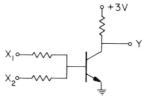

(c) not Gate Symbol

Figure 5.4 *not* Gate

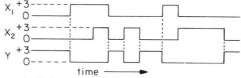

(a) Transistor nor Circuit

(b) Example Behavior

(c) nor Gate Symbol

Figure 5.5 *nor* Gate

The symbol for a *nor* gate is drawn in Figure 5.5 (c). Since *nor* is a complete operator (Section 4.4.1 and Exercise 22 in Chapter 4), it can be used to implement any switching function. Gates for other operators, such as *or*, *and*, and *nand*, can also be constructed from transistors.

Bit Storage

We have seen how gates may be directly used to perform logical operations on signals. But a computer must *store* information as well as process it. For this purpose, a large number of electronic, magnetic, and electromechanical memory devices are available.

The fastest bit storage element produced on a practical scale is the *flip-flop* (*FF*). It is normally used to implement the internal registers of the central processing unit. An example of a simple kind of flip-flop is shown in Figure 5.6 (a); the circuit is formed by cross-connecting two *nor* gates (or, alternatively, using *and* and *not* gates to implement the *nor* function).

The output lines are designated Q and Q' because one line is always the logical complement of the other. Assuming that the inputs S (*S*et) and R (*R*eset) are never "1" simultaneously the device has two stable states:

$$\text{State "1": } Q = 1 \text{ and } Q' = 0$$
$$\text{State "0": } Q = 0 \text{ and } Q' = 1$$

To see this, consider the following possibilities for S and R:

1. $S = 1$ and $R = 0$. Q' will become 0 because the upper *nor* gate input has $S = 1$ and Q will be 1 (state "1"), regardless of their previous values. *No* further changes will occur if S is now made 0; the feedback coupling of the *nor* gates will maintain the "1" state.
2. $S = 0$ and $R = 1$. State "0" will result, regardless of the previous values of Q and Q', since $R = 1$ guarantees that $Q = 0$, and $Q = 0$ and $S = 0$ guarantee that $Q' = 1$. Again, the new state persists if R is now set to 0.

The *timing diagram* of Figure 5.6 (b) shows how the output signals Q and Q' change in response to different values of S and R. It is convenient to describe the *FF* behavior by a table:

Current State (Q)	Inputs		New State (Q)
	S	R	
0	0	X	0
0	1	0	1
1	X	0	1
1	0	1	0

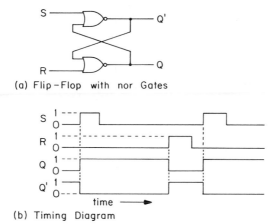

(a) Flip–Flop with nor Gates

(b) Timing Diagram

Figure 5.6 Simple Flip-Flop

The X in the table is a "don't care" indicator; either a 0 or a 1 could be present. The first row is *read*:

"If the *FF* is in state 0, the S line is 0, and R is either 0 or 1, then the new state of the *FF* will also be 0."

The remaining rows are read in a similar fashion.

Thus, the function of the set line S is to set the *FF* to state 1, while that of the reset line R is to reset the *FF* to state 0. In other words, S writes a "1" bit and R writes a "0" bit into this one-bit storage cell. As long as S and R are both 0, the bit remains stored. The bit can be read by examining either the Q or Q' lines.

A simple version of this *FF* is obtained by the circuit of Figure 5.7 (a). The resulting *FF* has *one input*, labelled D for "Data", and *one output*. The state of the flip-flop directly reflects the signal on the input line, as tabulated below:

Current State (Q)	Input D	Next State (Q)
X	0	0
X	1	1

Unfortunately, this device is not yet capable of *retaining* its state. We add a *control* line C, as in Figure 5.7 (b). Now, both *nor* gate inputs are 0 (the S

and R lines are both 0), until the C line is pulsed; the FF state is *not* changed unless the control line is pulsed. This behavior can be expressed in the Algolic

$$\text{if } C \text{ then } Q := D$$

where Q denotes both the state of the flip-flop and its output. We will use this type of FF, called a D flip-flop, for the remainder of the chapter and represent it by the diagram of Figure 5.7 (c).

Flip-flops can be extremely fast and change state in a small number of *nanoseconds* (one nanosecond $= 10^{-9}$ seconds). They come in a variety of forms with different state-changing and state-retention properties. Generally, FF's are more complex than the ones we have presented, primarily because of the need to isolate inputs from their outputs and still permit logical feedback paths from FF output lines to their inputs.

Because of their relatively high expense and power consumption, flip-flops are not normally used for main computer storage. *Magnetic cores* were the most popular bit storage elements for large main memories until the early 1970's. These are very small ferromagnetic "donuts" that can be magnetized in either a clockwise or counterclockwise direction, one polarity representing a binary "1" and the other, a binary "0". Memories are built by threading a matrix of wires through the cores. To write a bit, one passes a sufficient electrical current through the wires to magnetize the core; the direction of the current determines the polarity of magnetization (Figure 5.8). Reading is accomplished by writing, say a zero, and sensing any resulting change in magnetization of the core; this is a "destructive" read and the previous state must be restored. A central memory of 2^{15} words, each of 32 bits, would contain 2^{20} individual cores.

Magnetic cores have been replaced by *MOS semiconductor storage cells*[7] for use as the central memory of computers. The simplest cell of this type contains a capacitor and a transistor. A binary digit is stored as an electric charge on the capacitor; zero charge may denote a binary "0" while a small charge might represent "1". The capacitor is connected to the rest of the system through the transistor which acts as a switch. Information can be read or written with these cells in the order of several hundred nanoseconds.

---

[7] MOS stands for *metal-oxide-semiconductor* and denotes a particular semiconductor technology. It should be noted and emphasized that device and memory technologies are extremely dynamic, with many changes constantly occurring and predicted for the near future.

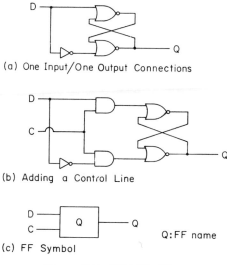

(a) One Input/One Output Connections

(b) Adding a Control Line

(c) FF Symbol

Q:FF name

Figure 5.7 *"D"* Flip-Flop

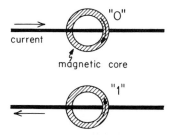

"0"

current

magnetic core

"1"

Figure 5.8 Writing Magnetic Cores

MOS memories are called *dynamic* because they must be constantly regenerated due to both a destructive read and the leakage of the capacitor charge. This is in contrast to *static* memories, such as flip-flops, that do not require regeneration mechanisms. Semiconductor gates and storage elements are not manufactured as individual discrete components, but are produced as very small ("microelectronic") *integrated circuits*, often containing hundreds and thousands of transistors and their interconnections.

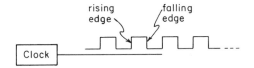

Figure 5.9   Clock Producing Timing Signals

Clocks and Clock-Controlled Flip-Flops

Modern computers also require producers of regularly-spaced timing signals, that is, one or more clocks. A clock device is an electronic oscillator that produces a continuous train of digital signals at a fixed frequency (Figure 5.9). All circuit changes—changes of "state"—are initiated at well-defined time units determined by these clock signals.

Signals from a master clock are distributed throughout a computer system so that all activities may be properly synchronized. Typically, the clock frequency is in the order of 10's of millions of cycles per second.

Flip-flops, such as the *D FF* outlined in Figure 5.7, are often designed internally to be sensitive to the rising or falling *edge* of a *control* or *clock* pulse, rather than the control line being high or low. This permits a more precise synchronization and can be used to ensure that, at most, one state change can occur per clock cycle. We will assume that our *D* flip-flop has been expanded internally so that it is *edge-triggered* by the signal on the *C* input. The *C* line will normally contain the output of an *and* gate:

$$C = \text{Clock} \cdot \text{Control}$$

where Clock is the clock signal and Control is a controlling signal from some other circuit.

Other hardware elements, such as power supplies and a variety of analog circuits, are also required in computer systems. However, these other components play a somewhat peripheral role. The processing and memory functions of computers are implemented mainly from logic gates and storage cells, controlled by clock signals.

5.4   DIGITAL LOGIC

5.4.1   Combinational Networks

We have shown how logic gates can be constructed from basic electronic computers. Combinational circuits or networks that realize switching functions can be formed by connecting gates in a tree-like fashion.

To review briefly some of the ideas covered in the last chapter, consider a combinational circuit for the *odd parity* function on four variables:

$$P_4(a, b, c, d) = \begin{cases} 1 & \text{if there is an odd number of 1's in } a, b, c, \text{ and } d. \\ 0 & \text{otherwise.} \end{cases}$$

A switching algebra expression for this function, say in *DNF*, could be easily produced by tabulating the value of P for each of the 16 possible inputs:

a	b	c	d	P_4
0	0	0	0	0
0	0	0	1	1
		.		
		.		
		.		
		.		
1	0	1	1	1
		.		
		.		
		.		
1	1	1	1	0

However, it may be observed that

$$P_4(a, b, c, d) = ((a \oplus b) \oplus (c \oplus d))$$

where $\oplus$ is the exclusive-or operator. To see this informally, we note that

1. $(x \oplus y)$ is the odd parity function on two variables
2. if the function P_n yields the odd parity function on n variables and P_m implements the function on m variables, then the odd parity function on $n + m$ variables

$$P_{n+m} = (P_n \oplus P_m).$$

(This result can be proven formally. See Exercise 8.)

The circuit of Figure 5.10 implements the function P_4. The remainder of this section presents several interesting examples of more complex circuits.

Example 1: A Parallel Adder

A combinational circuit design for a full one-bit adder *FA* was given in Section 4.4 (Figure 4.7). With input augend, addend, and carry-in bits X, Y

and C_{in}, respectively, the sum bit S and carry-out bit C_0 were given by the expressions:

$$S = ((X \oplus Y) \oplus C_{in})$$

$$C_{out} = (X + Y) \cdot C_{in} + X \cdot Y$$

Suppose two n-bit numbers are represented by the bit strings X_{n-1}, X_{n-2} ... X_0 and Y_{n-1}, Y_{n-2} ... Y_0. Then the *full n-bit addition* of these

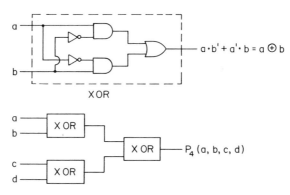

Figure 5.10   Combinational Circuit for Odd Parity Function on Four Variables

numbers can be performed by passing the bit signals to n FA's connected in tandem as shown in Figure 5.11. The carry-out line of FA_i is made identical to the carry-in line of FA_{i+1}, $i = 0, \ldots, n - 2$, thus ensuring that the carries are propagated correctly through the FA's.

We call this device a *parallel* adder because all digits are added almost concurrently. The complete sum is available as soon as all carries have passed through the FA's. On modern machines, such adders take on the order of tens of nanoseconds to perform addition of two words.

Example 2: Two's Complement Circuit

The purpose is to design a combinational circuit that produces the two's complement of a string of four bits. The circuit will thus have four input lines, denoted X_3, X_2, X_1, and X_0, and four output lines, denoted Y_3, Y_2, Y_1, and Y_0, such that

$$Y_3 Y_2 Y_1 Y_0 = \text{two's complement } (X_3 X_2 X_1 X_0) \text{ (Figure 5.12 (a))}.$$

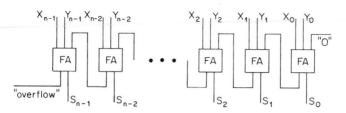

$$X_{n-1}\ X_{n-2}\ \cdots X_1 \quad X_0$$
$$+\ Y_{n-1}\ Y_{n-2}\ \cdots Y_1 \quad Y_0$$
$$\overline{S_{n-1}\ S_{n-2}\ \cdots S_1 \quad S_0}$$

Figure 5.11 Parallel Adder

We could proceed by tabulating the values of the outputs Y_i for each of the 16 possible inputs, but as in the odd parity function example, it is possible to arrive quickly at a neater solution by just thinking about the problem. In particular, we may recall that an easy way to get the two's complement of a number is to take the one's complement and add 1 as shown in Figure 5.12 (b). The addition of 1 in the first column can generate a carry that propagates through the remaining columns. If C_{in} represents the carry-in for the ith digit and C_{out} is the carry-out, then a simple case analysis yields the expressions:

$$Y_i = X_i{}' \cdot C_{in}{}' + X_i \cdot C_{in}$$
$$C_{out} = X_i{}' \cdot C_{in}$$

A single circuit for realizing these expressions can be replicated four times and connected together to compute the required two's complement (Figure 5.12 (c)).

Example 3: Binary to Decimal Decoder

Data and instructions are *encoded* in binary in computers. A *decoder* is a device that takes a coded string of bits and produces a unique output for each possible input sequence. In its most general form, a decoder has 2^n output lines for n input lines, with each output corresponding to one of the 2^n different input possibilities (Figure 5.13 (a)). Decoders are used throughout computer systems, for example to select a particular address line to storage, to determine specific operations from coded computer instructions, and to convert binary-coded character codes to unique character signals.

Consider a binary to decimal digit decoder that takes a 4 bit BCD coding of a decimal digit and generates a different output for each decimal digit represented. Letting "i" be the output function corresponding to the BCD string for decimal digit i, $i = 0, \ldots , 9$, we can tabulate the *10* output functions:

BCD				Output Functions					
X_3	X_2	X_1	X_0	"0"	"1"	"2"	"3"	$\ldots$	"9"
0	0	0	0	1	0	0	0		0
0	0	0	1	0	1	0	0		0
0	0	1	0	0	0	1	0		0
0	0	1	1	0	0	0	1		0
0	1	0	0	0	0	0	0		0
0	1	0	1	0	0	0	0		0
0	1	1	0	0	0	0	0		0
0	1	1	1	0	0	0	0		0
1	0	0	0	0	0	0	0		0
1	0	0	1	0	0	0	0		1

The functions can be expressed in switching algebra:

$$\text{"0"} = X_3{}' \cdot X_2{}' \cdot X_1{}' \cdot X_0{}', \qquad \text{"1"} = X_3{}' \cdot X_2{}' \cdot X_1{}' \cdot X_0,$$
$$\text{"2"} = X_3{}' \cdot X_2{}' \cdot X_1 \cdot X_0{}',$$
$$\text{"3"} = X_3{}' \cdot X_2{}' \cdot X_1 \cdot X_0, \qquad \ldots, \qquad \text{"9"} = X_3 \cdot X_2{}' \cdot X_1{}' \cdot X_0$$

This leads to the decoding circuit of Figure 5.13 (b).

Note that only 10 of the $2^4 = 16$ possible inputs have been used here. The other six codes would be error conditions, since none is a legitimate BCD code. If we wished to take this type of error into account, we could add another output line with the error function:

$$\text{error} = X_3 \cdot (X_2 + X_1)$$

An alternative implementation would employ a 4 to 2^4 decoder, and either ignore six of the output lines or pass them to error processing circuits.

One major application of decoders and other combinational networks is the logic circuits that control and address various parts of computer storage and provide for transfer of information among storage elements.

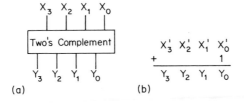

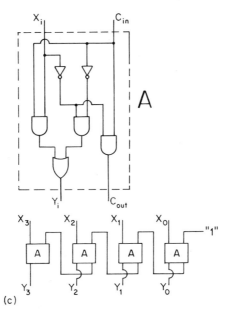

Figure 5.12 Two's Complement Circuit

5.4.2 Storage Systems

Bit storage elements are connected with combinational and other circuitry to form higher level memory units that may be accessed, read, and written. These units, in turn, are the building blocks for the two principal types of storage systems in machines—the main computer memory and the registers of the central processing unit.

Registers

A *register* is a set of bit storage cells that is used to store a logical unit of data for immediate or short term processing. In its simplest form, an n bit

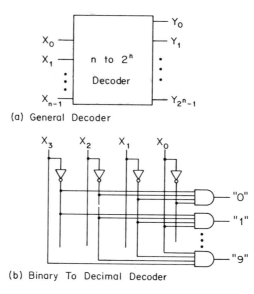

(a) General Decoder

(b) Binary To Decimal Decoder

Figure 5.13   Decoders

register consists of n cells, normally flip-flops, as shown in Figure 5.14. A given machine usually has a variety of registers of different sizes; for example, one computer might have registers of size 1, 2, 4, 8, 16, 24, 32, and 64 bits.

Much computer processing involves *transferring* information from one register to another. This task requires that data be *read* from a source register and *written* into a destination register. One simple circuit for accomplishing a register-to-register movement is illustrated in Figure 5.15. Here, the data in the four bit register A is read and copied to B under control of a transfer signal T. The T line is connected to the C input of each B flip-flop and is assumed to include a clock pulse *and* 'd with the transfer control signal. The transfer occurs only when the controlling Transfer line T is pulsed. The net effect of the circuit can be expressed in a higher level manner in Algolic:

if T then $B:= A$

Note that the data in A is *not* destroyed on the transfer; it is merely copied.

The transfer circuit also indicates how storage can be read and written. In order to write in a controlled manner, the data is placed on the appropriate

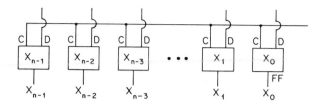

Figure 5.14 n Bit Register With n Flip-Flops

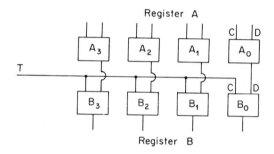

Figure 5.15   Register-to-Register Transfer

input lines and a write line is pulsed to start the operation. Similarly, the flip-flop outputs become available only when a read pulse occurs. In our example, the Transfer line acts as both a read and write line.

A central processing unit might have a "bank" of, say, eight identical registers $R_0, R_1, \ldots, R_7$. These registers can be individually identified by a unique three bit address. (Figure 5.16.) To select a particular register, the register address is passed through a 3 to 8 decoder. A decoder output, i.e., a register select line, could be connected to *both* input and output of each flip-flop of the register, thus permitting selection for either reading or writing.

A small storage system is constructed with the registers by adding Read and Write control lines, and DataIn and DataOut lines, as outlined in Figure 5.16. The Read and Write lines would be pulsed with clocked read and write signals, respectively. The DataIn and Write lines are connected to the input of all registers using appropriate combinational logic; similarly, the DataOut and Read lines would connect to the output of all registers. Switching algebra expressions for the C and D signals on flip-flop i of register R_j are:

$$D = \text{DataIn}_i$$

$$C = \text{Write} \cdot R_j$$

where DataIn_i is the ith line of DataIn.

The ith output line DataOut_i satisfies the following expression:

$$\text{DataOut}_i = \text{Read} \cdot (R_0 \cdot X_{i0} + R_1 \cdot X_{i1} + \cdots + R_7 \cdot X_{i7})$$

where X_{ij} is the *output* line of flip-flop i of register R_j.

In simpler terms, DataIn is written into the register selected by the decoder when a Write signal is given; and the contents of the selected register will be copied to DataOut whenever a Read signal is presented. The operation of the small register system may be described at a higher architectural level by the Algolic statements:

if *Read* **then** *DataOut* $:= R[ra]$
else
if *Write* **then** $R[ra] := DataIn$

Main Store

Main storage systems are much larger and slower than the register systems discussed above, and are used for longer term storage of programs and data. They have the general structure of Figure 5.17. Storage and retrieval of data is done through registers. The address of an element, such as a byte or a word, to be accessed is first sent to a *Storage Address Register* (SAR). The data that is read or written is stored temporarily in the *Storage Data Register* (SDR). These registers effectively isolate or buffer the storage from the rest of the computer.

If we represent storage as an array M, the memory operation can be expressed in Algolic:

if *Read* **then** $SDR := M[SAR]$
else
if *Write* **then** $M[SAR] := SDR$

Typically, main memory is organized internally as rectangular arrays that are addressed by x and y "coordinates"; for example, a 12 bit address for a 4

K word memory[8] could be divided into two 6 bit parts, and a 6 to 64 decoder would be used to select each coordinate.

In combinational circuits, the output is only a function of the input. Circuits consisting of both gates and flip-flops, such as some of those introduced

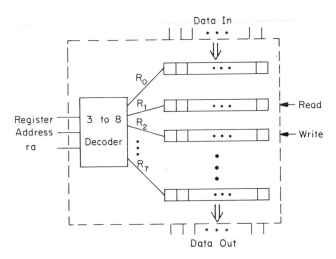

Figure 5.16   Register Bank

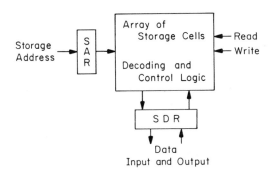

Figure 5.17   Main Storage System

---

[8]K stands for 1024 (2^{10}). Storage size is commonly expressed in this unit.

above, have outputs that depend not only on the input but also on the *state* of the flip-flops. The register bank system provides an obvious example; on a write, the circuit output, namely the *DataOut* lines, depends not only on the input *ra* and *Write* signals but also on the state of the selected register. Such circuits are called *sequential circuits* to reflect the fact that we are also interested in their behavior over time.

5.4.3   Sequential Circuits

Sequential circuits consist of networks of combinational logic and flip-flop registers controlled by clock signals. The *state* of a sequential circuit is defined as the states of its individual flip-flops. Changes of state can occur only when *FF* inputs change; and these changes are constrained to take place at discrete time units determined by clock pulses. At a detailed level, the complete processing capability of a computer is implemented with these circuits. As noted in Section 5.3, we will assume an edge-triggered *D*-type flip-flop constructed so that only one state change can occur per clock cycle.

Shift Registers

One important class of sequential circuits is the shift register. Shift registers are devices that store bit strings and can shift the strings one bit to the left or one bit to the right under control of some input signal. For example, consider a six bit shift register that shifts left; if the register initially contains the string 110101, successive left shifts yield:

$$110101 \xrightarrow{\text{left shift}} 101010 \longrightarrow 010100 \longrightarrow 101000 \ldots$$

where 0's have been introduced at the right at each shift.

Shifting has many applications. It provides an easy way to read and write bit strings, one bit at a time in sequence. Data can be sequentially moved out of a shift register for bit-by-bit examination; similarly, a shift register can be loaded by introducing the new bits at each shift. Shifting left (right) is also an easy way to multiply (divide) by two.

Shift registers can be constructed by connecting flip-flops in sequence through a small number of gates. To illustrate such a circuit and its operation, let us examine a four bit device that shifts right one bit at each shift pulse (Figure 5.18). Let the register initially contain the bits $b_3b_2b_1b_0$, i.e., b_i is in flip-flop X_i initially; then the following changes will occur:

$$b_3b_2b_1b_0 \xrightarrow{\text{shift pulse}} \quad 0b_3b_2b_1 \longrightarrow \quad 00b_3b_2 \longrightarrow 000b_3 \longrightarrow 0000.$$

The input lines to flip-flop X_i are connected such that at each shift pulse:

$$X_i \leftarrow X_{i+1}, \quad i = 0, 1, 2$$

X_3 is directly set to 0 by the constant "0" on its D input. The functional behavior of the circuit can be described by the Algolic:

if *Shift* **then**
begin
    for $i := 0$ **upto** 2 **do** $X[i] := X[i + 1]$;
    $X[3] := 0$
end

where the state of *FF* X_i is stored in $X[i]$.

Note that one can easily arrange to transfer a bit into the leftmost flip-flop rather than set it to 0; similarly the rightmost bit can be examined and/or stored by connecting appropriate circuits to X_0.

Sequential Adder

Shift registers are a necessary part of a sequential adder. Given shift registers for the augend X, addend Y, and sum Z, the sum $Z = X + Y$ can be obtained with a single one-bit full adder (FA) and a flip-flop to store a carry bit. Figure 5.19 contains a block diagram of the circuit. At each "add" pulse, a new bit is shifted into the FA from each of X and Y and the *Carry FF*, a new sum bit S is shifted into Z, and a new carry out C_{out} is stored in the *Carry FF*.

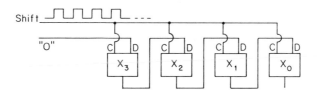

Figure 5.18   Shift Register

Let the X, Y, and Z registers be represented by n-element arrays indexed from 0 to $n - 1$. Then, the sequential adder circuit is a straightforward hardware realization of the algorithm:

Carry := 0;
for *Add* := 1 **upto** *n* **do**
{Complete addition takes n pulses, one per bit.}
begin
  {Add the bits.}
  $S := (X[0] + Y[0] + Carry)$ **mod** 2;
  if $(X[0] + Y[0] + Carry) \geq 2$ **then** *Carry* := 1 **else** *Carry* := 0;
  {Now shift X, Y, and Z registers.}
  last := $n - 2$;
  for $i := 0$ **upto** *last* **do**
  begin $X[i] := X[i + 1]$; $Y[i] := Y[i + 1]$; $Z[i] := Z[i + 1]$ **end**;
  $X[n - 1] := 0$; $Y[n - 1] := 0$; $Z[n - 1] := S$
end

Sequential adders are slower than parallel ones that contain only combinational circuits, since the former require one "Add" pulse per bit. However, the parallel adders require much more circuitry.

Counters

Another useful class of sequential circuits is the counter. This is a circuit that keeps a count of the number of input signals it receives. One application is in devices where timing pulses are counted, such as computer timers and

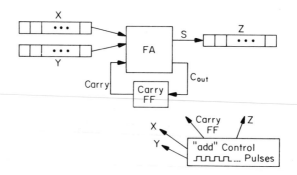

Figure 5.19   Sequential Adder

digital watches. Yet another application is the instruction counter of computers which is normally incremented by 1 after each instruction is executed. A counter consists of a register to store the current count and some combinational logic to increment the count, i.e., change the register state at each "count" signal.

Let us design a *two-bit binary counter* that successively counts 00, 01, 10, 11, 00, 01, ..., under control of a *Count* signal. The current count is stored in two flip-flops X_1 and X_0. In this example, we will informally introduce some parts of the standard design methodology for sequential circuits. The methodology is based on an enumeration of the possible circuit states and the state changes that result in response to different clocked inputs.

For our binary counter, the circuit state is the states of X_1 and X_0 and the single input is a *"Count"* signal. The desired behavior of the counter can be specified in a *state transition table* which lists the next state, the values of X_1 and X_0, that should result from each possible current state and input.

Current State		Input	Next State	
X_1	X_0	*Count*	X_1	X_0
0	0	0	0	0
0	0	1	0	1
0	1	0	0	1
0	1	1	1	0
1	0	0	1	0
1	0	1	1	1
1	1	0	1	1
1	1	1	0	0

The table specifies that the two-bit binary counter is incremented by 1 modulo 2 whenever a *Count* pulse (*Count* = 1) occurs. Note that X_1 and X_0 can also be interpreted as the value of the X_1 and X_0 output lines of the *FF*; for example, if X_1 is in the 0 state, then $X_1 = 0$.

The circuit has four states, one corresponding to each of the binary possibilities for X_1 and X_0, 00, 01, 10, and 11; name these states *S, T, U,* and *V,* respectively. The table above can then be represented in a more abstract form as a *state transition diagram,* as shown in Figure 5.20 (a). The circles designate states, the directed edges lead to the next state, and the labels on the edges denote input values. Thus if the system is in state *S* and receives input 0, it remains in state *S*; an input of 1 while in state *S* causes a transition to state *T*.

The state transition diagram is normally developed before the required flip-flops can be identified and the table produced. Generally, there is also an output associated with each state change. A state change has the form of Figure 5.20 (b). The interpretation is:

"If the system is in state S and receives input i, it produces output o and enters state T."

Our counter example is sufficiently simple that the diagram is not needed in order to derive the flip-flop requirements and table.

The next design task is to translate the specifications listed in the state transition table into the appropriate combinational logic for the input of each flip-flop. Consider the second line of the table. FF X_1 does not change its 0 state but FF X_0 goes from state 0 to 1. By maintaining D_1 at 0, X_1 will continue in state 0; to change X_0 to 1, the input D_0 must be set to 1. (Recall the FF behavior table presented in Section 5.3.) Using similar reasoning, each line of the table can be extended to include the FF inputs required for the state change; D flip-flops are particularly easy since their next state is identical to their input.

Current State		Input	FF Inputs		Next State	
X_1	X_0	*Count*	D_1	D_0	X_1	X_0
0	0	0	0	0	0	0
0	0	1	0	1	0	1
0	1	0	0	1	0	1
0	1	1	1	0	1	0
1	0	0	1	0	1	0
1	0	1	1	1	1	1
1	1	0	1	1	1	1
1	1	1	0	0	0	0

Each FF input column in the above table can also be interpreted as the definition of a *switching function* of the current state variables X_1 and X_0 and the input *Count*; the function can then be implemented with appropriate combinational logic since the lines X_1 and X_0 are available from the FF's. Using the table, we can obtain expressions for each function:

$$D_1 = X_1' \cdot X_0 \cdot Count + X_1 \cdot X_0' \cdot Count' + X_1 \cdot X_0' \cdot Count + X_1 \cdot X_0 \cdot Count'$$
$$= X_1' \cdot X_0 \cdot Count + X_1 \cdot X_0' \cdot (Count' + Count) + X_1 \cdot Count' \cdot (X_0' + X_0)$$
$$= X_1' \cdot X_0 \cdot Count + X_1 \cdot X_0' + X_1 \cdot Count'$$

$$D_0 = X_1' \cdot X_0' \cdot Count + X_1' \cdot X_0 \cdot Count' + X_1 \cdot X_0' \cdot Count + X_1 \cdot X_0 \cdot Count'$$
$$= X_1' \cdot (X_0' \cdot Count + X_0 \cdot Count') + X_1 \cdot (X_0' \cdot Count + X_0 \cdot Count')$$
$$= (X_1' + X_1) \cdot (X_0' \cdot Count + X_0 \cdot Count') = X_0' \cdot Count + X_0 \cdot Count'$$

The sequential circuit of Figure 5.21 is directly produced from these equations.

Now that we have examined several examples of sequential circuits, it is appropriate to take a more general view of their structure and design.

State Machine Design

A sequential circuit, sometimes called a *state machine,* can be described by the general block diagram of Figure 5.22. The *FF* outputs and some external input pass through combinational logic to generate the next state signals, *FF* inputs, and some external output. Changes of state occur only in synchronization with the clock.

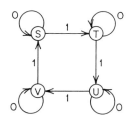

(a) State Transition Diagram For Binary Counter

(b) General Form

Figure 5.20 State Transition Diagram

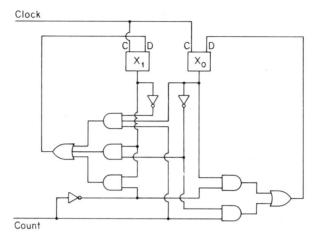

Figure 5.21   Binary Counter

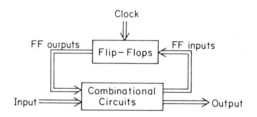

Figure 5.22   Block Diagram of a Sequential Circuit

The design technique was illustrated by the last counter example. Given a functional specification of a machine in terms of inputs and outputs, a state transition diagram that describes the desired behavior is produced. The number k of states in the diagram determines the number of flip-flops required; since n FF's can store 2^n states, k states will need $\lceil \log_2 k \rceil$ FF's.[9] The state transition table can then be directly obtained and extended with entries for the input of each FF and for the output; the present state and inputs, and desired next state, are used to derive the required signals for the

---

[9] $\lceil x \rceil$, called the *ceiling* of x, denotes the smallest integer greater than or equal to x.

output and *FF* inputs. Switching algebra expressions for the *FF* inputs and the circuit outputs are determined from the table. Finally, combinational logic implementing these expressions is connected to the *FF*'s to form the desired state machine.

A Design Example: Recognizing a String of Three One's

The problem is to design a sequential circuit that outputs a one for each non-overlapping string of three consecutive one's that it receives.

e.g.:
Input String   01100111000011111101111000111111111100
Output   00000001000000100100010000001001010000

The state diagram of Figure 5.23 (a) was obtained by noting that the basic task is to count one's; in state *One,* a single one has been encountered while in state *Two,* two consecutive one's have been received. The algorithm represented by the diagram can be stated in Algolic:

{Either 0 or 3 one's have been counted. Start again.}
Start: *read*(i); {Get next input bit i.}
        write('0'); {Output a 0 bit.}
        if $i = 1$ **then go to** *One* **else go to** *Start*;
{A first "1" has been received.}
One: *read*(i); *write*('0');
        if $i = 1$ **then go to** *Two* **else go to** *Start*;
{Two consecutive one's have been input.}
Two: *read*(i);
        if $i = 1$ **then** *write*('1') {three one's in a row}
        else *write*('0');
        go to *Start*

The input string 010111 causes the following state changes (equivalently, control to transfer to the Algolic labels):

$$Start \xrightarrow{0/0} Start \xrightarrow{1/0} One \xrightarrow{0/0} Start \xrightarrow{1/0} One \xrightarrow{1/0} Two \xrightarrow{1/1} Start$$

Since there are three states in the diagram, we require two flip-flops. Call these *A* and *B,* and arbitrarily assign the states as follows:

$$Start: A = 0 \quad B = 0$$
$$One : A = 0 \quad B = 1$$
$$Two : A = 1 \quad B = 0$$

Note that the fourth possible *FF* state, $A = 1, B = 1$, is not used.

The extended state transition table is now constructed; the X entries indicate "don't care" conditions:

	Current State		Input	FF Inputs		Output	Next State	
	A	B	I	D_A	D_B	0	A	B
(*Start*)	0	0	0	0	0	0	0	0
	0	0	1	0	1	0	0	1
(*One*)	0	1	0	0	0	0	0	0
	0	1	1	1	0	0	1	0
(*Two*)	1	0	0	0	0	0	0	0
	1	0	1	0	0	1	0	0
(Not used)	1	1	0	X	X	X	—	—
	1	1	1	X	X	X	—	—

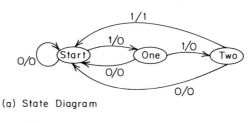

(a) State Diagram

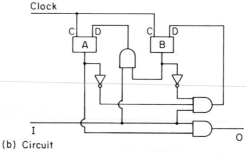

(b) Circuit

Figure 5.23   Recognizing Strings of Three One's

The *FF* input and *O* functions are:

1. $D_A = A' \cdot B \cdot I$

    However, note that the terms from the last two rows of the table can also be used if desired, since D_A could be 0 or 1 for the "don't care"'s. Using only the last line, we get
    $$D_A = A' \cdot B \cdot I + A \cdot B \cdot I = B \cdot I$$

2. $D_B = A' \cdot B' \cdot I$

3. $O = A \cdot B' \cdot I$

    Including the term from the last row, we obtain
    $$O = A \cdot B' \cdot I + A \cdot B \cdot I = A \cdot I$$

The circuit of Figure 5.23 (b) follows from these expressions.

A considerable theory, the theory of finite state machines or finite automata theory, is concerned with the power and behavior of machines that can be represented by state diagrams. These diagrams can also act as a finite model of computers. A somewhat different but related model with both states and storage is presented in Chapter 7. We should also emphasize that there are a number of practical issues, especially related to timing and synchronization, that we have not discussed and yet are very important for correct circuit design; moreover, we have restricted ourselves to one particular *FF* type. The large scale integrated circuit technology of the 1970's has also generated some new approaches to state machine design and structure. However, even though the technology continues to change dramatically, the underlying principles presented here remain valid.

5.5   COMPUTER ARCHITECTURE: AN EXAMPLE MACHINE

Assuming the various processing and storage capabilities provided by combinational and sequential circuits and storage systems, we can now describe some aspects of the architectural level of computer hardware. It is easiest to consider first the organization of a specific machine and then to use this machine as a basis for discussing other possibilities. Because we are treating a complete machine, it is also convenient to include programming level topics here.

The example machine is a modified and somewhat more realistic version of the one presented in Chapter 2. In the first part of this section, the machine is specified from a programmer's point of view. A possible architecture implementing this description is then presented. The last part outlines some additions and variations of the example machine that are commonly found.

5.5.1 Programmer's Specification

The computer, which we will call SAM (for *S*imple/*Sa*mple *M*inicomputer), has the general organization outlined in Figure 5.24. Main storage consists of 4 K 16 bit words, addressed from 0000 to 4095 (2^{12} − 1). The *central processing unit* (CPU), containing the control and arithmetic/logical components, has a single 16 bit accumulator register, AC, that is accessible to the programmer. SAM assumes a *two's complement* representation for integers and performs its arithmetic and tests accordingly. A typewriter terminal is used for input and output during program execution. Facilities for manually starting and stopping program execution, loading programs, and examining machine registers and storage are provided in the console.

The instruction format and instruction set of SAM are presented in Figure 5.25. At the right of each instruction is a mnemonic for easy reference, for example, *H*, *BLZ*, or *COM*. The instructions are grouped by function:

1. Control (*H, B, BZ, BLZ, BGZ*)

    As in almost all computers, SAM executes instructions from consecutive storage locations unless dictated otherwise by a control instruction. *B* is an unconditional transfer of control or branch to the address given in the operand field. *BZ, BLZ,* and *BGZ* will result in a branch only if the contents of the accumulator satisfy the given condition. *H* halts the computer; the "start" button on the console must be pressed to restart SAM.

2. Arithmetic (*ADD, SUB, INC*)

    Addition, subtraction, and incrementing by one are done assuming two's complement numbers. The machine will halt on *overflow*, i.e., if an arithmetic operation would produce a result greater than 2^{15} − 1 or less than -2^{15}. The *INC* instruction is useful for iterating through loops and other simple counting tasks.

3. Logical (*AND, COM*)

    AND does a bit by bit logical *and* of the AC and contents of α, while *COM* just complements each bit of the AC.

    Examples: Let AC = 1101 0011 0000 1111 and [32] = 0110 1101 1111 1100
    (1) instruction: 0100 0000 0010 0000
    AC = 0100 0001 0000 1100 after execution of this *AND* instruction.
    (2) instruction: 0101 XXXXXXXXXXXX (*X*: "don't care")

This instruction complements the AC giving AC = 0010 1100 1111 0000.

4. Shift (*RS, LS*)

The AC is interpreted as a 16 bit string. The low order four bits of the operand field are treated as an integer giving the number of bits to be shifted. Zeros are introduced at the left (*RS*) or right (*LS*) during the shift.

> **Example:** Let AC = •1011 0101 1111 0110. The instruction 0110 0000 0000 0101 shifts the AC right by five bits resulting in AC = 0000 0101 1010 1111.

5. Move (*LD, ST*)

These instructions load and store the AC.

6. Input-output (*RD, WR*)

RD and *WR* provide for reading or writing *one character* at a time. The system uses the eight-bit ASCII code. An *RD* operation reads the next character entered from the typewriter terminal into the *low order eight bit positions of the* AC; the instruction does not execute, but waits until a character has been entered by a user. For a *WR* operation, the character represented by the *low order eight bits of the* AC is printed on the typewriter. If the typewriter is already in the midst of printing a character when the *WR* is given, SAM will wait until the printing has completed before starting the new *WR*.

Programs are entered into storage and initiated through the console. We will ignore this aspect of the machine until the beginning of the next chapter. In addition to a functional description of the computer's components, storage, accumulator register, and instruction set, a complete specification must also include basic timing information. Execution times of instructions

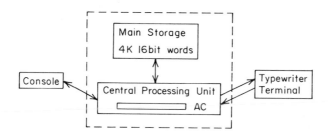

Figure 5.24 Components of SAM

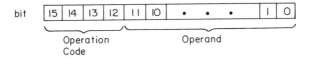

(a) Instruction Format

Operation Code	Meaning	(α denotes operand field)
		([α] denotes contents of cell with address α)

1. Control

  0 0 0 0   halt (H)

  1 1 0 0   go to α (B)

  1 1 0 1   if AC = 0 then go to α (BZ)

  1 1 1 0   if AC > 0 then go to α (BGZ)

  1 1 1 1   if AC < 0 then go to α (BLZ)

2. Arithmetic

  0 0 0 1   AC ← AC + 1 (INC)

  0 0 1 0   AC ← AC + [α] (ADD)

  0 0 1 1   AC ← AC − [α] (SUB)

3. Logical

  0 1 0 0   AC ← and (AC, [α]) (AND)

  0 1 0 1   AC ← complement (AC) (COM)

4. Shift

  0 1 1 0   AC ← right-shift (AC, α) (RS)

  0 1 1 1   AC ← left-shift (AC, α) (LS)

5. Move

  1 0 0 0   AC ← [α] (LD)

  1 0 0 1   [α] ← AC (ST)

6. Input-Output

  1 0 1 0   read (AC) (RD)

  1 0 1 1   write (AC) (WR)

(b) Instructions and Meaning

Figure 5.25 Instruction Format and Instruction Set

and input-output are needed for estimating the run time of programs. A typewriter terminal is a slow device, typically printing at a maximum rate of a few characters per second. Consequently, SAM's *WR* instruction might take 10's of milliseconds to complete. Reading (*RD*) has approximately the same maximum speed but also involves a "wait" for the user to enter information. The other instructions would normally execute in a small number of microseconds.

A Small Program for SAM: Reading Integers

A universal programming problem is to convert numbers entered through an input device to their internal binary representation. In the SAM environment, we consider the following variation. A user will type in one or more decimal digits followed by a blank, denoting a positive integer. The problem is to convert the input sequence of ASCII characters into the binary number that it represents.

Example:

Suppose the user types, in order, the characters '3', '6', and '␣', denoting the number 36 (base 10). The ASCII codes entered into the AC by the *RD* instruction would be:

$$0011\ 0011\quad (\text{ASCII '3'})$$
$$0011\ 1010\quad (\text{ASCII '6'})$$
$$0010\ 0000\quad (\text{ASCII '␣'})$$

Our program will convert this into the bit string: 0000 0000 0010 0100 (36_{10} in binary).

This is really a base conversion problem as discussed in Chapter 3. The data is entered in a coded version of base 10 and we wish to convert to base 2. We first present an algorithm in Algolic for reading integers:

```
        {Convert character string to a number.}
        x, digit : integer;  c : character;
        x := 0; {Number will be stored in x.}
loop:   read(c); {Get next character.}
        if c = '␣' then go to alldone ; {Check for termination condition.}
        {Convert c to a digit.}
        if c = '0' then digit := 0
        else if c = '1' then digit := 1
                        .
                        .
                        .
        else digit := 9;
        x := x × 10 + digit; {Build x.}
        go to loop;
alldone:        .
                .
                .
```

The Algolic segment is written so that it can be readily translated into a SAM program. First, consider the conversion of an input character to a digit. Examining the ASCII code for digits, it should be evident that we just have to eliminate the high order four bits of the character. This can be accomplished by reading the character into the AC and "*and*"ing the string 0000 0000 0000 1111. Similarly, a blank character test can be made by "*and*"ing the AC with 0000 0000 1101 1111 and then comparing the AC with zero.

Next, note that x must be *multiplied* by 10. Multiplication can be performed by *shifting* here. Since $10_{10} = 1010_2$, we have $x \times 10 = (x \times 2^1) + (x \times 2^3)$. But $x \times 2^k$ can be obtained by a *leftshift*(x, k). Therefore, $x \times 10$ can be computed with *leftshift*(x, 1) + *leftshift*(x, 3).

The SAM program is now straightforward. In order to make the program readable, symbols are used for the operation codes, operands, and instruction addresses; the program is in an assembly language, as introduced in Chapter 2. Thus, if the first instruction *LD ZERO* were stored in, say, location 1000, then *LOOP* would be synonymous with address 1001 and *ALLDONE* would correspond to location 1016. Assuming *DMASK* was stored in address 2052 ($2^{11} + 2^2$), then the *AND DMASK* instruction would be: 0100 1000 0000 0100.

Our program is incomplete in two ways. We have tacitly assumed that the number x is less than 2^{15} and that the user types only a sequence of digits followed by a blank. In any practical implementation, we must also test for overflow and the input of incorrect characters.

Address	Operation	Operand	Remarks
		.	
		.	
		.	
	LD	*ZERO*	Set $x = 0$ initially.
LOOP	*ST*	*X*	Store result in *X*.
	RD		Read character and store in *C*.
	ST	*C*	
	AND	*BTEST*	Test for *C* = '⊔'.
	BZ	*ALLDONE*	
	AND	*DMASK*	Obtain digit in *C*.
	ST	*DIGIT*	
	LD	*X*	Start $X \leftarrow 10 \times X$
	LS	1	Multiply by 2

	ST	X2	$X2 \leftarrow 2 \times X$
	LS	2	$AC \leftarrow X \times 8$
	ADD	X2	$AC \leftarrow 10 \times X$
	ADD	DIGIT	$AC \leftarrow 10 \times X + DIGIT$
	B	LOOP	Repeat.
ALLDONE	.		
	.		
	.		

Data

Address	Contents	Remarks
ZERO	0000 0000 0000 0000	
BTEST	0000 0000 1101 1111	Mask to test for blank.
DMASK	0000 0000 0000 1111	Mask to extract digit.
X	-----	Storage for X.
C	-----	Storage for character.
X2	-----	Temporary storage for $2 \times X$.
DIGIT	-----	Storage for digit.

5.5.2 Data Flow And Instruction Processing

A possible architecture for SAM is outlined in Figure 5.26, showing the principal units, registers, and control and data lines. Each line is labeled with a lower case alphabetic character for future reference. The ALU (*A*rithmetic *L*ogic *U*nit) in the central processing unit contains circuits for arithmetic and logical functions, and is used by all instructions that require comparisons, counting, arithmetic, and logic operations. In addition to the previously described accumulator (AC), SAM has the following registers:

1. 12 bit instruction counter (IC) for storing the instruction address.
2. 16 bit instruction register (IR) that contains the current instruction.
3. 12 bit storage address register (SAR) for the location of a main storage word involved in a memory read or write.
4. 16 bit storage register (SDR) for storing either a word to be written into *M* or a word read from *M*.

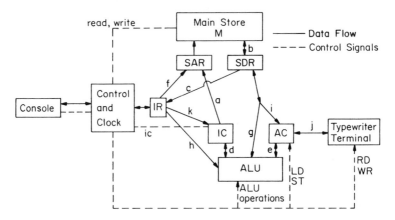

Figure 5.26   SAM Architecture

The purpose of the control unit is to control the retrieval and execution of each program instruction; this retrieval/execution sequence is called the *instruction cycle* because it is repeatedly performed. The retrieval or *"fetch"* part of the instruction cycle involves the operations:

1. Transfer the contents of the IC to the SAR in preparation for reading the next instruction from main store. (SAR ← IC)
2. Initiate a storage read. This reads the instruction from M into the SDR. (SDR ← M[SAR])
3. Transfer the contents of the SDR to the instruction register. (IR ← SDR)
4. Increment the instruction counter to be ready for the next instruction. (IC ← IC+1)

For the execution phase the *ADD* instruction, for example, is broken down into the elementary operations:

1. Transfer the operand field of the instruction to the SAR, in preparation for reading. (SAR ← OperandField(IR))
2. Read the operand from main store. (SDR ← M[SAR])
3. Transfer the SDR and AC to the ALU and initiate an *ADD* operation, returning the result to the AC. (AC ← AC+SDR)

The transfer and processing of data that occur during the instruction cycle are described by the Algolic program below. In order to relate the program to Figure 5.26, we have identified by comments the data lines involved in each elementary operation.

```
{Instruction Cycle of SAM Computer.}
cycle:   {Fetch Next Instruction into IR.}
         SAR := IC; {Data Line a}
         SDR := M[SAR]; {b. Read storage M.}
         IR := SDR; {c}
         {Increment instruction counter.}
         IC := IC + 1; {d}
         {Obtain operation and operand fields of instruction.}
         addr := GetOperandBits(IR);
         oc := GetOperationCodeBits(IR);
         {Decode operation code bits and execute instruction.}
         if oc = 0 then {H} WaitUntilStartButtonIsPressed
         else
         if oc = 1 then {INC} AC := AC + 1 {e}
         else
         if oc = 2 then {ADD}
         begin     SAR := addr; {f}
                   SDR := M[SAR]; {b}
                   AC := AC + SDR {e, g}
         end
         else
         if oc = 3 then {SUB}
         begin     SAR := addr; {f}
                   SDR := M[SAR]; {b}
                   AC := AC - SDR {e, g}
         end
         else
         if oc = 4 then {AND}
         begin     SAR := addr; {f}
                   SDR := M[SAR]; {b}
                   AC := and(AC, SDR) {e, g}
         end
         else
         if oc = 5 then {COM} AC := compl(AC) {e}
         else
         if oc = 6 then {RS} AC := rightshift(AC, addr){e, h}
         else
         if oc = 7 then {LS} AC := leftshift(AC, addr){e, h}
```

    else
    if oc = 8 **then** {LD}
    begin SAR := $addr$; {f}
                SDR := $M[SAR]$; {b}
                AC := SDR {i}
    end
    else
    if oc = 9 **then** {ST}
    begin SAR := $addr$; {f}
                SDR := AC; {i}
                $M[SAR]$:= SDR {b}
    end
    else
    if oc =10 **then** {RD} $read(AC)$ {j}
    else
    if oc =11 **then** {WR} $write(AC)$ {j}
    else
    if oc =12 **then** {B} IC := $addr$ {k}
    else
    if oc =13 **then** {BZ}
    begin   **if** AC = 0 {e} **then** IC := $addr$ {k} **end**
    else
    if oc =14 **then** {BGZ}
    begin   **if** AC > 0 **then** IC := $addr$ {k} **end**
    else {oc = 15, BLZ} **if** AC < 0 **then** IC := $addr$; {k}
    go to $cycle$

We have already seen how most of the elementary operations and storage functions may be individually implemented with combinational and sequential circuits and storage cells. Thus, we can build circuits for comparing bit strings, counting, transferring data between registers, decoding, arithmetic, and shifting. What has not yet been explained is how the *control* may be realized. In particular, the sequencing as specified by the Algolic statements must be implemented.

In the fetch part of the instruction cycle, we must assume that the operation SAR := IC is followed by SDR := $M[SAR]$, and that IC := IC + 1 is not performed before SAR := IC (IC := IC + 1 and SDR := $M[SAR]$ could proceed concurrently). Similarly, for each operation code, the proper sequencing of the information transfers and ALU activities must be provided. In terms of Figure 5.26, these requirements are met by sending out appropriate *control signals* at the right time.

The correct sequencing can be accomplished by dividing the instruction cycle into a fixed number of time periods, called *minor* cycles, each of sufficient duration to perform an elementary operation. The minor cycle time is some small multiple of the master clock cycle time. Suppose that an instruction cycle is divided into four minor cycles C_0, C_1, C_2, and C_3, where the instruction fetch occurs during C_0 and C_1 and execution proceeds within C_2 and C_3. This situation is illustrated in Figure 5.27 (a), where a minor cycle is defined for every master clock period. The C_i signals can be obtained by connecting a two bit binary counter to a two to four decoder as indicated in Figure 5.27 (b). By connecting the C_i to selected control signal lines, we can now initiate different operations at each minor cycle time.

A straightforward control for SAM would require six or eight minor cycles for the instruction cycle, since the three fetch operations $SAR := IC$; $SDR := M[SAR]$; $IR := SDR$ must be carried out in strict sequence, one minor cycle per operation, and the execution of, say, an *ADD* also involves three operations in sequence. The six or eight minor cycle pulses, C_i, can be produced with a three bit binary counter followed by a three to eight decoder, analogous to that in Figure 5.27 (b). The first minor cycle signal of SAM's control, C_0, would initiate the transfer from IC to SAR; at C_1, a read request signal is transmitted to the main storage system; C_2 controls the transfer from SDR to IR; and so on.

This completes our description of the SAM computer. We have omitted many details, especially those related to the console and typewriter input-output. However, what we have covered should convince the reader that SAM can indeed be constructed to operate in the manner depicted by the Algolic instruction cycle.

5.5.3 Extensions and Variations

SAM is a small machine by modern standards—a rather primitive representative of the microcomputer or minicomputer class. Normally, computers have much larger instruction sets and some additional features. It should be noted, however, that SAM's instruction set is certainly sufficient for any computational task; in fact, there is some redundancy in that operations, such as *SUB* and, say, *BGZ* and *BLZ*, can be programmed using the other instructions.

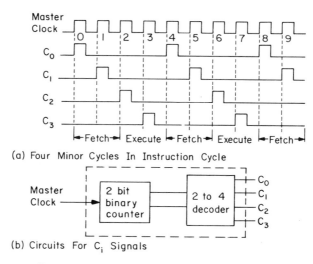

(a) Four Minor Cycles In Instruction Cycle

(b) Circuits For C_i Signals

Figure 5.27   Sequencing Signals For Control

Most machines have an extensive repertoire of machine language instructions, typically from 64 to several hundred different ones. Most of these can be classified in terms of the functional groupings that we employed for SAM—control, arithmetic, logical, shift, move, and input-output. For example, there may be instructions for: multiplication and division, decimal arithmetic, floating point arithmetic; circular shifts; or, exclusive-or; move between two storage locations, swap or interchange of two words; and so on.

Operand Addressing Methods

Many instruction variations result from the availability of more than one program-accessible register combined with more flexible operand addressing methods. Instead of one fast AC register, we might have a bank of fast registers that are used by the CPU for short term storage and processing; multiple registers reduce the number of memory loads and stores required for general ALU operations, and are also specifically useful for indexed address calculations and simple counting, discussed below.

Almost all of the operands of SAM's instructions are obtained by a direct addressing technique. There are at least five addressing methods in common use, all of which may be available on the same computer.

1. Direct
   The operand address directly appears in the computer instruction.
   e.g., In the following *ADD* instruction of SAM:

   0010 0000 0011 0000,

   the operand is *directly* obtained from storage address 48 (0000 0000
   0011 0000).

2. Relative
   An operand field of an instruction contains a *displacement* relative to
   the address of the instruction. For example, one might program, in
   symbolic form, the relative branches:

   B   +15   {Branch to the instruction 15 words from here.}
   BZ −4   {If AC = 0 then transfer back four instructions.}

3. Immediate
   The *operand itself, not* its address, appears in the instruction. A main
   store read for the operand is thus not needed. SAM's shift instructions
   (*LS, RS*) are of this type since the number of units to be shifted is
   specified in the operand field. It is customary to have arithmetic and
   logical immediate instructions, such as an *ADD* immediate where the
   bit string in the operand field is one of the arguments of the addition.

4. Indirect
   The *address of the address* of the operand is stored in the operand
   field. Indirect addressing is analogous to finding a letter in your
   mailbox that contains the address of another mailbox which has the
   letter. Indirect addressing is particularly useful when one wants to apply the same instructions to different operands, *without* modifying the
   instructions.

5. Indexed
   The need and concept of indexing can best be explained by an example. Consider the following simple calculation:

   $$sum := 0;$$
   $$\textbf{for } i := 1 \textbf{ upto } 20 \textbf{ do } sum := sum + x[i]$$

   Suppose the elements of the array x are stored in locations *addrx,*
   addrx + 1, ..., *addrx* + 19. To code this problem for SAM, we
   would then either
   (a) repeat the code for *sum := sum + x[i]* twenty times, with a
   different address *addrx* + *i* − 1 for each repetition—an
   impractical approach that does not generalize for large arrays, or

(b) use only one code sequence for *sum* := *sum* + *x*[*i*], but modify the instruction operand field to address a different *x*[*i*] each time through the loop.

The second solution in symbolic form is:

Address	Operation	Operand	Remarks
NEXT	LD	*SUM*	AC ← *sum*.
XINSTR	ADD	*X*	This instruction is modified each time through loop.
	STO	*SUM*	*sum* ← *sum* + *x*[*i*].
	LD	*I*	AC ← *i*.
	BZ	*FINISHED*	*i* = 0?
	SUB	*ONE*	*i* ← *i* − 1.
	STO	*I*	
	LD	*XINSTR*	Modify "*ADD X*"
	INC		to "*ADD X* + 1"
	STO	*XINSTR*	and store.
	B	*NEXT*	Repeat loop.
FINISHED			

Data	
Address	Remarks
SUM	Stores sum. Initially zero.
X	Address of *x*[*i*]. Initially *x*[1] (*addrx*)
XINSTR	Initially contains binary for "*ADD X*," but is modified each time through loop.
I	Loop index, used for counting. Initially contains 19.
ONE	Contains 1.

The operand part *X* of the instruction labeled *XINSTR* takes successively the values *addrx, addrx* + 1, ..., *addrx* + 19, so that the execution of this instruction gives *sum* + *x*[*i*], *i* = 1, ..., 20. The counting variable *I* counts from 19 down to 0.

In the earlier "von Neumann" machines, this was the standard technique for simple looping, counting, and running through a table of data. However, these indexing operations are so common and instruction modification is so error-prone, that special index registers and a new addressing method were developed to simplify programming. An operand address has two components in indexed addressing—a direct part, say D, and an index part, I, where I designates a register. During execution, the *address* of the operand is computed by hardware as $D + [I]$; i.e., the register contents are added to D. By just changing the contents of I, the same instruction can be used for different operands.

Instruction modification can thus be avoided with indexed addressing. This is not a minor point since much of the obscurity and errors in machine language programming were caused by the intricacies of such execution time changes. New instructions were also devised for assisting in common looping and counting; in particular, single operations that incremented (decremented) a register, inspected its contents, and then branched conditionally were added to instruction sets.

Variations also exist in the word length of the machine and in the number of operands specified in each instruction. Typical word lengths range from 8 bits to 64 bits. SAM is an example of a *one-address* machine, in that the address of one operand at most appears in an instruction. If other operands are required, their addresses are implicit in the instruction; thus SAM's AC is implicitly addressed by all arithmetic, logical, shifting, moving, and conditional branching instructions. Other organizations include:

1. Three-address instructions
   Instructions contain three operand addresses—two for the arguments of, say, an arithmetic or logical operation, and one for the result. In symbolic form, an *ADD* instruction:

$$ADD\ X\ Y\ Z$$

   would perform the processing:

$$[X] \leftarrow [Y] + [Z]$$

   or a conditional branch may be

$$BEQ\ X\ Y\ L$$

   with the interpretation:

   if $[X] = [Y]$ **then go to** L

2. Two-address instructions
    Instructions may contain two addresses. The addresses may be used, for example, to specify operand and result locations.

    e.g., $ADD\ X\ Y$ $[X] \leftarrow [X] + [Y]$

3. Zero-address instructions
    Here operands are accessed from fixed registers or are addressed by registers. The best examples of computers using this type of instruction are machines with hardware "stacks." (A stack is an interesting data structure discussed in Chapter 6.)

    e.g., ADD {This might have the effect $R1 \leftarrow R1 + R2$, where $R1$ and $R2$ are registers.}

Auxiliary Storage

One component that is essential for practical general purpose computing, and that is missing in SAM, is *auxiliary* or *secondary* storage. This is a very large store, with capacity frequently in excess of millions of words, that is connected to main memory (Figure 5.28). Under direct or indirect control of the CPU, blocks of information may be transferred between these two storage units. Auxiliary store provides a large temporary or permanent repository for files of data and programs.

One device commonly used for this auxiliary storage function is a rotating magnetic disk ressembling a phonograph record (Figure 5.28 (b)). A disk contains a number of concentric *tracks,* each of which may be divided into sectors. Information is stored magnetically along a track and is accessed in large blocks such as sectors. Multiple disks are often arranged on a spindle with mechanically movable read-write mechanisms as illustrated in the figure.

IO Processing and Interrupts

In the standard von Neumann architecture, input-output (IO) operations are not treated differently from other instructions; an IO instruction is executed to completion before the next instruction is initiated. However, there is an enormous disparity between the fast internal (electronic) speeds of the central processing unit and main store, and the slow electro-mechanical speeds of IO devices such as typewriters, card and paper-tape units, and auxiliary storage devices. Consequently, an IO instruction often takes several orders of magnitude longer to complete than the other internal operations.

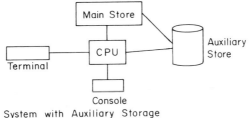

(a) System with Auxiliary Storage

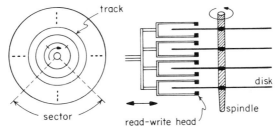

(b) Typical Disk Organization

Figure 5.28   Auxiliary Storage

The system can be run much more efficiently if the input-output operations *overlap* the other operations. This is accomplished by using a separate IO system that controls the complete execution of these instructions; the CPU merely initiates an IO operation. Communication between the central computer system and its IO subsystems can happen in at least two ways:

1. Polling.
    The CPU may interrogate the status of the IO system, where the IO status is recorded in registers. If, for example, an IO operation is in progress, the CPU can continue executing other instructions under program control, rather than wait for the IO to complete.
2. Interrupts.
    When an IO operation is completed, the CPU may be interrupted from its current task to continue the original program sequence that initiated the IO instruction. Interrupts provide much flexibility but lead to complex programming problems that are often best left to systems software specialists.

Hardware interrupts and polling exist in almost all machines. At the architectural level, an interrupt is implemented by setting a register that is tested at the end of every instruction cycle; if the register is set, the CPU transfers control to some *fixed* location in main store to get the next instruction. A simplified form of the basic instruction cycle of a computer including interrupts is:

cycle: *Fetch next instruction*;
              $ic := ic + 1$;   {Unless there is a branch or an interrupt, the next instruction is at *ic*.}
              Execute instruction;
              if *Interrupt* **then** $ic := InterruptLocation$;
                       {Change *ic* if the *Interrupt* register is set.}
              go to *cycle*;

The IO subsystem may be a complete computer itself. Polling and interrupts are also the hardware mechanisms that permit different computer systems to communicate.

Microprogrammed Control

Consider once again the Algolic description of the instruction cycle of SAM. We argued in Section 5.5.2 how this cycle could be completely realized by the electronic circuits presented previously. An alternative in common use is to implement the computer's control by *microprogramming*. With a microprogrammed architecture, the instruction set S presented to the normal user is not the set that is "hard-wired" into the machine; instead, S is *programmed* in terms of more primitive *micro-instructions* that are provided by the machine. Such micro-instructions are at about the level of the individual Algolic statements in SAM's instruction cycle; thus, a "micro-instruction" set may include operations for transferring data between two registers, initiating storage reads and writes, activating the ALU for specific operations, and conditional branching based on register values and addresses. The central processing unit has a *control store,* normally a read-only memory (*ROM*) that cannot be changed. The instruction cycle of the user machine is programmed and stored permanently in the ROM. These instructions are executed by the instruction cycle of the real micro-machine.

Programming at this level is called microprogramming. It is a more flexible and easier way to implement machines since one can modify the machine by changing the microprogram rather than by changing circuits. Higher-level languages and other systems software are also candidates for microprogram implementation, resulting in computers that do not have low-level machine languages accessible to the applications programmer. Microprogramming, first appearing in machines of the early 1950's, was promoted by the English computer pioneer M. Wilkes.

5.6 COMPUTER SYSTEMS AND TECHNOLOGY

Central processing units, memories, and input-output systems can be organized and connected in many different ways to form complete systems, depending on the current technology and the intended application. The spectrum ranges from a small personal computer consisting, for example, of a CPU, main store, disk auxiliary storage, typewriter terminal, and a video graphics display, to a large multi-user computer utility containing a network of computers with many processing elements executing concurrently. From another viewpoint, the possibilities include *centralized* systems where the computer's components are all "tightly-coupled" electronically and physically located together, to highly *distributed* systems consisting of autonomous processors and storage modules that are geographically separate and "converse" by passing messages over a communications network.

The most significant technological advances in computer hardware in the 1970's have occurred as a result of developments in *microelectronics.* Instead of connecting discrete components together by wires to produce a circuit, complete circuit "patterns"—components and interconnections—are placed on semi-conductor wafers photographically. Such integrated circuits may contain up to many thousands of components on a chip less than one centimeter square. The principal advantages of microelectronic circuits are that they are reliable and inexpensive, and do not consume much power.

The full range of computer building blocks are available on microelectronic chips; these include decoders, counters, memory units, complete central processing units called microprocessors, and even complete microcomputers. The imaginative computer architect can configure these basic blocks in endless ways. The practical consequence of the availability of flexible and low-priced digital modules has been to extend vastly the applications of computers. Small digital computers are the central controlling mechanism in a large number of consumer products, including watches, automobiles, and washing machines. They are used in measuring instruments, such as frequency counters and voltmeters, for guiding machines such as machine tools, and for controlling industrial processes. Computers are now used for signal processing in telephone, radio, and television communication systems. The more "traditional" tasks of data processing and scientific computing have been approached in different ways and applied to both smaller and larger problems.

Microelectronics are also having an impact on the science of computing. Algorithms are normally designed, analyzed, and implemented in terms of a *sequential* model of computing that emphasizes costs of performing logical and arithmetic operations and of data storage. While these considerations are still of major importance both practically and theoretically, one now should also treat seriously the possibility of *concurrent execution* of different algorithms or different parts of the same algorithm, and also consider the costs of message passing among the concurrent elements. It has become feasible to have many computer modules executing in parallel, with a resulting decrease in total execution time of an algorithm; the costs of microelectronic chips are relatively inexpensive compared with the costs of connecting modules together and communicating among modules.

EXERCISES

1. Trace the history of machine tools from the 16th through the 19th century.

2. Discuss a concept that was "ahead of its time"—in other words, a correct theory that was not practical for the level of contemporary technology.

3. The slide rule and the spring scale are both analog computers. Trace the history of the development of analog computers.

4. "The crucial breakthrough in the logical design of machines was the idea of a store that treated data and instructions in a uniform manner." Elaborate on this statement.

5. Write a short biography of either (a) Leibniz, (b) Pascal, or (c) von Neumann.

6. Use finite difference methods to tabulate the polynomial $p(x) = x^2$ for $x = 0, 1, \ldots, 8$.

7. Prove that the nth differences of a polynomial of degree n, $\sum_{i=0}^{n} a_i x^i$, $n \geq 1$, are identically equal to the constant $n! a_n$, where $n! = n \times (n - 1) \times (n - 2) \ldots \times 2 \times 1$.

8. Prove that the odd parity function

$$P_n(a_1, a_2, \ldots, a_n) = \begin{cases} 1 & \text{if there are an odd number of one's in } a_1, a_2, \ldots, a_n \\ 0 & \text{otherwise} \end{cases}$$

   ($n \geq 2$) can be implemented using only the exclusive-or operator $\oplus$; i.e., prove that

$$P_n(a_1, \ldots, a_n) = a_1 \oplus a_2 \oplus \cdots \oplus a_n.$$

   (Hint: Use induction on n.)

9. Design a full n-bit parallel subtractor. (See also Exercise 18 of Chapter 4.)

10. BCD encoder. Let the bit string $x_3x_2x_1x_0$ represent an unsigned binary number

$N = \sum_{i=0}^{3} x_i 2^i$. Design a combinational circuit with inputs $x_3x_2x_1x_0$ and outputs

$y_3y_2y_1y_0$ and C such that

   (a) $y_3y_2y_1y_0$ is the BCD code for the low order decimal digit of N and
   (b) C is the carry into the next digit position.

i.e. $N = 10 \times C + \sum_{i=0}^{3} y_i 2^i$ and $\sum_{i=0}^{3} y_i 2^i \le 9$.

e.g. if $x_3\,x_2\,x_1\,x_0 = 1101$ then $N = 13$, $y_3\,y_2\,y_1\,y_0 = 0011$, and $C = 1$.

11. Consider the register bank described in Section 5.4.2 (Figure 5.16). Let X_{ij} be flip-flop i of register R_j. Draw the combinational circuits connecting the register select, *Read, Write, DataIn* and *DataOut* lines to any X_{ij}.

12. Modify the shift register of Figure 5.18 so that it becomes a *circular shift register*; i.e., at each clock signal, we have $X_i = X_{(i+1) \bmod 4}$, $i = 0, 1, 2, 3$.

13. Design a sequential subtractor, analogous to the sequential adder of Figure 5.19.

14. Design a sequential circuit that outputs a one whenever it receives a bit string containing an odd number of one's followed by a zero.

e.g., Input   001101000111101111001110 ...
      Output 000000100000010000000001 ...

15. Assume that the SAM instruction set does not contain *BGZ* or *BLZ*. Implement these two instructions in terms of the remaining ones, i.e., write SAM program segments that have the same effect as *BGZ* and *BLZ*.

16. Assume that the SAM instruction set does not contain *SUB*. Implement *SUB* using the remaining instructions.

17. Consider the SAM program for reading integers. Modify the program to accept signed decimal integers. The input may be an optional sign ('+' or '−'), followed by one or more decimal digits and a blank.

18. Write a SAM program that prints out the bit contents of a storage word, starting from the *low* order bit of the word. For example, if the word contains 0110 1001 0000 1111, the output should be the characters '1', '1', '1', '1', '0', '0', '0', '0', '1', '0', '0', '1', '0', '1', '1', '0'.

19. Describe the architecture of some contemporary microcomputer, minicomputer, medium scale computer, or "super" computer.

ADDITIONAL READINGS

Mano, M. *Computer System Architecture.* Englewood Cliffs, N.J.: Prentice-Hall, 1976.

"Microelectronics." *Scientific American,* Vol. 237, No. 3 (September, 1977).

Randell, B. ed. *The Origins of Digital Computers.* New York: Springer-Verlag, 1973.

Tanenbaum, A. S. *Structured Computer Organization.* Englewood Cliffs, N.J.: Prentice-Hall, 1976.

Chapter 6

PROGRAMMING LANGUAGES AND SYSTEMS

The last chapter described the hardware architecture of a computer, including the basic instruction execution cycle of the control unit. The most obvious way to realize a computation on a machine is to express the algorithm as a *machine language program* that can be directly executed or interpreted by the computer hardware. This manual translation of an algorithm into machine code is a time-consuming, tedious, and error-prone task. In this chapter, we consider programming languages and systems that simplify the implementation and execution of algorithms on computers.

An early advance in computing was the development of *symbolic programming languages* and their corresponding *translator* programs that automatically translate symbolic programs into equivalent machine language code. The Algolic language used in this book is a simple example of a symbolic programming language. A common alternative to language translation is *interpretation*: instead of translating a program into machine code, each program statement is analyzed and directly executed by an *interpreter* program.

Language processors, such as translators and interpreters, are called *systems programs* or *systems software* because they are normally part of the total computer system presented to a user. In addition to language processors, most systems contain a wide variety of other software to simplify user programming and manage the computer's resources; these systems programs are either part of or controlled by an *operating system*, usually the most complex component of the computer software. Thus, the "machine" viewed by a user is rarely the real computer but is the machine defined by the operating system, language processors, and other systems programs that sit between the hardware and the user. This user machine is called a *virtual machine*.

In the next section, we examine some of the principal software components of computer systems and the virtual machines that they define. Programming languages are then discussed within the context of Algolic and several extensions to it. Section 6.3 covers some interesting problems in language processing. Several important aspects of operating systems are treated in the last section of this chapter. Throughout, we will present many examples of algorithms that are generally useful in non-numeric applications.

6.1 SOFTWARE COMPONENTS OF COMPUTER SYSTEMS

Loading and Executing Machine Language Programs

Let us start our software discussion by looking at the lowest possible programming level, machine language. Suppose that we have a "raw" computer with no software support and we have written a machine language program to solve some problem. Our task is to load the program into the computer and cause it to execute.

The operator's console of a computer has a large number of switches, buttons, and lights for manually entering information into storage, initiating and controlling execution, and interrogating and displaying the state of the machine. Assume that our machine language program P consists of words of instructions and data, $v_1, v_2, \ldots, v_n$, which are to be loaded into storage locations $s, s + 1, \ldots, s + n - 1$, respectively; and that execution is to start with instruction v_1. A simple manual procedure for loading and executing P on a typical machine is:

1. Set console switches to next storage address a. ($a = s + i, 0 \leq i \leq n - 1$).
2. Press "Load Address" button. (Enters a into the storage address register.)
3. Set console switches to next program word d. ($d = v_{i+1}$.)
4. Press "Load Data" button. (Enters d into storage at address a.)
5. If P is not completely loaded ($a \neq s + n - 1$), go to step 1.
6. Set switches to s, the first location.
7. Press "Load IC" button. (Enters s into instruction counter register.)
8. Press "Run" button. (Starts execution of program.)

This procedure takes a great deal of time and is practical only for *very* short programs. We can automate the loading process by first entering a short *loader* program that will load P. In Algolic, the loader program has the instructions:

$$f := s + n - 1 ;$$
$$\textbf{for } a := s \textbf{ upto } f \textbf{ do } read(M[a])$$

where we assume that the computer memory is represented by an array M of words. Execution of P can be automatically initiated by adding the statement:

go to s

after the simple loader. (Note that s is not really a legitimate Algolic label in this context.)

Loading and execution of P can now be performed as follows:

1. Manually load the short program:
    $$f := s + n - 1 ;$$
    for $a := s$ **upto** f **do** $read(M[a])$;
    go to s
    into some storage locations $t, t + 1, \ldots$, using steps 1 to 5 of the manual procedure.
2. Perform steps 6–8 to start execution at location t.

The automatic loader above works only for programs of length n which are to be stored in locations s to $s + n - 1$. A more general loader would permit programs of any length to be loaded into any contiguous set of storage locations. Let us assume that a machine language program P is preceded by two words of data, the address s of the first word of the storage area to be allocated to P and the length n of P. Then, loading and execution of any such P can be accomplished with the program:

Loader: $read(s)$; $read(n)$;
$f := s + n - 1 ;$
for $a := s$ **upto** f **do** $read(M[a])$;
go to s

Variations of this loader program appear in all computing systems and are the starting points for any software development on a machine. Because it is universally required, an elementary loader is usually built into the architecture of a computer, either as a permanently resident program or microprogram, or as hard-wired circuitry; a "Load" button is available on the console to activate the loader.

One of the first systems programs normally loaded by the basic built-in loader is a more sophisticated loader that performs program *relocation* as well as loading. Relocating loaders can load the *same* machine language program into *different* areas of storage by modifying the address fields of instructions during loading. Automatic relocation is useful because it permits several machine language programs to be easily combined into one large program, and for large systems, it allows several different programs to be resident in the machine at the same time.

Because language translators do not know, in general, where a particular translated program is going to be placed in storage, they produce machine code assuming some standard fictitious starting location, usually zero; during loading, the machine code is then relocated according to the memory locations allocated to it by a storage allocation program. A language translator program thus generates code for a virtual machine with fictitious storage addresses. This simple virtual storage system is implemented by a relocating loader, storage allocator, and other systems software.

Symbolic Languages and Their Processors

Machine language programming requires that the programmer use numeric codes and addresses to encode algorithms. Keeping track of such detail is very tedious. Pre-1950 coding was done in machine language, typically from flow chart specifications. In the early 1950's, symbolic machine languages were developed, called *assembly languages* (AL).

The basic idea is to use symbolic names for the binary, octal, or decimal digit sequences that denote operation codes, address fields, and data areas in machine language instructions and programs. A translator program, called an *assembler*, is then necessary to translate the symbolic code into equivalent numerical machine language. AL has a very close correspondence to machine code and is called a *low-level* language to distinguish it from such *high-level* languages as Algolic that are more oriented toward user problems.

As an example in assembly language programming, we consider an algorithm for computing the nth *Fibonacci* number F_n where we assume that $n \geq 2$. Recall from Chapter 2 that F_n is defined by the formula $F_n = F_{n-1} + F_{n-2}$, with $F_0 = 0$ and $F_1 = 1$. We will present an AL version of the following Algolic program for finding F_n:

```
NEWFIB := 1 ; OLDFIB := 0 ;
for I := 2 upto N do
begin
    TEMP := NEWFIB ;
    NEWFIB := NEWFIB + OLDFIB ;
    OLDFIB := TEMP
end
{NEWFIB contains F_N.}
```

Assume a single register machine similar to the one presented in Chapter 5. A program for F_n written in assembly language is given in Figure 6.1. The lines with operation code *WORD* are directives to the assembler to reserve and initialize a word of storage; the other lines each correspond to a machine language instruction. The *Label Field* permits the programmer to assign symbolic names to instruction and data words so that they may be easily referenced. The *Operation Code* fields contain pre-defined names that either correspond to the numeric operation codes of the computer or, as in the case of *WORD*, are instructions to the assembler, while the *Operand Field* contains programmer-defined names that will eventually translate into instruction and data addresses.

The central task of an assembler is to translate symbolic instruction and data references to real or virtual machine addresses; given the value for each programmer-defined symbol and the pre-defined values of the operation code names, the machine language version of an AL program can be easily generated. In practice, assembly languages are more complex than indicated by our example above and assemblers can be intricate programs.

Label Field	Operation Code	Operand Field	Comments
	⋮		
			AC is register name
LOOP	LD	N	$AC \leftarrow N$ (load)
	SUB	I	$AC \leftarrow AC - I$ (subtract)
	BLZ	*FINI*	branch to *FINI* if $AC < 0$
	LD	*NEWFIB*	$AC \leftarrow NEWFIB$ (load)
	ST	*TEMP*	$TEMP \leftarrow AC$ (store)
	ADD	*OLDFIB*	$AC \leftarrow AC + OLDFIB$
	ST	*NEWFIB*	$NEWFIB \leftarrow AC$
	LD	*TEMP*	$AC \leftarrow TEMP$
	ST	*OLDFIB*	$OLDFIB \leftarrow AC$
	LD	I	$AC \leftarrow I$
	INC		$AC \leftarrow AC + 1$
	ST	I	$I \leftarrow AC$
	B	*LOOP*	branch to *LOOP*
FINI			*NEWFIB* contains F_n
	⋮		
N	WORD		initialized to value of n
I	WORD	2	initialized to 2
NEWFIB	WORD	1	initialized to 1
OLDFIB	WORD	0	initialized to 0
TEMP	WORD		temporary storage
	⋮		

Figure 6.1   Assembly Language Code for Computing F_n

The assembler provides a virtual machine interface to the user—the assembly language machine—that permits machine language coding in symbolic rather than numerical terms. However, execution of an AL program involves several more steps. The assembler must first be loaded, the AL program translated, and the resulting machine code loaded and executed.

Programming at the machine level, even with an AL, requires great patience and attention to detail; the programmer must deal with many hardware allocation issues, such as register and storage allocation, that often have little apparent connection with the algorithm being implemented. A truly significant breakthrough in the mid-1950's was the creation of high-level *problem-oriented* languages that are independent of any particular computer and are more convenient for users. An enormous number of such languages have been developed and many are in widespread use today. Translators for high-level languages are called *compilers*. Compilers may directly produce machine code or AL code, or they may generate code in some other intermediate language that is later translated or interpreted; thus several layers of translation software may exist between the machine and a high-level language program.

Inevitably, the machine code generated by a high-level language translator is not always as efficient as the code that could be produced by a good programmer working directly in AL. However, for most applications, human and machine efficiency dictates the use of high-level languages. AL programming is done only where machine time and storage space are severely constrained or where high-level language software does not exist.

The virtual machine presented to a programmer in a high-level language is one that directly executes the high-level language. The fact that several layers of software—for example, compiler, assembler, and loader—may be required to implement this machine should be of little or no concern to the high-level language programmer; similarly, the details of the particular computer, such as instruction sets and registers, are also not relevant to this programmer. Thus, for example, the Algolic language defines an Algolic virtual machine that may be implemented on a variety of computers. The Algolic machine could be constructed with the following software on a particular machine:

COMP: a compiler that translates Algolic code to assembly language
ASM: an assembler that translates AL to relocatable machine code
RL: a relocatable loader that translates relocatable machine code to absolute machine language.

The execution of an Algolic program on this machine is illustrated in Figure 6.2.

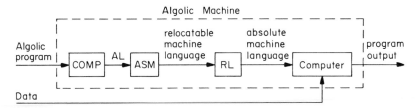

Figure 6.2   Example of an Algolic Machine

Software Aids for Program Preparation and Execution

Modern computer systems offer a large number of software utilities and subsystems that simplify the preparation, running, sharing, and maintenance of user programs.

Typically, practical programs consist of many hundreds of program statements. It is almost impossible to program, debug, and maintain such programs correctly if they are treated as one unit. Instead, a program is broken into a number of smaller and more manageable *subprograms,* and these are first independently written and tested. In addition, there exist many common computational procedures that are generally required as subprograms in a wide variety of applications; for example, many scientific applications use subprograms to compute the trigonometric functions sin, cos, and tan. These commonly used subprograms are collected together in systems libraries that are stored in auxiliary storage files. In order to combine a set of user subprograms and a selected set of library programs into one large program, a *linker* program is invoked; the linker modifies addresses so that one subprogram can properly transfer to another and so that data can be passed among the subprograms. The linker is a fundamental piece of systems software that often appears as a unit with the relocatable loader.

In the 1950's and early 1960's, the preparation and modification of programs were done off-line from the machine. Users would write their programs on paper using pencil and eraser, punch the program on cards, and submit the cards to the computer through a card-reader device; program changes were made by punching new cards and removing cards from the program deck. While this method is still in use, it is rapidly being replaced by a more efficient *on-line* technique. Users sit at a console with a typewriter keyboard, and directly enter and modify their program text by interacting with a software subsystem called a *text editor*. The text editor implements a virtual textprocessing machine with commands for inserting, deleting, appending, and searching strings of textual characters.

Programs are rarely without error. Software debugging aids that are useful for finding errors include *trace* programs that display the particular instructions executed and *dump* programs that display the "state," the storage contents and instruction counter, of the real or virtual machine during execution.

Much of the systems software resides on auxiliary storage and is loaded when needed. Similarly, files of data and programs, such as libraries and files produced by a text editor, normally reside on secondary storage. The software component responsible for maintaining and accessing these files is the *filing system*. The filing system is part of the machine's operating system.

Operating Systems

The use of language processors, such as assemblers, interpreters, and compilers, the invocation of a loader and linker, the execution of user programs, and the selection of programming aids described above are all controlled by the computer's *operating system* (OS). For relatively small systems that service one user at a time, the OS is primarily responsible for file management—storing, retrieving, and modifying auxiliary storage files of user programs, systems programs, and data; the OS also usually provides simplified input-output facilities to the user and handles the allocation and administration of main and auxiliary storage. In larger systems where several user jobs may be in execution at the same time, the OS is also responsible for switching control from job to job, scheduling jobs, and, in general, managing all of the computer's hardware and software resources.

From the user point of view, the OS is that part of the machine that responds to commands to load, translate, and execute programs, to do input-output, to manage files, and to allocate hardware resources. The operating system defines an elaborate virtual resource scheduling and filing machine.

Virtual Machine Hierarchy

The major software components can be organized in a virtual machine hierarchy above the real physical computer as shown in Figure 6.3. Each level of the hierarchy implements new virtual machines in terms of facilities provided by machines at lower levels. Thus the OS uses the real machine features to present a new abstract (OS) machine to users above it; similarly, the

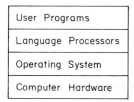

| User Programs |
| Language Processors |
| Operating System |
| Computer Hardware |

Figure 6.3   Levels of System Software

language processors are constructed with the OS and real machines that exist below it. Finally, the users have a wide range of language processing machines as well as the OS machine, within which they can define their algorithms. This software hierarchy is an extension of the hardware levels presented in Section 5.2.

6.2   PROGRAMMING LANGUAGES

The meaning of "programming languages" in this section will be restricted to high-level, general purpose programming languages. In particular, we will not be concerned with assembly languages or languages that are designed for very specific applications or types of machines. After a brief discussion of the history of programming languages, some aspects of syntax specification, data types, and procedures will be developed, using Algolic as our base language.

6.2.1   Historical Perspectives

Many hundreds of different programming languages have been implemented since the early 1950's and many ten's are in active use today. No wonder that the field has been likened to a tower of Babel! Computers are such universal symbol processing devices that it is very hard indeed to resist the temptation to design and implement a new language for each set of applications that arises. Despite the continued proliferation of languages, there exist only a few major *classes* of programming languages and only a few languages that are *widely* accepted either for their practical, aesthetic, or descriptive qualities. We will briefly cover the major classes and major languages below.

The first languages evolved from the "bottom-up" and were essentially extensions of assembly languages. Features that were typically added included floating point arithmetic, multiple address "pseudo-codes" such as defining a three-address machine on top of a real single-address machine, and simple arithmetic expressions and assignments such as $A = B + C$ or $C = (A + B) \times D$.

Languages for Scientific Computing

FORTRAN was the first high-level language that was accepted by a large user community (the acronym "FORTRAN" derives from *Formula Translating System*). It was developed in 1954 by John Backus and his associates at the IBM Corporation. FORTRAN was designed for engineering and scientific computing and its modern version is still the most popular language for this application area.

One of the reasons for the early success and acceptance of FORTRAN was that the designers took great pains to ensure that it could be compiled into reasonably efficient machine code. This accounted for the appearance of such strange statement forms as the arithmetic *IF* statement:

$$IF\ (e)\ i_1,\ i_2,\ i_3$$

where e is an arithmetic expression, and i_1, i_2, i_3 are each integer statement labels. The IF statement has the meaning, in Algolic:

> **if** $e < 0$ **then go to** i_1
> **else if** $e = 0$ **then go to** i_2
> **else go to** i_3 $\{e > 0$ here$\}$

FORTRAN also has the following statement types:

1. assignment: $v = e$, where v is a variable and e is an expression
2. several variations of **go to** statements
3. simple **if/then:** *IF* $(e)\ s$, where e is a logical expression and s is a simple statement, equivalent to the Algolic **if** e **then** s
4. *looping statement: DO n v* $= m_1,\ m_2,\ m_3$
    Repeat a set of statements up through the statement labelled n, for $v = m_1$, in steps of m_3, up to or down to m_2.
5. elaborate *read* and *write* statements
6. subprogram definition and use

FORTRAN is quite rudimentary but is widely used because it is relatively simple, can be compiled into efficient machine code, is available on most computers, was there first, and, finally, is supported by IBM which has the major share of the computer market. It is slowly evolving into a more expressive and structured language, but it still remains an awkward notation for communicating algorithms to machines and people. Nevertheless, FORTRAN has influenced the design of many other languages and compilers, and permitted computing to be done by non-computer professionals on a large scale.

In the late 1950's, an international group of academic and industrial computer scientists designed a new scientific programming language called Algol (for *algo*rithmic *l*anguage); several versions of this language were proposed and finally culminated in the revised Algol 60 report. This effort had enormous impact on the practical and theoretical developments in programming languages and compilers. A new notation, now called Backus-Naur Form (BNF) after its creators J. Backus and P. Naur, was used for precisely specifying the syntax of Algol. Variations of BNF are now the accepted method for describing the syntax of any programming language. In addition, the notation has been the catalyst for developing techniques for *parsing* languages (analyzing their form and structure) and for theoretical studies of language specification.

The Algol language is more general than FORTRAN in the sense that it imposes fewer restrictions on the use of various constructs; it also has several new features, such as compound statement (**begin ... end**), structured conditional and looping statements, and a "block structure" that permits variables to be defined only in local pieces of code. The new and more general language features stimulated and challenged compiler builders, and much of modern complier theory and practice can be traced to the problems of compiling Algol 60 code.

Algol 60 was used extensively in education, industry, and government applications in Europe; with the exception of academia, it was not widely accepted in North America where FORTRAN was too firmly entrenched. Many Algol-based languages were produced in the 1960's and 1970's, but perhaps the most significant successor is the Pascal language, designed by N. Wirth in 1970. Pascal has more elaborate mechanisms for creating and handling data structures and files, and is useful for text, symbol, and data processing programs, as well as numerical computations. It is a popular teaching language at many universities and is also the basis for several home computer and industrial languages.

Business Data Processing

About the same time that FORTRAN was being constructed for scientific programming, a parallel but apparently independent effort was reaching fruition in business data processing. The aim here was to produce a business programming language whose statements and commands resembled English and could consequently be used and understood by non-technical and relatively untrained business people. The first such language, FLOWMATIC, was specified in 1955. This was followed several years later by the well-known COBOL (*common business oriented language*). COBOL was designed in 1959 by a committee of American computer manufacturers, users, and the Defense Department. COBOL is certainly the most commonly used language in business work. It is probably true that more lines of COBOL are processed in computing systems than any other programming language.

In addition to the English-like syntax, COBOL has extensive file definition features that permit the programmer to specify large files of data conveniently. The file definition and processing facilities of COBOL are the most interesting innovations in this language and have had a broad impact beyond business data processing languages. Following is a COBOL example of part of the file definition for a simple employee file.

```
FD   EMPLOYEE FILE
     BLOCK CONTAINS 10 RECORDS
     LABEL RECORDS ARE STANDARD
        ⋮
01   PERSONAL-DATA
     02   EMPLOYEE-NAME
          03   FIRST-NAME PICTURE X(12)
          03   MIDDLE-INITIAL PICTURE X
          03   LAST-NAME PICTURE X(12)
     02   BIRTH-DATE
          03   DAY PICTURE 9(2)
          03   MONTH PICTURE 9(2)
          03   YEAR PICTURE 9(2)
        ⋮
01   EMPLOYEE-DATA
     02   LOCATION
          03   BRANCH PICTURE X(8)
          03   MAIL-STOP PICTURE X(2)
          03   TELEPHONE-EXTENSION PICTURE 9(5)
     02   WAGES
          03   RATE-OF-PAY PICTURE 9(7)
        ⋮
```

A COBOL file is composed of a number of records. Each record has the "structure" indicated by the above list, with each field of a record given a name, such as BIRTH-DATE. The PICTURE specification gives the length and type of each field; for example, FIRST-NAME consists of 12 characters (X) while DAY is composed of 2 decimal digits (9).

General Purpose

A committee representing the largest IBM computer users group, SHARE, and employees of the IBM Corporation set out in the early 1960's to design a multipurpose programming language that would be used for both scientific and business data processing. The result was the PL/I language. PL/I borrowed features from FORTRAN, Algol, COBOL, and several other languages and incorporated these to form a very complex and large language. While PL/I has not supplanted FORTRAN and COBOL on IBM machines, it is used widely.

Some Other Significant Languages

Table 6.1 lists several other programming languages that were pioneering and influential efforts, and are still used.

6.2.2   Syntax Specification

Natural languages, such as English or French, and artificial languages, such as programming languages or Morse code, have much in common. Any such language can be defined as a set of *sentences*, where each sentence consists of a sequence of atomic elements, such as words or symbols. The atomic elements are called the *vocabulary* of the language. The *syntax* or structure of a language is given by a set of composition rules, called a *grammar*, that define the elements and structure of any well-formed sentence. Associated with each well-formed sentence of a language is its *semantics* or meaning; the semantics depends on both the particular words in the sentence and the structure of the sentence.

To illustrate the ideas informally, consider a small fragment of English. Let the vocabulary be {HE, MARY, DRIVES, WALKS, GOES, TO, FROM, TOWN, SCHOOL} and the grammar be given by the rules:

```
sentence → subject predicate
subject → noun        subject → pronoun
predicate → verb      predicate → verb prepositional-phrase
noun → MARY           noun → SCHOOL        noun → TOWN
pronoun → HE
verb → DRIVES         verb → WALKS         verb → GOES
prepositional-phrase → preposition noun
preposition → TO      preposition → FROM
```

Some well-formed sentences based on these rules are:

HE GOES TO TOWN   MARY DRIVES FROM SCHOOL
HE WALKS   TOWN DRIVES TO MARY

Table 6.1   Some Other Important Programming Languages

Language	Inventor(s)	Year	Purpose	Special Features
LISP	J. McCarthy	1959	list processing	functional programming, list data structure
SNOBOL	D. J. Farber R. E. Griswold I. P. Polonsky	1962	string manipulation	pattern matching
APL	K. E. Iverson	1962	general purpose	vector and array operators, concise notation
BASIC	T. E. Kurtz J. G. Kemeny	1964	interactive teaching language	simplicity
SIMULA	K. Nygaard O-J. Dahl	1965	simulation	coroutines, classes

While all the sentences are *syntactically* correct, only the first three are meaningful using the normal semantics of English.

An analysis of a sentence that produces its structure or syntactical components is called a *parse*. For the example grammar above, a parse is conveniently represented as a *tree*, as shown in Figure 6.4(a).

The language in the example is *finite* in that only a finite number of sentences can be generated by the grammar; *subject* generates four possible phrases, MARY, SCHOOL, TOWN, and HE, and *predicate* generates $3 + (3 \times 2 \times 3) = 21$ possibilities, leading to 84 possible sentences. Each sentence is also bounded in length, being no longer than four words.

In order to permit an infinite number of sentences and an unbounded length in each sentence, one can use *recursive* rules. The simplest example of a recursive rule is one where the *left part*, the element being defined, also appears in the *right part* of the rule. Taking our example grammar again, we add the recursive rules:

sentence → subject predicate AND sentence

sentence → subject predicate OR sentence

sentence now appears on both sides of these rules. In addition to the sentences previously generated, the augmented grammar now produces longer sentences such as HE GOES AND MARY DRIVES FROM TOWN OR MARY GOES TO SCHOOL AND MARY DRIVES; a parse of a longer sentence appears in Figure 6.4(b). The combined rules are a convenient way of stating that a "sentence" consists of any number of "subject predicate" pairs connected with either AND or OR. The language described by the

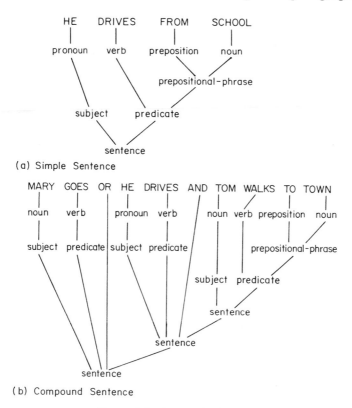

(a) Simple Sentence

(b) Compound Sentence

Figure 6.4   Parse of a Sentence

augmented grammar has an infinite number of sentences and there is no upper bound on the length of each sentence. Most languages have these features and we can be pleased that there are finite description methods for these infinite sets of unbounded strings.

These ideas were first formalized and developed for the domain of natural language syntax by the linguist Noam Chomsky in the 1950's. Chomsky's work spawned an intellectual revolution in linguistics, resulting in many new insights into the nature of language and language acquisition. This work also formed the underlying basis for many advances in natural language understanding systems, computer systems that can communicate in fragments of a natural language. More significantly from our point of view, parts of the Chomsky model of syntax have been successfully adapted for programming languages, where it has proven useful for specifying languages and, in the case of compilers, for parsing programs.

We mentioned in our brief history of programming languages the development of the BNF notation as part of the Algol project. This notation was the first adaptation of Chomsky's methods to programming language specification. We will now define and discuss the BNF notation and some of its variants.

We start with a simple example, the BNF definition of integers in terms of digits and + and −; the vocabulary will be $\{0, 1, 2, \ldots, 9, +, -\}$. A BNF definition, G_{int}, of integers is:

⟨integer⟩ ::= ⟨sign⟩ ⟨digit sequence⟩ | ⟨digit sequence⟩
⟨sign⟩ ::= + | −
⟨digit sequence⟩ ::= ⟨digit⟩ ⟨digit sequence⟩ | ⟨digit⟩
⟨digit⟩ ::= 0|1|2|3|4|5|6|7|8|9

The notational conventions are:

1.   Elements of the vocabulary, sometimes called *terminal symbols*, appear only in the right parts of rules.
2.   Syntactic components, or *nonterminal symbols,* appear on both the left and right parts of rules and are distinguished by enclosing them by the brackets "⟨" and "⟩". Thus ⟨integer⟩ and ⟨sign⟩ are nonterminal symbols.
3.   The symbol "::=" means "is defined as"; alternative terms are "generates," "produces," "may be rewritten as," and "consists of."
4.   The symbol "|" is used to separate alternative right parts so that several rules may be combined into one. Thus, instead of writing ⟨sign⟩ ::= + and ⟨sign⟩ ::= −, the two rules are combined into ⟨sign⟩ ::= + | −.

Thus, the first rule may be read as "An ⟨integer⟩ is defined as either a ⟨sign⟩ followed by a ⟨digit sequence⟩ or it is a ⟨digit sequence⟩." The third rule is recursive and defines a ⟨digit sequence⟩ to be a sequence of one or more ⟨digit⟩'s. A parse of an integer is shown in Figure 6.5.

BNF and languages are now defined formally. A *BNF grammar* is defined by a 4 tuple $G = (N, V, R, S)$ where:

N is the set of nonterminal symbols,
V is the set of terminal symbols,
N and V are disjoint $(N \cap V = \emptyset)$,
R is a set of rules of the form: $v ::= \alpha_1 | \alpha_2 | \cdots | \alpha_n$
where $v \in N$, $n \geq 1$, α_i is a string of the form x_{i_1}
$x_{i_2} \cdots x_{i_n}$ with $x_{i_j} \in (N \cup V)$ and $i_n > 1$, and
S is a distinguished member of N called the *start* symbol.

Example:

In the grammar for ⟨integer⟩'s presented above, we have

$G_{\text{int}} = (\{0, 1, \ldots, 9, +, -\}, \{\langle \text{integer}\rangle, \langle \text{sign}\rangle, \langle \text{digit sequence}\rangle, \langle \text{digit}\rangle\},$
  $R, \langle \text{integer}\rangle),$

where R is the listed set of rules.

A BNF grammar specifies a *language*. This language is the set of terminal strings or *sentences* that can be generated from the *start* symbol. In order to define this precisely, we first need to describe the intermediate results of a sentence generation, called a *sentential form*. Let $G = (N, V, R, S)$ be a BNF grammar. A sentential form is defined by the following rules:

1. S is a sentential form.
2. If $\alpha\, v\, \beta$ is a sentential form where $v \in N$ and each of α and β are either empty or strings containing elements of N and V, then $\alpha\gamma\beta$ is also a sentential form if $v ::= \ldots |\gamma| \ldots$ is in R.

A *sentence* generated by $G = (N, V, R, S)$ is a sentential form containing no non-terminal symbols. The *language* $L(G)$ generated by the BNF grammar G is the set of sentences generated by G.

Example:

Consider grammar G_{int} again. Some sentential forms of G_{int} are ⟨integer⟩, ⟨sign⟩ ⟨digit sequence⟩, $-$⟨digit⟩ ⟨digit⟩, ⟨sign⟩ 345, -1367. A sentence generated by G_{int} is 386. $L(G_{\text{int}}) = \{0, 1, \ldots, 9, +0, +1, \ldots, +9, -0, \ldots, +\,456, +457, \ldots\} = $ the set of all signed and unsigned integers.

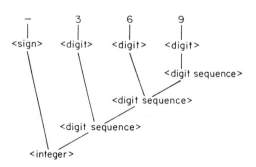

Figure 6.5   Parse of an Integer

One form that appears frequently in programming languages in different guises is *nested opening and closing brackets,* such as parentheses and **begin/end** pairs. Well-formed nested bracket structures can be defined as follows: An open bracket "(" followed by a closing one ")" is a well-formed pair, i.e, ( ). If S is a well-formed structure, then so it (S); if S_1 and S_2 are well-formed structures then so is $S_1 S_2$.

Examples are ( ), ( ) ( ), (( )), ( )(( )( ), (( )( )) ((( )( ))). The language of all such well-formed structures is generated by the BNF grammar[1] $G_{(\ )}$:

$$\langle \text{pairs} \rangle ::= \langle \text{simple pairs} \rangle \mid \langle \text{simple pairs} \rangle \langle \text{pairs} \rangle$$
$$\langle \text{simple pairs} \rangle ::= (\ ) \mid (\langle \text{pairs} \rangle)$$

Figure 6.6 shows a parse of a parentheses string according to this grammar.

A grammar should be designed not only to produce the correct sentences of the language but also to have syntactic categories that correspond to the semantics of the language. Simple arithmetic expressions provide a good example of this point. Consider the following BNF grammar G_{expr} for simple arithmetic expressions:

$$\langle \text{expression} \rangle ::= \langle \text{term} \rangle \mid \langle \text{addop} \rangle \langle \text{term} \rangle \mid$$
$$\qquad\qquad\qquad \langle \text{expression} \rangle \langle \text{addop} \rangle \langle \text{term} \rangle$$
$$\langle \text{term} \rangle ::= \langle \text{factor} \rangle \mid \langle \text{term} \rangle \langle \text{multop} \rangle \langle \text{factor} \rangle$$
$$\langle \text{factor} \rangle ::= \langle \text{unsigned integer} \rangle \mid \langle \text{variable} \rangle \mid (\langle \text{expression} \rangle)$$
$$\langle \text{addop} \rangle ::= + \mid -$$
$$\langle \text{multop} \rangle ::= \times \mid /$$
$$\langle \text{unsigned integer} \rangle ::= \langle \text{digit} \rangle \mid \langle \text{unsigned integer} \rangle \langle \text{digit} \rangle$$
$$\langle \text{digit} \rangle ::= 0 \mid 1 \mid 2 \mid 3 \mid 4 \mid 5 \mid 6 \mid 7 \mid 8 \mid 9$$
$$\langle \text{variable} \rangle ::= \langle \text{letter} \rangle \mid \langle \text{variable} \rangle \langle \text{letter} \rangle \mid \langle \text{variable} \rangle \langle \text{digit} \rangle$$
$$\langle \text{letter} \rangle ::= A \mid B \mid \cdots \mid Z$$

A parse for the expression $A + B \times C + (E - F)$ is shown in Figure 6.7. The grammar is designed so that the $\langle \text{multop} \rangle$'s take precedence over the $\langle \text{addop} \rangle$'s in parsing; for example, the grammar takes an expression such as $A + B \times C$ and syntactically decomposes it into A, $+$, $(B, \times, C)$ rather than say $(A, +, B)$, $\times$, C. This is convenient for generating the correct machine language code from such an expression.

The BNF notation has been extended in a variety of ways to make it even more convenient and useful. One particularly appealing addition eliminates those simple recursions where it is desired to express the iterative generation

---

[1] In most cases, it is sufficient to just give the rules R for the grammar; the start symbol is normally the left part of the first rule and the N and V sets are usually obvious.

of 0 or more instances of a string. We use the notation $\{\alpha\}$ to denote 0 or more instances of α. Thus, for example, in G_{int}, the ⟨digit sequence⟩ rule can be replaced by the simpler:

⟨digit sequence⟩ ::= ⟨digit⟩{⟨digit⟩}.

In $G_{(\ )}$, the ⟨pairs⟩ rule can be expressed as:

⟨pairs⟩ ::= ⟨simple pairs⟩{⟨simple pairs⟩}

and in G_{expr}, we can have simple rules for ⟨unsigned integer⟩ and ⟨variable⟩:

⟨unsigned integer⟩ ::= ⟨digit⟩{⟨digit⟩}
⟨variable⟩ ::= ⟨letter⟩{⟨letter⟩ | ⟨digit⟩}

The new rule for ⟨variable⟩ states that "a ⟨variable⟩ is defined as a ⟨letter⟩ followed by 0 or more elements, each of which is a ⟨letter⟩ or a ⟨digit⟩."

A concise and easy-to-understand notation for representing each rule in a grammar is the two-dimensional *syntax diagram*. Non-terminal symbols are enclosed in rectangles and terminal symbols appear in ovals or circles; the rectangular and oval boxes are connected by arrows. Examples are given in Figure 6.8. Generation occurs by tracing the arrows in the diagram; on reaching an oval box, the contained symbol is generated; a rectangular box means to transfer to the rule corresponding to the box contents and then returning after this latter rule has been used. Note that the diagrams permit

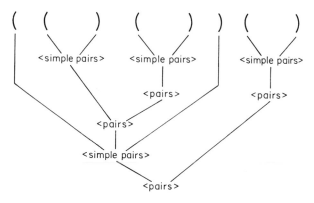

Figure 6.6   Parse of a Parenthesis String

the elimination of recursion in those cases where a simple iteration is described. The Appendix contains a complete specification of Algolic in both an extended BNF notation and also in terms of syntax diagrams.

Before leaving BNF, we should briefly note some of its limitations. The syntax of many languages cannot be described in BNF. A classic example is the language $\{a^n b^n c^n : n \geq 1\}$, where the notation x^n means n instances of the symbol x; it is a theorem that a BNF grammar does not exist for this language. Most programming languages cannot be completely described by BNF. For example, to describe syntactically the constraint that identifiers must be declared before they are used is not possible. Nevertheless, the notation is useful for handling most aspects of programming language syntax and represents a good compromise between convenience and tractability on the one hand and completeness on the other.

A great deal of work has been done on language syntax and it is a reasonably well understood area, at least for programming languages. Syntax, however, is just a small part of language specification, albeit an important one. One is ultimately only interested in semantics; formal syntax methods provide a systematic approach to examining the meaning of sentences in a

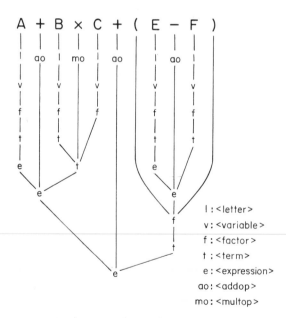

Figure 6.7   Parse of an Expression

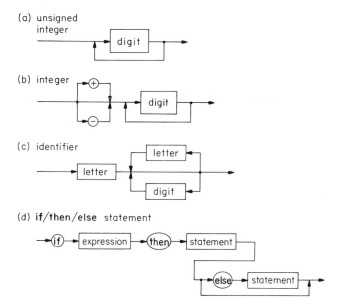

Figure 6.8   Grammar Rules in Syntax Diagram Form

language in terms of the meaning of their structural components. Unfortunately, useful techniques for expressing language semantics are not nearly as advanced as those for syntax; this is one of the more active areas of computer science research. At this point, the semantics of a programming language is usually expressed in ordinary English, as we have done for Algolic in the Appendix.

6.2.3   Data Types and Structured Data

The Algolic language provides four basic data types for variables—integer, real, Boolean, and character. Associated with each type is a set of values. Thus a variable of type *integer* can have any value from the set of integers and a variable of type *Boolean* can assume any value from the set of Booleans {true, false}. Because most languages have a variety of data types and it has proven useful to be able to construct new types, we define the notion of type more precisely:

A *data type T* is a set. The elements of *T* are called the *values* of the type. A variable of type *T* can only have values from the set defining *T*.

We use the notation

$$\text{\textbf{type} } name = set$$

for illustrating different types, where *name* is the name given to the data type and *set* specifies the assumable values of *name*.

Examples:

1. **type** *day* = {*Sun, Mon, Tues, Wed, Thurs, Fri, Sat*}
   If *x* is a variable of type *day*, then *x* may take on values only from the given set.
2. **type** *month* = {*Jan, Feb, Mar, April, May, June, July, Aug, Sept, Oct, Nov, Dec*}
3. **type** *evenint* = {*2i : i* an integer}
   This denotes the set of even integers.
4. **type** *vowel* = {*a, e, i, o, u*}
5. **type** *sex* = {*male, female*}

For each data type *T*, there is a corresponding set of *operators* for manipulating and testing the values of the type. Thus, for the type *integer*, the normal arithmetic operators and relational operators are defined, whereas for type *Boolean*, there is a set of logical operators. Many data types have a natural *ordering* that can be employed for testing operations. In Example 1 above, one reasonable definition for type *day* is *Sun* < *Mon* < *Tues* ... < *Sat*; this permits a programmer to make tests of the form $x = y$, $x < y$, or $x > y$, where *x* and *y* are of type *day*.

It is also useful to have *predecessor* and *successor* operations on ordered types, defined by:

$y = pred(x)$ means that $y < x$ and there does not exist a *z* such that
    $y < z < x$.
$y = succ(x)$ means that $y > x$ and there does not exist a *z* such that
    $x < z < y$.

The type *integer* has the normal $pred(x) = x - 1$ and $succ(x) = x + 1$, while the ordering above for *day* gives the function: $pred(Sun)$ = undefined, $pred(Mon) = Sun$, ..., $pred(Sat) = Fri$, and $succ(Sun) = Mon$, $succ(Mon) = Tues$, ..., $succ(Sat)$ = undefined. Similarly the *character* data type has a natural ordering, called the collating sequence, for which $"A" < "B" < "C" < \cdots$.[2]

The values of the types discussed so far are atomic or *scalar*; they are unstructured and are not decomposable into other types. We saw in Chapter

3 how the elements of the standard scalar types may be represented as bit sequences. Similarly, other scalar types can easily be coded for computer storage and manipulation.

A Program Example with New Scalar Types: Computing Tomorrow's Date.

Let us assume that a programming language permits the definition of the new scalar data types defined in the examples above. We can declare and manipulate constants and variables of these types as illustrated by the following program.

Suppose that today's date is defined by four variables:

$d : day ;$ $m : month ;$ $n : integer ;$ $year : integer ;$

For example, Tues May 5 1978 is represented as $d = Tues$, $m = May$, $n = 5$, and $year = 1978$.

The purpose of the program is to compute tomorrow's date; e.g., Wed May 6 1978. A computation of this type is necessary in a digital watch that always displays the current date.

```
{Compute tomorrow's date.}
changemonth: Boolean; n, year: integer;
d: day;      m: month;
{Today's data is given by d, m, n, year.}
changemonth := false;
if n ≥ 28 then {possible month change}
begin
    if (m = Feb) and ((year mod 4 ≠ 0) or n = 29) then
        changemonth := true {month is Feb. Check also for leap year.}
    else if (n = 30) and (m = Sept or m = April or m = June or
        m = Nov) then
        changemonth := true {month is a 30 day month.}
    else if n = 31 then changemonth := true
end;
```

---

[2] One must be careful about special characters such as "." and "$", since there is no single ordering that is universally accepted. The ordering is normally based on the character code that is used.

if *changemonth* **then** {new month}
begin *n* := 1; {first day}
  if *m* = *Dec* **then** {new year}
  begin *m* := *Jan*; *year* := *year* + 1 **end**
  else *m* := *succ*(*m*)
end
else *n* := *n* + 1;
if *d* = *Sat* **then** *d* := *Sun* **else** *d* := *succ*(*d*)
{Tomorrow's date is now in *d, m, n, year*.}

The simplest example of a *structured* data type is the array, introduced in Chapter 3. Structured data types are composed of elements of other types and ultimately are defined in terms of scalar data types. Thus, the array *x* : **array** [1..10] **of** *integer* is composed of 10 elements of type *integer*. Similarly, the operations that can be performed on structured data are specified in terms of defined operations on their scalar components. The computer representation of structured types is based on the representation of their scalar components.

6.2.3.1 Arrays

An array type may be defined with the notation:

type *name* = **array** [*lb*..*ub*] **of** *ComponentType*

where *name* is the name of the particular array type and *ComponentType* gives the type of the array elements.

Example: **type** *X* = **array** [1..10] **of** *integer*

denotes an array type named *X* with 10 components indexed by the integers 1 through 10, each component assuming a value of type integer. To use this type, we might declare *a* and *b* to be of type *X* with a declaration

$$a, b : X$$

We can now use $a[e_1]$ and $b[e_2]$ in program statements to access components of *a* and *b*, where e_1 and e_2 are expressions that evaluate to integers in the range 1 to 10.

Of course, for arrays, we simplify this declaration process considerably by combining the type declaration with the declaration of variables of the type:

$$a, b : \textbf{array} [1..10] \textbf{ of } integer$$

The array components could be of any scalar type; for example,

$$year: \textbf{array} [1..365] \textbf{ of } day$$

declares the array variable *year* to have 365 components, so that any element *year*[*i*] is of type *day*.

Generalizing this notion, the *ComponentType* of an array can also be any structured type. Multi-dimensional arrays are obtained by declaring the *ComponentType* to be also of type **array**. Thus, for example,

$$A: \textbf{array} [1..n] \textbf{ of array } [1..m] \textbf{ of } character$$

specifies an $n \times m$ character array (matrix) *A*. *A* has *n* elements, *A*[*i*], $i = 1, \ldots, n$, each of which is an array of *m* character elements. The *j*th component of *A*[*i*] is denoted *A*[*i, j*] using conventional programming notation; similarly, the declaration is abbreviated to

$$A: \textbf{array}[1..n, 1..m] \textbf{ of } character$$

A three-dimensional array can be analogously declared; for example,

$$M: \textbf{array}[1..3, 1..6, 0..4] \textbf{ of } Boolean$$

specifies the 90 Boolean elements $M[1, 1, 0]$, $M[1, 1, 1]$, $\ldots$, $M[3, 6, 4]$.

Program Examples:

1. Matrix Multiplication
   If *a* is an $n \times r$ matrix and *b* is an $r \times m$ matrix, then the matrix product $c = a \times b$ is given by:

$$c_{ij} = \sum_{k=1}^{r} a_{ik} \times b_{kj} \qquad i = 1, \ldots, n; \qquad j = 1, \ldots, m$$

This computation can be performed by the program segment:

```
a:array[1..n, 1..r] of real ;
b:array[1..r, 1..m] of real ;
c:array[1..n, 1..m] of real ;
x:real ;      i, j, k: integer ;
for i := 1 upto n do
  for j := 1 upto m do
  begin x := 0 ;
    for k := 1 upto r do x := x + a[i, k] × b[k, j] ;
    c[i, j] := x
  end
```

2. Display of a Three-Dimensional Board Game

Consider a computer version of three-dimensional "Scrabble," where words may be constructed in any of the front view, side view, or top view planes of a three-dimensional board (Figure 6.9). The board can be represented by an array:

Board : **array**[1..15, 1..15, 1..15] **of** *character*;

The following program segments will display all the 45 planes of the board. The program uses the output function

$$writeln(a_1, \ldots, a_n)$$

which writes the items $a_1, \ldots, a_n$ and then *skips to the next line*.

```
{Display front view planes.}
for k := 1 upto 15 do
begin writeln('front view—plane', k);
   for i := 1 upto 15 do
   begin for j := 1 upto 15 do write(Board[i, j, k]);
      writeln {Write a blank line}
   end
end;
{Display side view planes.}
for k := 15 downto 1 do
begin writeln('side view—plane', k);
   for i := 1 upto 15 do
   begin for j := 1 upto 15 do write(Board[i, k, j]);
      writeln
   end
end;
{Display top view planes.}
for k := 1 upto 15 do
begin writeln('top view—plane', k);
   for i := 15 downto 1 do
   begin for j := 1 upto 15 do write(Board[k, j, i]);
      writeln
   end
end
```

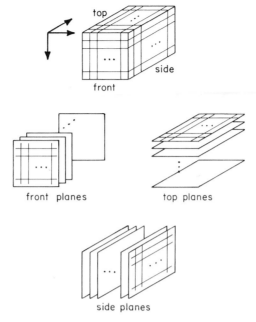

Figure 6.9   Three-Dimensional Board

6.2.3.2   Records

All components of an array must be of the same type and are referenced uniformly through their indices. It is also extremely useful to have structures where each component may be of a different type and can be referenced with different identifiers. The record types provide this capability. A record type is defined by the syntax:

⟨record type⟩ ::= **record** ⟨field list⟩ **end**

where the ⟨field list⟩ specifies one or more fields of the record. Each field is given by the syntax:

⟨field⟩ ::= ⟨identifier⟩ {,identifier} : ⟨type⟩

Examples:

1. The date used in the program example given at the beginning of Section 6.2.3 can be conveniently defined as a record type:

   type *date* = **record** *d*: *day*;
                    m: *month*;
                    n: *integer*;
                    y : *integer*
       end

   The record type named *date* has four fields, denoted *d, m, n,* and *y* respectively.

2. Complex numbers are mathematically represented by the form $a + bi$, where a and b are real numbers and $i^2 = -1$. When one performs computations with complex numbers, a record of type complex is often useful:

   type *complex* = **record** *re, im* : *real*
                         end

   The record type named *complex* has two fields, named *re* and *im* respectively.

   Let t be a record type with fields identified by $f_1, f_2, \ldots, f_n$. Then, a variable x of record type t can be defined with the declaration $x:t$. A component of x is accessed by $x \cdot f$, where f is the field name of the record component; i.e., $x \cdot f_1, x \cdot f_2, \ldots, x \cdot f_n$ reference each of the components of x.

Examples :

1. Using the record type *date* of the last example, the declaration *today: date* declares *today* to be a record variable of type *date. today·d, today·m, today·n,* and *today·y,* are used to access the components of *today*.

2. A variable z of the *complex* type defined in the last example is declared by: *z:complex*. The "real" field of z is referenced by $z \cdot re$ while the "imaginary" part is given by $z \cdot im$.

Program Example in Complex Arithmetic

If $z = x + yi$ and $w = u + vi$ are two complex numbers, with $x, y, u,$ and v real and $i^2 = -1$, then the complex sum $c = z + w$ and complex product $f = z \times w$ are defined:

$$c = (x + u) + (y + v)i \quad \text{and} \quad f = (xu - yv) + (xv + yu)i.$$

This computation can be easily programmed:

z, w, c, f: *complex* ;
$c \cdot re := z \cdot re + w \cdot re$;
$c \cdot im := z \cdot im + w \cdot im$;
$f \cdot re := z \cdot re \times w \cdot re - z \cdot im \times w \cdot im$;
$f \cdot im := z \cdot re \times w \cdot im + z \cdot im \times w \cdot re$

6.2.3.3 Dynamic Structures

The data types and structures we have considered so far are fixed in size; each has a predetermined constant number of components and each component is of fixed length. Structures of *dynamic* size also appear naturally in computations. By "dynamic size," we mean that the number of components of the structure can grow or shrink as a computation proceeds. Unless one is willing to waste much storage space, a mechanism for dynamically allocating storage to the structure during growth and freeing storage when the structure shrinks is required. The complexity and inherent inefficiency of dynamic storage allocation and liberation are the main drawbacks of these types of structures. However, they are so useful that they appear in most advanced programming languages.

One example of a type that often logically changes in size is the *string*, introduced earlier in Chapter 3. The definition of a string as a *sequence of zero or more characters* leads to a natural implementation as an array of characters. Thus the string $x = $ '*abc*' can be constructed by first declaring x as an array:

$$x: \textbf{array}[1 . . 3] \textbf{ of } character$$

and then making the assignments:

$$x[1] := \text{'}a\text{'}; x[2] := \text{'}b\text{'}; x[3] := \text{'}c\text{'} ;$$

To permit one form of dynamic sizes, one might expand the array declaration so that *variables* as well as constants can be included in the upper and lower bound specifications. For example, the above declaration could be changed to

$$x: \textbf{array}[1 . . n] \textbf{ of } character$$

When the array declaration is processed during program execution, the particular value of the variable n determines the actual upper bound size. Such dynamic array facilities are available in a number of languages and are widely used. However, they are not particularly helpful for dealing with strings. What is needed is a more direct scheme for specifying strings and their operations—one that treats strings directly as sequences. We present such a scheme below.

A string is a sequence of 0 or more characters enclosed in quotation marks; examples are 'abl', 'XY23X', '' (the null string), and 'Example'. *String* is a type in the sense that we have used it; i.e., the type *string* is a set of character sequences. The declaration

$$x: string$$

declares x to be a variable of type *string*. Typical operations on strings and string variables are:

1. concatenation, denoted by the operator **cat**:
   Let a and b be strings. Then a **cat** b produces a new string consisting of b concatenated onto the end of a.

Examples:

   (1) if a = '123' and b = 'xy', then a **cat** b = '123xy'.
   (2) 'main' **cat** 'loop' = 'mainloop'.

2. substring, denoted by the function *substr:*
   Let s be a string and i and j be positive integers, $i \le j$. Then $substr(s, i, j)$ produces a string consisting of the ith through jth characters of s.

Examples:

   (1) if s = '12345', i = 2, and j = 4, then $substr(s, i, j)$ = '234'
   (2) $substr('xyz', 2, 2)$ = 'y'
   (3) $substr('xyz', 1, 2)$ = 'xy'
   If s has fewer than i characters, then $substr(s, i, j)$ = ' ', the *null* string; if s has fewer than j characters, say $k < j$, then $substr(s, i, j)$ = $substr(s, i, k)$.

3. $length(s)$, where s is a string, returns the number of characters in the string s.
   Thus $length('xyz')$ = 3.
   The *null or empty* string ' ', has $length(' ')$ = 0.
   Note that the following relation holds:

$$s = substr(s, 1, i) \textbf{ cat } substr(s, i + 1, length(s))$$

Searching for a Substring

We consider an instance of the following common problem in text processing. Given a string s, count the number of times that the substring r appears in s. For our example, let r be the string '⎵at⎵'. A straightforward but relatively inefficient counting and matching algorithm is:

```
s, cs: string: count: integer ;
count := 0; cs := s; {cs will hold the current string.}
while length(cs) ≥ 4 do
   if substr(cs, 1, 4) = '⎵at⎵' then
   begin count := count + 1;
      cs := substr(cs, 4, length(cs))
   end
   else cs := substr(cs, 2, length(cs))
```

Producing the String Representation of an Integer

Let x be a positive integer. The problem is to produce the character string representing x; for example, if $x = 135$, we wish to compute the string '135'. This is similar to the computation that an output routine must perform in order to write out a number—the integer representation must be converted to the corresponding character string representation. The conversion algorithm uses our familiar mechanism for obtaining each digit of x:

```
s, c: string ; x, digit: integer ;
read(x) ;
{x contains integer to be converted to a string s.}
s := ' ' ; {Initial string is null.}
while x ≠ 0 do
begin digit := x mod 10 ;
   x := x ÷ 10 ;
   if digit = 0 then c := '0'
   else if digit = 1 then c := '1'
         ⋮
   else c := '9' ;
   s := c cat s {Build string.}
end ;
if s = ' ' then s := '0'   {just in case x = 0 initially}
```

Two dynamic structures have been introduced so far: dynamic arrays and strings. A third one of great importance is the *list structure*. These are used extensively in symbol manipulation problems that occur in artificial intelligence research (Chapter 9), symbolic mathematical computations such as symbolic algebra, symbolic integration, and theorem proving. Lists are analogous to dynamic records and were briefly described in Chapter 3.

6.2.4 Procedures and Functions

Procedures, functions, subroutines, and subprograms are all names given to self-contained program modules that can be invoked and executed at more than one place in a program by simply "calling" them. Without these mechanisms, it would be necessary either to repeat all the statements of a module wherever they are to be used in a program, or to transfer explicitly to the module and at the same time record a return location so that the module can properly transfer back upon completion. Procedures[3] also are natural organizational tools that make large programs easier to structure into subparts. Because of its usefulness, all major programming languages provide a procedure facility.

As an introductory example, suppose it is necessary to switch or interchange the values of two variables x and y at several places in a program. The code for this task can be placed in a procedure named *Switchxy*, defined as follows:

procedure *Switchxy* ;
begin $t := x$; $x := y$; $y := t$ **end**

Whenever the x-y interchange is desired, the programmer inserts a procedure *call*:

Switchxy

The language's compiler produces code to transfer to the first statement of the procedure and transfer back at the end of the procedure to the calling program.

Usually, it is convenient to pass *parameters* or arguments to procedures so that the same code can be executed with different variables. For example, suppose that we wish to interchange many variables in the program, not just x and y. Rather than have a separate procedure for each pair, the variables to be interchanged are passed as parameters. The procedure definition then becomes:

---

[3] We will use the terms "procedure" and "function" here because they are closest in spirit to Algolic. When it is not necessary to distinguish between them, the term "procedure" will include "function" also.

procedure *Switch*(*a*, *b*) ; {*a* and *b* are dummy names for the parameters.}
begin *t* := *a* ; *a* := *b* ; *b* := *t*   **end**

Now the call *Switch*(*x*, *y*) will interchange the values of *x* and *y* while the call *Switch*(*u*, *v*) will interchange the values of the variables *u* and *v*. When the procedure is called, the *actual* parameters (the parameters in the call) are systematically substituted for the *formal* or dummy parameters given in the procedure definition.

The temporary variable *t* in the *Switch* procedure is of no concern outside the procedure. It is often necessary to use several such variables that are *local* to the procedure. To ensure this locality, these variables are usually declared inside the procedure. The types of the parameters of a procedure are also specified in the procedure definition. The types of the actual parameters must then match the declared types or an error is flagged; this type checking greatly aids in debugging programs. Assuming that all variables are of type *integer*, our *Switch* procedure becomes:

procedure *Switch*(*a*: *integer*, *b*: *integer*); *t*: *integer*;
begin *t* := *a* ; *a* := *b* ; *b* := *t*   **end**

Examples:

1. Below is a procedure *Sort3* that sorts three integers in ascending sequence. Thus on return from a call *Sort3*(*u*, *v*, *w*), the values of the variables will have been permuted so that *value*(*u*) ≤ *value* (*v*) ≤ *value*(*w*). *Sort3* uses the *Switch* procedure declared above and illustrates how one procedure may call another.

```
procedure Sort3(a, b, c: integer) ;
begin
  if a > b then Switch(a, b) ;
  if b > c then
  begin
    Switch(b, c) ;
    if a > b then Switch(a, b)
  end
end
```

2. The *gcd* algorithm described in Chapter 2 can be defined as a procedure:

```
procedure gcd(m: integer, n: integer); r: integer ;
begin
  while n ≠ 0 do
  begin r := m mod n ; m := n ; n := r   end
end
```

This procedure may be invoked, for example, in a program:

$x := 15; y := 80; gcd(x, y); write(x);$
$a := 66; b := 75; gcd(a, b); write(a);$
$read(x, y); gcd(x, y); write(x)$

This program segment would produce the output 5, 3, and the *gcd* of the two numbers read by *read(x, y)*.

3. The dot product of two vectors a and b with n components is defined

$$c = a \cdot b = \sum_{i=1}^{n} a_i b_i$$

A procedure that computes a dot product, with a, b, and n as parameters is:

procedure *dotproduct(a, b: vector, n: integer, c: real)*;
i: integer;
begin
  $c := 0$;
  for $i := 1$ **upto** n **do** $c := c + a[i] \times b[i]$
end

where vector is a type declared as follows:

type *vector* = **array**$[1..n]$ **of** *real*

The last two examples return a single value, either the *gcd* of two numbers or the dot product, respectively. These procedures are implementations of mathematical *functions*. Often, it is desirable to use the results of such functions in expressions without necessarily assigning the result to a variable. Common mathematical functions such as logarithm, square root, and the trigonometric functions are frequently used in this way. Using our Algolic framework, a **function** can be declared in a manner similar to a **procedure**, except that we declare the type of value returned and indicate this result by "assigning" it to the function name. Example 2, *gcd*, can be rewritten as a function:

function *gcd(m, n: integer) : integer*;
r: integer;
begin
  while $n \neq 0$ **do**
  begin $r := m$ **mod** n; $m := n$; $n := r$ **end**;
  $gcd := m$ {returned result}
end

Then, for example, the call *gcd*(30, 75) will return the value 15. *gcd* could then be used in an expression, such as 25 + *gcd*(30, 75) ÷ *x*; if *x* has the value 5, this expression evaluates to 25 + 15 ÷ 5 = 28.

6.3   COMPILERS

A compiler is a translator program that takes programs written in some high-level language and translates them into equivalent programs in some lower-level language, usually machine or assembly language. The high-level input language is called the *source language* while the output is called the *target or object language.*

The translation process can be logically broken into three phases as illustrated in Figure 6.10. The purpose of *lexical analysis* is to decompose the source program into its elementary symbols or *tokens*, such as variable names, constants, operators, and special symbols. The tokens are fed to the *syntax analysis* component which parses the source program and checks that it is syntactically correct. The output of the syntax analysis phase is passed to *code generation* where the equivalent target machine program code is produced. In order to introduce these processes and some of their associated data structures in more detail, we will trace through the compilation of an Algolic statement into a hypothetical assembly language as illustrated in Figure 6.11.

The tokens or elementary components of the source language statement are: **if**, *b*, =, 15, **then**, *x*, :=, (,*a*, +,*b*,), /, *x*, **else**, *y*, :=, *x*. It is convenient to divide the tokens into five classes:

1. Identifiers(ID):   *b, x, a, c, y*
2. Constants (CONST):   15
3. Keywords of the language(KW):   **if, then, else**
4. Arithmetic and logical operations(OP):   =, +, /
5. Special symbols (SP):   :=, (,)

As the source code is processed by the lexical analyzer or scanner, the class of each token is determined and a unique numeric identifier is assigned to each symbol. Thus, the scanner might produce the following sequence of (token class, numeric identifier) pairs from the example source statement:

(KW, 3), (ID, 7), (OP, 6), (CONST, 25), (KW, 12), (ID, 5), (SP, 11), (SP, 10), (ID, 13), (OP, 2), (ID, 11), (SP, 12), (OP, 8), (ID, 5), (KW, 19), (ID, 18), (SP, 4), (ID, 5).

where (KW, 3) represents the token "**if**", (ID, 7) represents "*b*", (OP, 6) stands for "=", and so on.

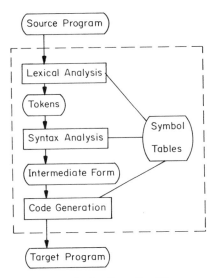

Figure 6.10   Compiler Phases

This representation of the token sequence is convenient for the parser.

The detailed description of each token is stored in a *symbol table*. Keywords, operators, and special symbols are placed in the symbol table at the beginning of the compilation process while identifiers and constants are inserted in the table as they are encountered for the first time by the scanner. When a token is discovered by the scanner, the symbol table is searched and the unique numeric identifier is returned.

The parser transforms the source program, represented by the token sequence, into an equivalent intermediate language that can be handled easily by the code generator. One of the most common and useful forms of parser output is *Polish postfix* notation. This form closely resembles the source program except that operators follow their operands in expressions and branching instructions are inserted where necessary. For an **if/then/else** statement:

   if ⟨Boolean expression⟩ **then**⟨statement 1⟩ **else** ⟨statement 2⟩,

the Polish postfix is:

   Polish postfix for ⟨Boolean expression⟩
   *IFJUMP L*1 {Transfer if ⟨Boolean expression⟩ is false.}
   Polish postfix for ⟨statement 1⟩
   *JUMP L*2 {Transfer to end of statement.}
   *L*1: *Polish postfix for* ⟨statement 2⟩
   *L*2:

A possible postfix form of our example statement produced by a parser is:

b, 15, =	{Polish postfix of b = 15. Evaluates to true or false.}
*IFJUMP L*1	{Transfer on false.}
x, a, c, +, x, /, :=	{Polish of $x := (a + c)/x$. true part of **if/then/else**}
*JUMP L*2	{Transfer to end of statement.}
label 1: y, x, :=	{Polish for $y := x$. **else** part of statement}
label 2:	

The next section discusses Polish postfix notation in more detail.

"Semantic" checking and analysis are also performed during the parsing phase. This process includes such tasks as checking that variables are declared before being used and that variables are used correctly. For example, an identifier declared to name an array cannot subsequently appear as a simple unsubscripted variable; or, in the arithmetic expression $a + c$, a and c cannot be type Boolean.

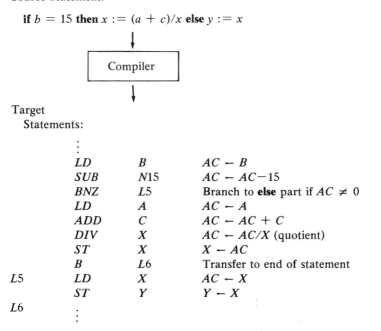

Source Statement:

   if b = 15 **then** $x := (a + c)/x$ **else** $y := x$

Compiler

Target
Statements:

	LD	B	$AC \leftarrow B$
	SUB	N15	$AC \leftarrow AC - 15$
	BNZ	L5	Branch to **else** part if $AC \neq 0$
	LD	A	$AC \leftarrow A$
	ADD	C	$AC \leftarrow AC + C$
	DIV	X	$AC \leftarrow AC/X$ (quotient)
	ST	X	$X \leftarrow AC$
	B	L6	Transfer to end of statement
L5	LD	X	$AC \leftarrow X$
	ST	Y	$Y \leftarrow X$
L6			

Figure 6.11   Example of Source and Object Statements

The Polish postfix form of our source statement is now passed to the code generation phase. In preparation for actually generating the code, the postfix instructions might first be transformed into another more convenient form called *quadruples*. A quadruple is a list of four items $(op, a1, a2, r)$, which is interpreted as "perform the operation op on the operands $a1$ and $a2$ and store the result in x." Quadruples obtained from the postfix code might be:

1:	$(=, b, 15, T1)$	$\{T1 \leftarrow (b = 15)\}$
2:	$(BNZ, T1, 6,)$	$\{$**if** $T1 \neq 0$ **then go to** quadruple 6$\}$
3:	$(+, a, c, T2)$	$\{T2 \leftarrow a + c\}$
4:	$(/, T2, x, x)$	$\{x \leftarrow T2 / x\}$
5:	$(BR, 7, ,)$	$\{$**go to** quadruple 7$\}$
6:	$(ST, y, x,)$	$\{y \leftarrow x\}$
7:		

Here, $T1$ and $T2$ are new *temporary* variables that are generated internally to store the results of the operations.

The quadruples are useful for some forms of program optimization and also for the machine storage and register allocation which are performed during code generation. The final assembly language target statements are now synthesized from the quadruples.

The particular intermediate languages that were employed for the example are not unique but are typical. Similarly, there is a large variety of possible compiler organizations, most of which correspond generally to that of Figure 6.10. This brief discussion has omitted many details and complexities; our purpose has been to present an introductory overview of the various compilation tasks. In the next two sections, we examine in more depth the Polish postfix notation and some aspects of symbol table organization and processing.

6.3.1 Polish Postfix Notation

Binary operators appear between their operands in ordinary mathematical and programming language expressions. In this form, the expression is said to be in *infix* notation. Postfix notation was first used by the Polish logician J. Lukasiewicz and is consequently also termed Polish postfix. Here, operators immediately follow their operands. Thus, the infix expression $a + b$ has the postfix form $a \; b \; +$.

Example:

Infix: $a \times (b + c) - d$

Postfix: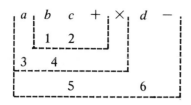

The operator $+$ has the operands denoted by 1 and 2; $\times$ has the operands 3, 4; and $-$ has the operands 5, 6.

Polish postfix is a convenient intermediate language for compilers as illustrated in the last section. It is also a language that can easily be directly interpreted or executed by computers; because of this convenience, postfix notation appears directly as the machine language of some computers, called stack computers, as well as electronic calculators. It is widely used in compilers, interpreters, and machines because the left-to-right order of appearance of operators is exactly the right order for invoking these operators; it is also parenthesis-free and thus uses fewer symbols than infix notation.

Conversion to Polish Postfix

We will first consider an algorithm to convert *fully-parenthesized* arithmetic expressions into Polish postfix; assume that the expressions use only single-letter variable identifiers.

1. Define the set AE of fully-parenthesized arithmetic expressions as follows:
   (a) $\alpha \in AE$ where $\alpha \in \{a, b, \ldots, z\}$ i.e., simple variables are AE's.
   (b) If $e_1 \in AE$ and $e_2 \in AE$, then $(e_1 \, \theta \, e_2) \in AE$ where $\theta \in \{+, -, \times, /\}$. Examples of members of AE: b, $(a + b)$, $((x + y)/z)$, $((f - (g \times h)/(j + k))$.
2. The postfix form of any member of AE is given by the following recursive definition:
   (a) Postfix$(\alpha) = \alpha$ for $\alpha \in \{a, b, \ldots, z\}$.
   (b) Postfix$((e_1 \, \theta \, e_2)) = $ Postfix(e_1) Postfix$(e_2) \, \theta$ for $e_1, e_2 \in AE$ and $\theta \in \{+, -, \times, /\}$.

Examples:

Postfix(a) = a

Postfix($(a + b)$) = Postfix(a) Postfix(b) + = a b +

Postfix($((x + y)/z)$) = Postfix($(x + y)$)   Postfix(z)   /

$\qquad\qquad\qquad$ = Postfix(x)   Postfix(y) + z /

$\qquad\qquad\qquad$ = x y + z /

Our infix to postfix conversion algorithm will use a dynamic data structure called a *stack*. A stack is most concisely described as a last-in first-out (LIFO) data structure because elements are removed from the structure in LIFO order. There are two operations associated with a stack:

1.   Push(x)   Insert the element x onto the top of the stack.
2.   Pop   Remove the top element from the stack.

The term stack is particularly appropriate since the Push operation is analogous to a stacking operation, and the Pop operation is analogous to unstacking. For example, stacking one tray on top of another in a cafeteria is similar to a Push and removing trays from the top first corresponds to a Pop.

A stack can be easily implemented using an array. Suppose we wish to use a stack S of integers. S can be defined as an array of sufficient size:

S: **array**[1..500] **of** *integer*

Let *top* be an integer, used as an index to point to the top element of the stack; thus $S[top]$ will always contain the last element Pushed onto the stack. Initially, $top = 0$. The stack is drawn schematically in Figure 6.12(a). The Push and Pop operations are defined:

1.   Push x onto S: $top := top + 1$; $S[top] := x$
2.   Pop: $top := top - 1$
$\qquad$ { An alternative definition stores the top element first;
$\qquad$ e.g., $x := S[top]$; $top := top - 1$}

These operations are illustrated in Figure 6.12(b) and (c). We should also take into account the possibilities of stack overflow ($top > 500$) on a Push and stack underflow ($top < 1$) on a Pop; however, these boundary conditions will be ignored here for simplicity.

The following algorithm will convert a character string representation of a fully-parenthesized arithmetic expression into its equivalent Polish postfix form.

1. The input is an array of characters, *Infix*[1], *Infix*[2], ..., *Infix*[n], $n \geq 1$, denoting a member of *AE*. The input is assumed to be error-free with no blanks; also it is convenient to let *Infix*[n] = ';'.

   Example: $((a + b) - ((c \times d)/e))$; is represented by *Infix*[1]= '(', *Infix*[2]= '(', *Infix*[3]= 'a', *Infix*[4]= '+', ..., *Infix*[17]= ')', *Infix*[18]= ';'

2. The output is an array of characters, *Polish*[1], *Polish*[2], ..., *Polish*[m], $m \geq 0$, representing the Polish postfix form of the input.

   Example: $\text{Postfix}(((a + b) - ((c \times d)/e))) = a\ b + c\ d \times e\ / -$ *Polish*[1] = 'a', *Polish*[2] = 'b', *Polish*[3] = '+', ..., *Polish*[9] = '−'.

The algorithm will also use the variables:

1. an array S of characters, employed as a stack
2. *top:* integer pointer to current top of stack
3. *i*: index into *Infix* array
4. *p*: index into *Polish* array
5. *c*: current input symbol ($c = Infix[i]$)

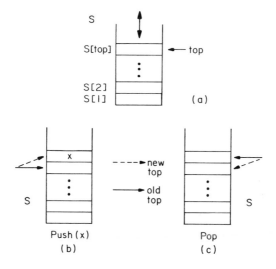

Figure 6.12   Stack Operations

The algorithm almost directly follows from the definition of Polish postfix and processes each successive symbol c of the *Infix* array as follows:

Value of c	Processing
variable $(a, b, \ldots, z)$	Move c directly to output array. (The order of variables is retained.)
operator $(+, -, \times, /)$	Push c onto stack. (c is not output until Postfix of its operands are output.)
'('	Ignore c.
')'	Output top of stack and Pop stack. (End of a sub-expression has been reached; operands have already been output.)

This can be translated into the Algolic code:

```
top := 0 ; p := 0 ; i := 1 ; c := Infix[1] ;
while c ≠ ';' do
begin
   if c = ')' then {Move top of stack to output and Pop.}
   begin p := p + 1 ; Polish[p] := S[top] ; top := top − 1 end
   else
   if (c = '+') or (c = '−') or (c = '×') or (c = '/') then
   {Push operator onto stack.}
   begin top := top + 1 ; S[top] := c end
   else
   if c ≠ '(' then {c must be a variable. Move to output.}
   begin p := p + 1 ; Polish[p] := c end ;
   i := i + 1 ; c := Infix[i]
end
{Polish[j], j = 1, ..., p, contains Polish postfix of input. }
```

To illustrate its operation, we will trace through an example. Let *Infix* contain the expression $((a + ((b - c)/\text{d})) \times e)$; the table below gives the contents of c, S, and *Polish* before and after the main **while** loop is executed:

Next Input Symbol $c = Infix[i]$	Stack S After Processing c	Polish After Processing c
(	—	—
(	—	—
a	—	a
+	+	a
(	+	a
(	+	a
b	+	a b
—	+ —	a b
c	+ —	a b c
)	+	a b c —
/	+ /	a b c —
d	+ /	a b c — d
)	+	a b c — d /
)	—	a b c — d / +
×	×	a b c — d / +
e	×	a b c — d / + e
)	—	a b c — d / + e ×
;	—	a b c — d / + e ×

It is not obvious that the above conversion algorithm always works, but it can be proven correct by working directly from the definition of the postfix form of an *AE*.

Evaluating Polish Postfix

As mentioned earlier, Polish postfix is also useful for directly evaluating arithmetic expressions. Suppose each variable c appearing in an expression has a value associated with it, denoted *value*(c). We will now present an *interpreter* that evaluates arithmetic expressions in Polish postfix. Again, a stack will be a central part of the interpreter algorithm. At any time an operation is to be performed, the top two elements of the stack will contain the values of the operands; the result of the operation becomes the new top stack element, replacing the previous two operands.

Let *Polish*[i], $i = 1, \ldots, m$, $m > 1$, be a character array containing the Polish postfix form of an expression; for convenience, assume that *Polish*[m] = ';'. The program below uses a stack S as before; the program terminates with the value of the expression in $S[1]$.

```
top := 0 ; i := 1 ; c := Polish[1] ;
while c ≠ ';' do
begin
  if c = '+' then
  begin S[top − 1] := S[top − 1] + S[top] ; top := top − 1 end
  else
  if c = '−' then
  begin S[top − 1] := S[top − 1] − S[top] ; top := top − 1 end
  else
  if c = '×' then
  begin S[top − 1] := S[top − 1] × S[top] ; top := top − 1 end
  else
  if c = '/' then
  begin S[top − 1] := S[top − 1] / S[top] ; top := top − 1 end
  else {c must be a variable. Stack its value.}
  begin top := top + 1 ; S[top] := value(c) end ;
  i := i + 1 ; c := Polish[i]
end
```

The simplicity of this algorithm is one of the reasons why postfix is so popular. Let us trace through an example. Suppose the array *Polish* contains $a \, b \, c - d \, / + e \times$; and the variables $a, b, c, d,$ and e have the values 6, 15, 5, 2, and 3, respectively; e.g., $value('a') = 6$, $value('e') = 3$. Then, the expression evaluation proceeds according to the table:

Next Input Symbol $c = Polish[i]$	Stack After Processing c
a	6
b	6, 15
c	6, 15, 5
−	6, 10
d	6, 10, 2
/	6, 5
+	11
e	11, 3
×	33
;	33

We have developed the postfix notation starting with fully-parenthesized infix expressions. At the expense of a more complicated infix to postfix algorithm, parentheses can be optional as in the standard forms of expressions.

In the absence of parentheses, priorities are defined for operators to reflect their precedence; for example '$\times$' has higher priority than '$+$' so that $a + b \times c$ is equivalent to $(a + (b \times c))$. The more general algorithm will not be presented.

We have also assumed that all operators are *binary* operators, requiring two operands. Unary operators can be easily added to the notation. As an example, we will add a *unary minus*. Designate the unary minus by the character '#' to distinguish it from the binary minus. Then, the definition of the set *AE* is augmented with:

$$(c) \text{ if } e \in AE, \text{ then } (\#e) \in AE$$

Similarly, augment the Polish postfix definition with

$$(c) \text{ Postfix}((\#e)) = \text{Postfix}(e) \text{ \# for } e \in AE$$

The change in the infix to postfix conversion algorithm to include # is left as an exercise.

Similarly, other "operators" such as the assignment operator $:=$ and the Boolean operators **and, or,** and **not** can also be included in Polish postfix. It has proven useful to develop postfix forms for all data elements and statements in a language; thus, declarations, subscripted variables, conditional statements, and looping statements have all been given a variety of postfix-like forms. The principle employed is that all operands be immediately followed by their operators.

6.3.2   Symbol Tables

Tables are used in systems and applications software to store symbolic identifiers and their meanings. A symbol table contains a set of *entries*, each entry consisting of an *(argument, value)* pair. The argument field is a character string such as an identifier, keyword, operator, or special symbol. The meaning or attributes of the argument symbol are stored in the value field; in the compiler case, the value of a symbol might include its token class and numeric identifier, and the type and storage location assigned if the symbol is a variable identifier. The argument part of each entry is unique in the table. An example is sketched in Figure 6.13, where the value fields are integers.

The four most common operations that are performed on a symbol table are:

1. Search
    Given a particular symbol, search the table looking for an entry with that symbol as argument. If an entry exists, return the value field.

Argument	Value
X	175
MAIN	0
Y3	−5
IRA	1000
POSTFIX	3765
ALAN	1000
TOP	−1
B	916
FILEID	14
⋮	⋮

Figure 6.13   Symbol Table

2. Insert
    Given an (argument, value) pair, insert it in the table. Insert is often
    preceded by the Search operation to see if the given entry is already in
    the table.
3. Delete
    Delete a given entry from the table. Delete is often preceded by a
    Search to find the location of the entry in the table.
4. Display
    Print the contents of the symbol table in some convenient format.

For the discussion that follows, we will ignore the value fields and represent a symbol table as an integer array *Table* of arguments. Each argument
entry *Table* [i] thus contains a fixed length integer rather than a variable
length character string. (We could retain variable length character strings
using character arrays or the string techniques described in Section 6.2.3.3,
but is is simpler to present the algorithms in Algolic using integers.) The index i for an entry *Table* [i] is considered the *address* of the entry.

The easiest and most straightforward way to maintain the table is as an
unordered linear list. At any time, *Table* [i], $i = 0, 1, \ldots,$ *new* is full and
Table [i], $i = new + 1, \ldots, n - 1$ is unused, where n is the length of the
Table array. A new entry *arg* is inserted in the table with the code:

new := *new* + 1 ;
Table [*new*] := *arg* : {Ignoring check that *new* ≤ $n - 1$}

The table is searched for an argument *arg* by just sequencing through all the
elements:

```
for i := 1 upto new do
    if Table[i] = arg then go to found ;
notfound: ... {arg is not in table.}
    ⋮
found: ... {Table[i] = arg}
```

For entries that are in the table, this process takes $new/2$ iterations through the loop on the average. Thus, new entries can be inserted efficiently but searching is rather slow.

An entry $Table[i]$ in the middle of the table is deleted by either compacting the table (set $Table[j]$ to $Table[j + 1]$ for $j = 1, \ldots, new - 1$, and then set new to $new - 1$) or by tagging the entry with some "undefined" indicator. The compacting solution is relatively slow, requiring about the same amount of work as the searching operation, while the tagging method wastes space. The table can be easily displayed in the order $Table[1]$, $Table[2]$, $\ldots$, but this sort of display can be inconvenient for a human to study unless the table is short.

A more convenient table display is obtained if the table is *ordered* according to the arguments. The table is ordered in *ascending* or *descending* sequence depending on whether $Table[i] > Table[j]$ or $Table[i] < Table[j]$ respectively for all $i > j$. Such a table can be searched efficiently using a *bisection or binary* search in approximately $k \log_2 n$ operations, where n is the size of the table and k is a constant. However, insertions are slow since the table must be reordered whenever a new entry is added. Techniques for ordering a table are called *sorting* methods. Both binary search and sorting methods are discussed in Section 8.4.

One particularly efficient scheme for performing table searches, insertions, and deletions is based on *hashing*, also called hash coding or hash addressing. The address of each entry in a table is obtained by computing some simple logical or arithmetic transformation, say h, on the entry argument; h is called the hash function. One hashing method is to square the numeric representation of the argument and select the central bits or numbers of the result as the table address.

Example:

Suppose that the symbol argument '*XI*' is to be inserted in an array *Table,* that '*XI*' is encoded numerically as 3275, and that we wish a 2-digit address.

Then $h('XI') = 3275^2 \mid$ middle $= 10725625 \mid$ middle $= 25$
       2-digits   2-digits
Then the desired entry is at $Table[25]$.

This method of address calculation should be contrasted with those required for ordered tables. In the latter, an entry address depends entirely on the order of the argument relative to the remainder of the arguments in the table.

Other common hash functions are:

1. Exclusive-OR on parts of the argument
    Break the argument into several bit strings of equal length and take the Exclusive-OR of these. (AND and Inclusive-OR are not satisfactory because they are biased in favor of producing O's and 1's, respectively.)
2. Division
    Divide the numerical representation of the argument by the table size and take the remainder as the argument.
3. Arithmetic summing
    Break the argument into several bit strings of equal length and add the corresponding binary numbers together.

A good hashing function will distribute the argument addresses uniformly over the table. Unfortunately, even with a good function, it is possible that two or more arguments will hash to the same address. This situation is called a *collision*.

Let us be more precise about hashing and collisions. Suppose that *Table* is searched for an entry *arg*. The hashing function *h* is applied to produce the address $adr = h(arg)$. Three possibilities exist at *Table*[*adr*]:

1. *Table*[*adr*] = *arg*
    The search is successful, with the desired entry at *Table*[*adr*].
2. *Table*[*adr*] is undefined.
    The entry *arg* is not in the table. If desired, the entry can now be inserted; this is the standard way to perform insertions. Note that we are assuming some tag or indicator that represents an undefined or vacant entry.
3. *Table*[*adr*] = *arg'* and *arg'* ≠ *arg*
    An address collision has occurred, because either $h(arg') = h(arg)$ or *arg'* was inserted at *adr* by the collision handling mechanism.

Two classes of methods for handling collisions are *rehashing* and *chaining*. Let $adr = h(arg)$ for some argument *arg*. If a collision occurs at *adr*, then rehashing is done by applying a *collision function*, say *c*, to compute a new address; the new address might also involve a collision and *c* is applied again until a vacant or matched entry is found. In general *c* is a function of *adr* and the number of times it has been called for that particular search. The complete address calculation can be expressed by the algorithm:

$adr := h(arg)$; $a := adr$; $i := 1$;
while $Table[a] \neq arg$ **and** (**not** $vacant(a)$) **do**
begin $a := c(adr, i)$; $i := i + 1$ **end**
{a contains the final successful address.}
{This algorithm works as long as the table either contains arg or has at least one vacant entry.}

There are a large number of collision functions that have been successfully used. It is desirable that c "cover" the whole table, so that a vacant entry is eventually found if one exists. One simple way to produce new addresses is to generate them *linearly* from $adr = h(arg)$; this gives the function

$$c(a, i) = (a + i) \bmod n.$$

The linear technique works well if the table is "sparse", i.e., has relatively few entries, but results in many rehashes, i.e., large values of i in $c(a, i)$, before success as the table becomes full.

Better performance is obtained by generating an offset from $h(arg)$ using a "pseudorandom" number generator, say $random(i)$ which generates an i th "random integer between 1 and $n - 1$:

$$c(a, i) = (a + random(i)) \bmod n.$$

$random(i)$, $i = 1, \ldots, n$ should generate all integers between 1 and $n - 1$ so that failure at $c(a, n)$ indicates that all entries of the table have been tested.

The chaining methods are faster than rehashing but require additional storage. The general idea is to link together all entries that hash to the same address, in a manner similar to that described in Section 3.6. We will not present any details of these methods.

The main criteria of "goodness" for any hashing scheme is the expected number E of address computations, sometimes called *probes*, that are necessary to find or insert an entry. E is an increasing function of the fraction α of the table that is occupied. Other goodness factors are the complexity of the hashing and collision handling computations and the amount of storage required. In general, using good standard methods, one should obtain a value of E of approximately 2 with a table about 90 percent full; this impressive performance accounts for the popularity of hashing. It should also be noted that hashing schemes deteriorate rapidly as the table becomes full and, as a consequence, "more than enough" storage must be allocated to the table.

This high performance assumes that the arguments are well-behaved with respect to the hashing and collision functions. In practice, it is possible to obtain poor results; for example, a large number of the particular entries encountered may all hash to the same address. The particular scheme used should be empirically tested against representative sets of arguments in order to catch such problems.

The major advantages of hashing over ordered table techniques are fast insertion of new items, fast deletions, and fast searching. Compared with unordered tables, hashing produces faster searches and deletions. These benefits are somewhat offset by the need for extra storage and *a priori* experiments with particular sets of arguments.

6.4   OPERATING SYSTEMS

Operating Systems (OS's) were briefly introduced in Section 6.1. Their primary functions are to manage and allocate the resources of the computer to user jobs and to provide users with software facilities to simplify the preparation, execution, and maintenance of programs.

OS's may be one or more of the following types according to the kinds of user jobs that they accept:

1. Batch processing
   There is no interaction between users and their jobs during processing. Jobs are submitted in sequential batches on input devices such as card readers, and job results are similarly received in batches from output devices such as printers. The earliest OS's were of this kind; most current systems provide batch services, especially for lengthy "compute-bound" jobs.

2. Interactive
   Users may engage in a variety of "conversations" with the system relevant to their jobs, including interactive program creation, execution, debugging, and maintenance. Jobs are usually submitted through a typewriter-like terminal and/or display device, and interactions occur through these same devices. Most modern general purpose systems provide conversational access.

3. Real-time
   The "user" in this case is one or more external processes (machines, devices, instruments, . . .) that are attached to the computer system, and command the attention of the system by setting hardware flags or generating interrupt signals. Generally, these signals and their associated data must be handled promptly within strict timing constraints or else the external process is seriously degraded or misrepresented.

The earliest systems in the late 1950's processed one user job at a time. However, the economics of computing made it more efficient to share the resources of a computer system among several users simultaneously and to take advantage of the parallel operation of some of the systems hardware components, primarily parallelism between the CPU and IO processors. This led to the development of *multiprogramming* OS's, where more than one job is maintained in main storage at the same time. A particular OS might handle any or all of batch, interactive, or real-time jobs, through the techniques of multiprogramming. Interactive systems that provide computational services to more than one on-line user concurrently are called *time-sharing* systems, because the CPU time is shared among the users. In general, the methods for sharing hardware resources such as CPU's, main and auxiliary storage, IO devices, and IO processors, and for sharing software such as programs and data, are classified as part of multiprogramming.

Because hardware costs have decreased dramatically, some of the original arguments for multiprogramming are no longer compelling. However, regardless of hardware costs, there still remains a *logical* need to share data among user jobs; some examples are inventory, banking, and reservation applications, where several users, often at different locations, require immediate access to the same set of files or data—inventory files, financial files, or reservations data, respectively. In addition, there are many applications where the speed increase due to concurrent operation of physical hardware devices is important and necessary.

User jobs directly or indirectly invoke the OS in two different ways. During user program execution, OS components are called to perform input-output and filing services, to allocate and free resources, and to respond to interrupts and errors. The other method is through statements in a *command and control* language (CCL) that precede each part of a job; these languages are also called *command* languages, *control* languages, or *job control* languages. Statements in a CCL contain either declarative data or requests related to programs, resources, or files. Typically, there are three classes of CCL statements:

1. Job initiation and termination
    The first statement of any interactive or batch job is a CCL command that identifies the user and job, and "logs" them into the system. As part of this job initiation, the command might include such information as user name, job name, user password, account number, job priority, resource limits of the job such as the maximum amount of CPU time and maximum number of output lines, and resource reservations such as the amount of main storage required and the number

of tape units needed. Similarly, the last statement of a job is an implicit or explicit CCL command to terminate the job.

2. Program management

    These are the CCL statements that direct the OS to link, load, and execute user programs, language processors, and utilities. For example, there might be commands to (a) load and execute the Algolic compiler, with the source program coming from the card reader, (b) link and load the compiler output with the Algolic library routines, and (c) execute the program resulting from (b). These commands might also have resource limit and reservation data, as well as the identification of files to be used.

3. File processing

    These statements describe the files required by the particular job phase and request resources related to file processing. Examples include the identification of the primary input and output files; allocation of IO devices; specification of the resources, organization, and access restrictions of a file; and specific editing operations to be invoked such as merging, copying, or modifying a file.

The CCL is often a powerful programming language that may be identical to the standard user language. The user can then express both the operating system control and his or her program in the same language.

6.4.1   OS Architecture

Some understanding of the organization and requirements of an OS can be obtained by means of a simple, yet realistic, example. Consider a multiprogramming system designed to run user jobs that are written in a single high-level language L and submitted in a batch mode on cards. Assume that an interpreter for L is permanently resident in main storage; thus, each user program will be executed directly by the interpreter. The underlying computer consists of the following hardware components: card reader, line printer, operator's console, CPU, main store, a disk unit, and channels connected to the IO devices that permit concurrent operation of the CPU, card reader, line printer, and disk.

At any time, there may be several user jobs in different stages of execution occupying main storage. The main storage allocated to an executing job, called the job's *workspace*, will contain the source program and any required data areas; this is stored in one contiguous area of memory. Workspaces are of variable length, depending on the job; two different jobs will require different size workspaces in general. One function of the OS is to manage these workspaces as jobs enter and leave the system. The OS and language interpreter are assumed to occupy fixed areas of storage.

Figure 6.14 illustrates the allocation of main storage to the operating system, interpreter, and several jobs. In the figure, three jobs have been loaded for execution and have corresponding workspaces.

Let us trace the flow of a user job J as it moves through the system (Figure 6.15). Globally, J passes successively through an Input Spool, Run, and Output Spool phase. The acronym *spool* stands for *S*imultaneous *P*eripheral *O*perations *OnL*ine, and refers to a technique for using the computer IO hardware efficiently. Instead of allocating the card reader and printer to an *executing* job, a virtual card reader and printer are provided on auxiliary storage. Jobs are collected together on auxiliary storage prior to their execution; this phase is called *input spooling*. The job output is written on auxiliary storage during execution. At a convenient later time, the output is written on the printer; this is the *output spooling* phase. There are many advantages to these procedures: a job scheduler can select a job waiting on auxiliary storage for loading and execution, according to the characteristics of the waiting jobs and the jobs already in execution; virtual input-output operations are faster, thus decreasing the amount of time that a job remains in storage; and the load on card readers and printers can be evenly balanced across jobs. The processing in each phase may proceed as follows.

1. Input Spool

    The entire job—control cards, source program, and data cards, if any—is read into main storage and written onto the disk in an incremental manner. During this process, disk space for J must be allocated. At this time, the resource requirements of J are extracted, including main storage, estimated CPU time, input length (number of data cards), and estimated output size (number of print lines). J becomes known to the system by storing its characteristics in a *job table* maintained by the OS.

2. Run

    There may be a large number of jobs that have passed through the Input Spool phase and are waiting on disk for the next step. Eventually, J is selected for loading and execution, and enters the Run phase. Main storage is allocated for J's workspace and the source program is loaded. J is now ready to run and it joins a queue of other active *processes* in the system. These processes may include other jobs that have been loaded and are in various stages of execution, tasks associated with input-output and spooling operations, and other parts of the operating system.

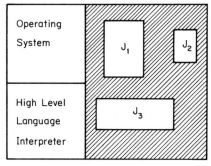

J_i : work space for user job i

▨ : free space

Figure 6.14   Allocation of Main Storage

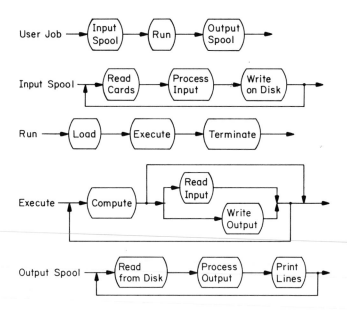

Figure 6.15   User Job Flow

After J is allocated the CPU by the *process scheduler*, the source program is interpreted; this starts the Execute part of the Run phase. Whenever J requests an input record or produces output, the IO is performed through virtual card and print files on the disk. J may lose the CPU while it is waiting for IO completion or due to pre-emption by a higher priority process. In the former case, if J issues an IO request, it normally will have nothing to do until the IO is completed. Other processes may be waiting for the CPU, and J then relinquishes the CPU to permit more efficient multiprogramming; J then enters a *wait* or *blocked* state until the IO completes and it can proceed. In general, J will share the CPU with a number of other processes during its execution. The process scheduler is responsible for allocating the CPU among the active processes.

J's execution will terminate either naturally, because the end of the program has been reached, or as a result of an error condition. J's workspace is then freed and the final resource usage record for the job is stored on disk.

3. Output Spool

    J's output file, including source program, accounting record, and the execution-time output, is then read from disk and printed on the line printer. J's files are then destroyed, and the disk space dedicated to J is released to the system.

The system just described has both *physical* and *logical* parallelism. The CPU and IO processors provide hardware concurrency. From a logical point of view, the user jobs that are active in main storage are also executing concurrently. It is also convenient to view many of the operating system components as parallel activities; for example, input spooling, loading, and output spooling can be treated as separate concurrent tasks. Such logically concurrent software components are called *processes*.

Our example system can be organized according to the process structure of Figure 6.16. Each process can be identified with one or more functional requirements of the system. The J_i are the user job processes and correspond to the resident jobs in execution. The *Loader* is responsible for loading a job from disk to main storage. The J_i and *Loader* are controlled by the *Job Supervisor* process that selects the next job to be loaded, creates and initiates the J_i processes, and terminates job execution. Input and output spooling are handled by the *Spoolin* and *Spoolout* processes, respectively.

Directly communicating with and controlling each IO device is an IO driver process. Spoolin communicates with the *Card Reader Driver* while Spoolout is connected to the *Line Printer Driver*. The *Disk Driver* process

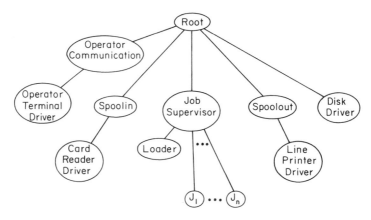

Figure 6.16   Example Process Structure

handles disk IO and services requests from *file system* routines invoked by Spoolin, Loader, and Spoolout; the file system is responsible for the creation, storage, retrieval, and deletion of all files on disk storage, including user job files, accounting records, and systems performance statistics. The IO driver processes handle the idiosyncrasies of particular IO devices and processors, and provide a uniform IO interface to the internal processes.

The *Operator Communication* process implements one- and two-way conversations with the operator's console through the *Operator Terminal Driver*. It provides such services as error handling, updating of user accounting records, retrieval of systems performance statistics, and display of current activities and job queues. *Root* is the creator of all the other components and also acts as an "idle" process when all other processes are in a blocked or waiting state.

The process structure gives one view of an OS, but it hides some aspects such as the file system, resource managers, and process scheduling mechanism. Another view of software architecture is sketched in Figure 6.17. In order to simplify the design, construction, maintenance, and understanding of OS's, the software can be defined and organized as a hierarchy of virtual "machines," where each level of the hierarchy implements a new virtual machine in terms of the facilities provided at lower levels.

The first level above the actual computer hardware is the OS kernel or nucleus. This component provides a set of data structures and routines for implementing higher-level strategies for process and resource control; examples are interrupt-servicing routines, process schedulers, message passing operations through which processes can interact, and queue manipulation

Figure 6.17   OS Virtual Machine Hierarchy

facilities. The hardware resource management level is concerned with the administration and allocation of resources, such as main and auxiliary storage, channels, and IO devices. At the next level, the file management system is responsible for creating, destroying, organizing, reading, writing, modifying, moving, and controlling access to data files. For example, there may be systems programs for maintaining a file directory that identifies and locates all data files accessible to user and system processes; for making a file active and ready for use ("opening" the file), and closing an active file (making it inactive); for loading and unloading a file; and for checking that the use of and access to a file are legitimate. An example of the latter is a situation in which a file owner might specify that his or her file is to be accessed only by a specified group of users in read-only fashion.

The functions of job management are to control the flow of individual and multiple jobs through the system. With the exception of the IO driver processes, most of the processes in the example system of Figure 6.16 perform job management tasks. Other job management functions include the interpretation of command language statements, job scheduling, and job execution control. At the highest level are the user jobs, which run on the virtual machine defined by the OS.

We have presented an outline of the organization and functions of general purpose OS's, using a simple batch processing system as an example. The same gross structure appears in time-sharing systems. Jobs do not pass through a spooling phase but instead are directly entered into the system in real-time by users at their terminals. The processes generated by a user job change between the active and blocked states as they communicate with the terminal, and request and receive resources from the system.

6.4.2 Interactions Among Concurrent Programs

A multiprogrammed OS and the user jobs executing within it can be logically described and implemented as a set of concurrent programs called processes. These processes may interact in two different ways. They can communicate by sending messages and synchronization signals to one another, and they can interact indirectly by competing for systems resources. Both kinds of interactions occur in the example OS presented in the last section.

Examples from Section 6.4.1:

1. Internal processes desiring IO services send appropriate messages to the IO processes.
2. The Spoolin process may send a message to a dormant Job Supervisor whenever it completes spooling of a "first" job.
3. Common data structures may be accessed by several processes; for example, the job table may be updated and/or read by the Spoolin, Job Supervisor, Spoolout, and Operator Communications processes.
4. Disk space is required by the Spoolin process to store jobs and by the user processes for storing job output during virtual output operations.

Ultimately, most interactions occur through *common* variables and data structures that may be accessed by several processes.[4] We will examine some interaction problems and solutions using a common memory model as illustrated in Figure 6.18. n processes, $p_1, \ldots, p_n$, are executing with a common memory M, containing the programs and private data $P_1, \ldots, P_n$, respectively, for each process, and a common data area D through which they interact. The processes may be running on separate central processors or they can be implemented by sharing a single machine among the p_i. In either case, it is useful to think of these processes as running concurrently.

The first problem that we will discuss is the *critical section* problem. Suppose that D may be updated by any of the processes. It is then necessary to

---

[4] We will not discuss interaction mechanisms in computer *networks* where independent computer systems communicate over telecommunications lines.

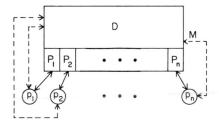

Figure 6.18 Processes With Common Memory

protect D from being simultaneously changed by two or more processes; if this protection is not provided, the data may not reflect the intended changes after the updates. A simple example will illustrate the problem.

Example:

Suppose processes p_1 and p_2 are both executing the statement $s := s + 1$ where s is stored in the common area D. Thus, the programs P_1 and P_2 for p_1 and p_2 appear as follows:

$$P_1: \textbf{begin} \ldots s := s + 1 ; \ldots \textbf{end}$$
$$P_2: \textbf{begin} \ldots s := s + 1 ; \ldots \textbf{end}$$

Assume that p_1 is running on a processor CPU_1 with internal register R_1 and p_2 is running on a different processor CPU_2 with register R_2. Then the following execution sequence could occur over time:

$$p_1: R_1 \leftarrow s ; R_1 \leftarrow R_1 + 1 ; s \leftarrow R_1 ; \ldots$$
$$p_2: \quad \ldots \quad R_2 \leftarrow s ; \quad R_2 \leftarrow R_2 + 1 ; s \leftarrow R_2 ; \ldots$$
$$t_0 \quad \text{time} \rightarrow \quad\quad\quad\quad\quad\quad\quad\quad\quad t_1$$

Let s contain the value 15 at time t_0; then at time t_1, s will contain the value 16 since both p_1 and p_2 read 15 for s into their internal registers. If s represented the number of blocks of memory allocated in an OS and the two processes were each updating s to indicate a new allocation of 1 block, then the final value of s is incorrect. Similarly, if p_1 and p_2 were part of an airlines reservation system and s represented the number of seats available on a flight, such an incorrect update would be intolerable. The correct result should clearly be 17 and both updates must count. The solution to this problem is to permit only one process at a time into its "critical section" (CS) $s := s + 1$. Note that the problem could still occur if p_1 and p_2 were sharing a single processor with control switching between the processes, since the internal CPU register would be saved and treated as private for each process.

In general, the critical section consists of those statements that access and update common variables and data structures. In operating systems and other systems with concurrency, the CS will normally contain many statements.

The CS problem was first studied seriously by Dijkstra in the mid-1960's. While there exist programming solutions using conventional machine instructions or conventional programming language constructs, these programs are extremely complex and mystifying. In order to solve the CS problem and handle other process communications requirements, Dijkstra invented two new instructions, *wait* and *signal*[5] that operate on special variables called *semaphores*. Semaphores may only take on non-negative integer values. The operations are defined below, where S is a semaphore variable.

1. *wait(S)*
    If $S > 0$, then decrement S by 1; otherwise ($S = 0$), wait until $S > 0$.
2. *signal(S)*
    Increment S by 1.

The testing and decrementing of S is assumed to be one *indivisible* operation in *wait(S)*; similarly, the signal operation is assumed indivisible. With the exception of initialization, a semaphore variable can only be accessed through the wait and signal instructions.

If a process is delayed on a wait operation because the semaphore is zero, the waiting can be implemented in either of two ways. The process invoking the *wait(S)* can do a *busy wait* by looping, or the process can release the CPU and remain inactive until $S > 0$. The only way that a process waiting on a semaphore S can proceed is when another process issues a *signal(S)*.

Suppose the n processes $p_1, \ldots, p_n$ each have critical sections of code $CS_1, \ldots, CS_n$, respectively in their programs. Then the critical sections may be protected by surrounding them with waits and signals as follows:

> *lock: semaphore;* {*lock* is declared to be of type *semaphore.*}
> $\vdots$
> *lock* := 1; {Initialize *lock* semaphore.}

P_1 : **begin** ... *wait(lock)*; CS_1 ; *signal(lock)* ... **end**
P_2 : **begin** ... *wait(lock)*; CS_2 ; *signal(lock)* ... **end**
$\vdots$
P_n : **begin** ... *wait(lock)*; CS_n ; *signal(lock)* ... **end**

---

[5] These operations were called P and V, but wait and signal have more mnemonic significance in English.

lock has a value of 0 whenever any process is in its CS and has a value of 1 if no process is in its CS. If *lock* = 1 and two processes attempt a *wait* (*lock*) simultaneously, then the operations will proceed *sequentially,* and only one will succeed and enter its CS; the other process will be delayed on the wait until a signal occurs. Several processes may be delayed on a *wait* (*lock*); when a *signal* (*lock*) occurs, only one of these processes will be permitted to complete the wait and enter its CS.

Another problem that involves critical sections and a more interesting application of semaphores is the *readers-writers* problem. Suppose that some processes need to read or interrogate the data area *D* while other processes need to write or update *D*. It is logically possible for any number of processes to read *D* simultaneously, but *D* must be considered a CS for writing purposes; also, because *D* might be temporarily inconsistent during a write, we wish to exclude any reading during the write operations. This set of constraints occurs in many operating systems and data base systems. For example, there may be some processes in an OS that need to examine a job table and other processes that update the table; an airlines reservation system may have some processes that read flight reservations data and other processes that write it.

The following solution permits simultaneous reads and enforces the restriction that only one write can proceed at a time and reads cannot overlap a write. Processes that need to read *D* are represented by a single program named *readerprogram*, and processes for updating *D* are represented by the program *writerprogram*.

```
lock, writeperm: semaphore;    readercount: integer;

{Initialize variables.}
lock := 1; writeperm := 1; readercount := 0;
readerprogram : begin ...
                wait(lock);
                readercount := readercount + 1;
                if readercount = 1 then wait(writeperm);
                signal(lock);
                Perform reading of D;
                wait(lock);
                readercount := readercount - 1;
                if readercount = 0 then signal(writeperm);
                signal(lock);
                ...
         end
```

writerprogram : **begin** ...
             wait(*writeperm*);
             Perform writing of D;
             signal(*writeperm*);
             ...
      end

The semaphore *writeperm* represents "permission to write." *writeperm* is used in a writer process to protect the critical section "Perform writing" and thereby ensure that only one writer at most can be in its CS; it is also used by a reader process to delay a first reader (*readercount* $= 1$) in the case where writing is being performed and to wake up a waiting writer when the last reader (*readercount* $= 0$) leaves. The *lock* semaphore is used on entry and exit to reading to protect the updating of *readercount* and to define unambiguously the particular case when *writeperm* is adjusted.

The last problem that we will introduce is the *deadlock* problem. This problem occurs frequently in resource sharing systems where processes may dynamically request and release resources. It is possible to arrive at a system state where some processes are waiting for resources that will *never* become available; the waiting processes may, for example, be delayed at a *wait*(*S*) operation on some semaphore *S* associated with the resource. The wait is eternal because the processes that have the desired resources are themselves waiting for resources that, in turn, are held by waiting processes. Such a state is called a deadlock state and can effectively terminate the operation of a system unless some drastic action is taken.

As an example, consider two processes p_1 and p_2 that both update a file *D* and require a printer *T*. Assume that the routine *Request*(*r*) will allocate the resource *r* to its caller on an exclusive basis and that the routine *Release*(*r*) will return on free *r*; if *r* is not available on a *Request,* the calling process is delayed until *r* becomes free. In our case *r* is *D* or *T*. Then p_1 and p_2 may execute the programs shown on page 255.

Suppose that p_1 and p_2 reach a_1 and a_2 at the same time: for example, p_1 gets *D*, then p_2 gets *T*, then p_1 reaches a_1, and finally p_2 reaches $a_2 \cdot p_1$ holds *D* and is waiting for *T* at a_1 while p_2 holds *T* and is waiting for *D* at a_2. Neither process can proceed until the other one executes and releases its resource. One could recover from this situation by either pre-empting resources or destroying processes, but both solutions are in general unsatisfactory.

p_1:
$\quad\quad\quad$:
$\quad\quad$ *Request(D)*;
$\quad\quad$ {p_1 now has D.}
$\quad$ a_1: *Request(T)*;
$\quad\quad$ {p_1 now has T, as well
$\quad\quad\quad$ as D.}
$\quad\quad\quad$:
$\quad\quad$ *Release(T)*;
$\quad\quad$ {T is now available.}
$\quad\quad$ *Release(D)*;
$\quad\quad$ {D is now available.}
$\quad\quad\quad$:

p_2:
$\quad\quad\quad$:
$\quad\quad$ *Request(T)*;
$\quad\quad$ {p_2 now has T.}
$\quad\quad\quad$:
$\quad$ a_2: *Request(D)*;
$\quad\quad$ {p_2 now has D, as well
$\quad\quad\quad$ as T.}
$\quad\quad\quad$:
$\quad\quad$ *Release(D)*;
$\quad\quad$ *Release(T)*;

Three subproblems are associated with deadlock:

1. Detection
   How can it be determined if some subset of a system of processes is deadlocked?
2. Recovery
   Given that deadlock has occurred, how can the deadlock be eliminated without disrupting the system too much?
3. Prevention
   How can deadlock be prevented from ever occurring?

We will not discuss the detection and recovery methods but will informally cover two simple deadlock prevention schemes. One straightforward prevention method is to require that each process request and acquire at *one* time all the resources it may conceivably need. Deadlock is impossible here because either each process has no resources or it has all of its resources; therefore, it cannot be both waiting for a resource and holding a resource that some other process needs. This policy has been used in a number of systems but it is not very efficient. Resources will often be allocated long before they are used, and they would also have to be allocated for those cases where there is only a chance that they might be required.

A more efficient prevention policy is an *ordered resource* scheme, originally devised by Havender in the 1960's. Resources are divided into n classes $C_1, \ldots, C_n$. A process is permitted to request and acquire resources from any class C_i provided that it has no allocations from classes $C_i, C_{i+1}, \ldots, C_n$; that is, if a process has already acquired resources up to and including class C_i, it cannot ask for any more from classes $C_1, \ldots, C_i$ and can only request resources in the higher classes $C_{i+1}, \ldots, C_n$. Note that this policy reduces to the first one above when $n = 1$.

Example:

Suppose that

$C_1 = \{d_1, \ldots, d_a\}$, where each d_i is a file,
$C_2 = \{m_1, \ldots, m_b)$, where each m_i is a main storage block, and
$C_3 = \{t_1, \ldots, t_c\}$, where each t_i is an IO device.

Then, a process with no resources can request anything from C_1, C_2, or C_3; a process with files (C_1) can only request storage(C_2) or IO devices(C_3); a process with C_1, C_2, and C_3 resources cannot request anything. If C_3 represents the most expensive or scarcest resources, then this policy permits one to defer requests for the most valuable resources until they are actually needed.

It can be proven that deadlock is impossible with the ordered resource scheme. The key part of the proof is that resources from the highest class C_n will eventually become available because processes that have elements of C_n can make no further requests until their C_n resources are released.

EXERCISES

1. "Time flies like an arrow." Give several parses and meanings for this sentence.

2. Consider the grammar for a simple fragment of English presented at the beginning of Section 6.2.2 and augmented with recursive rules. Parse the following sentences according to this grammar:

   (a) MARY WALKS TO SCHOOL
   (b) HE GOES TO TOWN AND MARY DRIVES FROM SCHOOL OR HE DRIVES

3. Parse the string $+9101$ according to the grammar G_{int}.

4. Show that $\langle\text{sign}\rangle$ $\langle\text{digit}\rangle$ $\langle\text{digit sequence}\rangle$ is a sentential form generated by G_{int}.

5. A "tick" and a "tock" are defined by the BNF rules:

$$\langle\text{tick}\rangle ::= ? \mid * \mid \langle\text{tick}\rangle ? \mid * \langle\text{tock}\rangle$$
$$\langle\text{tock}\rangle ::= \$ \mid * \langle\text{tick}\rangle \mid ? \langle\text{tock}\rangle$$

Indicate whether each of the following is a $\langle\text{tick}\rangle$, a $\langle\text{tock}\rangle$, both, or neither:

$$*\$ \quad *? \quad *?\$ \quad ??\$ \quad \$*$$

6. A binary floating-point constant has been defined in English as follows:
   "A binary floating-point constant consists of a field of binary digits followed by
   the letter E, followed by an optionally signed decimal integer exponent followed
   by the letter B. The field of binary digits may contain a decimal point."

   Examples: 1011001E5B   101.101E12B   11101E-28B   .001E-2B

   Write a BNF grammar for binary floating-point constants.

7. Represent the grammars $G_{(\ )}$ and G_{expr} as syntax diagrams.

8. Let $c[1]$, $c[2]$, ..., $c[n]$, $n \geq 1$, be an array of characters such that each element
   $c[i]$ contains either '(' or ')'; for example, $c[1] = $ '(', $c[2] = $ ')', $n = 2$. Write an
   Algolic program fragment that determines whether or not the parentheses sequence in c is a sentence of $G_{(\ )}$.

9. Suppose that today's date is given by a pair of integers (i, y) representing the ith
   day of year y; e.g., (116, 1980) denotes the 116th day of the year 1980. Write an
   extended Algolic program that converts the day number i to the conventional
   data representation as a day name (e.g., Tues), month name (e.g., Nov), and
   day within month (e.g., 15), given the day name for Jan 1 of the year. The input
   and output variables are declared:

   > i, y: integer; firstday: day; {Given date and day of Jan 1}
   > d: day; m: month; n: integer; {Output variables containing conventional
   > date}

   For example, if $i = 65$, $y = 1981$, and firstday = Wed, your program should
   compute $d = $ Thurs, $m = $ Mar, and $n = 5$.

10. A picture can be represented digitally as an $n \times n$ matrix P of non-negative real
    numbers such that the value of any P_{ij} is the "intensity" at the coordinates (i, j).
    It is frequently desired to smooth P by changing each P_{ij} to the average value of
    P_{ij} and all its immediate neighbors. The new value of each P_{ij}, say Q_{ij}, is
    defined:

    $$Q_{ij} = (P_{ij} + P_{i+1,j} + P_{i-1,j} + P_{i,j+1} + P_{i,j-1})/5 \text{ for } i = 1, \ldots, n \text{ and}$$
    $$j = 1, \ldots, n.$$

    (Assume fictitious rows 0 and $n + 1$ and columns 0 and $n + 1$, with each ele-
    ment having value 0.)
    Let P and Q be defined:

    > P : **array**$[0 .. n + 1, 0 .. n + 1]$ **of** real;
    > Q : **array**$[1 .. n, 1 .. n]$ **of** real;

    Given P, write a program segment in extended Algolic that computes Q using
    the above smoothing algorithm.

11. Consider the three-dimensional board described in Section 6.2.3.1. Assume that the board is initialized with blanks and that the game is played by inserting characters in the board squares; that is, at any time, any *Board*[*i*, *j*, *k*] will contain either a blank or some non-blank character. Let a *word* be defined as a sequence of non-blank characters. Write a program that computes the *longest* word in any row or column of any of the 45 board planes.

12. Give a program that determines whether or not a string *S* is a palindrome in the following two cases:

    (a) *S* is represented as an array of characters.
    (b) *S* is declared to be a string (*S: string*). Use the string operations defined in Section 6.2.3.3.

13. Let a *word* be defined as a sequence of non-blank characters surrounded by one or more blanks on either end. Given a string *S*, write a program that computes the number of words and the length of the longest word in *S*, in the following two cases:

    (a) *S* is represented as an array of characters.
    (b) *S* is declared as a string.

    (Assume that *S* is "padded" with a blank on either end.)

14. Suppose the character string *I* represents a signed integer, consisting of an optional sign followed by a string of characters from the set {'0', '1', ..., '9'}; for example, '+15', '−328', '9', '475'. Write a program that converts *I* to an integer *x*, in the following two cases:

    (a) *I: **array**[1..n] **of** character; x: integer;*
    (b) *I: string; x: integer;*

15. Write a procedure that computes the *n*th Fibonacci number. Use the heading:

    procedure *Fibonacci(n, F: integer)*; {Return F_n in F.}

16. Repeat question 15 using a function:

    function *Fibonacci(n: integer): integer;*

17. Write a procedure that rearranges the *n* elements of a vector *a* such that the last element of *a* becomes the new first element, the second last element becomes the new second element, and so on; for example, if *a* originally contains, in order, the values 15, 18, 35, 17, the new arrangement of *a* will be 17, 35, 18, 15. Use the heading:

    procedure *Reverse(a: vector, n: integer)*;

    Do not use any other arrays or vectors in the procedure.

18. Convert the following expression into Polish postfix notation:

$$(a - ((b + (c + d)) / ((d \times e) - (f \times g))))$$

19. Convert the following Polish postfix expression to fully-parenthesized infix form:

$$a\ b \times w + x\ y \times z - /$$

20. Write a BNF grammar for the set AE of fully-parenthesized arithmetic expressions.

21. Trace the execution of the Polish postfix conversion algorithm on the character string:

$$((a - (b \times c)) / (d + e));$$

Show the contents of c, the stack S, and the output array *Polish* after each execution of the main **while** loop.

22. Modify the Polish postfix conversion algorithm to include the unary minus operator #.

23. (a) Modify the Polish postfix *interpreter* algorithm to include the unary minus operator #.

(b) Trace the execution of your modified algorithm on the postfix expression:

$$a\ b\ \#\ c + \times\ d\ e + +$$

where the variables a, b, c, d, and e have the values 25, 3, -10, 15, and 18, respectively. Show the contents of c and the stack after each execution of the main **while** loop.

24. Let x be an integer in the range $0 \le x \le 2^{32} - 1$. Write an Algolic algorithm to produce an integer y in the range $0 \le y \le 2^8 - 1$, using the exclusive-OR hashing method.

25. Let two processes p_1 and p_2 execute the programs P_1 and P_2, respectively:

S_1, S_2: *semaphore;*
$S_1 := 1; S_2 := 1;$
P_1: **begin** ... *wait(S_1);* ... *wait(S_2);* ...
               signal(S_1); ... *signal(S_2);* ...
    end
P_2: **begin** ... *wait(S_2);* ... *wait(S_1);* ...
               signal(S_1); ... *signal(S_2);* ...
    end

Show how p_1 and p_2 can deadlock. Show how both p_1 and p_2 can execute without deadlock.

26. Suppose disk space is dynamically allocated when needed for input spooling of jobs and for job output. Assume that a Spoolin process requests disk space when entering a new job into the system, that a user job process requests disk space when performing virtual output, and that a Spoolout process releases or frees disk space after a job has been printed. Show how it is possible to deadlock these processes when the disk becomes full. Can you think of any ways to prevent this type of deadlock?

ADDITIONAL READINGS

Elson, M. *Concepts of Programming Languages.* Palo Alto: Science Research Associates, 1973.

Freeman, P. *Software Systems Principles—A Survey.* Palo Alto: Science Research Associates, 1975.

Gries, D. *Compiler Construction for Digital Computers.* New York: John Wiley & Sons, 1971.

Sammet, J. *Programming Languages: History and Fundamentals.* Englewood Cliffs, N.J.: Prentice-Hall, 1969.

Shaw, A. C. *The Logical Design of Operating Systems.* Englewood Cliffs, N.J.: Prentice-Hall, 1974.

Wirth, N. *Algorithms + Data Structures = Programs.* Englewood Cliffs, N.J.: Prentice-Hall, 1976.

Wirth, N. *Systematic Programming: An Introduction.* Englewood Cliffs, N.J.: Prentice-Hall, 1973.

Zelkowitz, M. V.; Shaw, A. C.; and Gannon, J. D.; *Principles of Software Engineering and Design.* Englewood Cliffs, N.J.: Prentice-Hall, 1979.

Chapter 7

TURING MACHINES
AND COMPUTABILITY

The previous chapters have presented many examples of algorithms as well as machines and circuits that realize them. In this chapter, we precisely define the notion of an algorithm and explore the limits of what is algorithmic or *computable*. The basis for our study will be the work of the British scientist Alan Turing (1912-1954).

We have seen and used an assortment of notations for describing algorithms. These languages ranged from the informal use of English to a reasonably rigorous programming language—*Algolic*. To analyze the idea of what is algorithmic, we require a formalism that is simple enough for logical analysis and, at the same time, is sufficiently general to describe all processes that could be reasonably called algorithms. For these purposes, Turing invented a class of formal devices, now called Turing Machines.

7.1 TURING MACHINES AND THE
CHURCH-MARKOV-TURING THESIS

Turing decided that what was minimally needed for describing computations was

1. An external storage to record and store input and output.
2. A means for reading from and writing on the external storage.
3. A control unit to determine the unambiguous actions to be taken.

We will follow his construction of a machine, a *Turing Machine,* embodying these three elements.

External storage is represented by a *tape* that is a linear strip divided into squares. The tape is *unbounded* in that another square can always be added to either end if necessary. Each square is either *blank* or contains a *symbol.*

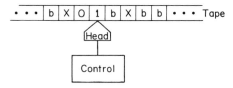

Figure 7.1   Components of a Turing Machine

The symbols are from a finite set of characters called the *alphabet* of the machine. At any instant, a *tape head* points at a single tape square. The head is capable of reading the symbol found in that square; when directed it will write a new symbol on the square. The tape head receives its direction from *control*. Control can cause the head to write a new symbol and then to move to either the left or right neighboring tape square. A Turing Machine is shown schematically in Figure 7.1, where *b* denotes a blank square and 0, 1, and *X* are non-blank symbols from the alphabet.

Control acts by selecting and executing an appropriate *quintuple* from a finite set of quintuples available to it. These quintuples collectively comprise the machine's *program*. A quintuple consists of:

1. An internal (current) state
2. An input (read) symbol
3. An output (written) symbol
4. An internal (next) state
5. A head movement

An *internal state* is one of a finite number of distinct state symbols. At a particular instant, control has a *current state*. The current state and the tape symbol under the tape head (the input symbol) together determine the quintuple to be executed.

We now describe the machine more formally. A Turing Machine (TM) is specified by:

1. A finite external tape alphabet S, including the blank symbol b.

$$S = \{b, s_1, \ldots, s_m\}$$

2. A finite set of internal states Q, including the halt state h.

$$Q = \{h, q_1, q_2, \ldots, q_k\}$$

3. A program consisting of a finite set of quintuples of the form:

$$q_i \, s_j \, s_k \, q_l \, M$$

where $q_i, \, q_l \in Q$, $s_j, \, s_k \in S$, and M is either L or R. L stands for "move tape head left one square" and R means "move tape head right one square." Each quintuple must be defined *uniquely* by its first two symbols; i.e., there *cannot* exist two distinct quintuples $q_{i_1} s_{j_1} s_{k_1} q_{1_1} M_1$ and $q_{i_2} s_{j_2} s_{k_2} q_{1_2} M_2$ such that $q_{i_1} = q_{i_2}$ and $s_{j_1} = s_{j_2}$.

4. A tape that has a finite number of non-blank squares, each square containing a symbol from S. This defines the *initial tape configuration*.
5. The *initial internal state* which is an element of Q.
6. The *initial tape head position* which is a specific tape square pointed at by the head.

The exact operation of a TM is given by the flow chart of Figure 7.2. A computation proceeds by executing program quintuples sequentially until a halt condition occurs. The next quintuple to be executed is determined by the current state and symbol scanned. These must match the first two symbols of a unique program quintuple. This quintuple then directs the next execution cycle. A single instruction will do three jobs:

1. Rewrite the scanned tape symbol.
2. Change the current state of control.
3. Move the tape head one square.

The machine halts if it enters the halt state h or if the current state and symbol scanned do not match the first two symbols of any quintuple. If the machine halts, the output of the computation is represented by the contents of the tape.

Examples of Quintuples:

1. $q_1 \, A \, B \, q_3 \, L$
   This quintuple is interpreted as follows:
   If control is in state q_1 and the tape symbol read is A,
   then (1) A is rewritten as B,
         (2) control is changed to state q_3, and
         (3) the tape head is moved one square left. (Figure 7.3(a)).
2. $q_1 ** \, q_1 \, L$
   If control is in state q_1 and the tape symbol read is *,
   then (1) * is unchanged (* is rewritten as *),

(2) q_1 remains the state of control, and

(3)   the tape head is moved one square left. (Figure 7.3(b)).

3. $q_5 * 0 h R$

If control is in state q_5 and the tape symbol read is *,

then   (1)   * is rewritten as 0,

(2)   control is changed to state h (halt),

(3)   the tape head is moved one square right, and

(4)   the machine halts. (Figure 7.3(c)).

We will now illustrate a complete but very elementary TM that takes a tape with a string of A's and rewrites them as 8's. The machine will start in state q_1 and move to the right rewriting A's to 8's. The machine halts on the first blank square.

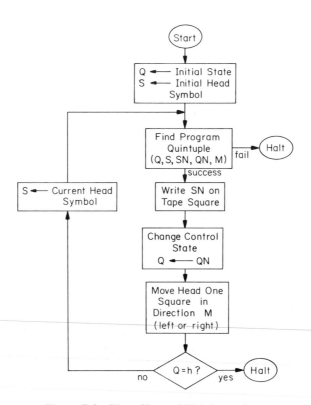

Figure 7.2   Flow Chart of TM Operation

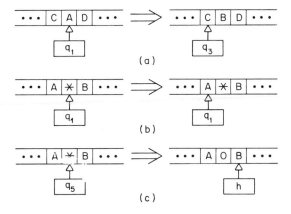

Figure 7.3   Execution of Single Quintuples

The machine specifications are:

1. Alphabet $S = \{b, A, 8\}$
2. States $Q = \{h, q_1\}$
3. Program: $\{q_1\,A\,8\,q_1\,R,\ q_1\,b\,b\,h\,L\}$
4. The machine starts on the leftmost A in state q_1.

Let us trace the execution of this machine on an initial tape given by Figure 7.4(a). At the initial configuration, $q_1\,A\,8\,q_1\,R$ is the unique matching program quintuple; the execution of the quintuple results in the configuration of Figure 7.4(b). Again $q_1\,A\,8\,q_1\,R$ is applicable leading to Figure 7.4(c). Finally $q_1\,b\,b\,h\,L$ is executed causing the TM to enter the halt state (Figure 7.4(d)). It should be apparent that this simple TM will rewrite an arbitrary number of contiguous A's as 8's and halt. The initial tape description is the input for the TM, and its output is the tape description upon halting.

A computation is a constructive specification of an input-output relationship. A TM specification is patently an *effective* procedure; the operation of the device involves only the simplest of bookkeeping operations. Given that the tape is as large as is necessary, i.e., that a computation never runs out of tape, it is easy to see that arbitrary inputs and outputs can be expressed on the tape. In constructing a TM, the programmer can designate any finite set of quintuples to accomplish the desired transformations. What is difficult to see is just what computations are possible as TM's. For example, can one devise a TM to multiply two decimal numbers? Without some practice in writing TM programs, it is not immediately evident that computations such as multiply are possible.

Turing himself felt that these machines could be made to realize *any* effective calculation! This is known as the Church-Markov-Turing thesis[1], more simply called *Turing's thesis*:

> "Every effectively calculable function is computable by some Turing Machine."

Another way of stating this thesis is that *every algorithm* can be realized by a Turing Machine. In this form, we have a precise definition of an algorithm as a TM computation.

It is hard to believe such a comprehensive claim for such a simple class of device. Yet, to date, all the evidence points to its validity. Every attempt to define algorithm or effective procedure has led to the same class of computable functions. As we shall see, even today's most powerful computers can be imitated by a Turing Machine. Some computer scientists believe that in a fundamental sense the brain can also be so simulated.

7.2 SOME EXAMPLES OF TM COMPUTATIONS

We will now develop in detail several TM algorithms. As the programmer of a TM, we are allowed to specify the starting state of control and the initial tape square to be scanned. We will choose a tape alphabet and coding conventions to make our programming job as easy as possible. As we design and exhibit TM's for successively more difficult computations, the reader should develop a deeper appreciation for Turing's thesis.

A TM to check parity

A string of one's will be of *odd parity* if there are an odd number of one's in the string. We want a TM to scan a string of one's and print T (for true) if the parity is odd and F, if not.

The machine, called TM_{parity}, is defined: $S = \{b, 1, T, F\}$,
$Q = \{h, q_{odd}, q_{even}\}$, and the quintuples are $\{q_{odd} 1 1 q_{even} R, q_{odd} b T h R, q_{even} 1 1 q_{odd} R, q_{even} b F h R\}$.

---

[1] Church and Markov are two theorists who had a similar insight.

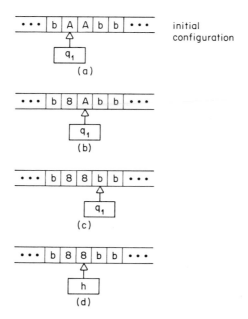

Figure 7.4   Execution Trace

The conventions for the initial configuration are

1. q_{even} is the initial state.
2. The tape head is pointing at the leftmost one.
3. The input is a contiguous string of one's surrounded by blanks.

TM$_{parity}$ marches across the tape reading each symbol once until it encounters the first blank square. At this point it writes out the answer T or F and halts. Figure 7.5 traces the execution of this machine for a sample input. Note how the state keeps track of the parity of the tape.

Only four quintuples were used to specify this program. With such a short program, there is no difficulty in writing the quintuples down. More difficult problems benefit from a condensed tableau representation of a TM.

Tableau Representation for TM$_{parity}$

		state	
		q even	q odd
tape alphabet	1	1 q odd R	1 q even R
	b	$F\,h\,R$	$T\,h\,R$
	T	– – –	– – –
	F	– – –	– – –

Each entry is indexed by its initial (state, symbol) pair; if an instruction (quintuple) exists, its three outcomes—the rewritten symbol, the new state, and its move—are displayed. We may further simplify this representation by the following conventions:

1. If the state is not changed, do not include it in the entry.
2. If the tape symbol is not rewritten, do not include it in the entry.
3. If the new state is h, do not necessarily include a tape move.
4. An empty entry implicitly represents a halt state.

The condensed tableau for TM parity is:

		state	
		q even	q odd
tape alphabet	1	q odd R	q even R
	b	$F\,h$	$T\,h$
	T	– – –	– – –
	F	– – –	– – –

A TM That Copies a String of A's and B's

It is frequently useful to modify the input but retain the original information for some further part of the computation. One way to accomplish this is

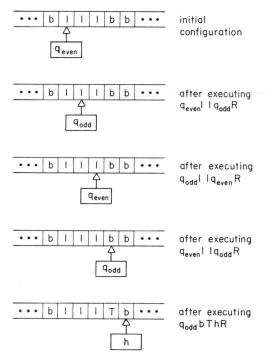

Figure 7.5 Executing TM$_{parity}$

to copy the original input onto another part of the tape. The copy can then be modified or destroyed while the original is preserved. We will construct a machine called TM$_{copy}$ which, when presented with a sequence of A's and B's followed by the symbol "Δ," will copy that string to the right of the Δ. The purpose of Δ is to act as a boundary mark on part of the tape; such a symbol is called a *delimiter* or *sentinel*.

Example:

initial tape

		b	A	B	A	Δ	b	b		

final tape

		b	A	B	A	Δ	A	B	A	b	

The machine will use two standard TM programming techniques:

1. The original tape information is preserved with a reversible substitution code; as the computation proceeds, A will be temporarily changed to X and B will be changed temporarily to Y in the original input. The purpose of this technique is to distinguish between that part of the input that has been copied and that part which has yet to be copied.
2. Delimiters are used to terminate tape searches. Searching is performed by scanning the tape in a single direction until a particular delimiter is encountered.

The algorithm for TM_{copy} proceeds as follows:

1. Initially the tape head starts at the leftmost non-blank square. If it is Δ, then halt.
2. If the head reads A, then change to X and go to step 4.
3. If the head reads B, then change to Y and go to step 5.
4. Move right until the first blank is encountered and write an A. Go to step 6.
5. Move right until the first blank is encountered and write a B.
6. Go left past the Δ until an X or Y is encountered. Rewrite it to A or B as appropriate.
7. Move right one square. If it contains Δ, then halt; otherwise go to step 2.

Converting these requirements to a TM tableau, we have:

TM_{copy}

	q_{scan}	q_X	q_Y	q_{return}
Δ	h	R	R	L
A	$X\ q_X\ R$	R	R	L
B	$Y\ q_Y\ R$	R	R	L
b		$A\ q_{return}\ L$	$B\ q_{return}\ L$	
X				$A\ q_{scan}\ R$
Y				$B\ q_{scan}\ R$

Note how the program steps under q_{scan} perform steps 1–3, q_X does step 4, q_Y does step 5, and q_{return} executes steps 6–7. The state q_{scan} is a test on the symbol scanned and has one of three outcomes. The state q_X examines the tape moving right until it hits b serving as a delimiter. In effect, q_X moves the head to the right preserving the fact that it needs to write an A. The trick in easily writing TM programs is to organize states to perform the relevant subtasks of the computation clearly and simply.

It is also interesting to see that extending TM_{copy} to other symbols requires little added effort. For example, if we wanted to copy a string of A, B, and C's, we would add a q_Z column similar to q_X and adjoin two rows for C and its encoded form, say Z.

How efficient is the algorithm given by TM_{copy}? One standard measure of efficiency is the number of instructions executed as a function of the length of the input. Let the input string of A's and B's be of length n ($n \geq 0$). For each element of the input string, it requires $n + 2$ instructions to read the symbol, move through to the copy area, and copy the symbol. It then takes $n + 1$ instructions to move left back to the original symbol and reverse its substitution code. Consequently, $2n + 3$ instructions are performed for each input element. For n elements, we then execute $n(2n + 3) = 2n^2 + 3n$ instructions. Including the final halt, the number of instructions executed is therefore $2n^2 + 3n + 1$.

A TM That Checks For Palindromes

We will construct a TM that determines whether an arbitrary string of A's and B's is a palindrome. Our algorithm will successively pick up the leftmost unexamined symbol and compare it with the rightmost unexamined symbol. Each matching pair is crossed off until the middle of the string is reached, indicating that the string is a palindrome. If at any point the symbols do not match, the string is not a palindrome and the computation halts. The method is akin to the peeling of an onion, layer by layer, outward in.

Initially, the tape head points at the leftmost non-blank symbol in state q_{scan}.

e.g.,

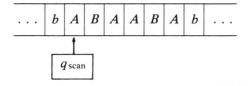

When the machine halts, the tape will contain an N if the string was not a palindrome or a P if the string was a palindrome.

$TM_{palindrome}$

	q_{scan}	q_A	q_B	q_{Acheck}	q_{Bcheck}	q_{return}
A	$b\,q_A\,R$	R	R	$b\,q_{return}\,L$	$N\,h$	L
B	$b\,q_B\,R$	R	R	$N\,h$	$b\,q_{return}\,L$	L
b	$P\,h$	$q_{Acheck}\,L$	$q_{Bcheck}\,L$	$P\,h$	$P\,h$	$q_{scan}\,R$

Note how q_{scan} converts the tape symbol into state information while q_A and q_B go off looking for the first right blank. This algorithm destroys the original string. If we wished to preserve the original string, we could make use of TM_{copy} first, or we could have converted the A's and B's to other characters and reconverted back after the answer had been computed.

A TM that adds

The final example in this section will be a familiar algorithm, addition of two binary numbers. The fact that a TM can be constructed to accomplish this operation should help convince the reader that TM's can be constructed to carry out all binary arithmetic and logical operations—in effect an argument that all digital computer operations can be so simulated.

The TM, called TM_{add}, will carry out the standard binary addition algorithm. For each successive digit position, it will compute a carry-out and a sum digit. Let us first program a one bit full add. An initial configuration is shown below:

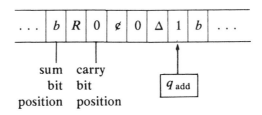

Δ delimits the two bits to be added,
$\mathcal{\not c}$ marks the carry position (both carry-in and carry-out), and
R marks the result.

$\text{TM}_{\text{OneBitAdd}}$

	q_{add}	q_0	q_1	q_{0+}	q_{1+}	q_2	q_{1c}	q_{2c}	q_{0c}
0	$q_0 L$			$q_0 L$	$q_1 L$		$q_1 L$	$1\ q_0 L$	$q_0 L$
1	$q_1 L$			$q_1 L$	$q_2 L$		$q_0 L$	$q_1 L$	$0\ q_1 L$
Δ		$q_{0+} L$	$q_{1+} L$						
¢		$q_{0c} L$	$q_{1c} L$			$q_{2c} L$			
R		L	L						
b		$0\ h$	$1\ h$						

Notice how the states keep track of the current sum. The initial state q_{add} retains the bit found by entering either q_0 or q_1. The state q_0 moves the head left through one of the delimiters Δ, ¢, or R. If a Δ is found, it enters q_{0+} and notes the appropriate one bit addition to perform by changing to state q_0 or q_1. If a ¢ is found in q_0, the state q_{0c} (carry) is entered and the new carry bit is computed. If an R is scanned in q_0, state q_0 is reentered and the blank to the left of R is replaced by the sum bit 0. The states q_1, q_{1+}, q_2, q_{1c}, and q_{2c} perform analogous functions.

To extend $\text{TM}_{\text{OneBitAdd}}$ to a general binary adder, we need a state that returns to a new position ("column" to be added) and a means of marking the next position to be added. We assume that TM_{add} starts in state q_{add} looking at the rightmost non-blank symbol. The same delimiters as before are used to separate the augend, addend, carry, and result fields; the augend and addend are assumed to contain the same number of bits. Marking is accomplished by changing each bit position that has been added to an X. To return from the result field to the first non-blank on the right, the TM will enter a return state q_{ret}; after returning, q_{add} is entered and the tape is scanned left until the first non X is found.

Example:

Initial configuration

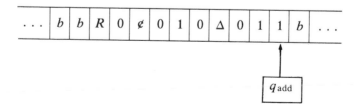

Final configuration

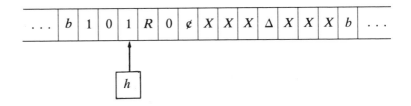

Combining $\text{TM}_{\text{OneBitAdd}}$ with the above changes, we get the following tableau for TM_{add}:

TM_{add}

	q_{add}	$q0$	$q1$	$q0+$	$q1+$	$q2$	q_{1c}	q_{2c}	q_{0c}	q_{ret}
0	$X\ q0\ L$	L	L	$X\ q0\ L$	$X\ q1\ L$	L	$q1\ L$	$1\ q0\ L$	$q0\ L$	R
1	$X\ q1\ L$	L	L	$X\ q1\ L$	$X\ q2\ L$	L	$q0\ L$	$q1\ L$	$0\ q1\ L$	R
Δ	L	$q0+\ L$	$q1+\ L$							R
¢	L	$q_{0c}\ L$	$q_{1c}\ L$			$q_{2c}\ L$				R
R	$h\ L$	L	L							R
b		$0\ q_{\text{ret}}\ R$	$1\ q_{\text{ret}}\ R$							$q_{\text{add}}\ L$
X	L			L	L					R

7.3 TM COMPOSITION

In $\text{TM}_{\text{palindrome}}$, the original tape information was destroyed. If we wished to preserve it, we could first call TM_{copy}; rather than halting when TM_{copy} finishes, we could then invoke the start state of $\text{TM}_{\text{palindrome}}$. This is the method of *composition*. The TM tableaux are combined and appropriate transition states are invented to transfer control from one TM to the next. Typically this can be done by carefully examining all instances of the halt state. We used just such a technique to construct TM_{add}.

In a similar fashion, we can readily compose a set of basic routines into a large and complex library of programs. Once a routine is in the library, it can be thought of as a single operation which may be recombined with other such programs. The increased computing power obtained through function composition gives further credence to Turing's thesis.

For a TM to be meaningful, it must have an interpretation of its external alphabet that is understandable. The TM writer must explain what the input and output mean. For example, when the tape is encoding numbers, the particular coding scheme must be explained. Once a TM is displayed for a particular function, it is by definition a computable function. In fact, by Turing's thesis, we argue that *only* those functions that can be realized by TM's are computable. The question that remains is are all well-defined functions computable?

7.4   THE UNIVERSAL TURING MACHINE

In order to demonstrate that a particular function is computable, we have had to construct a particular TM that computes the function. Turing, however, was able to construct a single Turing machine that is capable of imitating the operation of any other TM; such a machine is called a *Universal Turing Machine*, abbreviated UTM. This machine is the theoretical analogue of a general purpose digital computer. It will turn out that the UTM will allow us to demonstrate a most remarkable result, namely that some well-defined functions are not computable.

In the TM examples of this chapter, the reader checked the description of the machines by simulating its operation. In a strict sense the reader, possibly aided by pencil and paper, was a universal machine imitating the behavior of an arbitrary TM. We wish to embody these processes in a UTM.

To construct a UTM, we must have two essentials:

1.   A uniform method of describing any TM in a finite symbol set (this description will appear on the tape of the UTM), and
2.   A set of TM programs that perform the TM basic cycle.

Encoding an arbitrary TM

It has already been demonstrated how the binary system can be used to encode the integers. Let us use the binary system to encode the various finite sets that describe a particular TM. For example TM_{parity} has three tape symbols $\{1, T, F\}$ and blank (b), and it has two states $\{q_{odd}, q_{even}\}$ and halt (h). Since h and b are always involved, they can represent themselves; the other symbols can be converted to the binary numbers 1, 10, 11, 100, and 101. Thus we have for TM_{parity}:

Original	Code
q_{odd}	1
q_{even}	10
1	11
T	100
F	101

We can leave the move notation as $\{L, R\}$ since it always appears. Finally, a *
can be inserted between each binary code to separate each encoded symbol.

Example quintuple: q_{odd} 1 1 q_{even} R becomes 1 * 11 * 11 * 10 * R

The UTM will require that an arbitrary TM program can be encoded on its
tape. Our notation is satisfactory for this requirement as each program quintuple is readily separated by its move character.

In order to complete the description, it is necessary that the current state,
current symbol, tape head position, and tape be encoded. We can perform
each of these encodings in binary and simply mark each area with its own
delimiter.

Example: UTM tape

program quintuples	¢	current state	*	current symbol	$	simulated tape	H	simulated tape

The symbols ¢, $, and H have been added to mark special positions on the
UTM tape; H is a marker for the tape head position. Our encoding uses the
symbols 0, 1, *, ¢, $, H, L, R, b, h, a total of 10 symbols; of course, other en-
codings are also possible.

Imitation algorithm overview

Given a description of a TM and its tape encoded on the UTM tape as
described above, the UTM program acts on that description executing the
quintuples of the encoded machine as follows: [2]

1.   The UTM matches the current state-symbol pair to the state-symbol
      pairs in the program listed to the left of ¢. If no match occurs, the
      UTM halts.

---

[2] Note that the simulated tape as shown is only unbounded on the right. In order to expand on
the left, the tape can be copied and shifted right.

2. The UTM copies the new state number into the current state squares immediately to the right of the ¢.
3. The UTM copies the new symbol immediately to the right of H.
4. The UTM moves the symbol H either left or right a number of squares equal to the length of the tape symbol encoding.[2]
5. The UTM copies the new tape square symbol on the right of H into the current symbol area.
6. If the current state is not a halt, then go back to step 1; otherwise, halt.

The imitation algorithm of the UTM needs a matching routine that will look up the current state-symbol pair, a copying routine for recording new states and symbols into appropriate tape locations, and a number of simple bookkeeping routines to maintain encoded information properly from cycle to cycle. The reader's experience with various TM constructions should be convincing enough to demonstrate that each of these routines is programmable as a TM. More detailed descriptions of such routines can be found in Minsky (1967) or Davis (1958).

7.5 THE HALTING PROBLEM

We have now developed a sufficient set of tools for exploring the limits of computability. Is every well-defined function computable? We will see that the powerful notion of the universal machine is to an extent self-defeating, in that it raises questions that are too complex for a UTM itself to answer. There are simpler problems in logic that have the same flavor. Before we undertake to prove rigorously that there exist *non-computable* functions, it is instructive to look at some simple paradoxes first.

The Paradox of the Barber

There is a town that has one male barber and a number of other adult males. The barber shaves all and only those men who do not shave themselves. All men in the town shave or are shaved. Who shaves the barber?

Clearly, there are but two possibilities: either the barber shaves himself or he doesn't shave himself. If the barber does not shave himself, then the barber is an adult male who doesn't shave himself and is shaved by the barber. Ah, but if the barber shaves the barber, he shaves himself. This is not allowed. Each of the two apparent possibilities leads to an impossibility. The only way out of this difficulty is to say no such town exists. In effect the non-existence of the postulated town was proved by contradiction.

Grelling's Paradox

The word "autological" means adjectives that apply to themselves. For example, the word "English" is English; the word "short" is short; the word "polysyllabic" is polysyllabic. The word "heterological" means adjectives that do not apply to themselves. Some examples are "monosyllabic", "long", and "Spanish." Is "heterological" heterological or autological?

Again the reasoning parallels that of the barber paradox. Each possibility leads to a contradiction. However, one could escape the barber paradox by saying "no such town exists"—but heterological patently exists. It is right here in the preceding paragraph along with its definition.

One approach to understanding this difficulty is to see how a Turing Machine could decide if a word was heterological, just as it could decide if a word was a palindrome.

A TM which decided heterological needs to see if a word was true of itself (this is an imaginary "Gedanken" experiment as no one has an adequate understanding of natural language to program such a function). In applying this $TM_{heterological}$ to the word "heterological" one would end up continually applying the definition, i.e., heterological is heterological if heterological is heterological ... In other words, its definition contains its own description. The attempt to compute $TM_{heterological}$ (heterological) would lead to a non-terminating reapplication of the definition. Naturally one can ask whether such non-terminating situations can be foretold. It would save a large amount of useless computation to know in advance that a given program acting on a given input tape did not halt.

A Hypothetical TM That Decides The Halting Problem

Let us imagine a TM, call it H (for halting), which given a description of an arbitrary TM, call it M, will decide whether or not machine M halts when given T as its input tape. This can be expressed by the notation:

$$H(M, T) = \begin{cases} 0 & \text{if } M(T) \text{ does not halt.} \\ 1 & \text{if } M(T) \text{ halts.} \end{cases}$$

For example, the TM consisting of the single quintuple $q\ b\ 1\ q\ R$ will never halt when given a blank tape. It will instead move right, writing an infinite string of one's. The same machine started on a non-blank tape square immediately halts. Both of these cases are easily understood. Considering that we can use a UTM to simulate any other machine, it may seem that a minor modification to a UTM would solve the halting problem. If a UTM were allowed to run up to 10^6 imitation cycles, we could detect many halting situations. But, this is a strict upper bound; for many machines, one could (in principle) provide an input tape that exceeds this limit. For example, let the palindrome detector work on a tape of length $10^6 + 1$ (actually this is much larger than is necessary (see Exercise 7.10)); it would still halt but not in the limits imposed by our simple attempt to construct H.

In reality, H cannot be constructed. The proof of this is similar to the proof by contradiction in the Barber's paradox.[3] Namely the existence of such a TM will lead to an impossible situation. We will also tie this argument into related questions in mathematics in a later section.

Theorem: There can be no TM that solves the halting problem.
Proof: Assume $H(M, T)$ exists—do not forget that we are talking about a Turing Machine to compute this function. Therefore, machine H has on its tape a description of an arbitrary machine M and its input tape T. This can be encoded in the same manner as it was done for the UTM. Now fashion a new TM called H_s, having only one argument M:

$$H_s(M) = \begin{cases} 0 & \text{if } M(M) \text{ does not halt.} \\ 1 & \text{if } M(M) \text{ does halt.} \end{cases}$$

H_s answers whether a machine M will halt when given as input its *own* description. If H is available then H_s is easily constructed. We use the copy TM to recopy the single argument M and pass as output the tape "M, M" to H, i.e. $H_s(M) = H(M, M)$. It is critical to the proof to understand that H_s is a simple construction given H.

Consider a further construction, a machine P which works as follows:

$$P(M) = \begin{cases} \text{if } H_s(M) = 1 \text{ then } loop. \\ \text{if } H_s(M) = 0 \text{ then halt with 1.} \end{cases}$$

P is a simple composition given H_s. Namely when H_s halts with a 1, P enters a loop or if it halts with 0, it rewrites this as 1. We have shown how to construct P given that H_s is available. The following well-defined question then arises:

What is $H_s(P)$??

---

[3] Review also the discussion in Section 4.1.2

Case 1: $H_s(P) = 1$.
This means that $H(P, P) = 1$. Then $P(P)$ must halt. However if $H_s(P) = 1$, then $P(P)$ will loop. *Contradiction.*

Case 2: $H_s(P) = 0$.
This means that $P(P)$ does not halt. However if $H_s(P) = 0$, then $P(P)$ halts with output 1. *Contradiction.*

Since P and H_s are computable given H, H cannot be computable. $\square$

7.6   NUMBERS, INFINITY AND DIAGONALIZATION: ANALOGUES TO THE HALTING PROBLEM

While Turing proved the non-constructability of the halting machine in 1936, his proof rested on ideas that were first understood in the late 19th century by the German mathematician Georg Cantor. These matters are deeply tied to the concept of infinity, written ∞, as a number. In this section, we will examine this notion and its relation to the halting problem. There are two reasons for doing this: (1) it is one of the most elegant abstractions in the history of mathematics and as such has intrinsic appeal, and (2) it ties computability and self-description to the idea of counting.

When counting systems were first developed, it became clear that there was no largest number. The Greek philosopher Zeno (3rd century B.C.) baffled his contemporaries with several paradoxes based on infinity. His most famous was the problem of Achilles and the tortoise.

Achilles, the fastest of the Greek warriors, was asked to race a tortoise 1000 meters in which the tortoise was given a lead of 100 meters. Achilles was twice as fast as the tortoise and accepted the race wagering a large sum on himself. Achilles covered the first 100 meters, but the tortoise had now run 50 meters further. Achilles raced to this point only to find the tortoise 25 meters further. Each time Achilles reached the tortoise's old position, the tortoise had travelled an additional distance. Achilles was never able to pass the tortoise and could not collect on his wager. This problem arose because the Greeks had no simple way of handling the successive subdivision of the race into, eventually, an infinite number of pieces—a situation readily dealt with by modern calculus.

A more disturbing aspect of infinite sets is that they are equinumerous with their own subsets. Consider the function $f(n) = 2n$, where each natural number 1, 2, 3, . . . , is related to an even number 2, 4, 6, ... There is a one-to-one correspondence between all natural numbers and the even numbers; the latter are a proper subset of the former. This confusing set of affairs is of course impossible for finite sets. While this disturbing fact was known about infinite sets, it was largely ignored until Georg Cantor began investigating such questions.

We will denote the size of the set of natural numbers, $N = \{1, 2, 3, 4, \ldots\}$ by the number $\aleph_0$ (read aleph null). A set of cardinality $\aleph_0$ is called *countable*. We can show that an infinite set is countable by giving a one-to-one mapping of it onto N. The number $\aleph_0$ has many remarkable properties distinguishing it from its finite counterparts:

1. $\aleph_0 = \aleph_0 + 1$
2. $\aleph_0 = \aleph_0 + \aleph_0$
3. $\aleph_0 = \aleph_0 \times \aleph_0$

For example, property 2 is seen in the equivalence of N and its proper subset, the even numbers. Property 3 is a more interesting one and Cantor proved it by demonstrating that the rational numbers were countable. A rational number is a number of the form p/q, where p and q are natural numbers.

Theorem (Cantor): The natural numbers are equinumerous with the rationals, i.e., the rationals have cardinality $\aleph_0$.
Proof: Write out all the rationals as a two-dimensional matrix:

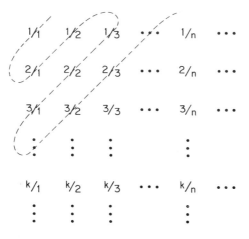

It is obvious that all rationals appear somewhere in this matrix. We draw the curly line through each diagonal, where each diagonal contains all p, q such that $p + q = r$. The position of a rational on the curly line is its mapping into the natural numbers. We have therefore demonstrated by this mapping that the rationals are $\aleph_0$. $\qquad\square$

The next set of interest to mathematicians is the reals. We will examine all real numbers in the interval (0, 1) and see if they have cardinality $\aleph_0$. These numbers can be written as an infinite string of decimals digits

$$0 \cdot a_1 a_2 a_3 \ldots a_n a_{n+1} \ldots$$

For example, $1/3 = 0.3333 \ldots$
$1/2 = 0.5000 \ldots$
$\pi - 3 = 0.14159 \ldots .$

The Greeks had already known that the rationals did not contain the $\sqrt{1/2}$. The rationals are a proper subset of the reals, just as the integers are a proper subset of rationals. Cantor proved that the reals were not countable.

In the proof that the rationals are $\aleph_0$, there is an ingenious way to list the rationals. In order to show that no listing of the reals is possible, we must again resort to proof by contradiction. The proof contains deep parallels to the proof of the non-existence of H, the TM for solving the halting problem.

Theorem (Cantor):   The reals are not countable.
Proof: Assume that the reals are countable, namely that an indexed list of reals is available:

$$1. \leftrightarrow 0. \, a_1^{(1)} \, a_2^{(1)} \, a_3^{(1)} \ldots$$
$$2. \leftrightarrow 0. \, a_1^{(2)} \, a_2^{(2)} \, a_3^{(2)} \ldots$$
$$3. \leftrightarrow 0. \, a_1^{(3)} \, a_2^{(3)} \, a_3^{(3)} \ldots$$

$$\vdots \quad \vdots \quad \vdots \quad \vdots$$

$$k. \leftrightarrow 0. \, a_1^{(k)} \, a_2^{(k)} \, a_3^{(k)} \ldots$$

$$\vdots \quad \vdots$$

The subscript represents the digit position, and the superscript gives the position of the real in the list. For example, $a_i^{(j)}$ is the ith digit in the jth number in the list. We now construct a "diagonal" number d, where the ith digit of d is given by the formula $d_i = (a_i^{(i)} + 1) \bmod 10$. The number d in decimal notation is $0.d_1 d_2 d_3 \ldots$ and is obviously a real number in the interval (0, 1). If our list is complete, this number must appear in some position in the list. Assume d appears in position k. By the diagonal construction of d we have $d_k = (a_k^{(k)} + 1) \bmod 10 \neq a_k^{(k)}$. Therefore d differs from the number in position k. It will, indeed, differ in at least one digit from any number in our list. Therefore no such list can be constructed and the reals are not $\aleph_0$.

□

Cantor's argument relied on a construction called the *diagonalization* procedure. In effect the machine P used in our proof of the halting problem was also a diagonalization argument. This can be seen more directly in the following alternate proof of the nonexistence of a TM for the halting problem.

Theorem: A TM that solves the halting problem cannot exist.

Proof: When encoding TM's in constructing a UTM, we made use of 10 symbols $\{0, 1, *, c, \$, H, L, R, h, b\}$. Equate these symbols to the 10 decimal digits. Then each TM and each tape are encoded into a unique integer (why?). Let us list the tapes and the TM's in ascending order along a two dimensional matrix as was done for the rationals.

	Tape 1	Tape 2	Tape 3	...	Tape j	...
TM_1	halt(1, 1)	halt(1, 2)	halt(1, 3)	...		
TM_2	halt(2, 1)	halt(2, 2)	halt(2, 3)	...		
TM_3	halt(3, 1)	halt(3, 2)	halt(3, 3)	...		
$\vdots$	$\vdots$					
TM_i					halt(i, j)	...
$\vdots$						

Assume the existence of a TM called H that computes whether machine i halts on tape j. Imagine the entries in the above table to be computed by H and defined as follows:

$$\text{halt}(i, j) = \begin{cases} 0 & \text{if } TM_i \text{ does not halt on Tape } j. \\ 1 & \text{if } TM_i \text{ halts on Tape } j. \end{cases}$$

Let us construct a "diagonal" TM called D. D will halt on Tape i if TM_i does not halt on Tape i, and D will loop on Tape i if TM_i does halt on Tape i. D is clearly constructable if H is. Therefore it must appear at some position k in our list of machines. That row in the table is represented by an infinite string of binary digits. However, our construction of D is such that it cannot have its kth digit correct—since this digit was diagonalized. Therefore, D cannot be in the list. But this means H cannot exist since D is clearly constructable from H. *Contradiction.*   □

The existence of non-computable functions is a part of a revolutionary understanding of the foundations of logic, mathematics, and computation.

These insights, starting with the work of Cantor in the 19th century and extending into the 20th century with the work of Turing, Gödel, and others, clarified many enigmas associated with the infinity of numbers—enigmas which had been troubling philosophers and mathematicians since antiquity.

7.7 VARIANTS ON THE HALTING PROBLEM

The halting problem argument is difficult to grasp because there is no intuitive underlying model. Real world intuition extends only to finite sets and numbers for which no such problems exist. One immediate question that arises is: Are there other non-computable functions?

Reducibility

In arguing the unsolvability of the halting problem, a TM was constructed that computed the halting functions only for machines applied to their own descriptions—H_s. This machine led to an impossible situation. Since it could be easily constructed if H was available, H could not exist. Now if some machine M could be transformed into H (or H_s), the same reasoning would allow us to conclude that M could not be constructed. This is called *reducibility* to the halting problem. Reducibility is the fundamental method of proving that other functions are not computable.

The Blank Tape Halting Problem

Consider the halting problem for machines started on a blank tape. This is a sub-case of the halting problem. However, it can be reduced to the ordinary halting problem.

Define the machine: $H_{\text{blank}}(M) = H(M, \text{blank tape})$.

Consider machine M_{any} operating on tape T and replace it by machine M_{writeT} composed with $M_{\text{any}} \cdot M_{\text{writeT}}$ will start by writing tape T on a blank tape with a series of quintuples of the form $q_i\, b\, S_i\, q_{i+1}\, R$, where S_i is the ith symbol on the tape T. Since only a finite number of tape cells may be initially non-blank, only a finite set of such quintuples is necessary. After writing the tape, it calls M. So,

$$H(M,\ T) = H_{\text{blank}}(M_{\text{writeT}} \circ M)$$

where $\circ$ denotes composition of machines. Hence the problem reduces to the unsolvability of the ordinary halting problem.

The Equivalence Problem for Two Computations

Is it possible to have an algorithm that decides whether two TM computations give the same result for all halting computations? Let E be the TM for equivalence and let M_1 and M_2 be arbitrary TM's.

$$E(M_1, M_2, T) = \begin{cases} 0 & \text{if } M_1(T) = M_2(T) \text{ or if } M_1(T) \text{ and } M_2(T) \\ & \text{both don't halt} \\ 1 & \text{otherwise.} \end{cases}$$

This would be a very useful computation. If someone reprogrammed a computer in a more efficient way and wished to be sure that the new program produced the same results as the old, the new program could be checked by E.

Let M_{loop} be a machine which does not halt. Then, it can be shown that

$$E(M_{\text{loop}}, M, T) = H(M, T)$$

Therefore the equivalence problem reduces to the halting problem.

Many other general computations can be reduced to the halting problem and hence can be shown to be unsolvable.

7.8   ALTERNATIVE FORMS OF COMPUTABILITY

A Turing Machine could be constructed to simulate a computer. It would be a long and tedious program. The random access of information in computer memory would be replaced by linear searches along the TM tape. The operations of a computer can be simulated in a manner similar to the TM_{add} example of Section 7.2.

A computer program can be written to simulate a UTM. Such a program demonstrates that the computer is an alternate model for computability. All general purpose computers, and even many special purpose computers, can be programmed to simulate a UTM given *arbitrary* external memory such as an unlimited supply of magnetic tape. Let us program a UTM simulator in Algolic.

A Turing Machine Simulator

Given a suitable Algolic encoding of a Turing machine M, the program P_{UTM} will simulate the activities of that machine. Let the quintuples of M be stored as five integer arrays:

CurrentState[i], *CurrentSymbol*[i], *NewSymbol*[i], *NewState*[i], *Move*[i], $i = 1, \ldots, n,$

where the symbol and state arrays are integer encodings of the corresponding entities of M, and $Move[i] = +1$ means R while $Move[i] = -1$ denotes L. Let the tape be represented as an array $Tape[i]$, $i = 0, \pm 2, \ldots, \pm m$. $Tape[i]$ would contain an encoding of the symbol contained in the ith square of M's tape. We could let $m = 1000$, say; if we "run out" of tape, the array bounds may be extended or we could start using auxiliary storage.

The following variables are employed to represent the "state" of the machine M being simulated by P_{UTM}:

Q: current state of M

$head$: current head position (the read/write head of M is prepared to read or write $Tape[head]$)

S: current symbol ($S = Tape[head]$)

Assume that $HaltS$ denotes the halt state, $InitialState$ is the initial state of M, $head = 0$ initially, and that the array $Tape$ is initialized with M's initial tape. The Algolic program segment for P_{UTM} follows the flow chart of Figure 7.2:

P_{UTM}:

```
    head := 0; Q := InitialState; {Initialize.}
    while Q ≠ HaltS do
    begin
      S := Tape[head]; {Read next symbol from tape.}
      {Search the n quintuples for (Q, S, ., ., .).}
      i := 1;
      while (i ≤ n) and (not (CurrentState[i] = Q and CurrentSym-
        bol[i] = S)) do i := i + 1; {inefficient but simple sequential
        search}
      if i > n then Q := HaltS {(Q, S, ., ., .) not in quintuples}
      else
      begin {Search successful at quintuple i.}
        Tape[head] := NewSymbol[i]; {Write new symbol on tape.}
        head := head + Move[i]; {Move head.}
        Q := NewState[i] {Change state of M.}
      end
    end
    {Simulation terminates. Tape contains output of M.}
```

As we have noted, several mathematicians proposed alternate formal models for computability. These models of Kleene, Markov, Church and others, have been shown equivalent, i.e., they can be used to simulate a UTM and in turn can be themselves simulated by a Turing Machine. Each such formulation that has remained an actively used vehicle for exploring computability is characteristically more useful than the other formulations for some set of problems. The ordinary programming languages and machine languages are of course practical tools—used when writing programs for real computers. The formal schema generally are more satisfactory for theoretical problems, where the simple structure illuminates rather than obscures a mathematical proof. (After all, what is more atomic and naive than a TM?) The converse is generally true—a real computation expressed as a TM is usually more obscure than the same computation in a high-level programming language like Algol.

While we will not investigate alternate formal models of computability here, the existence of a wide variety of such models is important support for Turing's thesis. We are thus strongly inclined to treat *effectively computable* and *Turing Machine computable* as identical.

7.9   THE SIGNIFICANCE OF NON-COMPUTABILITY

That there are interesting problems that have no complete computational solution has, of course, tremendous practical significance. The alchemists of the middle ages were searching for the philosophers' stone—a catalyst for changing dross to gold. Similarly programs that solve the halting problem or the equivalence problem are unavailable. Just as the new science of chemistry was founded on an understanding that basic constituent materials were immutable, a similar understanding of non-computability frees computer scientists to pursue practical sub-cases. For example, the halting function can be computed when the programs are loop free. In the next chapter, some issues of practical concern will be discussed.

The Turing result as indicated earlier is one of a number of similar results. The logician K. Gödel in 1931 proved that any consistent axiom system sufficiently rich to represent elementary number theory could have true statements that were not provable within the axiom system. The flavor of this theorem is similar to knowing that a TM either halts or does not halt but having no way of always predicting which will happen. The Gödel result is proved by showing that well-formed statements of number theory can be uniquely numbered. These numbers are called Gödel numbers. A "diagonalized" number is then constructed which corresponds to a well-formed statement of number theory. This diagonalized formula is the equivalent of H in TM theory. Both Turing and Gödel demonstrated the limitations of formal constructive systems.

These results have been used to imply that machines are limited in a way man is not. It is argued that man is intuitive, inconsistent, creative, and superrational, and hence has no limits. Machines are deterministic, plodding, uncreative, and strongly limited in the sense of Gödel-Turing.

However, the Gödel-Turing result limits mathematicians in the *exact* same way. A mathematician cannot produce a deductive proof of a non-provable proposition without abandoning the system within which the limitation exists. The computer using the same meta-system would also avoid the Gödel-Turing limitations. Indeed one could, as Turing pointed out, program an inconsistent set of axioms into a computer and totally avoid the Gödel limitation.

A further insight of the Turing work is that the difficulty springs from the UTM's ability to interpret and imitate any other machine in the system. Only in systems that allow internal mimicry do unsolvable problems exist. Metaphorically, only self-conscious reasoning systems create unanswerable metaphysical questions. The mystical cyclic quality of *amor fati*[4] becomes in machine terms an inability to solve the halting problem. The problems of consciousness become in these terms an epiphenomenon of the "universal" computing facility of the human brain.

The debate on the philosophical significance of the Gödel-Turing results continues. The controversies have been further stimulated by work in artificial intelligence—the area of computer science that attempts to write programs that imitate human intelligence. Some results of this work will be examined in Chapter 9.

The Cantor-Gödel-Turing work in logic and mathematics is part of a 20th century revolution in all scientific thinking. The observer is condemned to live in the universe and, constrained by his subjectivity, never to completely know the "state" of the universe. The quantum mechanics and relativity theory both insist on this condition. In consequence, modern philosophy is dominated by positivists who no longer ask unanswerable metaphysical questions.

EXERCISES

1. Give one advantage and one disadvantage of using English, Algolic, and TM machines as algorithmic notations.

---

[4] literally, "love of fate"

2. For the tape:

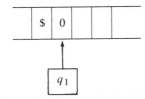

what is the effect of the following instructions:

(a) $q_1\,0\,0\,q_2\,R$
(b) $q_1\,0\,1\,q_1\,L$
(c) $q_1\,\$\,0\,q_1\,R$
(d) $q_1\,0\,0\,h$

3. Write the simplest possible TM program that will always halt.

4. What would be the problem with having $q_1 * * q_3 L$ and $q_1 * A\, q_2 R$ appear in the same TM program?

5. Change TM_{parity} so that it erases the tape as it scans.

6. Extend TM_{parity} to a program that computes the one's parity of a string of one's and zero's—i.e., only taking into account the parity of one's, e.g. TM_{parity} $(11010) = TM_{parity}\,(0111) = T$.

7. Change question 6 to output two answers—one for the parity of one's and the other for the parity of zero's. Try to write this program in two different ways (1) in which you only scan the tape once from right to left and (2) in which you scan the tape twice.

8. Change TM_{parity} to a TM that computes whether the number of one's on the tape is divisible by 3.

9. Let the initial tape for TM_{copy} be:

Execute TM_{copy} on this tape until the machine halts. After each quintuple is executed, show the tape, head position, and new tape.

10. Consider $TM_{palindrome}$. For a string of length n, how many instructions are executed in showing the string to be a palindrome.

11. Change $TM_{palindrome}$ so that it can deal with strings of A, B, and C.

12. Suppose an integer x is coded in *unary* on a Turing machine tape as follows:

If $x > 0$, then x is represented by a string of $2x$ one's.
If $x \le 0$, then x is represented by a string of $2|x| + 1$ one's.

Examples: +2:

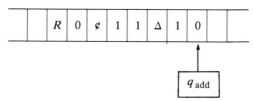

4 one's

−2:

... | b | 1 | 1 | 1 | 1 | 1 | b | ...

5 one's

(a) Exhibit a TM that computes the function $f(x) = x - 1$, where x is an integer.
(b) Describe a TM that computes the function $g(x) = 2x$.
(c) Using the machines of (a) and (b) and composition, describe a TM that computes the function $h(x) = 2x - 1 = f(g(x))$.

13. Simulate the action of TM_{add} on the tape:

| | R | 0 | ¢ | 1 | 1 | Δ | 1 | 0 | | |

q_{add}

Show the contents of the tape each time the TM enters state q_{ret}.

14. Construct a TM named $TM_{OneBitSubtract}$ that subtracts two one bit binary numbers; include a bit for the "borrow."

15. Suppose a positive integer is coded in unsigned binary on a TM tape.

Examples:

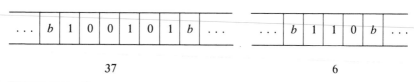

37   6

Describe a TM that computes the function $f(x) = x + 1$, where x is a positive integer.

16. Exhibit a TM that computes the two's complement of a bit string.

Examples:

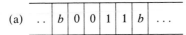

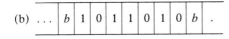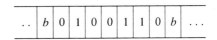

(a)

(b)

17. (a) Using the same encoding for the non-negative integers, exhibit the following three TM's:

$$
\text{(i) } TM_{m<n}\colon \text{Computes } f(m,\ n) = \begin{cases} T & \text{if } m < n \\ F & \text{if } m \geq n \end{cases} \quad (m,\ n \geq 0)
$$

(ii) $TM_{m \leftarrow m-n}$: Replaces m by $m - n$ for $m \geq n$

(iii) $TM_{n \leftarrow n+1}$: Increments n by 1 $(n \geq 0)$

(b) Using composition and the three machines of (a), give a $TM_{q,r}$ that computes the quotient q and remainder r on dividing m by n, where m and n are positive integers.

18. (Busy Beaver Problem) Write a TM which has an external alphabet $\{1\}$ and uses K states such that the TM writes on an initially blank tape as many one's as possible and then halts. Try this for $K = 1, 2, 3, 4, 5$.

19. Decode $10 * b * 101 * h * R$ as a quintuple of TM_{parity} using the UTM coding found in Section 7.4.

20. Draw a flow chart for the UTM.

21. Write a TM which can look up a state-symbol pair in a TM program encoded on a UTM tape.

22. What is the minimum length palindrome necessary to force $TM_{palindrome}$ to halt after 10^6 cycles?

23. Paradox has been of fundamental importance in the development of philosophy and logic. Develop this theme by examples from antiquity up until modern times.

24. Consider the problem of Achilles and the tortoise. When Achilles reached the finish line, where would the tortoise be?

25. Are the powers of 2, i.e., 1, 2, 4, 8, 16, 32, .. equinumerous with the integers? Prove your answer.

26. Provide a polynomial in p and q that maps the rationals into the integers.

27. What is the flaw in the following "proof" that the rationals cannot be counted?

(a) Write the rationals as a decimal expansion.
$$0 . a_1{}^{(1)} \, a_2{}^{(1)} \, a_3{}^{(1)} \, \ldots$$
$$0 . a_1{}^{(2)} \, a_2{}^{(2)} \, a_3{}^{(2)} \, \ldots$$
$$0 . a_1{}^{(3)} \, a_2{}^{(3)} \, a_3{}^{(3)} \, \ldots$$

(b) Construct a diagonalized number
$$b_i = \begin{cases} a_i{}^{(i)} + 1 & \text{if } a_i{}^{(i)} \neq 9 \\ 0 & \text{if } a_i{}^{(i)} = 9 \end{cases}$$

This number does not appear in the list of rationals; hence the list is incomplete and the rationals are not countable.

28. Prove that the class of all TM programs that "once started never move to the left of their starting square," constitutes a class of TM's for which the halting problem is unsolvable.

29. Contrast the operation of a TM with the operation of the digital computer. In what ways are they the same?

30. "If it can be shown that human intellectual skills cannot be simulated by machine, Turing's thesis will have been disproved." Elaborate on the meaning of this remark.

31. Examine the thesis that a sufficiently complicated system can never be fully understood whenever the observer is part of the system. Be sure to comment not only on the logical incompleteness of complex systems, but on analogous difficulties which have come to light in experimental sciences.

ADDITIONAL READINGS

Arbib, M. *Brains, Machines and Mathematics.* New York: McGraw-Hill, 1964.

Cohen, P. J. and Hersch, R. "Non-Cantorian set theory," *Scientific American.* December 1967.

Galler, B. and Perlis, A. *A View of Programming Languages.* Reading, Mass.: Addison-Wesley, 1970.

Minsky, M. *Computation: Finite and Infinite Machines.* Englewood Cliffs, N.J.: Prentice-Hall, 1967.

Nagel, E. and Newman, J. R. "Gödel's proof," *Scientific American.* June 1956.

Nievergelt, J. and Farrar, J. C. "What machines can and cannot do," *Computing Surveys,* Vol. 4, No. 2, June 1972, pp. 81–96.

Quine, W. V. "Paradox," *Scientific American.* April 1962.

Rogers, H., Jr. *Theory of Recursive Functions and Effective Computability.* New York: McGraw-Hill, 1967.

Trakhtenbrot, B. A. *Algorithms and Automatic Computing Machines.* New York: Heath, 1963.

Chapter 8

ANALYSIS OF ALGORITHMS

A computer program is meant to specify an algorithmic solution to a class of problems. We wish to be sure that the program *correctly* specifies such a solution; furthermore, it is desirable that the solution be an *efficient* one. This chapter covers some of the important techniques and ideas related to these two aspects of algorithm analysis.

Correctness

A program is correct if it terminates with answers appropriate to its input. How can one argue persuasively that a given program is correct? In many of our examples, we attempt this persuasion through *comments*. The comments are the program authors' description of what important pieces of program do. They are written both to document the program and to persuade the user that the program will work. We also frequently execute the program on sample input for which an answer is known. This can be done by hand-simulation or, more extensively, by running larger volumes of test data on a computer. A well-chosen set of tests often provides a convincing, if not perfect, argument for correctness.

These informal procedures for verifying that programs are error-free are not always satisfactory. Since many algorithms need to be correct over an infinite domain,[1] such as the set of all strings or the positive integers, no amount of testing can guarantee correctness. Even well-refereed published programs often contain bugs. In other areas of science, most certainty is assured by a rigorous proof. So it will be with programs; we will formally prove the correctness and termination of algorithms. It should be noted that

---

[1] Strictly speaking, the domain of computer-representable entities is finite, but it could be so large that for all practical purposes, it is best treated as infinite.

the proofs themselves can be in error—ultimately there is no complete guarantee of correctness, but the level of precision required in a rigorous proof is in itself an effective debugging technique.

Efficiency

For any problem, there are often many good candidate solutions. For example, there are numerous interesting sorting methods, and there are many books written on the variety of techniques for solving systems of linear equations. Typically, important computational problems have a variety of solution methods. In order to predict performance and to determine a preferred method to use, it is necessary to know how efficient an algorithm is with respect to such resources as memory space and computation time. Methods which take little space often require large numbers of instructions and methods conservative of instruction cycles often require comparatively large memory storage; this is spoken of as a time-space tradeoff.

Focusing on time and space measures frequently leads to improved algorithms. However, for many practical problems, there is a point beyond which improvements can no longer be made, and the algorithm is optimal. It is of great importance to know how efficient the best possible algorithms are for a given problem. Some interesting results on this question are presented in the latter half of this chapter.

8.1 PROGRAM PROVING

In Chapter 2, we introduced a formal technique for proving the correctness of a flow chart representation of an algorithm. We now outline an analogous method for proving programs correct. The central idea is to use assertions to indicate the effects of executing one or more program statements—what transformation is accomplished by the statement(s) and what is left unchanged.

Example: *before*: $\{z > 0\}$
$$x := 0; \quad y := 2 \times x; \quad r := z;$$
after: $\{x = 0, \quad y = 0, \quad r = z, \quad z > 0, \quad r > 0\}$

In the above example, given some input conditions (assertions) on the program variables ($z > 0$), the three assignments lead to a set of provable output conditions ($x = 0, y = 0, r = z, z > 0, r > 0$). Regardless of what else is going on in the program, the output conditions are true if the input conditions are true and the assignment statements are executed.

Given input assertions A_I and output assertions A_O for a program represented by statements S, the correctness of S with respect to A_I and A_O is established in two steps:

1. Prove that if A_I is true and S is executed, then A_O will be true when and if S terminates.
   We express this theorem with the notation: $\{A_I\} \, S \, \{A_O\}$.
2. Prove that S terminates.

The assertion proofs are made manageable by decomposing S into its constituent statements and providing appropriate assertions and proofs for each constituent.

Example: Consider the following annotated program for computing $10 \times a$ in a tricky fashion.

```
algorithm Tricky10×a;
a, a2, a8, a10: integer;
begin
    read (a);
    {A_I: a is an integer}
    a2 := a + a;
    {a2 = 2 × a}
    a8 := a2 + a2;
    {a8 = 4 × a}
    a8 := a8 + a8;
    {a8 = 8 × a}
    a10 := a8 + a2;
    {A_O: a10 = 10 × a}
    write ('a = ', a, ' 10 × a =', a10)
end.
```

Given the truth of A_I, i.e., that a proper integer is read into a, then $a10 = 10 \times a$, (A_O), when the program terminates. Each successive assertion is self-evidently true from the laws of arithmetic. The program terminates since there are no loops. The correctness of the input-output assertion is expressed:

$\{a \text{ is an integer}\} \, a2 := a + a; \, a8 := a2 + a2; \, a8 := a8 + a8;$
$\qquad a10 := a8 + a2 \, \{a10 = 10 \times a\}$

This example is, of course, a simple one, since it does not use the more difficult program statements such as conditional and **while** statements.

Statements and Input/Output Assertions

What kinds of assertions can be proven for various types of statements? Consider the *assignment statement*:

$$v := expr$$

Suppose we wish an output assertion $A_O = A(v)$ that states some relations involving the variable v; then $A(expr)$, the result of substituting $expr$ for all occurrences of v in A, must be satisfied *before* executing the assignment. Stated another way, if $A(expr)$ is true and "$v := expr$" is executed, then $A(v)$ will be true;

$$\text{i.e., } \{A(expr)\}\ v := expr\ \{A(v)\}$$

This rule expresses the meaning of an assignment statement and can be used as an *axiom* or *proof rule* in correctness proofs.

Examples:

1. $\{y + z = 5\}\ x := y + z\ \{x = 5\}$

   $\quad A(y + z) \qquad\qquad\quad A(x)$

2. $\{0 < v + 1 \le 10\}\ v := v + 1\ \{0 < v \le 10\}$

   $\qquad A(v + 1) \qquad\qquad\qquad A(v)$

   Simplifying $A(v + 1)$:

   $\{-1 < v \le 9\}\ v := v + 1\ \{0 < v \le 10\}$

3. Normally, we must also use logical implication. The statement "$a8 := a8 + a8$" in the program "$Tricky10 \times a$" has output assertion $A(a8)$: $a8 = 8 \times a$. By the assignment axiom, we can assume:

   $\{a8 + a8 = 8 \times a\}\ a8 := a8 + a8\ \{a8 = 8 \times a\}$

   $\qquad\quad A_I \qquad\qquad\qquad\qquad\qquad A_O$

   But assuming that the assertions preceding our statement have been proven, we have the truth of $\{a8 = 4 \times a\}$ which implies A_I.

The **if/then/else** statement has two alternate paths selected by the truth or falsity of its Boolean expression, but we wish to prove theorems of the form:

$$\{A_I\}\ \textbf{if } B \textbf{ then } S_1 \textbf{ else } S_2\ \{A_O\}$$

The result is established *if* we can prove the following theorems associated with each path:

1. $\{A_I \wedge B\}\ S_1\ \{A_O\}$
2. $\{A_I \wedge \neg B\}\ S_2\ \{A_O\}$

Example:

$\{x \in R,\ \text{the set of real numbers}\}$
if $x \geq 0$ **then** $y := x$ **else** $y := -x$
$\{x \in R \wedge y = |x|\}$

The reader should verify that the two theorems above are provable here,

$$\text{i.e.,}\ \{x \in R \wedge x \geq 0\}\ y := x\ \{x \in R \wedge y = |x|\}$$
$$\text{and}\ \{x \in R \wedge \neg(x \geq 0)\}\ y := -x\ \{x \in R \wedge y = |x|\}.$$

These can be easily proven using the assignment axiom.

The rule: "if $\{A_I \wedge B\}\ S_1\ \{A_O\}$ and $\{A_I \wedge \neg B\}\ S_2\ \{A_O\}$, then it can be concluded that $\{A_I\}$ **if** B **then** S_1 **else** S_2 $\{A_O\}$" is called the *axiom* or *proof rule* for the **if/then/else** statement.

The other important statements in Algolic are those that loop. We will only treat the **while** statement as it is most basic and other loops can be rewritten in terms of it alone. The form of the **while** is **while** B **do** S; internal to the **while** loop and before S is executed, the Boolean expression B is true. The statement S can thus assume that B is true, but its execution may change B. Any assertion except B that is always to be true *before* S is executed should also, in general, hold *after* execution of S since control can return to the top of the loop again. Upon exit from the **while**, B is false and all output assertions can also include $\neg B$.

These observations lead to the search for an *invariant* assertion—one that holds both before and after S, and before and after the **while** statement. Given such an invariant assertion, say A, if we can prove:

$$\{A \wedge B\}\ S\ \{A\}$$

then we may conclude:

$$\{A\}\ \textbf{while}\ B\ \textbf{do}\ S\ \{A \wedge \neg B\}$$

This proof rule or axiom for the **while** statement focuses our attention on finding appropriate invariants (A's) that express the intended meaning of the loop.

Examples:

1. Consider again the square root program given in Section 4.1.2. The program annotated with assertions is:

    $\{N \geq 0\}$
    $a := 0;$
    $\{A : a^2 \leq N\}$
    while $(a + 1) \times (a + 1) \leq N$ **do** $a := a + 1;$
    $\{(a^2 \leq N) \wedge \neg((a + 1)^2 \leq N)\}$

    To verify the **while** loop, we must prove:

    $\{a^2 \leq N \wedge (a + 1)^2 \leq N\}\ a := a + 1\ \{a^2 \leq N\}$

    $\{\quad A \quad \wedge \qquad B \quad\}\ \ S\ \ \{\ A\ \}$

    The axiom of assignment gives

    $\{(a + 1)^2 \leq N\}\ a := a + 1\ \{a^2 \leq N\}$

    But $A \wedge B$ implies B, i.e., $a^2 \leq N \wedge (a + 1)^2 \leq N \supset (a + 1)^2 \leq N$. It is therefore true that $\{A \wedge B\}\ S\ \{A\}$, given the above expressions for A, B, and S.

2. The following code is an example of a loop structure that appears frequently.

    $S := 0;\ i := 1;$
    while $i < 10$ **do begin** $S := S + a[i];\ i := i + 1$ **end**

    Let us verify the program by inserting appropriate assertions; the axioms that we have presented for each statement type can be used to prove each assertion. The program with inserted assertions is:

$$S := 0; i := 1;$$

$$\{i = 1 \wedge S = \sum_{t=1}^{i-1} a[t]\}$$

while $i < 10$ **do**

$$\textbf{begin } \{1 \leq i < 10 \wedge S = \sum_{t=1}^{i-1} a[t]\}$$

$$S := S + a[i];$$

$$\{1 \leq i < 10 \wedge S = \sum_{t=1}^{i} a[t]\}$$

$$i := i + 1$$

$$\{1 < i \leq 10 \wedge S = \sum_{t=1}^{i-1} a[t]\}$$

end

$$\{i = 10 \wedge S = \sum_{t=1}^{9} a[t]\}$$

The examples demonstrate how various assertions are realized from the axioms for each important Algolic statement type. There is no general rule for deriving such assertions. If there were, it would amount to a complete proof procedure for determining the effect of algorithms, a violation of the undecidability results of the previous chapter.

Termination

Where no loops exist, termination is self-evident;[2] when loops are present, termination must be proven. In the **while** loop of the last example, it is apparent that the variable i counts from 1 to 10 with $i = 10$ causing termination. The value of i increases monotonically by a fixed amount each time through the loop. The usual method of proof of termination is to find some variable or quantity that either increases or decreases until a termination condition occurs.

Example:

Suppose a loop has the general form:

while $x > 0$ **do begin** $x := x - e$; S **end**;

Assuming that $e > 0$ and S has no effect on e or x, it is clear that x monotonically decreases until it satisfies the property $x \leq 0$; consequently, the loop terminates.

---

[2] We are assuming that all operations in Boolean and arithmetic expressions terminate and are ignoring such problems as overflow, underflow, and divide by zero.

The Correctness of a GCD Program

We prove the correctness, including termination, of a program for Euclid's greatest common divisor algorithm. The program and proof are similar to those introduced in Chapter 2.

```
algorithm GCD;
M, N, m, n, r : integer;
begin {M > 0 ∧ N > 0}
   read (M, N);
   m := M; n := N;
   {gcd(M, N) = gcd(m, n)}
   while n ≠ 0 do
   begin
      {gcd(M, N) = gcd(m, n) ∧ m > 0 ∧ n > 0}
      r := m mod n;
      {gcd(M, N) = gcd(m, n) ∧ 0 ≤ r < n ∧ m = qn + r ∧ q ≥ 0}
      m := n; n := r
      {gcd(M, N) = gcd(m, n) ∧ m > 0 ∧ n ≥ 0}
   end;
   {n = 0 ∧ gcd(M, N) = gcd(m, n) = m}
   write ('GCD of M = ', M, 'and N = ', N, 'is', m)
end.
```

The critical point about the above assertions is that $gcd(M, N) = gcd(m, n)$ remains true throughout the execution of the **while** loop.

Theorem: $gcd(M, N) = gcd(m, n)$ is an invariant for the **while** loop.
Proof:
Case 1: upon loop entry.
$m = M$ and $n = N$. Therefore it is trivially true that $gcd(M, N) = gcd(m, n)$.
Case 2: after the loop is executed.
By Theorem 1 in Section 2.2.1, the assertion after "$r := m$ **mod** n;" is valid; by Theorem 2 in Section 2.2.1, $gcd(m, n) = gcd(n, r)$ after execution of this statement also. Therefore, the substitutions for m and n given by "$m := n$; $n := r$" maintain the invariance of $gcd(M, N) = gcd(m, n)$.   □

Theorem: At some iteration, $n = 0$ and the **while** loop terminates.
Proof: After "$r := m$ **mod** n," we have $0 ≤ r ≤ n - 1$ by the definition of the **mod** operator. Since n is then set to r, n is decreased by at least 1 each time through the loop. Hence n must eventually reach 0.   □

8.2 EFFICIENCY

When solving problems by computer, we want programs that are efficient, as well as correct and understandable. Let us examine the efficiency of a frequently occurring computation—the evaluation of polynomials. We will give three different algorithms for this problem and analyze the time and space used by each.

The first method is based on the decomposition of the polynomial

$$P(x) = a_n x^n + a_{n-1} x^{n-1} \cdots + a_1 x + a_o$$

into its $n + 1$ subexpressions of the form $s_i = a_i x^i$, $i = 0, \ldots, n - 1$, where each subexpression is evaluated separately. The following program $P1$ implements this approach.

algorithm $P1$;
    {Polynomial evaluation by computing each $s_i = a_i x^i$ separately.}
    n, i, j : *integer*; $x, polyval$: *real*;
    a, S **:array** [0..100] **of** *real;*
    {n is the degree of the polynomial $P(x) = $ a$[n]x^n + \cdots + $ a$[0]$. $S[i]$ will
      be used for the value $a[i]x^i$, *polyval* will store the value of $P(x)$.}
    begin
      read (x, n); {$0 \leq n \leq 100$}
      for $i := 0$ **upto** n **do**
      begin
        $S[i] := 1$; *read* $(a[i])$;
        for $j := 1$ **upto** i **do** $S[i] := x \times S[i]$;
        $S[i] := a[i] \times S[i]$
      end;
      polyval $:= 0$;
      for $i := 0$ **upto** n **do** *polyval* $:=$ *polyval* $+ S[i]$;
      write (*'value at'*, x, *'is'*, *polyval*)
    end.

Each $S[i]$ requires i multiplications to compute x^i and one multiplication for $a[i] \times S[i]$, for a total of $i + 1$ multiplications. To compute all n terms requires $\sum_{i=0}^{n} (i + 1)$ multiplications; summing this standard series, we have $(n + 2)(n + 1)/2$ total multiplications. *polyval* is obtained by the addition of $n + 1$ terms. Summarizing, we have for $P1$:

    $n + 1$ adds, $(n + 2)(n + 1)/2$ multiplies
    2 arrays that must be at least the size of the degree of the polynomial

By noticing that $x^{i+1} = x^i \times x$, $i = 0, \ldots, n - 1$, we can avoid a large amount of recomputation for the S terms. Algorithm $P2$ uses this relationship.

algorithm $P2$;
    {$P2$ is the same as $P1$ except that is uses the relationship $x^{i+1} = x^i \times x$}
    $n, i : integer$; $x, polyval : real$;
    $a, S, power$: **array** $[0..100]$ **of** $real$;
    {Variables are as in $P1$ except $power[i] = x^i$}
    begin
      $read(x, n)$; {$0 \le n \le 100$}
      $power[0] := 1$; $read(a[0])$; $S[0] := a[0]$;
      for $i := 1$ **upto** n **do**
      begin
        $read(a[i])$; $power[i] := x \times power[i - 1]$;
        $S[i] := a[i] \times power[i]$
        {$power[i] = x^i$, $S[i] = a[i] \times x^i$}
      end;
      $polyval := 0$;
      for $i := 0$ **upto** n **do** $polyval := polyval + S[i]$;
      $write('value\ at', x, 'is', polyval)$
    end.

Algorithm $P2$ requires

    $2n$ multiplications, $n + 1$ additions
    3 arrays of size at least as great as the polynomial degree

There is a significant reduction in the number of multiplications compared with $P1$. However, there is the additional storage used for the *power* array, but this array is not really necessary. (See Exercise 8.11.)

We now come to algorithm $P3$ which follows from the decomposition

$$P(x) = ((\ldots (a_n x + a_{n-1})x + a_{n-2})x + \cdots + a_1)x + a_0.$$

This method is known as *Horner's rule*. A similar scheme was previously used in Chapter 3 for number base conversion.

algorithm *P3*;
  {Polynomial evaluation by Horner's rule.}
  n, *i* : *integer*; *x*, *polyval* : *real*;
  a : **array**[0 . . 100] **of** *real;*
  begin
    read (*x*, *n*); {0 ≤ *n* ≤ 100}
    polyval := 0;
    for *i* := 0 **upto** *n* **do**
    begin
      read (*a*[*n* − *i*]); *polyval* := *polyval* × *x* + *a*[*n* − *i*]
    end;
    write ('*value at*', *x*, '*is*', *polyval*)
  end.

Horner's rule uses only $n + 1$ multiplications and $n + 1$ additions, and a single array to store coefficients. *P3* is thus a substantial improvement over *P2* in both time and storage. In fact, Horner's rule uses the theoretical minimum number of multiplications and additions required for evaluating an arbitrary polynomial.[3] Note that we could do away with the *a* array in all three algorithms by just using *a* : *real* and not retaining each coefficient.

The Order Notation

An "order" notation is often used to characterize the efficiency of an algorithm. If program *P1* operates on a polynomial of degree *n*, we say it takes $O(n^2)$ multiplications (to be read "order n^2"). Recall that it took $(n + 2)(n + 1)/2$ multiplications for *P1* to compute the value of an *n*th degree polynomial, so $O((n + 2)(n + 1)/2) = O(n^2)$. In effect we are saying the two expressions, $(n + 2)(n + 1)/2$ and n^2, are roughly comparable, say within a constant factor of each other—a true statement for large values of *n*.

More exactly, if $f(n) = O(g(n))$, then it is necessary and sufficient that there exist two numbers *a* and *M* such that

$$|f(n)| \le a \cdot |g(n)|, \qquad n \ge M$$

Example: Let $f(n) = (n + 2)(n + 1)/2$ and $g(n) = n^2$.

Then we can show by induction that if $a = 1$ and $M = 4$ then $(n + 2)(n + 1)/2 \le n^2$.

---

[3] Actually, Horner's rule requires only *n* multiplications and additions; this can be obtained in *P3* by initializing *polyval* to *a*[*n*] and changing the **for** loop to "1 **upto** *n*."

Proof: For $n = 4$, we have $(n + 2)(n + 1)/2 = 6 \times 5/2 = 15$ and $n^2 = 4^2 = 16$. Since $15 < 16$, the result holds for $n = 4$.

Induction step: Assume that the result is true for $n = 4, \ldots, k$. Let $n = k + 1$. Then $(n + 2)(n + 1)/2 = (k + 3)(k + 2)/2 = (k + 1)(k + 2)/2 + k + 2$ and $n^2 = (k + 1)^2 = k^2 + 2k + 1$.

By the induction hypothesis, the result holds for $n = k$; i.e., $(k + 1)(k + 2)/2 \le k^2$. Also from arithmetic, we have $k + 2 \le 2k + 1, k \ge 1$.

Therefore $(k + 3)(k + 2)/2 \le (k + 1)^2$ and the result is true for $n = k + 1$.   □

For most elementary functions such as polynomials, it is easy to show that the order notation makes use of the term that grows the fastest in the expression.

Examples:

1. $O(ax^7 + 3x^3 + \sin(x)) = O(ax^7) = x^7$
2. $O(e^n + an^{10}) = O(e^n)$
3. $O(n! + n^{50}) = O(n!)$

The order notation provides an approximate characterization of the growth of a function. For expressing the efficiency of a given algorithm, the variable n, say, in $f(n) = O(g(n))$, is some appropriate measure of the size of the problem. In the case of polynomials, the degree is a natural measure. The efficiency of an array processing computation is typically expressed as a function of the array size while a string algorithm might use string length as the "size" variable. Generally, the size of a problem is directly related to the size of the input.

8.3 THE EFFICIENCY OF SEARCHING AND SORTING

Computers are used more for non-numerical applications than for numerical scientific ones. Many non-numerical applications involve storing and retrieving data in some systematic fashion. Typically the information is ordered and stored according to a numerical or alphabetical key so that it may be retrieved and displayed conveniently. For example, the phonebook is ordered by last name; U.S. income tax files are ordered by social security number.

Linear and Bisected Retrieval

Assume that each information record of a file consists of a *key* part and a *data* part. Given a search key, the retrieval problem is to find that record, if any, that has a key identical to the search key. We will ignore the data part of each record and represent a file by an array $a[1]$, ..., $a[n]$, of keys. (This formulation is similar to that used for symbol tables in Section 6.3.2, where the terms table, entry, argument, and value were used for file, record, key and data, respectively.)

We will study two common ways to retrieve information. The first method—bisection search—requires that the information be ordered on the key. The second method—linear search—is independent of any ordering of the information.

In bisection search, we look midway in our ordered file and compare the key we are searching for with the key just found. If the keys are the same, the search is successful; otherwise, the comparison dictates a remaining half of the file where the key may be. The process is repeated on this half of the file. In effect, each search progresses by cutting the remaining search in half, i.e., "bisecting" the search. The name *binary search* is also used for this algorithm because the size of the file is reduced by a factor of two at each step. The following program implements these ideas.

```
{Searching by Bisection}
{Assume that a[1], ..., a[n] are ordered a[1] < a[2] < ··· < a[n].}
low := 1; high := n; mid := (low + high) ÷ 2;
read (key); {item to be searched for}
{key is assumed to be in the array a.}
while key ≠ a[mid] do
begin
   if key < a[mid] then high := mid − 1
   else low := mid + 1;
{Note: high is monotone decreasing and low is monotone increasing.}
   mid := (low + high) ÷ 2
end;
write('found at', mid)
```

To illustrate the operation of this search algorithm, let $n = 7$, $key = 28$, and the array a be:

i:	1	2	3	4	5	6	7
$a[i]$:	3	11	16	18	28	80	101

Each time control reaches the **while** loop test "*key* $\neq$ *a*[*mid*]", the values of the program variables (*low, high, mid*) are: (1, 7, 4), (5, 7, 6), and (5, 5, 5).

Theorem: The bisection algorithm works in $O(\log_2 n)$ comparisons.
Proof: By induction. Assume $n = 2^k + 1$ objects. We will show that no more than k executions of the **while** loop are required.

Case $k = 1$: $n = 2^1 + 1 = 3$. We have $a[1] < a[2] < a[3]$. If *key* is found in $a[2]$, then $mid = (1 + 3) \div 2 = 2$ will give the correct location immediately without executing the **while** loop. If *key* is in $a[1]$, then $key < a[2]$ is true and the **while** loop is executed once, setting *high* to $mid - 1$, namely $high = 1$; then $mid = (1 + 1) \div 2 = 1$ and *key* is found after one execution. The argument is symmetrical for *key* in $a[3]$.

Case general: Assume by induction hypothesis that the theorem is true for $k \leq m$. We now prove it for $k = m + 1$. The first calculation of *mid* gives $mid = (2^{m-1} + 1 + 1) \div 2 = 2^m + 1$. Thus the first comparison of *key* leaves two halves of the array each size 2^m. By the induction hypothesis, this search requires no more than m loop executions for a maximum of $m + 1$.

Therefore our proof has shown that for $n = 2^k + 1$, we require at most k loop executions. Since $\log_2 (n - 1) = \log_2 (2^k) = k$, this is just $O(\log_2 n)$. For n values which are not conveniently in this form, we can apply the same proof to $n' = 2^k + 1 = n + r$ with $0 \leq r < n$. These r elements can be interpreted as a list of elements of maximum value appended to a. Since two comparisons are made each time through the loop except the last, the number of comparisons is also $O(\log_2 n)$. $\square$

Binary search is thus extremely fast. For example, one million entries can be searched with no more than 20 comparisons.

A *linear search*, also called *sequential search*, would start from $a[1]$ and proceed to $a[n]$ checking each key in turn:

{Linear Search}
{$a[1], \ldots, a[n]$ are arbitrarily ordered.}
   $i := 1$; *read* (*key*); {key is assumed to be in the array a.}
   while $key \neq a[i]$ **do** $i := i + 1$;
   write ('*found at*', *i*)

Theorem: Assuming *key* is equally likely to be anywhere in a, the average number of comparisons for linear search is $O(n)$.
Proof: There are n possibilities for finding *key*, each requiring $1 \leq i \leq n$ comparisons. Therefore, the expected number of comparisons is

$$\frac{1}{n}(1 + 2 + \cdots + n) = \frac{1}{n}\sum_{i=1}^{n} i = \frac{1}{n}\frac{(n + 1)n}{2} = \frac{n + 1}{2} = O(n). \quad \square$$

For a million element array, a linear search requires an average of one-half million comparisons. Clearly, it is preferable to search an ordered list in $O(\log_2 n)$ if the list is the least bit large. However, we have ignored the work involved in ordering the list. The methods for doing this are called *sorting* algorithms.

Sorting

If one wishes to obtain the ordering $a[1] < a[2] < \cdots < a[n]$, then no two adjacent elements can end up with $a[i] > a[i + 1]$. We first present an algorithm based on interchanging any two adjacent elements which are out of order. The method is called a *bubble sort* because the largest element is "bubbled" to the top of the current list at each step.

{Order the array $a[1]$, ..., $a[n]$, in ascending sequence using a bubble sort.}
$n1 := n - 1;$
for $k := n1$ **downto** 1 **do**
   for $i := 1$ **upto** k **do**
       {Bubble largest element in $a[1]$, ..., $a[k + 1]$ to $a[k + 1]$.}
       if $a[i] > a[i + 1]$ **then**
          begin {interchange}
              $t := a[i + 1]; a[i + 1] := a[i]; a[i] := t$
          end
    {$a[1] < \cdots < a[n]$}

For a size n problem, the inner loop ("$i := 1$ **upto** k") is executed first $n - 1$ times, then $n - 2$ times, ... and finally 2 times. This leads to the summation

$$\text{inner-loop-executed} = \sum_{i=2}^{n-1} i = \sum_{i=1}^{n-1} i - 1 = \frac{n(n-1)}{2} - 1$$

which is $O(n^2)$. This is a natural measure of the efficiency of the bubble sort since most of the computation is performed in the inner loop.

The bubble sorting method is much more costly than either of the searching techniques discussed. Ideally, it would be a one-time cost, justified by the later use of bisection searches in $O(\log_2 n)$ time rather than $O(n)$ linear searches. Sorting in $O(n^2)$ is reasonable if the number of file searches are at least $O(n)$ before the sorted file is discarded. (Why?)

The bubble sort is a simple sort but not a very efficient one. There exist much better algorithms that sort in as little as $O(n \log_2 n)$ time. Where bubble sort would order 1000 elements in $a \times 10^6$ computation steps, a more efficient $O(n \log_2 n)$ algorithm could sort between 10^4 and 10^5 elements in the same amount of time.

One such algorithm which on the average works in $O(n \log_2 n)$ time is *quicksort*, invented by C. A. R. Hoare. Quicksort works by partitioning an array of elements into two parts, the low end of the array having elements all smaller than the high end of array. This is done by comparing each element to some randomly selected key and placing elements in one end of the partition based on their comparison with this key. Each subpartition is similarly treated until the array is in order. We illustrate by the following example.

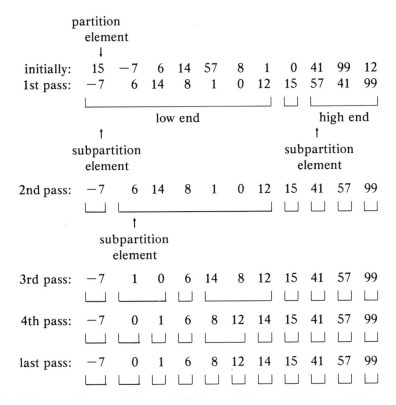

When we are fortunate, the partition element divides each subarray into two equal halves. If this were to happen each time, only $O(\log_2 n)$ passes would be required to sort the array. This is near enough to the average case behavior for large n—though we will not derive the result here. Each pass requires $O(n)$ comparisons with the various partitioning elements giving us a total effort of $O(n \log_2 n)$.

A large number of different sorting algorithms have been devised; for example, Knuth presents and analyzes 14 different methods in his encyclopedic volume on sorting and searching. The two we have discussed represent extremes in the sense that bubble sort is one of the least efficient (in time) general methods and quicksort is recommended as one of the best for general use. (These remarks are based on *average* time cost measures; quicksort has worst case behavior of $O(n^2)$ when the array is already in order, while a simple variation of bubble sort runs in $O(n)$ for this case.)

8.4 WHAT IS PRACTICALLY COMPUTABLE

A modern large scale computer can carry out approximately 10^{10} operations an hour. Assuming that this is proportional to the size of problem it can handle, we find the following relationships:

Complexity	Size	Operations
$\log_2 n$	$2^{10^{10}}$	10^{10}
n	10^{10}	10^{10}
n^2	10^5	10^{10}
n^5	10^2	10^{10}
2^n	33	10^{10}
$n!$	13	10^{10}

A problem that requires an exponentially or factorially complex algorithm is thus only solvable for very small-sized problems. We have already seen that certain problems, such as the halting problem, are undecidable. There are also problems which are not practically computable because they are exponentially or factorially complex, or worse.

Evaluating Satisfiability—NP Problems

A Boolean function is *satisfiable* if and only if there is some truth assignment to its variables that makes the function true. For example, $f(a, b) = (a \lor b) \land (\neg a \lor \neg b)$ is satisfiable since the function is true for the assignment $a = T$ and $b = F$ (also true for $a = F$ and $b = T$).

As we have seen in Chapter 4, a Boolean function has 2^n truth assignments for an n variable expression. It is clearly possible to compute satisfiability by exhaustively checking all 2^n assignments. However, this is an impractical approach as illustrated in the above table and one naturally asks whether it can be improved upon. Unfortunately, no better algorithm has been found for the general case, and it has been shown by work of J. Cook that it is likely that no such algorithm exists. If this is true, then the computation of satisfiability in the general case is $O(2^n)$.

Cook and others have shown that a large class of important and well-studied computations is in the same category of difficulty as the satisfiability problem—these are called the *NP complete problems*. Some NP complete problems are knapsack problems, travelling salesman and Hamiltonian problems, various difficult games such as checkers and go (suitably generalized), and numerous optimization, combinatorial, and graph problems. If any of these problems could be solved by a polynomial time algorithm, then all of them could. At the moment there is a strong suspicion in the theoretical community that NP problems are all inherently exponential.

While the existence of NP problems is a pessimistic result, there are means of coping with this class. Many of the above problems are solvable in polynomial time,[4] if restricted to certain sub-cases. Also many have algorithms which often work efficiently but occasionally run longer than some permissible prespecified time. There are also ways of finding approximate solutions to some of these problems, where the approximation is cheaply computed. As we shall see in the next chapter on artificial intelligence, there are various schemes for attacking intrinsically difficult problems.

EXERCISES

1. Give two reasons for comments in programs.

2. What is an invariant?

3. What is true after the following program segment? Illustrate with input/output assertions.

$$\textbf{if } x > 1 \textbf{ then } z := 5;$$
$$\textbf{if } x = -2 \textbf{ then } z := 10;$$

---

[4] A problem of size n is solvable in polynomial time if its time complexity or efficiency is $O(p(n))$ where $p(n)$ is a polynomial in n.

4. Prove as rigorously as possible that the following program computes $n!$

```
algorithm factorial;
    {computes n! for n ≥ 1}
    n, fct: integer;
    begin read (n); fct := 1;
        while n > 1 do
        begin
            fct := fct × n; n := n − 1
        end;
        write('factorial is', fct)
    end.
```

5. Prove that the following program terminates, for $t > 0$.

```
algorithm nonsense;
    t : integer;
    begin read(t);
    over: if t mod 2 = 1 then t := t + 1 else t := t ÷ 2;
        if t > 1 then go to over;
        write('finished')
    end.
```

6. How often is "over: ... " executed as a function of the value of t in the last exercise?

7. Write an Algolic program to compute the sum $a[1] + a[3] + a[5] + \cdots + a[2m + 1]$ and prove it correct.

8. The Fibonacci sequence is defined as: $F_0 = 0$, $F_1 = 1$, $F_n = F_{n-1} + F_{n-2}$ $(n \geq 2)$. Prove that $O(F_n) = 2^n$.

9. For what values of the integer n is $0.001 \times n^2 > 1000 \times n$; and in general for what values of n is $an^2 > b \times n$, $0 < a < b$?

10. Hand-simulate algorithms $P1$, $P2$, $P3$ for the polynomial $P(x) = x^3 - 2x + 5$ at $x = 3$.

11. Improve algorithm $P2$ by removing the array *power* and performing this calculation in array S.

12. Give a proof of correctness and termination for the bisection algorithm.

13. Reprogram bubble sort with a Boolean variable *"nochange"* which is false if no interchange occurs. Use this to stop sorting when all elements are in order. Discuss the improvement in efficiency relative to ordinary bubble sort.

14. $\{x > 0 \wedge e > 0\}$
    while $x > 0$ **do**
    begin
       $x := x - e;\ S$
    end
    $\{k \times e > x$ for some integer $k > 0\}$

    Prove that this program will terminate. Hint: k is the number of times the **while** loop is executed.

15. Prove that

    (a) $O(ax^7 + 3x^3 + \sin(x)) = x^7$
    (b) $O(e^n + an\,10^{10}) = O(e^n)$
    (c) $O(n! + n^{50}) = O(n!)$

16. Program quicksort.

17. Hand-simulate the sorting of the sequence 3 −17 4 −12 5 16 99 14 8, for both bubble sort and quicksort.

18. Show that sorting in $O(n^2)$ is reasonable compared with maintaining an un-ordered file if the number of file searches is at least $O(n)$ before a file is discarded.

19. Quicksort performs in its worst-case when the input is already sorted. Show that quicksort runs in $O(n^2)$ in this case and argue that this is indeed its worst-case.

20. Imagine having arrays
       bucket: **array** $[1..10000]$ **of** *Boolean*
         a: **array** $[1..100]$ **of** *integer*

    Now we are told that $1 \le a[i] \le 10000$ and that each $a[i]$ is unique. We want a sorting routine which sets $bucket[a[i]] = true$ and sorts by collecting all the indices j in order for which $bucket[j] = true$. Write such a routine in Algolic. What is the order of computation? Is it better than quicksort? Can you improve this "bucket" sort? (Notice the space-time tradeoff).

21. Are the following Boolean functions satisfiable and, if so, with what truth assignment:

    a) $(a \wedge \neg b) \wedge (\neg a \vee b)$
    b) $(a \wedge b \wedge \neg c) \wedge (\neg a \vee b \wedge a) \wedge (\neg a \vee \neg b)$
    c) $(a \vee b \vee c) \wedge (\neg a \vee \neg b \vee \neg c) \wedge (a \vee \neg b \vee c)$

22. Write an Algolic program for checking satisfiability.

23. The following problem is NP complete. Given n reals $a_1, a_2, \ldots, a_n$, divide them into two distinct sets such that the sums of the two sets are most nearly equal. (This is analogous to giving out two lists of assignments to two workers so

that both lists will be completed at most nearly the same time.) E.g., the set {5.3, 7.4, 1.8, 2.3} can be divided into two sets {7.4, 1.8} and {5.3, 2.3}, with most nearly equal sums 9.2 and 7.6, respectively. Write an $O(n^2)$ algorithm which tries to solve this problem. Will your method always get a best solution? Hand-simulate your method on a set of 10 numbers.

ADDITIONAL READINGS

Aho, A. V.; Hopcroft, J. E.; and Ullman, J. D. *The Design and Analysis of Computer Algorithms.* Reading, Mass.: Addison-Wesley, 1974.

Horowitz, E. and Sahni, S. *Fundamentals of Data Structures.* Potomac, Md.: Computer Science Press, 1976.

Knuth, D. E. *Fundamental Algorithms.* Reading, Mass.: Addison-Wesley, 1968.

Knuth, D. E. *Searching and Sorting.* Reading, Mass.: Addison-Wesley, 1973.

Liu, C. L. *Introduction to Combinatorial Mathematics.* New York: McGraw-Hill, 1968.

Manna, Z. *Mathematical Theory of Computation.* New York: McGraw-Hill, 1974.

Chapter 9

ARTIFICIAL INTELLIGENCE

A variety of unusual applications called artificial intelligence (AI) programs is examined in this chapter. We do this for several reasons. We wish to explore the potential future use of computers. We also want to demonstrate that computation is not limited to the mathematical or data processing applications most commonly discussed. Finally, we wish to motivate a discussion of the implications to society of computer use. AI programs most sharply focus our attention on these topics.

In the study *The Year 2000,* Herman Kahn and Anthony J. Weiner, two noted extrapolators, list a number of speculations about the year 2000 A.D. On a list of speculations, given as having a high degree of certainty, is the prediction that the use of computers for intellectual collaboration will be widespread by the turn of the century (it is arguably the case that this has already happened). A second list of speculations, titled "less likely but important possibilities," contains the prediction of "true" artificial intelligence. Since to some degree machines are already intelligent, the important issues are really the ultimate intelligence of programmed computers and the quality and use of this intelligence.

But first, *what is intelligence?* Our conception of intelligence is rooted in human behavior. Some aspects of intelligence are the ability to solve both concrete and abstract problems, to converse in natural language, to learn from experience using it to modify and improve on past behavior, and so on. Indeed, there is no simple characterization that fully defines it.

Given a problem in the integral calculus, such as $\int xe^{-x^2}\, dx$, most adults in our society would not be able to solve it. A few experts in the calculus would have no trouble solving it—these experts would include a program called MACSYMA. This program is now used by many scientists to augment their ability to solve symbolic integration problems. Is the existence of very high quality symbolic integration programs—ones that surpass in skill all but a few expert humans—an instance of intelligent programs, or is it an example of high level technique?

Functional adults in our society speak at least one natural language fluently, for example English; these individuals understand and can be understood by each other. Computer programs exist which can understand English in a limited fashion; typically their domain of discourse is also highly restricted. Is this limited performance merely a temporary technical road-block on the way to complete understanding or is it a sign of some more basic obstacles to machine intelligence? The universal human ability to speak and understand natural language is considered a better measure of general intelligence than the esoteric ability to solve symbolic integration problems. Intelligence enables man to speak natural language, write poetry, learn mathematics, conduct business, plan battles and negotiate peace. It is a general capacity to acquire and apply knowledge effectively. An AI program would be a mechanism with similar abilities.

9.1   TURING'S TEST AND DEFINITIONS OF AI

In Chapter 7 we covered some of Alan Turing's contributions in the theory of computers. Turing was also deeply interested in the question of machine intelligence. He believed that machines could be programmed to appear intelligent. In effect, this belief was an affirmation of his thesis. Remember that Turing's thesis stated that "any effectively computable function is computable by a Turing machine." Either man's intellect can be captured by a program or we have a counterexample of Turing's thesis (at least, one can present compelling arguments for the validity of this either/or proposition). To avoid having to define intelligence—a problem psychologists and philosophers have yet to resolve—Turing proposed a test that a program should meet to demonstrate intelligence. *Turing's test,* as it has come to be known, is to see if an AI program could imitate a human intelligence in a way that would deceive a skeptical human interrogator.

In Turing's test, a human interrogator may question party A or party B. The interrogator is told that one of these parties is a program and the other a person. The aim of the game is to distinguish correctly between the human and the machine. The interrogator questions the candidates via a teletype link in order to avoid the need for building speech recognition and generation equipment. Of course the program is prepared to lie in response to such questions as "Are you a machine?" Furthermore the program will respond inaccurately from time to time if asked to do arithmetic computations, and will answer such questions with speeds appropriate to human faculties. Turing felt that if an AI program could be devised that plays this "imitation game" well enough to deceive human interrogators, it will have demonstrated true artificial intelligence.

The imitation game neatly sidesteps the need to define intelligence. However, it is clear that the program must have an adequate understanding of natural language or the game would be lost immediately. Adult human conversation is a central problem of AI within which all other issues arise, such as deduction, common sense, and learning. Let us briefly illustrate these points by a hypothetical dialogue.

Interrogator: "Tell me what a cyborg is?"

A: "I don't know."

Interrogator: "A cyborg is a synthesis of animal and machine. The sensory and central nervous systems of the animal are used to augment and control the machine. An example could be linking a monkey's eyes and brain with an otherwise automated tank. Do you think this is feasible?"

A: "No. I am repelled by the notion."

Interrogator: "Why is it not feasible?"

A: "Because, neurophysiologists do not know enough to decode the signals from the central nervous system."

The above dialogue fragment illustrates how discourse requires that you learn new concepts such as "cyborg." And furthermore it demonstrates that discourse requires deductive skills and ways of focusing on appropriate knowledge. Party A deduced reasons for the infeasibility of cyborgs. To do so, A had to understand that neurophysiology was more critical to the problem than either electrical engineering or theology (however, it could be imagined that "intelligent" answers could be framed within these areas as well).

While the Turing test is one way of viewing the central task of AI, other definitions illuminate different attitudes to the field. AI could also be conceived as the science of the algorithmic processes underlying reasoning and perception, whose chief natural example is man; much as aerodynamics is the science of flight whose chief natural examples are birds.

Another definition is that AI is the category of computer applications that are "poorly" understood. It is the residue of computer applications that do not have strong theories and methodologies. In effect, AI is the "natural philosophy" of computer science. Medieval academies classified their studies into theology, mathematics, and natural philosophy, where the latter was the "everything else" category. Over the next centuries, astronomy, physics, chemistry and biology became distinct disciplines. These subjects acquired their own methodologies and languages. More recently, sociology, anthropology, and psychology solidified into distinct disciplines. Natural philosophy remains but has been whittled down considerably. Similarly, AI has lost subareas whenever the methods for their problems became adequate and routinized. This has happened in some parts of pattern recognition and symbolic manipulation. What remains are the more speculative areas where computational method is currently inadequate and lacking in a theoretical basis.

A person walking down a road loses a contact lens. What to do? A first approach would be to get down on the ground and randomly feel around for it. If this trial-and-error search fails, one may mark the position of the loss; and fetching a bucket of paint, inscribe concentric circles in the presumed vicinity of the lost lens. Each circle could be systematically searched, innermost first, until the lens was found. This last approach might be modified by favoring the direction of fall and searching this section first. Such a progression, (1) trial-and-error, (2) systematic-exhaustive search, and (3) preferential guided search, typifies the development of AI programs in various problem areas. One could conceive of a final refinement where the physics of the fall of the lens was so well understood that an exact location could be computed—avoiding any search. But this would take the program out of the domain of AI. Figure 9.1 illustrates these four solution possibilities.

9.2 GAME PLAYING

In practically every culture, a variety of difficult intellectual games has developed. Some of these games are so rich in complexity that their mastery requires talent and professional attention. Games such as chess, go, checkers, and duplicate bridge are in this category. These games are rigorously defined arenas for displaying certain important reasoning abilities, such as deduction, extrapolation, learning, planning, and evaluation. The fact that no one can play perfect chess or go, despite the fact that each has been played and analyzed for centuries, points to a fundamental richness. Such games can be simply programmed and can be tested against human players of ranked competence. The quality of decision making in a game can be tested in a way that no real world decision can be measured. A policy decision such as a business or governmental decision may succeed, but one does not know how it compares to making a different decision. The

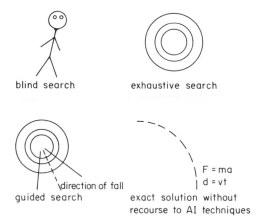

blind search   exhaustive search

guided search   exact solution without
                             recourse to AI techniques

Figure 9.1 Search Strategies

world cannot be reset like a chess board. For these reasons, game playing is a favorite experimental domain for AI programs.

Let us start our analysis with a familiar and simple game—tic-tac-toe, also known as "X's and O's." Tic-tac-toe is a zero-sum game of perfect information. This means that at any time in the game both players know the complete situation and can compute, in principle, all possible further positions. Furthermore, it is a finite game, limited in total number of plays. The game presents no challenge in its most elementary form and is quickly mastered by children.

Consider the following tic-tac-toe position

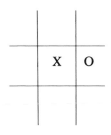

in which X made the first move. At this point, it is again X's turn to move and he can force a win:

This analysis of "you go here, I go there" until the result is clear is the standard method of analyzing such games. The analysis is called the *game tree, move tree,* or the *look-ahead* tree. Part of a move tree for tic-tac-toe is sketched in Figure 9.2.

A game tree is generated from an initial position by considering some number of legal moves. For each alternative, a number of the opponent's replies are considered. This procedure is continued until a *terminal* position is reached. A terminal position is one which can be evaluated. For simple games, one can often tell whether a position is a win, draw, or loss without much analysis. For example, in Figure 9.2, both branches on the left side

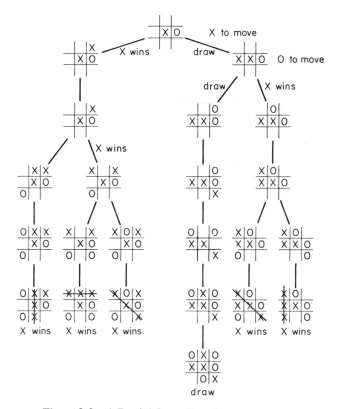

Figure 9.2   A Partial Game Tree for Tic-Tac-Toe

of the tree after O's move lead to a win for X, and that win can be "backed up" the tree to O's move.

The initial position, the "root" of the tree, is called a *depth* or *ply* 0 position. Each move adds 1 to this ply number in the analysis tree. The *value* of the original position is the outcome of the game where both players are assumed to be rational, i.e., assumed to be capable of making a best move. The following discussion shows how position values are obtained using this rational strategy.

Let white, the first player, be denoted by □ and black, the second player, be denoted by ○. If white wins, call this a result of 1; if black wins, call this a result of −1; and let a draw be a result of 0. Consider Figure 9.3(a). White has four alternatives and being rational will choose the third move from the left. This leads to a score of 1, a win for white. Black chooses the minimal valued position from among his alternatives. For example, in the rightmost case of Figure 9.3(b), this means choosing the position with value −1. The effect of these choices is to leave white the same choice as in the previous case.

When □ is offered a set of alternatives, he chooses the maximum valued move. When ○ is offered a set of alternatives, he chooses the minimum valued move. The result is the *minimax* value of the game. Obtaining this score is called *backing-up* the tree values. The value of a given nonterminal node is the maximum valued alternative for a □ move and the minimum valued alternative for a ○ move. If all the successors of a given node have values, the node can be evaluated. The nonterminal nodes nearest the terminal nodes are evaluated first and gradually the value is backed-up to the initial ply 0 position. The best move is the one that guarantees that the game's value will be this backed-up value. Figure 9.4 contains an example. In the first step, nodes *B* and *H* are evaluated since values exist on all their successors; *B* selects the minimum (3) and *H* selects a maximum (7) according to our rational strategy. The minimax value of the game, 6, is the final backed-up value at *A*. This represents the *best* score that □ can get starting at position *A*, assuming that ○ plays rationally.

A general algorithm for computing the minimax value from a game follows directly from our examples:

Backing-up Values

1. Choose an unscored non-terminal node *N*, all of whose successors are scored. If there are none, halt; all values have been backed up.
2. If *N* is a □ node, then score it the highest valued of its alternatives. If *N* is a ○ node, then score it the lowest value of its alternatives.
3. Go to step 1.

Tic-tac-toe has a small number of moves, so that a complete analysis using the above techniques is possible. Most interesting games, such as chess, have finite move trees, but the complete trees are too large to be feasibly enumerated. An ordinary chess game lasting 50 moves (100 ply) has an average of almost 40 responses per ply leading to a total move tree of 40^{100} positions. Even with clever reductions, no one can envision a computer capable of enumerating or storing this size tree. (Compare 40^{100} with the count of some other very large sets, such as the number of atoms in the universe!)

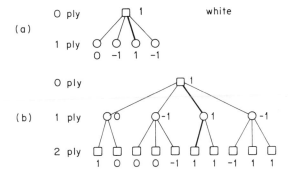

Figure 9.3 Examples of Rational Move Selection

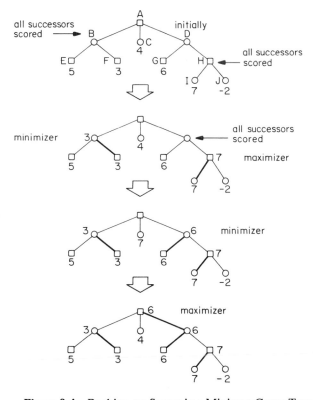

Figure 9.4 Backing-up Scores in a Minimax Game Tree

9.2.1   A Detailed Look at Playing Chess

Chess masters play good chess by being highly selective in their considerations of moves. They will frequently work out the consequences of only one or two moves, only expanding this choice if their analysis does not confirm the reasonableness of the original choice. With such careful selection, they can readily look 10 ply ahead examining only 100 or fewer positions. In certain forced situations involving checkmates or elementary endgames, masters may look ahead over 30 ply. This narrow a search is based on both deduction and extensive chess knowledge. When grandmaster Richard Reti was asked how many positions he examined before moving, he said, "One, the right one." This ideal is currently far from being achieved in chess programs. Such programs may look at up to one-half million positions to select a single move.

Chess programs must make three important decisions:

1. decide which moves to analyze,
2. decide when to stop analyzing, and
3. decide on the value of the positions generated.

Each such decision relies on chess knowledge built into the chess program. We will see how such knowledge is transformed to an algorithmically useful form—for this is frequently the heart of any AI project.

An average length chess game between players of equal ability takes about 50 moves. When players decide to stop playing, it is because the outcome is clearcut, even though a checkmate is possibly 20 moves away. Generally the game stops because of overwhelming material advantage for one player without any compensating advantage for the other player. "Overwhelming material advantage" at the beginner level is a queen and at the grandmaster level is often only a pawn. A person or program must strive for increasing his advantage until it becomes "overwhelming." If this strategy is not possible, one attempts to maintain the current balance. This implies that it is critical to determine which player has the advantage in a given position.

A large part of chess theory is concerned with different types of advantage; the most important of these are material advantage, control of space, king safety, and structural advantage. Structural advantages include advanced protected passed pawns, knight outposts, the two bishops in uncluttered positions, and numerous other recognizable features described in books on chess theory. An evaluation procedure would assign values to each of these features and combine them, ordinarily in a linear function, to give an overall score to the position. Table 9.1 contains a number of such features and typical values indicating their relative importance. We next illustrate their use in an evaluation procedure for a chess position.

A Hypothetical Static Evaluation Function:

$$\text{value(chess position)} = \frac{1}{\text{complexity}} \times (\text{Material}_{\text{white}} + \text{Territory}_{\text{white}} +$$

$$\text{Structural}_{\text{white}} - \text{Material}_{\text{black}} - \text{Territory}_{\text{black}} - \text{Structural}_{\text{black}}),$$

where *complexity* is a number reflecting the number of pieces remaining on the board. The idea is that a position in which one player is ahead by two pawns is more valuable if fewer pieces remain on the board.

Table 9.1   Positional Features Found in Chess Theory Books

feature	value in a linear function
1. Material queen, rook, bishop, knight, pawn	95, 50, 37, 35, 10
2. Territory controlled either by occupation or attack	1 per central square 1 per square in the neighborhood of the opponent's king
central squares, opponent's squares, squares in the king's neighborhood	½ per opponent's square (not including above) These values are to be increased by the square root of the number of times a chess-square is controlled.
3. Structural features passed pawn	4 (+4 more for each square nearer the 8th rank)
isolated pawn	−2
doubled pawn	−2
knight outpost	10
two bishops	5
rook on the back ranks	10
pins	2
open files	1
king safety (castled-uncastled)	−5 if uncastled
active vs. bad bishop	−8 if bad bishop
pawn majority on the queen's wing	3

The above type of function is not valid in a "dynamic" position, where values can rapidly change. A person who has sacrificed a piece for a mating combination must look beyond the position where the material is lost. In taking a rook with a queen, one is temporarily ahead by a rook; but if the queen is immediately captured, one ends up substantially behind. Certain moves are thus inherently dynamic. Examples are captures, checks, pushing pawns, and attacks; most captures involve recaptures, most checks waste time, and most pawn moves are structurally weakening. These types of moves may involve immediate and substantial changes in positional value if there is no appropriate countermove. Hence there is a need for a look-ahead tree in the analysis of games like chess. Figure 9.5 has a simple example.

The good chess program analyzes the most dynamic moves in a position until the position resolves itself. In generating a move tree, it must decide whether it can reliably evaluate a position using its static evaluation function; and if not, it must decide in what order it will consider further moves. These observations lead to the following program outline.

Basic Chess Program

1. Generate k_0 moves from the initial position. Produce the most dynamic moves first.
2. For each resulting position in the next ply, p, generate k_p moves. Continue this generation procedure until some maximum ply is reached.
3. Evaluate all resulting terminal positions, except those which are "overly" dynamic. Overly dynamic positions involve positions where checks and captures are possible.
4. Continue generating moves in overly dynamic positions until they can be reliably evaluated.
5. Back-up the terminal board evaluation and choose the best minimax move.

A typical chess program will investigate a tree of dimensions 10, 7, 5, 4, 2, and 2, where $k_0 = 10$, $k_1 = 7$, ..., and $k_5 = 2$. Thus 5600 moves would be generated assuming no further analysis is needed for overly dynamic positions.

This type of chess program is built on principles first outlined by Alan Turing and Claude Shannon. Both of these men are more famous for other contributions in the theory of computation, but both were also fascinated by the intellectual depth of chess. Each independently arrived at the above

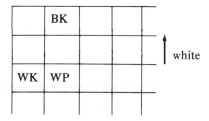

If white moves, he wins by pushing his pawn and forcing a queen; if black moves, he draws by moving over in front of the white king.

Figure 9.5   A Position Where Static Analysis Fails

formulation of a chess playing program in the late 1940's. Programs currently exist for playing checkers, chess, go and numerous other games of strategy, using ideas similar to those of this section. These programs have reached quite respectable levels of competence. The checker playing program of Arthur Samuel can play master level checkers. This program was a landmark in artificial intelligence work; developed in the late 1950's, it was the first program that attained a level of ability that compared to the ability of top human experts. The chess playing programs of the 1950's played at amateur levels of expertise. Chess playing programs developed in the 1970's can occasionally beat human chess masters.

9.3 HEURISTIC PROBLEM SOLVING

Move trees and special chess evaluation functions would not allow a machine to shop in a grocery store or make travel connections from Walla Walla, Washington, to Twente, The Netherlands. Humans can reason in general and "common sense" ways applicable to a wide range of previously unencountered problems. In order to understand and duplicate this capability, the team of Newell, Shaw,[1] and Simon of the RAND Corporation and Carnegie-Mellon University built a series of programs which attempted general-purpose problem solving. Their work and the later work of many other AI research groups, including the Edinburgh University Experimental Programming Unit headed by Donald Michie, has shown that programs with general search methods can be made to solve deductive problems over widely varying domains. The search methods incorporate problem dependent information to guide the solution attempts efficiently.

---

[1] Not the "Shaw" who coauthored this book.

In game playing, the minimax tree structure is such a general search technique; when applied to a specific game, it uses an evaluation function which is game-dependent to order its search and select good moves.

In AI, we use the term *heuristic* or heuristic function to mean information which can be applied to narrowing a search. A heuristic is "a rule of thumb"; e.g., "Large stores have cheaper prices than small stores" is a heuristic. It is a useful rule but may not always be correct. Nevertheless, the problem of finding cheap eggs in a large city may be attacked with a reasonable hope of success using the large store heuristic. Consider the heuristic, "the more traffic, the nearer the center of town." If a person were in a strange city and used this rule to find its downtown, he may instead end up at a truck terminal. Nevertheless, the rule frequently works and is useful in cutting the extent of the driver's search. Heuristics involve identifying problem domain features that are often successful in reducing search.

The Newell, Shaw, and Simon work, begun in the mid 1950's, was an attempt to achieve AI by modelling human problem solving. They proposed methods which they claimed humans used. Their programs were meant to be an information processing model of human problem solving behavior.

The problems they studied were deductive where the problem solver must go from starting place to some terminating place. The problem solver was to use moves, operations, deductions, or transformations, depending on the form of the problem. Examples are: find a checkmate from position S using the legal moves of chess, or prove theorem T using the deductions allowed in algebra.

At any instant in the process, the problem solver has found his way to a number of places, also called *states,* and can choose to search further from one of these points. To choose a good next place and a useful move or transformation from that place, Newell, Shaw, and Simon proposed a method based on "differences" which they called "means-ends analysis." Intuitively, when one is at state S and wishes to arrive at state T, there are *differences* in the description of the two states. A move, transformation, or operation is applicable if it can work on a relevant difference. The "ends" are to reduce the difference between S and T by some series of operations on S; the "means" are the choice of operators or transformations appropriate to the differences found between states.

Example:

The problem is to prove $A + B + A = 2 \times A + B$

Transformations: (a) $C + C = 2 \times C$

                        (b) $C_1 + C_2 = C_2 + C_1$

Start State S: $A + B + A$

Goal State T: $2 \times A + B$

Differences between S and T: There are fewer letters in the original expression, and the order in which B's and A's are written is different.

Solution: Apply (b) to the Start State, where $C_1 = A + B$ and $C_2 = A$. $A + B + A$ is then transformed to $A + A + B$. Apply (a) to this new expression. $A + A + B$ is transformed to $2 \times A + B$.

The example is a very simple one, but nevertheless contains the major ideas of Newell, Shaw, and Simon. Their first attempt to embody these ideas in a program led to the Logic Theorist (LT) written in 1956, which was a program to solve symbolic logic problems. The symbolic logic or propositional logic has been discussed in Chapter 4. The LT program tried to show that a logical expression was derivable from a set of axioms by repeated application of these axioms as steps that rewrote the initial expression into the goal expression. This was a modestly successful effort, and the Newell team set out to show that these methods could be applied to other problems. In 1959, they reported work on *GPS*—the General Problem Solver, which could do problems in approximately ten different areas.

GPS Applied to Symbolic Logic

GPS attempts to prove theorems in the propositional calculus by systematically manipulating an initial formula "towards" the goal formula. Consider the problem of showing that

$$((R \supset \neg P) \wedge (\neg R \supset Q)) \equiv \neg(\neg Q \wedge P)$$

is a theorem, where the left hand side (lhs) of the equivalence is the initial formula and the right hand side (rhs) is the goal. The lhs is longer than the rhs; the lhs also contains the variable R not found on the rhs, and it has different logical connectives from the rhs. If these differences are reduced by applying an appropriate rule, then there would be progress in solving the problem. In the symbolic logic problem, GPS is given the 12 rule types listed in Table 9.2 and an operator-difference table also illustrated in Table 9.2. The operator-difference table shows which operators (rules) can be used to reduce differences. For example, rule R6 is used to change logical connectives: thus,

$$(R \supset \neg P) \wedge (\neg R \supset Q) \xrightarrow{\text{R6}} (\neg R \vee \neg P) \wedge (R \vee Q),$$

where the $\neg \neg R$ was simultaneously replaced by R. GPS attempts continually to reduce differences until the rhs is found. As one measure of its success in the logic domain, GPS found proofs for 38 of the first 52 theorems in Russell and Whitehead's *Principia Mathematica.* [2]

An outline of GPS reveals an organization that is akin to the way in which naive human subjects attempt to solve deductive problems:

1. Identify the difference between the current state (form of the expression) and the desired state.
2. Select a transformation known to affect this difference and attempt to apply it.
3. If the transformation is not immediately applicable on the current state, transform that state to a new one for which the transformation selected in step 2 works.

In order to develop and test GPS as a model of human cognition, protocols of human subjects solving the same problems were compiled and analyzed. The protocol was an account of how the subject solved the problem. The subjects were instructed to "think aloud" paying special attention to why they chose a next step. These preferences were encoded in the GPS operator-difference table. When GPS was run, it would print a sequential trace of the steps it attempted in solving a problem, and this trace could then be compared to the human subjects' protocols.

Another important general model for heuristic programming is one where the heuristic quantifies progress. The GPS program tries to reduce a difference, any difference. Normally there are many differences—some difficult to reduce, others easy to reduce—yet GPS in its early descriptions ignores these distinctions. Several programs of the 1960's treat differences as measures of distance in the problem solving space. Such programs include the graph traverser of Doran and Michie and the heuristic path algorithm of Pohl. At any point in the search, these programs have reached some group of states. The heuristic function "measures" the difficulty in going from the reached states to the goal. It chooses the easiest or nearest state. If the heuristic estimator is accurate, these programs will efficiently find solutions even in very large spaces.

---

[2] B. Russell and Alfred N. Whitehead. *Principia Mathematica,* V. 1. 1910, V. 2. 1912, V. 3. 1913, Cambridge University Press.

Table 9.2   GPS Characterization of the Symbolic Logic Domain

RULES

R1. $A \wedge B \rightarrow B \wedge A$
$A \vee B \rightarrow B \vee A$
R2. $A \supset B \rightarrow \neg B \supset \neg A$

R3. $A \wedge A \leftrightarrow A$
$A \vee A \leftrightarrow A$
R4. $A \wedge (B \wedge C) \leftrightarrow (A \wedge B) \wedge C$
$A \vee (B \vee C) \leftrightarrow (A \vee B) \vee C$

R5. $A \vee B \leftrightarrow \neg(\neg A \wedge \neg B)$

R6. $A \supset B \leftrightarrow \neg A \vee B$

R7. $A \wedge (B \vee C) \leftrightarrow (A \wedge B) \vee (A \wedge C)$
$A \wedge (B \wedge C) \leftrightarrow (A \vee B) \wedge (A \vee C)$
R8. $A \wedge B \rightarrow A$
$A \wedge B \rightarrow B$
R9. $A \rightarrow A \vee X$

R10. $\left.\begin{array}{c} A \\ \\ B \end{array}\right] \rightarrow A \wedge B$

R11. $\left.\begin{array}{c} A \\ \\ A \supset B \end{array}\right] \rightarrow B$

R12. $\left.\begin{array}{c} A \supset B \\ \\ B \supset C \end{array}\right] \rightarrow A \supset C$

"$\rightarrow$" means an expression on the lhs can be rewritten by an expression on the rhs.
"$\leftrightarrow$" means either side could be rewritten, i.e., $C_1 \leftrightarrow C_2$ is equivalent to $C_1 \rightarrow C_2$
and $C_2 \rightarrow C_1$.

Differences

D_1   length of expression

D_2   order of letters

D_3   logical connectives

D_4   grouping by parentheses

Partial operator-difference table

	D_1	D_2	D_3	D_4
R_1		X		
R_2	X	X	X	
R_3	X			
R_4				X
R_5	X		X	
R_6	X		X	

Example: The 15 puzzle

The 15 puzzle is a popular game consisting of a 4×4 board containing
15 movable tiles, numbered 1 to 15. The remaining vacant board position,
the 16th one, changes its location on the board if a neighboring tile is
moved into it. Given some initial board position S (locations of the numbered tiles), the purpose of the game is to move the tiles as quickly as

possible into some final arrangements T. We will partially trace a sample puzzle, using a heuristic function h defined as

$$h(S) = \sum_{i=1}^{15} t_i(S)$$

where $h(S)$ is the estimate in going from state S to the final state and $t_i(S)$ is the number of units (horizontal + vertical "distance") that tile i in state S is from its final goal position in state T.

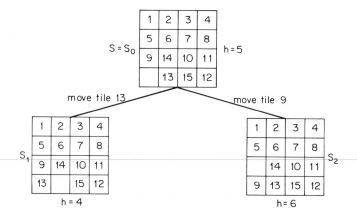

$$h(S) = 0 + 0 + 0 + 0 + 0 + 0 + 0 + 0 + 0 + 1 + 1 + 1 + 1 + 1$$
$$+ 0 = 5$$

since pieces 1 through 9 are "home" and the remaining pieces are each one square away from their goal position in T. The two possible moves from state S are illustrated below.

The move to S_1 is estimated to be closer to the goal since $h(S_1) < h(S_2)$. Choosing S_1 as the next state to transform we obtain

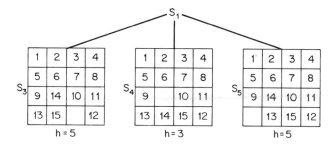

S_4 is chosen as nearest because it has the smallest h. The heuristic search continues until the goal state is reached or the program quits.

Heuristics are rules for recognizing useful, progress-making steps, obviating the need for exhaustively carrying out all steps. GPS and other heuristic search programs have demonstrated a general method for efficiently applying special-purpose knowledge to finding deductive solutions in many problem domains. Computers armed with general heuristic reasoning ability and search techniques can make sensible decisions in unanticipated situations. One major AI problem is to provide machines with such general abilities.

9.4 NATURAL LANGUAGE AND SEMANTICS

Computers understand FORTRAN, Algol, PL/I, and numerous other programming languages; but natural language, with its ambiguity and subtle nuance, is not yet fully understood by any computer program. Some philosophers and linguists say that a machine is too "rigid" to interpret properly many ambiguous sentences. (Consider the sentence, "He has an ace up his sleeve." In certain contexts, it refers to a real ace card literally hidden up a gambler's sleeve. In other circumstances, neither cheating nor real cards are implied; the sentence is a figurative statement to the effect that the person in question has a decisive surprise strategem on reserve.) These philosophers and linguists make the inference that a deterministic (read in the bias *limited*) computer program cannot possess the intellectual flexibility that allows the human mind to distinguish levels of meaning and humor in natural language. So far, they are right; but there is no proof of such a limitation that is inherent in computer programs.

ELIZA—An Attempt to Pass the Turing Test

Speaker: "Einstein's general theory of relativity predicts that light will be bent in a gravitational field."

Response: "What else is predicted by Einstein's general theory of relativity?"

Imagine a program capable of making the above response. How well must it understand natural language to accomplish this feat and others? It is remarkable that only a very limited set of mechanisms is necessary in order to maintain a conversation. Such a program, named ELIZA, was written by Joseph Weizenbaum of MIT in 1966.

A *decomposition rule* for ELIZA is a template for matching strings produced by the "speaker." An example that would fit the above speaker's sentence is

$$
\begin{matrix}
1 & 2 & 3
\end{matrix}
$$
$$
\text{(string 'predicts' string).}
$$

This rule has three parts, and it would match any sentence that has "predicts" in it.

1. 'Einstein's general theory of relativity' = string
2. 'predicts'
3. 'that light will be bent in a gravitational field' = string

A response is a "reassembly rule" which may or may not use pieces of the decomposition. The reassembly rule used for generating the above response is

('What else is predicted by' 1),

where 1 is the explicit string in the first position of the decomposition rule.

ELIZA scripts consist of decomposition rules that are sequentially matched against the speaker's input. Each decomposition rule has one or more reassembly rules. The program chooses the reassembly rule to generate a response. A script also includes default responses. If a sentence does not match any decomposition rule, the program generates the default response, for example, "Please go on," or "Can you explain that again?"

One script, dubbed DOCTOR, mimics a Rogerian therapist. This is a psychoanalyst who tries not to interject himself in the discussion; instead, he elicits from the patient a running stream of complaints. The patient performs self-analysis with the aid of the therapist as a prompter. The program uses the DOCTOR script to model a therapeutic dialogue.

A hypothetical dialogue might be the following:

Patient: "I am upset."
Doctor: "Why are you upset?"
Patient: "My wife ran off."
Doctor: "Did you like your wife?"
Patient: "Yes, I loved her deeply."
Doctor: "Tell me more about your wife."

The first sentenced was decomposed by a rule ('I' string 'upset'). The reassembly rule providing the response was ('Why are you upset'). The second patient sentence was decomposed by the rule ('My' string 'ran' string) with the response ('Did you like your' 2); 2 here refers to the second component of the decomposition. If the patient had said, "My car ran well," the response would be, "Did you like your car?" The Rogerian therapy setting is a very good context for such a program. The psycho-analyst is expected to be naive. His remarks are possibly enigmatic. The benefits of even such minimal understanding are enough so that wide-spread use of DOCTOR type programs has been proposed for seriously understaffed mental institutions.

ELIZA-like programs have passed a weak version of the Turing imitation-game test. They have for a short time deceived people who think in advance that they are talking to a human. The expectation is strong enough so that it takes some foolish utterance to alert a person to the fact that his respondent is a machine. While it would not pass the Turing test to most people's satisfaction, it is amazingly proficient for a limited mechanism.

A necessary extension to an "understanding" natural language system is a dictionary. It is easy enough to place dictionaries into computer memory. Many words, of course, have multiple definitions; the "right" one must be determined from context—not a simple problem. It is also easy to make a computer generate sentences of grammatical natural language; this can be done with syntactic schema similar to the ones introduced in Chapter 6. Unfortunately, grammatically correct sentences may have little or no meaning. Consider, for example, "John is a little large planet in the previous county." How is this sentence known to be nonsense? It is correct in its syntactic form—subject "is" object. But do planets reside in counties? Aha! *Knowledge* is the key. It must be available to even a sophisticated syntactic system to insure meaning and understanding. If the computer program has an adequate model of what is to be talked about, it might be able to converse intelligently.

First Abilities—STUDENT

STUDENT, a program written by Daniel Bobrow in 1964, is designed to solve algebra word problems.

Example:

Input sentences:
   Bill's father's uncle is twice as old as Bill's father. Two years from now Bill's father will be three times as old as Bill. The sum of their ages is 92. Find Bill's age.
STUDENT's analysis:
   The meaning of the first sentence is: Uncle $= 2 \times$ Father
   The meaning of the next sentence is: $3 \times$ (Bill $+ 2$) $= 2 +$ Father
   The meaning of the third sentence is: Bill $+$ Father $+$ Uncle $= 92$
Answer: Bill $= 8$, Father $= 28$, Uncle $= 56$

STUDENT interprets each sentence as a linear equation. It "knows" that it must end up with a consistent and solvable set of linear equations. It attempts to analyze each English sentence to satisfy this requirement. For example, the requirement that the linear equations be solvable is very powerful in deciding what pronouns reference.

Example: The number of soldiers the Russians have is half of the number of guns they have. The number of guns they have is 7000. What is the number of soldiers they have?

   In the last sentence, "they" must be interpreted as "the number of soldiers the Russians have."

A pronoun is equated with a variable in the linear system of equations. If solution is then possible, this interpretation is printed out; otherwise, STUDENT attempts to relate the pronoun to another variable. It could interpret a pronoun in two different ways if both interpretations were consistent with solving the resulting set of equations.

STUDENT can be used to solve a wide range of high-school algebra problems. It has an explicit *minitheory* for age problems. Whenever the program encounters words or phrases like "as old as," or "age," it invokes the model for extracting age information. This allows it to identify a specific person despite a welter of adjectival and possessive modifiers, such as in "Bill's father's uncle." If the information identifying all variables is

inadequate, the machine asks, "Do you know any more relationships between these variables," and lists the variables. Additional information is
also used in its attempt to solve a problem. For example, it has a global
dictionary which contains useful general relationships like "people means
more than one person" and "1 foot equals 12 inches." The combination of
STUDENT's precise world-view and its general flexibility in incorporating
heuristics for choosing appropriate sentence interpretation forms a powerful natural language question-answering system.

In 1971, Terry Winograd completed work on an integrated AI system
which had impressive natural language ability. His system allowed a one-
armed robot SHRDLU to receive English language commands. The robot
manipulated a table-top world containing an assortment of children's
building blocks. The robot would respond to such statements as "place
the blue pyramid behind the green block." It could carry on obviously
meaningful conversation about this BLOCKS-world. Within this framework, it could usefully reason and use the product of this reasoning to
disambiguate complicated English language sentences such as, "Will you
please stack up both of the red blocks and either a green cube or a pyramid." His program was a telling demonstration of the power of minitheory
semantics.

Minitheory systems of question-answering exist for calculus rate problems, for block-stacking problems, and for the analysis of weather information. In each of these programs, different semantical interpretations are
tried, according to what is allowed by the dictionary being employed, until
an understanding consistent with the program's minitheory has been
internalized.

As Seymour Papert of the MIT Artificial Intelligence Project points out,
it is likely that a human intelligence has hundreds or thousands of such
minitheories available. This large body of knowledge is difficult to assimi-
late under one general control structure, but this is not necessarily an
inherent limitation of a machine's abilities as some critics imply.

9.5 LEARNING

There are two schools of thought on the importance of learning. One
group, which includes many cyberneticists, pattern-recognition theorists,
and neural modelers, maintains that learning is the core problem of intelligence. They argue that a non-learning machine misses the point—
adaptation. Nonadaptive machines are rigid and have a level of performance

which is fixed. This level of performance, even when quite good, is only a reflection of the theory of the problem area. It is not a reflection on how well intelligence has been modeled.

The learning-first group, as they will be referred to here, is not homogeneous in its approach to learning. The neural modelers wish to understand how animal central nervous systems work and try to follow current neurophysiological theory. They model the functional abilities of various neurons and the interconnection patterns among neurons. Another segment of the learning-first group, the perceptron theorists and the cellular automatists, postulate artificial neurons or "mini-Turing-machines," which may be inspired by analogy to the real central nervous system but need not have a direct functional correspondence. Their neurons ordinarily calculate Boolean functions whose results are tied together in summation circuits where the pattern of interconnection is learned. The aim is to get powerful computational devices using artificial neural nets. A further subgroup studies learning independent of mechanism. These researchers generally approach the subject as a statistical approximation problem. The interest here is in classes of functions which can be used to classify patterns and whose coefficients can be changed by a learning procedure. They do not care what machines or neural nets are used to implement these functions. This subgroup of learning-first theorists begins to merge into the second school, which takes the position that learning is of lesser importance in modelling intelligence.

The second school of thought maintains that learning can always be implemented in an artificial intelligence program. The organization of the program will suggest where learning may be incorporated. Once programs are able to organize knowledge, they can be used to organize new knowledge. How much a program can learn is considered to be a function of its structure. Learning, in this view, is a secondary feature of an AI program, used to tune performance. Regardless of whether learning is conceived of as primary or not, it is a powerful AI technique.

Rote Learning

Rote learning is remembering explicitly a situation along with its effect. An early childhood instance of rote learning is "touch a glowing object and it burns your skin." If you play tic-tac-toe, it is helpful to remember all positions from which you lost, so that you will be able to avoid them thereafter. Tic-tac-toe is a simple enough game so that it is possible, after rote learning, to play perfect games. Other examples of rote learning are remembering telephone numbers, irregular spellings, "book" openings in chess, physical constants, birthdays, and mathematical formulas.

Rote learning uses much storage space. Each situation and its consequence must be individually stored. Other kinds of learning are more conservative of storage. For example, learning the equation $f(x) = x^2$ eliminates the need to learn the set of pairs (1, 1), (2, 4), (3, 9), ...; i.e., the table of squares. Consequently, with rote learning, one should preserve only highly referenced pieces of knowledge. For example, it is useful to remember that $\sin(\pi/2) = 1$ because $\pi/2$ is a common angle; similarly, it is important to remember that putting an "X" in the center of the tic-tac-toe board is the best first move.

Coefficient "Generalization" Learning

To exercise intelligence requires the ability to make distinctions and to evaluate these distinctions. Distinctions are recognizable features of the problem situation. The chess player confronted with the possibility of exchanging pieces must evaluate the relative value of the piece exchange. In specific instances, a pawn is worth more than a queen—if it can administer a checkmate, for example. Overall, however, it is useful for the chess player to assume an average value for a piece. This average value, being independent of the specific situation, can be used to reject routinely inappropriate exchanges without retaining every individual chess position.

The worth of a situation can often be expressed as a linear function: value(situation) $= a_1 f_1(\text{situation}) + a_2 f_2(\text{situation}) + \cdots + a_n f_n(\text{situation})$, where the f_i are a set of features that are possibly present and the a_i are coefficients, sometimes called "amplifiers," attached to these features. Then *generalization learning* consists in systematic modification of the a_i to reflect the "true" value of the situation.

Examples of features:

1. In tic-tac-toe, a center square is worth more than a corner square; a corner square is worth more than a side square.
2. In chess, a program that considers a bishop to be worth more than a rook should consistently play worse than one that considers a rook to be worth more than a bishop. (Of course, a completely naive program that does not know how to use a rook—for example, to seize open files or to penetrate the seventh rank—may, in fact, not perform better.)
3. In distinguishing a 'D' from an 'O', great attention must be paid to vertical straight lines, but not horizontal straight lines.

There are many computational techniques for adjusting coefficients. Typically, a set of *training* situations is evaluated for which known orderings exist—that is, value(situation$_1$) < value(situation$_2$) < $\cdots$ < value-(situation$_n$). After each situation, the trainer modifies the coefficients of the problem-solving program's evaluation function in a manner that produces the desired ordering.

These training schemes are sometimes very successful, especially in the area of pattern recognition. It is critical that the right set of features be used. Regardless of the sophistication of the training routine, a set of inadequate features will not make for useful discrimination. A classic case is the checker player who counts the number of black squares on the board in evaluating his position.

Outside of pattern recognition, the most successful application of learning is found in Samuel's checkers playing program. It uses sophisticated forms of generalization learning, gaining experience by evaluating "book" positions and by playing itself. In its book evaluation, the program assumes that it is desirable to produce the same moves as advocated by checkers masters in books and corrects its evaluation function when it fails to pick the advocated move. All of the features contained in its evaluation function were known useful features of the game, or were invented by Samuel. The program learned the relative utility or inutility of each feature but did not learn features of its own. We know of no instance in which a program has added to the theory of a human game by creating a new feature of importance. To do this would require an "inductive" learning scheme; and while a primitive theory of inductive learning is emerging, it cannot produce worthwhile induction on patterns as complex as "good" checkers or chess positions.

The most powerful method for developing programs capable of significant intellectual attainment has been to use human experts to "teach" the program the proper features of the problem space. Learning procedures that then suitably train and refine the program's weights produce improvement in task performance. However non-specific learning programs, such as a variety of neural-net machines, have had very limited success. The inspiration for this general learning approach is the evolutionary development that took billions of years to produce human intelligence. To simulate this achievement on even the very largest computer seems a naive hope.

9.6 ARTIFICIAL INTELLIGENCE: TRENDS, ACHIEVEMENTS, AND PROBLEMS

In the early years of artificial intelligence research (before 1960), computer scientists produced major new innovations and heralded the imminence of "truly" intelligent machines. Their failure to recognize the organizational complexity of building on these innovations caused them to be premature in their speculations on further progress. This led to a backlash from scientists upset by the notoriety the upstart field had achieved. These critics made absolutist claims that, inherently, machines could not achieve a creative intellect. The 1960's proved to be more mature years. Continuing solid achievements in the face of increasingly appreciated difficulties moderated the opinions of critics and computer scientists alike.

Computer programs can write music, conduct cocktail-party dialogue, play checkers at the level of weak master, solve a wide variety of mathematical problems, solve such difficult combinatorial puzzles as Instant Insanity, guide robots around rooms littered with obstacles, model human paranoia, and do well on the geometrical-analogies section of an IQ exam.

Many of the new programs go beyond an initial demonstration of doing problems of a given type. The 1960's saw the evolution of performance programs—programs with the ability of an expert in the field in question. The SIN-symbolic integration program of Joel Moses of MIT is such a program. It has built into it a theory of symbolic integration that allows it to perform above the ability of the average Ph.D. in mathematics. It decides most questions algorithmically and without search. Because it has an adequate performance theory of the problem domain—symbolic integration—it is no longer considered an artificial intelligence program. SIN and other symbolic mathematics programs contain a highly developed corpus of technique which has become a subdiscipline of computer science. Many problems in other areas, such as information retrieval and statistical pattern recognition, have made a transition from ill-understood artificial intelligence challenges to well-understood bodies of knowledge. The nonroutine progresses to the routine and is demystified.

Two important trends in artificial intelligence are *integrated systems* and *high-performance programs*. The latter trend has been mentioned already, examples being programs for symbolic mathematics, game playing, medical diagnosis, spectrography, and chromosome identification. These performance programs are normally the product of more than 10 man-years of work, which includes a collaboration of computer scientist and problem-domain expert.

A sophisticated medical treatment program, MYCIN, has been developed at Stanford University for prescribing antibiotic therapy in bacterial infections. MYCIN requires information on the patient's symptoms, medical history, and laboratory tests. It then applies some combination of its several hundred rules to deduce an applicable treatment. The rules are chiefly in the form of conditionals such as:

if infection is gram-positive and patient has fever and cough
then with certainty p we have infection x

The rules are phrased with certainty factors that human experts have derived from their experience. The system executes complicated deduction in the face of uncertainty and provides an explanation for its decision making. It is the synthesis of AI technique using notions taken from heuristic search theory and knowledge organization, and expertise extracted from doctors. MYCIN and other medical diagnosis programs are beginning to be used experimentally by doctors.

The second trend, integrated systems, has grown out of an accumulation of small successes in a number of areas of artificial intelligence. It comes from a realization that synthesis requires and produces a new level of understanding and that through synthesis more complex problems can be attempted. These systems are usually constructed around a robot and its environment. Typically the robot has an "eye"—a television-type scanner—and an "arm"—an electromechanical limb which is computer controlled. One environment is a world of toy blocks. The robot is able both to analyze its world and to manipulate blocks in its world. The robot can be given commands in English. These commands are understood if they are compatible with the robot's knowledge of its block's world. Such a system has been constructed at MIT; it is written using a specially designed AI programming language called LISP-MICROPLANNER. This system allows goal oriented searches to be specified without the need to describe the explicit search program—the MICROPLANNER routines have built-in heuristic search programs and general deductive mechanisms. Similar systems like STRIPS at Stanford Research Institute and QA4 at Stanford University exist for use in integrated problem-solving environments.

Such systems are far from achieving the "autonomy" or "consciousness" displayed by the computer HAL in the film *2001—A Space Odyssey*. However, the possibility of an integrated intelligence equipped with a set of learning routines bootstrapping its intelligence beyond the capabilities of the human designers of its programs is a distinct and awesome one. (A. Samuel's checkers program routinely beats its designer.) Current programs already have a complexity that limits the programmer's attempts to predict their performance.

One definition of consciousness is the ability to think about, or have a model of, oneself. In planning their actions, robots already have primitive representations of their world and of themselves in that world. The notion that a Universal Turing Machine can be given its own description already heralds, in the abstract, a "conscious" machine. This limited form of consciousness is of course not comparable to what certain theologians and philosophers mean by consciousness; for them, the understanding of consciousness can only be subjectively known. For these theorists, consciousness is not something one can test for in another organism or machine; there is not a consciousness "imitation game."

Societal Implications of Artificial Intelligence

Let us assume that we will have, by the year 2000, machines that

1. converse in ordinary English,
2. reason, in the sense of having a general common-sense intelligence,
3. learn, and
4. control robots—mobile machines that can receive sensory information and manipulate the environment via their own mechanical limbs.

The resulting uses of such machines might produce widespread unemployment. They might be used as a centrally-controlled police force. They might produce a cornucopia of goods and a generally affluent egalitarian society. Any number of possibilities, both threatening and beneficial, can be imagined. However the possibilities cannot be attributed only to the potential of artificial intelligence. Computer-aided instruction in education, information retrieval systems, and operations research applications all create problems of the same kind. The unique aspect is the realization that an "average" intelligence does not stand as a barrier. The intelligent learning machine will have a nearly "unlimited" eidetic memory and will continue to benefit from faster circuitry and improved programming at a rate unmatched by organic evolutionary refinement.

The Copernican revolution displaced Earth as the center of the universe. The industrial revolution shifted the "burden" of physical labor onto machines. The Darwinian revolution replaced destiny by evolutionary accident. All of these intellectual and societal shifts have acted to reduce "the place of man in the cosmos." They have acted to destroy a presumption of uniqueness. The development of intelligent machines, if it happens, is diminishing a last pillar of human stature. This diminution will occur in proportion to the degree and nature of intelligence created in computers.

It is impossible to predict the development of the field and the societal response to its achievements, but we can list some possibilities.

1. Limit the machines' development (turn off the machines is an extreme form of this response).

2. Integrate the machines' abilities into the human central nervous system—create "cyborgs."
3. Manipulate human genetics and accelerate the development of the human brain by biogenetic engineering and controlled breeding.
4. Strive for a close interactive cooperation between machine and man.
5. Accept a benevolent machine controlled economy and environment where everyone "drops out."

The above scenarios presume that the intelligent machines remain under control and subservient to man's purposes. While (2) and (3) are in the realm of technical possibility, they represent responses where the "solution" may be worse than the problem." It seems that (1) or (4) is the most desirable given our contemporary moral values. Response (1) allows human control of the society but limits the potential for growth that a machine-augmented intellectual environment could offer as in (4). On the one hand, society ponders the effects of computers and possible responses; and on the other hand, the technology itself continues its unrestrained development. The technological imperative continues while the existential dialectic remains unresolved.

EXERCISES

1. Give two distinct definitions of AI.

2. Is the use of natural language in conversation a sufficient criterion for intelligence?

3. Would Turing's imitation game be a better test if a group of Nobel Laureates was used?

4. If machines could provably not perform tasks that human intelligence can, would Turing's thesis on computability be violated?

5. Define some heuristics for choosing tic-tac-toe moves.

6. Using the heuristics of Exercise 9.5 play a game of tic-tac-toe, copying out the move tree.

7. Write an Algolic program to play tic-tac-toe.

8. What is the backed-up value of:

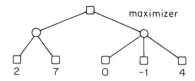

9. Give three reasons why chess is harder than tic-tac-toe. Is chess harder than checkers? Why?

10. Take some game you know and develop an AI framework for choosing good moves in that game.

11. List two heuristics that you use in everyday situations.

12. Given the same goal state as in the text example, what is $h(S)$ for the 15 puzzle:

1	2	6	3
4	5	7	10
15		14	9
13	12	11	8

S

13. Of the four possible moves in Exercise 9.12, which would you choose and why?

14. What are various interpretations for the sentence, "Bombers have targets?"

15. Make up a list of 10 ELIZA templates to be used in a script for talking about the weather, e.g.,

rule	response
$(X$ 'rain' $Y)$	('Did you wear a raincoat today?')
('Today it is' $Y)$	('I hope it is' Y 'tomorrow')

where X and Y are strings.

16. Why is STUDENT more interesting that ELIZA?

17. Discuss how a program could learn by playing itself tic-tac-toe.

18. Defend or refute the thesis that truly intelligent computer programs will be possible.

19. Defend or refute the thesis that truly intelligent computer programs will greatly benefit society.

ADDITIONAL READINGS

Feigenbaum, E. and Feldman, J. eds. *Computers and Thought.* New York: McGraw Hill, 1963.

Kahn, H. and Weiner, A. J. *The Year 2000.* New York: MacMillan Co., 1967.

Meltzer, B. and Michie, D. eds., *Machine Intelligence.* Vol. 5, Edinburgh: University of Edinburgh Press, 1970.

Minsky, M. ed. *Semantic Information Processing,* Cambridge, Mass.: MIT, 1968.

Nilsson, N. *Problem Solving Methods in Artificial Intelligence.* New York: McGraw Hill, 1971.

Raphael, B. *The Thinking Computer.* San Francisco: Freeman, 1976.

Weizenbaum, J. *Computer Power and Human Reason.* San Francisco: Freeman, 1976.

Winston, P. *Artificial Intelligence.* Reading, Mass.: Addison Wesley, 1977.

Chapter 10

COMPUTER USE AND ITS IMPLICATIONS

We have introduced some of the basic ideas of algorithms, programming, and computers. In our study of computation, a number of applications have also been mentioned. However, it would require several bookshelves to describe in any comprehensive way the full range of computer applications in our technological society.

Such is the range of computer use that popular works describe our era as the "computer age" or the "post industrial society"—a time when not only is physical labor accomplished by machine, but more significantly, mental labor as well. In this chapter, we present a number of different applications of computation. We discuss not only the how of each application, but also its social implications.

10.1 SOCIAL AND ETHICAL QUESTIONS

Computers are the capstone technology of our times. All technologies have their own dynamics and their own servants. One of the most powerful technologists of modern times was Albert Speer, the minister of war production in Nazi Germany. He served a twenty year sentence in Spandau as a war criminal and used this time to reflect on his experience. At the end of his memoirs,[1] he wrote:

> The catastrophe of this war has proved the sensitivity of the system of modern civilization evolved in the course of centuries. Now we know that we do not live in an earthquake-proof structure. The build-up of negative impulses, each reinforcing the other, can inexorably shake to pieces the complicated apparatus of the modern world. There is no halting this process by will alone. The danger is that the automatism of

---

[1] *Inside the Third Reich,* Avon Press, 1969, p. 658.

progress will depersonalize man further and withdraw more and more of his self-responsibility.

Dazzled by the possibilities of technology, I devoted crucial years of my life to serving it. But in the end my feelings about it are highly skeptical.

Computers affect society at many levels. The most global level is addressed by the Speer quotation. The major issue is whether or not a technological society is a humane society. For some, a humane society is not achievable by technological means.

At another level are the specific problems coming from the potential misuse of the computer. A much-discussed danger is the loss of privacy as a consequence of large central data banks. Another example is the unthinking replacement of human labor by machines.

Progress out of control is the distortion of the fairy godmother into the Golem—the mythical robot monster of the Eastern European village. Often the same computer methods can be used for good or ill. In Table 10.1, a list of different computer uses and their possible alternative effects portrays this dichotomy.

An oft-quoted remark of scientists is that "science and technology are morally neutral; the employment of science and technology for societal goals is not morally neutral." The science of nuclear physics, for example, produced both atomic bombs and diagnostic x-ray machines. The decision on how to employ technology is a political decision in which the whole society should participate. But it is the minimal responsibility of scientists to point out the possible consequences of employing new technology. They should have a sensitivity to the societal matrix that dictates potential use. Let us examine some specific examples of potential computer use and misuse, and later return to the general question of technology and society.

10.1.1   An Example of the Thin Gray Line of the Social Consequences of Technology

Real-time monitoring of the life signals of heart attack victims has drastically improved their chances of recuperation. In our society this form of medical technology is highly praised. The Shock Research Unit of the University of Southern California's School of Medicine has an intensive care system where temperature, cardiac input, venous pressure, respiration, urine output, and heart rate can all be continually monitored. A predefined undesirable reading of these life signals alerts a doctor or nurse.

Table 10.1 Optimistic and Pessimistic Expectations For Some Computer Applications

Use	Optimist	Pessimist
economic planning and automation	economy of abundance; end to drudgery	massive unemployment; rationalizing work effort to the point of complete alienation
central data banks	humane and effective social policy	police state surveillance; loss of privacy
computer aided education	uniformly higher levels of education	uniform indoctrination through central control over course content
artificial intelligence	synergistic collaboration of man and machine	human obsolescence
weather prediction	avoidance of natural disaster; greater agricultural production	use of weather as a weapon
urban and transportation planning	better housing and transportation	values sacrificed to efficiency
defense command systems	"pax machina"; ever vigilant machines maintain an armed truce	further escalation with a greater potential for catastrophic accident
computer psychotherapy	enhanced mental health	brainwashing

This ongoing monitoring of life signals is being extended to outpatient care; pacemakers, electrocardiograms taken over the telephone, and new telecommunications miniaturization are advances which lead to a continuing surveillance and maintenance of the defective heart beyond the hospital environment.

What can be done for physically debilitated people can in principle be done for mentally and emotionally debilitated people. There is a growing understanding of the electrical and chemical activity that accompanies emotional states. In the last few years, many efforts have been made using biofeedback to control emotional states. The alpha rhythm, a primary brain wave, is now linked to the meditative state. High adrenalin flow, heart rate, and brain wave activity can be monitored to determine exceptional emotional conditions. Increased physiological knowledge, coupled with improved telecommunications and other forms of remote sensing, can hypothetically be used to control defective emotional states in people.

For example, the parole officer who must monitor the activities of the released criminal could be augmented or supplanted by a computer sensing the parolee's emotional signals. Any instance of exceptional emotional activity could trigger a variety of responses, possibly including remote release of a tranquilizer in the parolee. Prisoners might prefer release under this form of control rather than continued imprisonment. Law and order can be safeguarded while the criminal attempts to reform. This potential application of real-time computer control would use the same technology as remote monitoring of cardiac patients.

Of course, what can be done for the emotionally defective can also be done for the "politically" defective. Any person judged as having an undesirable set of beliefs can be monitored and controlled. Thus, a pervasive behavioral dictatorship could be achieved by extending the use of the above computer application. This use could be seen as a natural outgrowth of the initially benevolent technology. Most certainly, this last stage of unmitigating universal behavioral surveillance and control is repugnant. But where is the line crossed from socially desirable use to socially dysfunctional use? Does the availability of the technology itself change the moral standard in a subtle, unpremeditated fashion?

The above scenario is hypothetical. While the technology exists, there are still many difficulties in reliably implementing such a system. However, a real-time computer technology that monitors the state of readiness of the nation's nuclear defense and estimates the ongoing threat of attack is of similar type and complexity to a potential system for monitoring dissidents.

10.2 COMPUTERS IN MEDICINE

Computers are used in medicine to do ordinary billing of patients, to keep medical records, to monitor life support systems, to provide intelligent instrumentation, to augment clinical and diagnostic reasoning, and to suggest treatment. Such applications as billing, record keeping, and hospital personnel scheduling are common to a host of organizations; the only distinction that could be made for their use in medical applications is the need for better standards of accuracy. It is one thing to receive the wrong dress from a department store and quite another to receive the wrong medication or treatment from a hospital. In this section we describe uses that are specific to the medical profession.

Advanced Medical Instrumentation

The perfect medical diagnostic machine would provide information without risk or bodily invasion. Invasive procedures include taking blood and tissue samples, or in more radical cases, exploratory surgery. Noninvasive procedures include taking temperature, pulse, or blood pressure. Invasive procedures are more hazardous, uncomfortable, and costly.

Electronic and computer-oriented instrumentation has greatly extended the realm of noninvasive data acquisition. One such device is the computer-aided X-ray tomagraphic unit (CAT). Conventional X-ray diagnosis uses shadowgraphs, a photographic technique that is sensitive to a 25 percent difference in X-ray absorption. A CAT records the beam attenuation from all angles; because of its computational prowess, it can process and separate absorption coefficients to a 0.25 percent difference. This is an improvement by a factor of 100 over the conventional techniques. Certain cancers or brain tumors can be detected reliably by the CAT that once required either exploratory surgery or radio-isotope injections—both very hazardous invasive procedures.

Prosthesis

Examples of simple prosthetic devices are a wooden arm and hook replacing an amputated arm and hand, and eyeglasses for correcting vision. With recent advances in computer science, especially in robotics, these elementary devices can be extended or supplanted. Computer assisted devices can replace sensory function to some degree. Organs, such as the eye, gather and interpret information; hands and arms are controlled by neural impulses. Prosthetic devices employing microprocessors and other electronic and computational devices can be substituted for many of these neural functions.

One such device to aid the blind is the Optacon. This device converts ordinary printed text to vibrations. The blind person places his fingers over a set of perforations and feels a vibrating image corresponding to the printed text. There are also devices which convert text to English vocalizations. The Optacon replaces braille. The computerized conversion of text to vocalization replaces readers for the blind. These devices are coming into widespread use. More exotic machines under test convert a general visual frame to tactile signals transmitted to a selected area of skin that serves as a pseudoretina.

Another aid for the blind and visually impaired is the Kurzweil Reading Machine. Developed over a period of ten years and incorporating sophisticated hardware and artificial intelligence techniques, this desktop device reads English printed text and produces continuous speech output. It is a synthesis of pattern recognition, linguistics and phonetics, voice synthesis, and digital hardware design. The machine uses over one thousand rules to pronounce phonetically the words that it has recognized by means of an optical character scan. Such devices are already installed in a variety of public facilities such as libraries and rehabilitation centers.

Research continues on computer-controlled hands and arms directed by neural and muscular signals sensed in the amputated limbs. Computerized arms that are to some degree self-controlling employ programs that have been developed in AI laboratories. The hope is that cheap and flexible bionic devices will soon be available. Robotic arms are already installed on automotive assembly lines as reliable replacements to human laborers in tedious, repetitive, and dangerous environments.

Diagnostic and Treatment Aids

MYCIN, already mentioned in the previous chapter, represents one of a number of newly developed diagnostic programs to aid the physician. Yet another is the Duke University Cardiovascular Information System. The Duke program classifies a coronary patient according to a large set of descriptors. These descriptors include the patient's medical history and the physical and laboratory findings of his or her examination. Once the patient is categorized, the doctor can review the treatment of any previous patient similarly grouped. While such a taxonomic process is conceptually simple, the enormous variety of pooled experience of the medical community could not be effectively summarized and accessed manually.

The most ambitious of diagnostic programs is the INTERNIST program developed at the University of Pittsburgh. This program simulates the reasoning of the expert clinician. INTERNIST has a database covering over 80 percent of the diagnoses of internal medicine. It is fed symptoms and laboratory data, and uses over 100,000 rules to deduce an appropriate diagnosis. The system associates a likelihood of finding a given symptom linked to a given disease. For each symptom, there is also an associated list of diseases in which it is known to occur. INTERNIST reasons probabilistically and deductively, and selects the most likely diagnosis. The program's expertise is comparable to a very skilled specialist in internal medicine.

Other programs exist for more restricted domains. CASNET provides a model of glaucoma and its treatment. PIP reasons in the realm of renal disease, while PUFF works in the area of pulmonary dysfunction. Such is the proliferation of general and special expertise, that one can predict that by the end of the 1980's all major medical centers will rely on such aids. Indeed, the physician may be asked to ratify routinely a machine produced diagnosis and treatment.

10.3   COMPUTERS AND DECISION MAKING

Today computer analysis is an integral part of planning and decision making in many large organizations. Computers are used to predict the effect of a given decision. Much of this is an outgrowth of Operations Research, a methodology for quantifying and selecting policy in complex environments.

The Origins of Operations Research

Operations research grew up with the computer, both being offsprings of World War II. Before the United States entered the war, Great Britain was enduring heavy German bombing. Its defenses included a small, highly skilled airforce, anti-aircraft, and radar. The British needed to utilize these limited resources in a maximally effective way and called upon a scientific team to analyze their defenses. They assessed radar site placement, fighter aircraft maintenance schedules, and other variables. Overall, scientists were able to devise policies that were twice as effective as those previously used.

A similar "operations research" team later investigated Japanese Kamikaze attacks on the Pacific fleet. There were two policy variables. A ship decided on the violence of its evasive maneuvers versus the effectiveness of its anti-aircraft fire. A study of 477 Kamikaze attacks showed that the strategy should depend on the size of the ship. A very large ship should undertake the most violent evasive maneuvers; these turns would have only a small effect on the precision of its anti-aircraft fire. Small ships were most effective in avoiding a Kamikaze hit if they did not maneuver, but instead maintained course to provide precise anti-aircraft fire. Ships which adhered to the operations research group's strategy were twice as likely to avoid Kamikaze damage. The remarkable success of these wartime studies gave a tremendous impetus to this budding methodology. The computer abetted the spread of operations research by providing a tool to evaluate larger and larger problems.

An Example: The Traveling Salesman Problem

A salesman based in city A must periodically travel to all other cities in his territory. He goes to each city once and only once and then returns to city A. All cities are connected by airline flights and he wishes to book the least costly tour of all cities. In Figure 10.1, the complete map of the salesman's territory is drawn. For any two cities there is a line between them labeled by the cost of using that connection. The salesman starts at city A and must trace a tour where a next city is one not yet visited. After all cities are visited, he returns to A. One such tour of cost 18 is shown in Figure 10.1. At this point, the reader should see if this value can be improved.

This small problem has $5! = 120$ possible tours (See Figure 10.2). The number of possible tours for an n-city problem is $(n - 1)!$. Practical problems that occur in transportation and communications may involve 50 or more locations. But evaluating one billion tours of a 50 city problem would be much less than a billionth of the total feasible tours—clearly, a method other than exhaustive enumeration is necessary.

Monte Carlo Algorithm for the Traveling Salesman Problem

Starting with city A, there are five remaining cities to visit. Choose one at random, say C, and visit it next. This leaves four cities unvisited. Again choose at random an unvisited city. Continue this process until the tour is complete. The resulting tour is called a Monte Carlo trial. It is simple to generate such tours. The larger the sample of such tours, the more likely a good tour will be found among them.

Example: Monte Carlo trials in the six-city problem

tour	length	
ABDFECA	18	
AEDCFBA	14	the best tour found
AEBCDFA	17	
AECBFDA	17	
ADFCBEA	18	
AFCEDBA	17	

(a sample of six trials out of 120 tours)

To perform a Monte Carlo trial, a computer must simulate a random process. Of course algorithms are deterministic, but simple functions exist which generate long sequences of numbers whose behavior satisfies statistical criteria of randomness. These functions are called pseudo-random number generators.

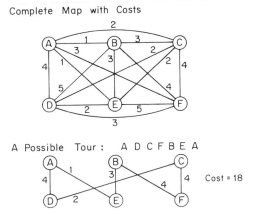

Complete Map with Costs

A Possible Tour :   A D C F B E A
Cost = 18

Figure 10.1   Traveling Salesman Map and Tour

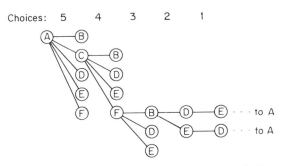

Choices: 5   4   3   2   1

After each previous choice there is one less further choice to make.

The diagram shows a portion of the possible decisions including two complete tours

ACFBDEA and   ACFBEDA.

Figure 10.2   Enumeration of Tours

Locally Good Heuristic Methods

A real salesman confronted with planning our tour might start at city A and select the nearest neighboring city, E or B. Say he chooses E and continues to select the nearest neighboring city not already visited. He can continue to use this easily computed heuristic until a tour is found. Recall that a heuristic is an *ad hoc* rule that is used to make decisions without any guarantee that the decisions so reached will be optimal.

Example: Nearest-Neighbor Tours

tour	*length*	
AEDCBFA	15	
AECDFBA	13	the best nearest-neighbor tour
ABCDEFA	16	
ABEDCFA	15	
ABCEDFA	14	
ABECDFA	14	

The nearest-neighbor method uses a specific local test to obtain a global solution. However, such local rules can go astray and not achieve a good solution (See Figure 10.3).

The traveling salesman problem is still being studied for methods which efficiently:

1. guarantee a near optimal solution,
2. have a high probability of being optimal, or
3. guarantee an optimal solution or give up.

Methods exist for each of these categories that solve multi-hundred city problems. However, the general problem is in the NP complete category. Thus it is expected in the worst cases to take exponential time to compute guaranteed optimal solutions.

Simulation

Operations research is closely related to the simulation approach to problem solving. Simulation is an attempt to predict events in the real world by creating a computer program to mimic it. The outcome of simulation experiments is used by decision makers as plausible predictions.

For example, suppose that a bank wants to decide between two different ways of serving customers. In one, all the customers wait in a single line or *queue* and the customer at the head of the queue goes to the first available teller. In the other, the customer goes to a particular teller's queue. The bank determines through surveys and clockings:

1. the average length of a transaction and
2. a person who waits in line more than 12 minutes is unhappy.

The bank's objective is to have the fewest unhappy customers using the least number of tellers. It cannot try each queuing pattern because of the inconvenience to its customers and the need to build service facilities according to the pattern chosen. Instead it simulates the behavior of its customers for each pattern and selects a design based on the outcome of the simulation.

Similar studies on traffic and housing patterns are made when a new highway is planned. They are used to predict urban growth and traffic impact from the new road and its exits. One such study showed that maximum traffic flow during rush hours through New York's Lincoln Tunnel occurred at 18 m.p.h.

The ability to simulate is not always the ability to predict. Many attempts have been made to predict the stock market; at best, these have met with limited success or are so specialized that they are rarely useful. On the other hand, extremely useful application has been made to the

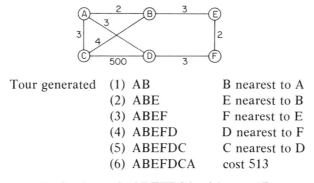

Tour generated	(1) AB	B nearest to A
	(2) ABE	E nearest to B
	(3) ABEF	F nearest to E
	(4) ABEFD	D nearest to F
	(5) ABEFDC	C nearest to D
	(6) ABEFDCA	cost 513

Optimal tour is ADFEBCA with cost 17.

In the fifth step of the nearest-neighbor solution the only remaining unvisited city was C, and the tour was stuck with visiting it.

Figure 10.3   The Nearest-Neighbor Tour Goes Astray

game of blackjack.[2] The computer simulated hundreds of thousands of blackjack hands where different strategies were used. In the process it found a strategy based on keeping track of discards from previous plays that allowed the gambler to have a better than even money advantage against the casino.

The difference between blackjack and the stock market is the validity of the model. The rules of blackjack and the laws of chance are well known. The variables affecting a given stock's performance are not. Confidence in simulation modeling is akin to confidence in any theory—have the predictions been confirmed, and are they more reliable than any competing model.

An Elementary Simulation: The Game of "Life"

The game of life is an archetypal checkerboard simulation. It was invented by the English mathematician John H. Conway for exploring certain formal situations involving reproduction and growth. The game is a successor to the work of John von Neumann on cellular automata.

A checkerboard simulation is a model where the world is broken up into a square array of cells. Each cell may interact only with its neighboring cells, the interactions occurring once per simulated clock pulse. The rules for a local change are well-defined and simple; but predicting global change is impractical without computer simulation. The game of life has the following rules:

1. A cell is either empty or alive (X).
2. Each cell is the center of a three by three square grid of cells which contains its eight neighbors.
3. A cell that is empty at time t becomes alive (X) at time $t + 1$ if and only if exactly three neighboring cells were alive at time t.
4. A cell that is alive at time t remains alive at time $t + 1$ if and only if either two or three neighboring cells were alive at time t. Otherwise it dies for lack of company (<2) or overcrowding (>3).
5. The simulation is conducted, in principle, on an infinite two-dimensional grid (See Figure 10.4).

The simulation starts with an initial configuration of X's on the grid. At each successive time step, a new configuration is computed according to

---

[2] E. O. Thorpe, *Beat the Dealer: A Winning Strategy for The Game of Twenty-One,* Vintage Books, 1962.

the rules. The simulation may be used to search for board patterns with certain properties. It is easy enough to come up with stable configurations or disappearing configurations, as shown in Figure 10.5(a) and (b). However, an initial configuration that can generate a constantly expanding population is difficult to discover. One such pattern, called "the glider gun," was found by a team of MIT students using a computer simulation. (Figure 10.4(c)).

Another configuration, as yet undiscovered but known to exist, is a "Garden of Eden" pattern. This is a pattern that cannot be generated from any other configuration—hence the name. For example, a blank configuration is not a Garden of Eden pattern because it can easily be generated from another configuration such as the one in Figure 10.5(b).

The game of life is a basic form of ecological simulation. By widening the class of objects that may exist or coexist in a cell, and by changing the rules for interaction between a cell and its neighborhood, a variety of complicated systems can be studied. Simulations of this form are used to study urban growth patterns, world economic cycles, stellar evolution, and the daily weather.

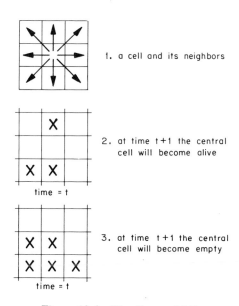

1. a cell and its neighbors

2. at time t+1 the central cell will become alive

3. at time t+1 the central cell will become empty

Figure 10.4 The Game of Life

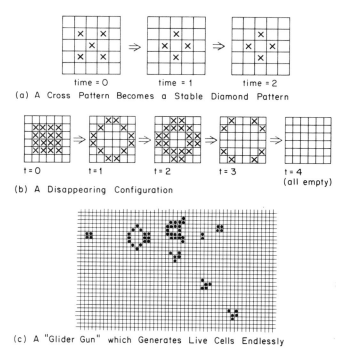

(a) A Cross Pattern Becomes a Stable Diamond Pattern

(b) A Disappearing Configuration

(c) A "Glider Gun" which Generates Live Cells Endlessly

Figure 10.5   Some Sample Life Configurations

Societal Implications

There are several important questions in using simulations and operations research techniques for prediction:

1. Is the model valid?
2. Is the model understandable?
3. Is the model inclusive?
4. Who determines the model's purpose?
5. Who is accountable for computer-based decisions?
6. Who has access to the system?

The above questions are neither exhaustive nor independent of each other, but provide a basis for an initial inquiry.

Question 1, the criterion of validity, is the same for computer theories as for other theories. Namely, a theory is valid if it predicts an observable reality more correctly than competing theories. A model of the weather that almost never makes accurate forecasts will not be relied on regardless of its imposing structure.

Validity becomes a difficult issue when only a single experiment can be attempted and this experiment has potentially irreversible consequences. The U.S. government, for example, has conducted a long series of underground nuclear weapons tests in the southwestern deserts and the Aleutian Islands off Alaska. Both areas lie in the middle of earthquake fault regions. There is some unknown probability that a nuclear test will trigger a massive earthquake. Before one Alaskan test, many responsible scientists felt that a substantial earthquake hazard existed and attempted to dissuade the Atomic Energy Commission from proceeding. The government responded with assurances that its simulations of the effects of this test showed that no earthquake was possible. However, there was no adequate model of earthquake prediction. If the government's analysis was in error, there would be the potential for monumental disaster. Yet, the test proceeded, and fortunately no major earthquake occurred. Was the government's model correct? All that can be ascertained is that it was not incorrect—since only the possibility of an earthquake was predicted by non-governmental scientists. Many such irreversible policy decisions are based on inadequate models, for example, starting a war, building a highway, and using non-biodegradable pesticides and detergents.

In ancient times, policy makers consulted oracles. The predictions were believed because only believers could secure a prophecy. The most famous oracle was the Delphic oracle of Greece; its prophetesses stood in divine communion with the god Apollo and received omens of the future. Anyone lacking in confidence in such predictive methods was unlikely to seek such advice. Similarly, a simulation program may be oracular. The user of a simulation program frequently believes its results without fully comprehending the model's relationship to reality. Indeed the rules of the simulation and their interactions are often obscure and incomprehensible. Such models that are not understandable should inspire little confidence.

Is the model inclusive? The model can be valid and explainable but not broad enough. A pesticide may indeed increase agricultural production, but will it interfere with a vital component of the ecological whole? The computer has allowed an increase in the ability to provide a comprehensive model, but reality is always approximated. The disasters occur not because 1000 or 10,000 variables are included, but because one variable or relationship is omitted.

Furthermore, it is relatively easy to quantify certain variables such as profit, and relatively difficult to quantify other variables such as political freedom. Typically, what is easily quantifiable will be used in the model.

The political or social policy based on such a model will not be sensitive to these omitted variables.

The fourth question is a political question. Consider the following example. In the mid 1960's, the U.S. Congress debated the emplacement of an anti-ballistic missile system. Lacking the resources to build a fully comprehensive system, Congress asked the Pentagon to prepare a priority list of cities to protect. The Pentagon invented a merit function based on such factors as population, economic value, and defense value. Its computer programs produced a list of cities in order of defensive priority. The top of the list had the expected major cities of the United States, with one exception. The exception was a small southern city of a population less than 100,000. This city was home base for the chairman of an important congressional committee which controlled many defense matters. One need not envision a deliberate insertion of this city into the high priority list. It is most probable that the weightings of the appropriate variables could be chosen for this to occur as a consequence. In this way, a political decision could be disguised in a seemingly objective computer-based analysis.

When decisions are taken based on computer analysis, who is responsible for their effects? A simple non-simulation example illustrates the problem. The consumer who has been incorrectly billed by computer often must spend an inordinate amount of time clearing up this error. The billing department blames the computer department and the computer department blames the software vendor, and they all conveniently blame the computer. The computer serves as a perfect scapegoat for avoiding responsibility.

The last question posed is the question of access. Consider the politician who has access to an analysis of demographic variables in his constituency. This analysis will suggest positions he should take on different issues. His opponent, lacking such analysis, is at a decided disadvantage. The means to predict reliably the effect of different policies is a source of great power.

Computer-based decision making can be either manipulative or responsive. The choice is essentially a political one. The technological problems are ones of implementing appropriate controls and guaranteeing correct systems.

10.4   INFORMATION RETRIEVAL AND PRIVACY

Information retrieval is the management and access of information by a computer on a machine readable store. Typically the data base is too large to be stored in the main computer memory and instead must be stored on cheaper and slower storage mediums such as magnetic tape or disk. The functions of an information retrieval system are to store large files of information, efficiently retrieve information, delete old information and insert new information, protect the integrity of the data base, and prevent unauthorized access to the data base. Not all information retrieval systems need worry about these functions to the same degree, but all systems share most of these requirements.

An Elementary Information System

Let us present a hypothetical information retrieval system for a credit bureau in a small community. Assume that the data base has 100,000 *records,* where each record contains the credit information on a particular person. An example record is given in Figure 10.6. A record is composed of several fields. These include ordinary data fields, such as name, salary, and occupation; a *pointer* field that contains the address of the next-of-kin record; and an *access code* which protects the record from unauthorized use.

The 100,000 records in this file are available on a disk. The information is stored alphabetically on consecutive tracks. A table of contents, called a *file directory,* precedes the information file. The file directory gives the disk address for each alphabetical grouping. The system can respond to several types of *queries.*

Examples:

1. query: retrieve X. ALT
   response: X. ALT, Cleric, $5,000, No, 2D, $589, D. F. ALT, 000, 1973

   This query would be performed by finding in the directory where the A's start and reading the A's into the computer main memory. There a search could retrieve "X. ALT" and print the associated information.

2. query: retrieve X. ALT and next-of-kin
   response: X. ALT, Cleric, $5,000, No, 2D, $589, D. F. ALT, 000, 1973
             D. F. ALT, Candlemaker, $893, Yes, 4C, $0, C. ALT, 000, 1971

   This query would find X. ALT's record and use the next-of-kin field to find D. F. ALT's record. The address stored in the pointer field of next-of-kin can be used to find D. F. ALT without any further search.

Pointer fields are included when search patterns occur frequently enough to justify the additional storage.

3. query: retrieve average-salary of occupation-Cleric
   response: $8,219

This type of statistical complilation requires a complete search of the 100,000 records. Each record's occupation field must be compared to Cleric and if a match occurs, the salary field is added in to the average. This is a very expensive query since it involves a check of all records.

Information which is located by a pointer field, or some sequence of pointer fields, can be found in at most k addressing operations where k is the length of the pointer chain. In our example, occupational information may be frequently requested. There could be many job classifications recognized by the system, including "Cleric." Then instead of listing the occupation, use this as a pointer field. Each Cleric's record will use the occupation field to point at the next cleric in the data base, as shown below.

Example: Cleric Pointers

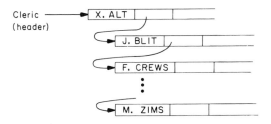

Now searching a file for information about a given occupation only requires searching the chained together records.

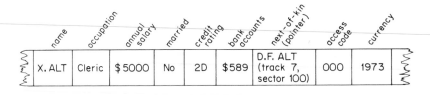

Figure 10.6   Example of Credit Bureau Record

Updating the File

Our credit bureau system needs to be periodically updated by removing out-of-date records and inserting new records. The more structured the file, the more difficult in general this updating becomes. Our alphabetically ordered file cannot have a new record inserted at its end; instead it must be inserted in its appropriate position in the ordered sequence. This requires moving records to create space for the new record. This in turn disrupts the current pointer information which must address the new locations. Similarly, deleting old information creates unused space.

Since these updating operations are relatively expensive, they are done as infrequently as possible. One way to accomplish the update is to use a secondary file. The spaces created by deleting information remain unused, while new information is added to the secondary file. When the secondary file gets large enough to warrant a complete file revision, its records are merged with the primary file's records. This process is analogous to an encyclopedia publisher putting out yearbooks (secondary files) until it decides to edit a new edition.

Protecting Access and Integrity

The access code field in the credit bureau record is a protection mechanism. A query must also contain an integer password which must match the access code. Unauthorized users would not have such a password. For example, if their password were "000," they would be entitled to access X. ALT's record. This authorization code technique provides a limited form of protection.

National Data Banks and the Right to Privacy

Information retrieval systems are an attractive solution to managing the information needs of an increasing complex bureaucratic government. But consider the *New York Times* headline of Sunday, June 28, 1970: "Federal Computers Amass Files on Suspect Citizens—Many Among Hundreds of Thousands Listed Have No Criminal Records—Critics See Invasion of Privacy." The story goes on to say that the government is compiling dossiers in several data bases, such as:

1. a Secret Service computer data bank containing over 50,000 persons who are of "protective interest,"—in other words, they may wish to do harm to the President.

2. a Justice Department data bank on individuals and groups who may participate in "civil disturbance." This group includes peace activists, racial minorities, interest groups, and "radical" political parties.
3. a Health, Education, and Welfare data bank on 300,000 children of migrant farm workers. The file contains scholastic records including teachers' judgements of the students' attitudes.

Nearly all government agencies as well as many private organization have access to, or maintain data files on the citizenry. These agencies believe that the data banks are necessary in order to act knowledgeably and efficiently. The collection, maintenance, and use of this data threatens a citizen's right to privacy.

Consider the guide-lines to determine who is of "protective interest" for the Secret Service data bank. In order of priority, they are:

Individuals or groups who are planning to harm physically or embarrass the President or other high government officials.

Individuals or groups who have in the past been involved in activities described in 1.

Individuals or groups who insist upon personally contacting high government officials for the redress of imaginary grievances.

Individuals who make oral or written statements which are either abusive, emotional, or threatening about high government officials.

Individuals who are gate crashers.

Individuals who may have access to concealed weapons or explosives.

Individuals who may have been involved in anti-American or anti-U.S. government demonstrations or civil disturbances.

The first category involves criminal behavior. The last category involves the rights of a free citizenry, which include petitioning high government officials about their grievances real or imagined and free assembly for purposes of protest. Where is the "thin gray line" separating the right to privacy from the need to protect the President? Senator Ervin, an expert on constitutional law and a vocal critic of the move toward a massive centralized national data bank, has stated that information retrieval technology and its uncontrolled use are creating "a mass surveillance system unprecedented in American history."

Government agencies, such as the Social Security System, the Internal Revenue Service, and the Census Bureau have computerized files on almost all adults in our society. Similarly, private organizations, such as insurance companies, banks, and credit bureaus have comprehensive economic profiles of tens of millions of Americans in their data bases. Who has access to this data? How is information entered and deleted and with what controls on the data's validity? How is the system protected from unauthorized use?

It has only been recently that real attention has been paid to the right of privacy, resulting in laws that partially protect the individual. In the frontier society of pre-20th century America, each homestead was sacrosanct. Privacy was a geographical and demographic imperative. Stringent trespass laws and lax gun control are our inheritance from this period. In the interconnected and delicately balanced modern industrial state, individual rights are often abridged to guarantee the security and welfare of the entire society. This abridgement has been accomplished, in part, by giving substantial authority to centralized government agencies. Without considerable sensitivity to individual privacy, computer technology allows an acceleration of this process.

10.5 FORECASTS

It would be foolish to attempt detailed predictions of a technology that sees major breakthroughs every three to five years. Nevertheless, it is important to appreciate and consider what is likely to happen in computer technology. Since 1945, computer technology has improved roughly one order of magnitude per demi-decade. This means that the general range of improvement from 1945–1980 is approximately 10^8. Now if we were born in 1945 and given \$10 to invest, then an investment that grew at the rate computer technology improved would leave us a billionaire in 1980.

The figure 10^8 represents an aggregate of improvements. The ENIAC used 140 kilowatts: a small microprocessor today uses less than three watts, a reduction in power consumption of 5×10^4. The ENIAC had 18,000 tubes occupying 3,000 cubic feet; today, very large scale integrated circuits contain an equivalent number of circuits in one millionth the space. Cost, power consumption, reliability, memory size, speed, physical size and ease of use have all improved by orders of magnitude. The expectation is that all these computing attributes will continue to improve.

The Very Largest Super Computers

The very largest machines of the 1970's, such as the CRAY 1 and ILLIAC IV, perform between 10^7 and 10^8 basic machine operations per second and access main memories of about 10^8 bits. These machines cost at least ten million dollars. By 1985, it is expected that the very largest computers will perform as many as 5×10^9 useful operations per second and have access to main memories of at least 10^{10} bits. These machines will continue to be only few in number (only one ILLIAC IV was ever built) and would be applied chiefly to large scale numerical computations such as weather modeling. Much of their ability to process large numerical problems comes from the easily orchestrated parallelism inherent in very large systems of equations. Like other very large scientific instruments, such as 200 inch telescopes and gigavolt accelerators, they help extend the frontiers of science.

The Very Smallest Computers

The very largest computers, while impressive in performance, are likely to have little effect on our daily lives. Instead it will be the computers on a chip that will most profoundly influence society. These devices have replaced mechanical timekeeping by digital timekeeping; mechanical calculators by digital calculators; and are in the process of replacing mechanical ignition timing and automotive engine control by digital controllers. Furthermore, there is the expectation that millions of households in the United States will have a home computer by 1985. The house of the 1980's will be littered with microprocessors built into appliances, toys, telephones, high-fi, and whatever else can benefit from limited intelligent control. Already, microwave ovens are programmable as are elaborate home thermostats. The home thermostat that can obey detailed instructions relating time of day and week to temperature control allows much greater flexibility and energy efficiency. We will talk to our appliances and they will answer back. It is now feasible to build an alarm-clock-radio that says, "Please wake up, Joe; today is Monday the 5th and you will be late for the office." Joe will, of course, be able to tell his intelligent alarm clock to let him sleep another half hour. Devices such as the Texas Instruments' "Speak and Spell" game have general programmable speech synthesis and cost under $50. Discrete word voice input circuits that control microprocessors are also available for as little as $100. It is mind-boggling to contemplate the effects that socialized machines' communicating with us in natural language will have.

Many companies are experimenting with chip manufacturing technologies that could mean 100,000 gates per chip and 1,000,000 bits of memory per chip. Microprocessors as powerful as the largest machines of the late 1950's will be available on single chips for no more than tens of dollars by 1990. Indeed, they will be throwaway items much as lightbulbs are. Any definable need will have a computation "socket" into which a microprocessor will be plugged.

Computers in the Work Place

Communication and record keeping are increasingly being computerized. The secretary is moving from typewriter to word processing station (terminal). The salesclerk is moving from the cash register to the (cashless, often) point of sale terminal. The bankteller is frequently being augmented or replaced by the electronic bank station. The record keeper is already a program and data base. We hear such terms as "word processing," "the cashless society," and "electronic funds transfer." Each refers to a growing integrated network of electronic communication and computation automatically manipulating information. Information as represented by records, cash, checks, and memos imprinted on paper is being phased out of intermediary transactions. Consider, for example, making an airline or hotel reservation. One calls up and a clerk inputs your request to a terminal; the terminal automatically accesses its database and without further human intervention, schedules you and records credit-card payment. What once required numerous clerks now requires one message taker. Indeed with home terminals it is possible to eliminate even the one human agent.

One possible extrapolation is the elimination of almost all middle-management from the labor force. There will be a front-line layer of employee. These will be the sales and service representatives, and the basic clerks or typists who will act as an entry point to a business or governmental agency. A second layer will be policy makers and technocrats, the senior-level management making non-routine judgments. Routine judgment, paper shuffling, bookeeping, and filing will be handled electronically and automatically.

So far the use of computers at work has not affected the level of employment. New services are generated which generate increasing demands. While the nature of work has changed for many, there is no conclusive evidence that work satisfaction is lessened. We are a society in transition, moving from an energy driven work place to an information driven work place. Warehouses, railroad tracks, freeways, and power generators are becoming secondary, while databases, phone networks, terminals, and processors are becoming primary.

10.6 TECHNOLOGY AND TECHNOCRACY: THE CHALLENGE TO MAN'S VALUES

The computer scientist constructs an extensive simulation model to aid policy makers. The model itself might allow a clear rational analysis of conflicting priorities, but it may also involve the manipulation of these priorities. The computer model can thus be used as a smokescreen to obscure. Scientific and technological expertise are often so used to transfer debate away from the general public to the rarified domains of this expertise. In this way, public decision making may be excessively influenced by technical experts—the so-called technocracy.

Theodore Roszak characterizes the technocracy as follows:[3]

> In the technocracy, nothing is any longer small or simple or readily apparent to the non-technical man. Instead the scale and intricacy of all human activities—political, economic, cultural—transcends the competence of the amateurish citizen and inexorably demands the attention of specially trained experts. Further, around this central core of experts who deal with large-scale public necessities there grows up a circle of subsidiary experts who, battening on the general social prestige of technical skill in the technocracy, assume authoritative influence over even the most seemingly personal aspects of life: sexual behavior, childrearing, mental health, recreation, etc. In the technocracy everything aspires to become purely technical, the subject of professional attention.

Critics of the increasing reliance of man on his machines, including Roszak, Jacques Ellul, D. N. Michael, Herbert Marcuse, Norman O. Brown, and Lewis Mumford, feel that technology threatens basic human values. For them, such values as dignity and freedom are mysteries that stand outside of the technological world. Are these critics only backward-looking naive idealists, afraid of loss of human stature? Historically, machines have been a freeing agent. They have allowed man to enlarge his scope and domain; for example, the telescope has enlarged man's knowledge of the universe. But these achievements have created a continuing tension by diminishing man's place in the universe.

The computer has extended this tension to our inner mental life. Each of us must decide and act on our own perceptions of the computer revolution.

---

[3] *The Making of the Counterculture,* Anchor Books, 1969, pp. 6, 7.

EXERCISES

1. Take one of the uses found in Table 10.1 and write a paper describing (a) current developments, (b) expected developments, and (c) societal impact.

2. Construct a moral continuum, similar to the one given in Section 10.1, for a different use of computer technology.

3. Outline two problems not mentioned in this chapter that are solved by operations research methods.

4. Prove that AECDFBA is an optimal traveling salesman tour in the example of Section 10.3.

5. The fact that an automobile owner pollutes the air because this marginal loss is more than compensated for by the convenience of personal transportation is an example of "the tragedy of the commons." Give some examples involving computer use.

6. Many critics of quantitative methods claim that certain objectives are not measurable. Argue this pro or con.

7. Investigate and outline the capabilities of an information retrieval system currently in operation.

8. Program a simple information retrieval system built along lines outlined in the text.

9. Investigate encryption methods for enciphering data to protect privacy.

10. How does your local bank protect the privacy of checking and savings account information from improper access?

11. Write a paper on the current capabilities and capacities of some national data bank, e.g., The National Crime Information Center.

12. "Science and technology are morally neutral." Defend or attack this thesis.

13. "An advanced technological state is harder to rule autocratically than a backward society because it is a finely tuned mechanism which is highly vulnerable to revolutionary sabotage." Argue this pro or con.

14. Should computer scientists have a professional code of ethics similar to that of the medical and legal professions? What should be its contents?

15. "Computer technology is its own imperative." Discuss.

ADDITIONAL READINGS

Ellul, J. *The Technological Society.* New York: Knopf, 1964.

Hoffman, L. J. ed. *Security and Privacy in Computer Systems*. Los Angeles: Melville, 1973.

Kahn, H. and Weiner, A. J. *The Year 2000*. New York: MacMillan Co., 1967.

Linvill, J. G. and Hogan, C. L. "Intellectual and Economic Fuel for the Electronics Revolution." *Science* Vol. 195, No. 4283 (March, 1977), 1107–13.

Miller, A. *The Assault on Privacy: Computers, Data Banks and Dossiers*. Ann Arbor: University of Michigan Press, 1971.

Mowshowitz, A. *The Conquest of Will*. Reading, Mass.: Addison-Wesley, 1976.

Rivlin, A. M. *Systematic Thinking for Social Action*. Washington, D.C.: Brookings, 1971.

Roszak, T. *The Making of the Counter Culture*. San Francisco: Anchor Books, 1969.

Taviss, I. *The Computer Impact*. Englewood Cliffs, N.Y.: Prentice-Hall, 1970.

Weizenbaum, J. *Computer Power and Human Reason*. San Francisco: Freeman Press, 1976.

Wiener, N. *The Human Use of Human Beings*. Boston: Houghton Mifflin, 1950.

Appendix

DEFINITION OF THE ALGORITHMIC LANGUAGE ALGOLIC

A.0 Purpose and Genesis

The Algolic language is a precise notation for describing algorithms so that they may be easily understood, designed, implemented as computer programs, and analyzed. Algolic can be translated in a straightforward way into any of a variety of common high-level programming languages, including BASIC, FORTRAN, PL/I, Pascal, and Algol 60. It has borrowed most heavily from Algol 60 and Pascal, and has many of the basic constructs contained in these languages.

A.1 Syntax Notation

The syntax of each Algolic construct is defined in an extended Backus-Naur Form. A *syntactic category* is denoted by a suggestive phrase surrounded by the brackets ⟨ and ⟩, for example, ⟨compound statement⟩. The construct ⟨*empty*⟩ will stand for the null sequence of symbols.

A *syntactic rule* is written

$$S ::= \alpha$$

where S is a syntactic category and α is a sequence of syntactic elements, each of which is either a syntactic category or a string of basic symbols. The formula is interpreted (read) as "S may be rewritten as α." The form

$$S ::= \alpha \mid \beta \mid \ldots \mid \gamma$$

is an abbreviation for the rules

$$S ::= \alpha$$
$$S ::= \beta$$
.
.
.
$$S ::= \gamma$$

where the symbol "|" indicates "or." For example, the rule:

⟨if statement⟩ ::= **if** ⟨Boolean expression⟩ **then** ⟨statement⟩ |
        if ⟨Boolean expression⟩ **then** ⟨statement⟩ **else** ⟨statement⟩

gives the two possible forms of the ⟨if statement⟩. Finally, the brackets { } are used to indicate 0 or more repetitions of their enclosing symbols; for example, the rule

⟨unsigned integer⟩ ::= ⟨digit⟩ {⟨digit⟩}

defines an ⟨unsigned integer⟩ to be a ⟨digit⟩ followed by 0 or more ⟨digit⟩s.

A.2 Programs

An algorithm is completely specified by an Algolic program[1] which has the syntax:

⟨program⟩ ::= **algorithm** ⟨identifier⟩; ⟨declarations⟩ ⟨statements⟩.

Example:

algorithm *GCD1*;
m, n, r: *integer*;
begin
  read(m, n) ; *write('The values of m and n are '*, *m, n)*;
  {Compute the greatest common divisor of *m* and *n*.}
  while $n \neq 0$ **do**
  begin $r := m$ **mod** n; $m := n$; $n := r$ **end**;
  write('The gcd is' , *m)*
end.

---

[1] The term "program" is used throughout the Appendix to mean an Algolic description of an algorithm.

The ⟨identifier⟩ provides a name for the algorithm. The ⟨declarations⟩ part defines the name and type of every variable used in the program. The ⟨statements⟩ component describes the instructions to be followed when executing the algorithm. An Algolic algorithm P is performed by executing the ⟨statements⟩ of P within the context of its ⟨declarations⟩.

A *comment* may be inserted at any point in a program except between the characters comprising an ⟨identifier⟩, ⟨number⟩, or ⟨special symbol⟩. A comment consists of any string of symbols surrounded by "{" and "}", for example,

$$\{\text{This is a comment.}\}$$

Comments have no effect on the meaning of a program and may be inserted and deleted at will.

A.3 Atomic Elements

The lowest level constituents or atoms of an Algolic program are ⟨identifier⟩, ⟨number⟩, ⟨special symbol⟩, ⟨quoted character⟩, and ⟨character string⟩.

1. An ⟨identifier⟩ is used to denote a program name, variable, or statement label.
   ⟨identifier⟩ ::= ⟨letter⟩ {⟨letter or digit⟩}
   A ⟨letter⟩ is any upper or lower case English letter.
   ⟨letter⟩ ::= $A|B|C \ldots X|Y|Z|a|b|c \ldots x|y|z$
   ⟨digit⟩ ::= $0|1|2 \ldots 8|9$
   ⟨letter or digit⟩ ::= ⟨letter⟩ | ⟨digit⟩

   Examples: $dGA37H$ $GCD1$ $A1000$

2. A ⟨number⟩ is expressed in the usual decimal notation.
   ⟨number⟩ ::= ⟨integer⟩ | ⟨real⟩
   ⟨integer⟩ ::= ⟨unsigned integer⟩ | ⟨sign⟩ ⟨unsigned integer⟩
   ⟨real⟩ ::= ⟨unsigned real⟩ | ⟨sign⟩ ⟨unsigned real⟩
   ⟨sign⟩ ::= $+$ | $-$
   ⟨unsigned integer⟩ ::= ⟨digit⟩ {⟨digit⟩}

   A ⟨real⟩ number may contain an integer scale factor. The factor appears at the end of the number, with the letter "E" acting as a separator. It is interpreted as a power of 10 to be multiplied by its preceding decimal number.

⟨unsigned real⟩ ::= ⟨unsigned integer⟩·⟨unsigned integer⟩ |
          ⟨unsigned integer⟩·⟨unsigned integer⟩ *E* ⟨integer⟩ |
          ⟨unsigned integer⟩ *E* ⟨integer⟩

Examples: 67 13.2 7.67E-56 87E12

3. ⟨special symbol⟩s consist of the special characters and words used as operators, delimiters, and punctuation.

⟨special symbol⟩ ::= ⟨special character⟩ | ⟨special word⟩
⟨special character⟩ ::= +|−|×|/|÷|⊔|:|:=|.|;|'|'|=|≠|..|
                    >|≥|<|≤|(|)|[|]

The symbol ⊔ denotes the blank character.
A ⟨special word⟩ is an underlined sequence of two or more characters that is treated as a single symbol. ⟨special word⟩s are reserved and may not be used as identifiers.

⟨special word⟩ ::= **algorithm|and|array|begin|do|downto|**
            else|end|for|go to|if|mod|
            not|of|or|then|upto|while

4. A ⟨quoted character⟩ is a single character enclosed by single quotation marks.

⟨quoted character⟩ ::= '⟨single character⟩'
⟨single character⟩ ::= ⟨letter or digit⟩ | ⟨special character⟩

Examples: '*d*' '*F*' '4' '≤' '/'

A ⟨character string⟩ is a sequence of one or more ⟨single character⟩s surrounded by quotation marks.

⟨character string⟩ ::= '⟨single character⟩ {⟨single character⟩}'

Examples: '*Algolic program*' '15' '*A + b*' '*c*'

A.4 Declarations, Types, and Denotations

All variables used in an Algolic program are uniquely named and must be declared at the beginning of the program. This declaration has the syntax

⟨declarations⟩ ::= {⟨identifier⟩ { , ⟨identifier⟩} : ⟨type⟩ ; }
⟨type⟩ ::= ⟨simple type⟩ | ⟨array type⟩
⟨simple type⟩ ::= *integer| real | Boolean | character*
⟨array type⟩ ::= **array**[⟨integer⟩ .. ⟨integer⟩] **of** ⟨simple type⟩

Examples: $x5$, A: *real* ;   *BBC* : **array**[3 .. 25] **of** *Boolean*;
                 n, *main*, *flow*: *integer* ;

The ⟨type⟩ of a variable defines the structure of the variable and the values it can hold. The ⟨simple type⟩s permit the following sets of values:

1. *integer*   : the set of integers
2. *real*   : the subset of real numbers representable by the syntax for ⟨real⟩
3. *Boolean*   : the truth values true and false, represented by the identifiers *"true"* and *"false."* These identifiers cannot be used as variables.
4. *character* : the set of single characters, denoted by the category ⟨quoted character⟩

The ⟨array type⟩ specifies *single* dimensional vectors in which each component has the same ⟨simple type⟩. The two integers within the square brackets, *lb* and *ub* say, define the lower and upper bounds, respectively, of the array, and declare that the array has $ub - lb + 1$ components, denoted $n[lb]$, $n[lb + 1]$, ..., $n[ub]$ where n is the array name.

A simple unstructured variable is referenced by its identifier. An array component is referenced by its identifier followed by an index expression in square brackets; the index expression must evaluate to an integer between the lower and upper bounds (inclusive) declared for the array. A variable denotation has the syntax:

⟨variable⟩ ::= ⟨identifier⟩ | ⟨identifier⟩ [⟨arithmetic expression⟩]

Examples: Ab $X15Y$ $B[35]$ $cd[a + 12]$

A.5   Expressions

Expressions describe the computation of values of ⟨simple type⟩. They may be composed of variables, constants, and operators.

⟨expression⟩ ::= ⟨arithmetic expression⟩ | ⟨character expression⟩ | ⟨Boolean expression⟩

An ⟨arithmetic expression⟩ produces a value of type *integer* or *real*.

⟨arithmetic expression⟩ ::= ⟨term⟩ | ⟨sign⟩ ⟨term⟩ | ⟨arithmetic expression⟩ ⟨operator⟩ ⟨term⟩

⟨term⟩ ::= ⟨variable⟩ | ⟨unsigned integer⟩ | ⟨unsigned real⟩ | (⟨arithmetic expression⟩)

⟨operator⟩ ::= $+|-|\times|/|\div|$**mod**

Examples: I $35/x$

$15.3 + (a[17]/(B - C + D))$
$(x \textbf{ mod } y) - (15 \times \text{U}[a + 6] + 11) \div 13$

The normal order of evaluation of arithmetic expressions is from left to right, except that the operators $\times$, $/$, $\div$, and **mod** take precedence over $+$ and $-$. Parenthesized expressions are evaluated before any immediately preceding or succeeding operator is applied. Thus $a + b/c - d + e$ evaluates in the order: $(((a + (b/c)) - d) + e)$. The variables and constants must be of type *real* or *integer*. The meaning of the operators and the type of the result obtained after applying an operator are defined in the following table:

operator	operation	type of operands	type of result
$+$	addition	*integer*	*integer*
$-$	subtraction	*real*	*real*
$\times$	multiplication	mixed (*real* and *integer*)	*real*
$/$	division	*integer*, *real*, mixed	*real*
$\div$	division with truncation	*integer*	*integer*
mod	modulus	*integer*	*integer*

A ⟨character expression⟩ is simply a variable of type character or a ⟨quoted character⟩. They are used primarily in ⟨Boolean expression⟩s for making comparisons.

⟨character expression⟩ ::= ⟨variable⟩ | ⟨quoted character⟩

Examples: 'A' '$<$' *CHARVAR*

A ⟨Boolean expression⟩ produces a value of type *Boolean*.

⟨Boolean expression⟩ ::= ⟨Bterm⟩ | **not** ⟨Bterm⟩ |
                         ⟨Boolean expression⟩ **and** ⟨Bterm⟩ |
⟨Bterm⟩ ::= ⟨variable⟩ | *true* | *false* | (⟨Boolean expression⟩) |
    ⟨arithmetic expression⟩ ⟨relational operator⟩ ⟨arithmetic expression⟩ |
        ⟨character expression⟩ ⟨character relation⟩ ⟨character expression⟩
⟨relational operator⟩ ::= = | ≠ | < | ≤ | > | ≥ |
⟨character relation⟩ ::= = | ≠

Examples: **not** *flag*   *human* **or** *animal* $I \geq J$
            a **and**(**not** b **or** c)) **or** (*true* **and** X[15])
            $(a \geq b)$ **and** $(c = d)$ $(a = \text{'}d\text{'})$ **or**(**not** $(b + 15/e \leq 35.7)$)

The normal order of evaluation is from left to right except that the arithmetic operators take precedence over the relational operators, the relational operators take precedence over the Boolean operators, and precedence (**not**) > precedence(**and**) > precedence(**or**). Thus *a* **or** *b* **and** *c* evaluates according to (*a* **or** (*b* **and** *c*)). As in ⟨arithmetic expression⟩s, parentheses are used to override the normal left to right order; parenthesized expressions are evaluated before any immediately preceding or succeeding operators are applied. The following table summarizes the meaning of the operators and gives the resulting type obtained after applying an operator.

operator	operation	type of operands	type of result
not	negation	*Boolean*	*Boolean*
or	logical "or"	*Boolean*	*Boolean*
and	logical "and"	*Boolean*	*Boolean*
=	equal	*real*	*Boolean*
≠	not equal	*integer*	*Boolean*
		character	*Boolean*
>	greater than	*integer*	*Boolean*
≥	greater than or equal	*real*	*Boolean*
<	less than		
≤	less than or equal		

A.6 Statements

The actions of an algorithm are specified by simple and structured statements. A statement may be identified by a label, permitting the statement to be a target of a **go to**; a given label cannot identify more than one statement.

⟨statements⟩ ::= ⟨empty⟩ | ⟨statement⟩ | ⟨label⟩ : ⟨statement⟩
⟨label⟩ ::= ⟨identifier⟩ | ⟨unsigned integer⟩
⟨statement⟩ ::= ⟨simple statement⟩ | ⟨structured statement⟩
⟨simple statement⟩ ::= ⟨assignment statement⟩ | ⟨goto statement⟩ |
⟨input-output statement⟩
⟨structured statement⟩ ::= ⟨compound statement⟩ | ⟨if statement⟩ |
⟨while statement⟩ | ⟨for statement⟩

A.6.1   Simple Statements

The ⟨assignment statement⟩ assigns the value of an expression to a variable, replacing its old value by the new one.

⟨assignment statement⟩ ::= ⟨variable⟩ := ⟨expression⟩

The ⟨variable⟩ and ⟨expression⟩ must be of the same ⟨simple type⟩, except that the ⟨expression⟩ may also be of integer type when the ⟨variable⟩ is real.

Examples: $x := (a + 15.6)/y$ $sn[i + 1] := sn[i] - x + y \times 6$
$a := b$ **and** $(c = d)$ $h[j] := \text{'}B\text{'}$

The ⟨goto statement⟩ transfers control during execution to the statement identified by a given target label.

⟨goto statement⟩ ::= **go to** ⟨label⟩

Examples: go to *main*   **go to** 15

The ⟨input-output statement⟩s allow an algorithm to communicate with its surroundings by requesting data ("reading" from an input device) and transmitting data ("writing" onto some output device). The inputs and outputs of an algorithm are defined by these statements in an Algolic program.

⟨input-output statements⟩ ::= *read*(⟨variable⟩{ , ⟨variable⟩ }) |
write(⟨item⟩ {, ⟨item⟩ })
⟨item⟩ ::= ⟨variable⟩ | ⟨character string⟩

Examples: *read*(x, y3, a[13])   *write*(bb, 'a string', x)

The *read* statement reads a sequence of data items from an input device, assigning the first data item to the first variable in the read list, the second data item to the second variable, and continuing in this fashion until all variables have been assigned. The *write* statement writes a sequence of data items on some output device. If an item is a ⟨variable⟩, then the value is output; if an item is a ⟨character string⟩, then the character sequence inside the quotation marks is transmitted.

A.6.2   Structured Statements

Structured statements provide the means for grouping statements together. A **go to** statement outside of a given structured statement cannot have as its target a statement inside the given structured statement.

The ⟨compound statement⟩ groups together a sequence of statements and specifies that they are to be executed in the sequential order that they are written.

⟨compound statement⟩ ::= **begin** ⟨statements⟩{ ; ⟨statements⟩} **end**

Example: begin $x := y + 6 ; y := x ; a := 15$ **end**

The ⟨if statement⟩ conditionally executes a statement or its alternative statement, if present, depending on the value of a ⟨Boolean expression⟩.

⟨if statement⟩ ::= **if** ⟨Boolean expression⟩ **then** ⟨statements⟩ |
               if ⟨Boolean expression⟩ **then** ⟨statements⟩ **else** ⟨statements⟩

Examples: if $a \le b$ **then** $c := e + f$
           if d **and** (**not** e) **then begin** $x := y; y := z$ **end**
           else begin $x := u ; u := y ; y := z$ **end**

If the ⟨Boolean expression⟩ evaluates to true, then the ⟨statements⟩ following the **then** are executed; otherwise, either no statement is executed or, if the **else** part is present, the ⟨statements⟩ following the **else** are executed. The ⟨statements⟩ following the **then** and the **else** cannot be labeled. When ⟨if statements⟩ are nested, they are interpreted from the inside out. Thus **if** be1 **then if** $be2$ **then** $s1$ **else** $s2$ is interpreted as: **if** $be2$ **then begin if** $be2$ **then** $s1$ **else** $s2$ **end**.

The ⟨while statement⟩ specifies that ⟨statements⟩ are to be executed repeatedly until a given ⟨Boolean expression⟩ becomes false.

⟨while statement⟩ ::= **while** ⟨Boolean expression⟩ **do** ⟨statements⟩

Examples: while $(a < b)$ **or** $(a > 15)$ **do** $a := a + c$
           while $(a[i] \ne$ 'c') **and** $(i \le n)$ **do**
           begin $x := x + y/z ; i := i + 1$ **end**

The meaning of the ⟨while statement⟩ can be expressed in terms of more elementary forms:

   while be **do** s is equivalent to:

   w : **if** be **then begin** s ; **go to** w **end**

The ⟨for statement⟩ specifies a fixed number of repetitions of a given statement and assigns to a *control variable* a different integer value during each repetition.

⟨for statement⟩ ::= **for** ⟨identifier⟩ := ⟨for list⟩ **do** ⟨statements⟩
⟨for list⟩ ::= ⟨start value⟩ **upto** ⟨final value⟩ |
                     ⟨start value⟩ **downto** ⟨final value⟩
⟨start value⟩ ::= ⟨identifier⟩ | ⟨integer⟩
⟨final value⟩ ::= ⟨identifier⟩ | ⟨integer⟩

Examples: **for** $i := 1$ **upto** 100 **do** $s[i] := s[i] + a[i]$
                   for $x := a$ **upto** $- 15$ **do**
                       begin $y := x + 5$; $u := u/z$ **end**
                   for $k := i$ **downto** j **do** $a := a + b[k]$

The ⟨statements⟩ part of the ⟨for statement⟩ cannot be labeled. The ⟨identifier⟩s in the above syntax must all be variables of type *integer* and cannot be altered by the repeated ⟨statements⟩. The ⟨for statement⟩ has the meaning:

for $v := s$ **upto** f **do** S

is equivalent to:

$v := s$; **while** $v \le f$ **do begin** S ; $v := v + 1$ **end**

for $v := s$ **downto** f **do** S

is equivalent to:

$v := s$; **while** $v \ge f$ **do begin** S ; $v := v - 1$ **end**

A7.   Syntax Summary

The syntax of Algolic is summarized in the syntax diagram of Figure A.1. Syntactic categories are referenced by rectangular boxes in the figure; the angular brackets, ⟨ and ⟩, are not used. Terminal symbols, the symbols contained in Algolic programs, and atomic elements appear inside oval or circular enclosures.

1. program

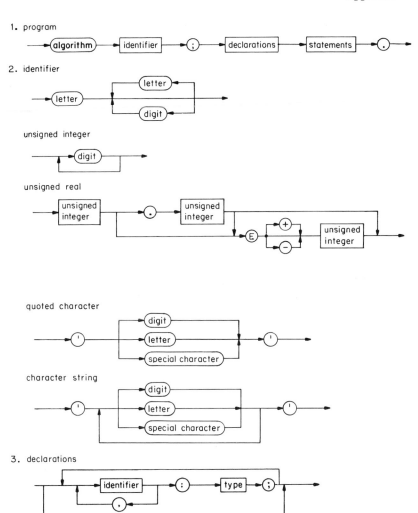

2. identifier

unsigned integer

unsigned real

quoted character

character string

3. declarations

Figure A.1 Syntax Diagrams for Algolic

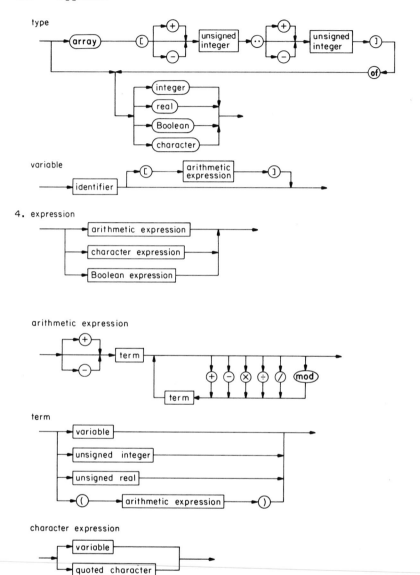

Figure A.1   Continued

Boolean expression

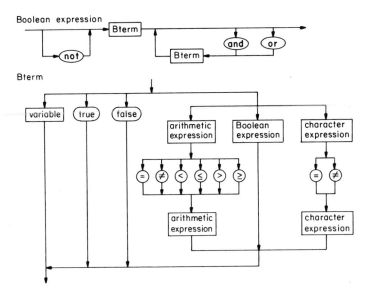

Bterm

5. statements

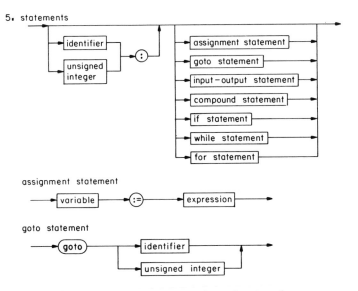

assignment statement

goto statement

Figure A.1 Continued

input – output statement

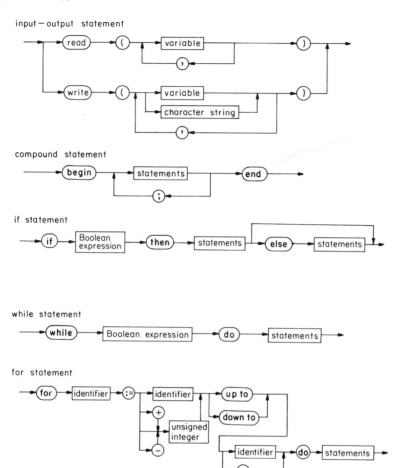

compound statement

if statement

while statement

for statement

Figure A.1 Continued

Index

minimax value, 322
minimum, algorithm for, 41–43
minitheory, 336–337
minor cycle, 181
Minsky, M., 277, 293, 346
minuend, 84
MIT, 119, 334, 337, 341, 342, 359
mod, 20
Monte Carlo algorithms, 354–355
Morrison, E., 135
Morrison, P., 135
MOS : metal-oxide-semiconductor, 150
Moses, J., 341
most significant digit, 75
move tree, 320
Mowshowitz, A., 372
multiplicand, 65
multiplication algorithms, ancient and medieval
  chessboard method, 62
  diagonal lattice scheme, 62–63
  doubling, 60–62, 69
multiplier, 65
multiprogramming, 243 (*see also* operating systems)
Mumford, 370
MYCIN program, 341–342, 352

Nagel, E., 293
nand operator, 125
nanosecond, 150
natural language, 205
natural language understanding, 316, 333–337
  DOCTOR program, 334–335
  ELIZA program, 334–335
  SHRDLU program, 337
  STUDENT program, 336–337
Naur, P., 203
nearest-neighbor method, 356
negation, 102
New York Times, 365
Newell, A., 9, 327–331
Newman, J. R., 293
Newton, 101
Nievergelt, J., 293
Nilsson, N., 346
non-computability, 287–288
non-computable functions, 283
nonterminal symbols, 208
nor circuit, 146–147
nor operator, 129
not, 109
not gate, 121, 146

not operation, 102
NP complete problems, 311, 356
nuclear physics, 348
nucleus of an operating system, 248–249
null string, 222
number systems, 51–79
  Arabic system, 57–58
  Babylonian, 53–55
  binary number system, 64–65
  decimal system, 63
  Egyptian hieroglyphic, 52, 54
  general positional system, 66–67
  hexadecimal number, 79
  history, 51–60
  Indian contributions, 57
  late Roman, 52, 54
  Mayan, 55–56
  octal number, 79
  place value notation, 54–60
  Sanskrit-Devanagari digits, 57
  Sumerian, 53–55
  ternary number, 79
numerical analysis, 46, 89
Nygaard, K., 206

object language, 227
octal number, 79
odometer, 131
one's complement code, 81–84
operand addressing methods, 182–186
operating systems, 193, 200, 242–256
  architecture, 244–249
  process structure, 247–248
  types, 242
  virtual machine organization, 248–249
operations research, 343, 353–362
  origins, 353
  simulation, 356
  traveling salesman problem, 354–356
operators, 377–379
operator's console, 194
Optacon, 351
or, 109
order notation, 304–305
order-of-magnitude, 142
ordered resouce policy, 256
ordering relations, 214
Organick, E., 50
or gate, 121
or operation, 103
orrery, 131
OS : operating system, 200
output spooling, 245–247